WINTHROP ROCKEFELLER

WINTHROP ROCKEFELLER

FROM NEW YORKER TO ARKANSAWYER, 1912–1956

JOHN A. KIRK

The University of Arkansas Press
Fayetteville | 2022

ISBN: 978-1-68226-195-8 (cloth)
ISBN: 978-1-68226-221-4 (paper)
eISBN: 978-1-61075-763-8

26 25 24 23 22   5 4 3 2

Manufactured in the United States of America

Designed by Liz Lester

⊚ The paper used in this publication meets the minimum
requirements of the American National Standard for
Permanence of Paper for Printed Library Materials Z39.48-1984.

Library of Congress Cataloging-in-Publication Data

Names: Kirk, John A., 1970–   author.
Title: Winthrop Rockefeller: from New Yorker to Arkansawyer, 1912–1956 / John A. Kirk.
Other titles: From New Yorker to Arkansawyer, 1912–1956 /
Description: Fayetteville: The University of Arkansas Press, 2022. | Includes bibliographical
    references and index. | Summary: "Why did Winthrop Rockefeller, the scion of one of the
    most powerful families in American history, move to a mountaintop in Arkansas from
    New York in the 1950s? In this richly researched biography of the former Arkansas
    governor, John A. Kirk delves into the historical record to fully unravel that mystery."
    —Provided by publisher.
Identifiers: LCCN 2021029489 (print) | LCCN 2021029490 (ebook) | ISBN 9781682261958
    (cloth) | ISBN 9781610757638 (ebook)
Subjects: LCSH: Rockefeller, Winthrop, 1912–1973. | Rockefeller family. | Industrialists—
    New York (State)—New York—Biography. | Philanthropists—Arkansas—Biography. |
    Arkansas—Politics and government—1951– | New York (N.Y.)—Biography.
Classification: LCC F415.3.R62 K57 2022 (print) | LCC F415.3.R62 (ebook) |
    DDC 976.7/053092 [B]—dc23
LC record available at https://lccn.loc.gov/2021029489
LC ebook record available at https://lccn.loc.gov/2021029490

In memory of my father William John Kirk

CONTENTS

ACKNOWLEDGMENTS

I am grateful to a number of people for their help, support, advice, and encouragement in writing this book.

The book's origins lie in my time spent as a scholar-in-residence at the Rockefeller Archive Center (RAC) in Sleepy Hollow, New York, in 2009. I began with the modest goal of examining the relationship between Winthrop Rockefeller and the civil rights movement in Arkansas. What I discovered convinced me to undertake a much larger study. Further grants-in-aid in 2009 and 2016 assisted with follow-up visits.

The RAC is a wonderful place to work for so many reasons, chief among them its beautiful setting, the always professional, knowledgeable, and friendly staff, and a large and ever-rotating number of impressive researchers. This made the RAC not just an archival repository, but also a valuable place to share thoughts and ideas. Thank you to RAC president Jack Meyers; vice president James Allen Smith; executive assistant Norine Hochman; assistant director and head of reference Michele Hiltzik Beckerman; director of research and education Barbara Shubinski; former assistant director, the late Kenneth W. Rose; former senior research archivist Erwin Levold; former grants administrator Camilla Harris; and archivists Bethany J. Antos, Brent Phillips, and Tom Rosenbaum.

The year after the scholar-in-residence award at the RAC, I moved from Royal Holloway, University of London, to accept a new position at the University of Arkansas at Little Rock as the George W. Donaghey Distinguished Professor of History and chair of the History Department. The endowed Donaghey professorship provided funding that aided my research.

The move also placed me in the same city as UA Little Rock's Center for Arkansas History and Culture (CAHC), home to the extensive Winthrop Rockefeller Collection. For over a decade, I kept a number of archivists busy with requests for materials. The same is true for Central Arkansas Library System (CALS) staff who work at the Butler Center for Arkansas Studies, which shares the reading room space. My thanks and appreciation go to Sarah

Bost, Adrienne Jones, Anna Lancaster, Shannon Lausch, Kaye Lundgren, Brian Robertson, Nathania Sawyer, Shirley Schutte, Rhonda Stewart, Colin Woodward, and a host of graduate assistants from the History Department's Public History MA program. Guy Lancaster, editor of CALS's excellent online resource the *Encyclopedia of Arkansas*, is a font of information on state history. We have held a number of discussions on a number of topics over a number of drinks throughout the years. Guy put me in touch with local historian Don Higgins, who kindly shared his research on Petit Jean Mountain and its environs with me. Deborah Baldwin is associate provost and director of CAHC, and David Stricklin was director of the Butler Center for most of the time I spent doing research there.

Winthrop Rockefeller's legacy lives on today in Arkansas in a number of ways, but most visibly through the various organizations that bear his name. The Winthrop Rockefeller Institute, part of the University of Arkansas system, is based on Petit Jean Mountain in buildings that used to belong to Winrock Farms. The Institute is a conference venue and facilitates "collaboration . . . in the free exchange of ideas as an effective way to solve problems." Executive director and CEO Marta M. Loyd has been particularly engaged with my research as someone who strongly believes that Winthrop Rockefeller's life experiences should centrally inform the Institute's mission. I always enjoy my visits up to the mountain, not least because there are so many other Rockefeller aficionados there. Among them are Joyvin Benton, Payton Christenberry, LaDonna Cole, Janet Harris, Chris O'Cain, Paulette Smith, and Cary Tyson.

I have also had the opportunity to work with the Winthrop Rockefeller Foundation, which seeks to "relentlessly pursue economic, educational, social, ethnic, and racial equity for all Arkansans." On a number of occasions, I have met with the Foundation's CEO Sherece Y. West-Scantlebury and her team members Corey Anderson, Brad Cameron, Lisa Dixon, Regan Gruber Moffitt, and Sarah McBroom. At Winrock International, where the focus is on international development programs, my main point of contact was Dave Anderson.

Lisenne Rockefeller, Winthrop Rockefeller's daughter-in-law, was encouraging throughout the research and writing of this book, and she was instrumental in helping to set up my interview with David Rockefeller. I certainly appreciated David taking the time out of his busy schedule to share his thoughts on his brother with me. I was also delighted at various points to discuss my research with two of Winthrop Rockefeller's grandsons, Winthrop Paul Rockefeller Jr. and Will Rockefeller, both of whom were born after their grandfather's death.

Peter J. Johnson facilitated arrangements for the interview with David

Rockefeller in New York. Peter's two volumes, cowritten with John Ensor Harr, *The Rockefeller Century* (1988) and *The Rockefeller Conscience* (1991), are benchmark works on the Rockefeller family that I returned to time and again. I am grateful for their exhaustive research, and for that of many other authors who have written on the topic and whose work is cited here. They have all made my job much easier.

Two anonymous reviewers for the University of Arkansas Press did a thorough and skillful job in assessing the manuscript's strengths and weaknesses. I am thankful to them for their guidance in making this a better book. Copyeditor Matthew Somoroff helped me to hone my prose and attend to the finer details. Appropriately enough, I completed the finishing touches on the manuscript while teaching at Arkansas Governor's School (AGS) in summer 2021. AGS is an extraordinary resource for students in the state, and Robin Lasey and Jeff Woods at Arkansas Tech University do an incredible job running it.

This volume continues my longstanding relationship with the press. A big shout-out to friends and colleagues there, including Mike Bieker, David Scott Cunningham, Melissa King, Charlie Shields, Jenny Vos, Janet Foxman, Liz Lester, and Sam Ridge. I greatly miss the late Larry Malley, Julie Watkins, and Brian King.

My family is the foundation of everything I do. My love as always to my mother Anne, my brother Alan and his wife Louise, my niece Annabelle and nephew Marcus, my late Aunt Edith, and my wife Charlene and daughter Sadie. My Arkansas in-laws, Bud and Linda Coker, head an extensive network of relatives in the United States.

This book is dedicated to the memory of my father, William John Kirk, who passed away while I was revising the manuscript for publication. That event made me think even more intently about what is involved in writing a life story, family relationships, and especially the relationship between fathers and sons.

WINTHROP ROCKEFELLER

Winthrop Rockefeller at Winrock Farms, Arkansas, in the
1950s. *Winthrop Rockefeller Collection, UA Little Rock Center for
Arkansas History and Culture.*

CHAPTER 1

Winrock

"THIS IS MY SHOW!" declared Winthrop Rockefeller, as he took *Saturday Evening Post* journalist Joe Alex Morris on a tour of his recently built Winrock Farms atop Petit Jean Mountain in Arkansas. "It doesn't have anything to do with any Rockefeller family project. This is all my own."[1]

It was September 1956, and Winthrop was forty-four years old. At six feet and three inches tall, and weighing in at a bulky 225 pounds, he was a commanding presence. He was still handsome, though the creeping signs of middle age were beginning to show in his thinning, dark, slicked back hair and receding hairline. Soft brown eyes hinted at an underlying shyness, contrasting with his more genial, carefree, and outgoing demeanor. Winthrop's aquiline nose was unmistakably inherited from his mother's Aldrich side of the family. Full and shapely lips formed a big, cheery, welcoming smile to guests, which revealed tobacco-stained teeth, a product of the strong-tasting, unfiltered Picayune cigarettes he liked to habitually smoke. Winthrop's work shirt and khakis were standard issue. When he was out working on the farm, he liked to blend in with everyone else. He wore his favorite hand-stitched cattleman's boots, but their fancy swirling patterns and the *WR* initials emblazoned on the shins remained modestly tucked away underneath his pant legs. The *WR* trademark was visible everywhere around Winthrop's various enterprises. It took pride of place above the corrals at Winrock Farms, and it was seared into the hides of his four hundred cherry-red Santa Gertrudis cattle herd purchased from the King Ranch in Texas, including his $31,000 (equivalent to about $297,000 in 2020 dollars) showpiece bull called Rock.[2]

Winrock Farms had fast become one of Arkansas's top tourist attractions. It was located just outside the town of Morrilton and some sixty-five miles northwest of the state capital of Little Rock. More than sixty thousand people traveled from near and far to stare in wonderment at the miracle that had occurred on Petit Jean Mountain. In just three short years between 1953 and 1956, and at a cost of $2 million (equivalent to $19.1 million in 2020 dollars)—

an eye-watering amount anywhere in the United States, but especially so in one of the poorest states in the nation—Winthrop had transformed the scrub and woodland into a model cattle-breeding operation. After an initial purchase of a 927-acre tract of land, Winrock Farms had grown to 2,400 acres split between the top of the mountain and the valley below.[3]

Everyone told Winthrop that it was far more sensible to build Winrock Farms entirely down in the valley, right next to the water supply that it needed to operate. But the view was better from the mountaintop, and Winthrop's ever ebullient enthusiasm never stopped him from believing that any obstacle could be overcome. Engineers devised a system that included constructing four lakes, a riverside pumping station, a 25-gallons-a-minute filter plant, auxiliary power plants, three miles of underground waterlines, and two miles of portable aluminum sprinkler pipes to defy the received wisdom and keep the green grazing pastures on the summit irrigated. Over 350,000 tons of rock was shifted for fill or retaining walls. Another 50,000 tons of rock was crushed to build roads to make the farm accessible. Three large barns were erected, along with two 300-ton silos to hold feed, cattle corrals with iron fences, horse stables, a fully equipped garage and machine shop, underground storage for 3,000 gallons of gasoline, a firehouse with a fire engine, a laundry, a locker room with shower facilities for farm workers, and a suite of air-conditioned offices for administrators. Winrock Farms even had its own airfield, complete with a hangar, a waiting room, and a 4,600-foot lighted runway that was large enough to accommodate a four-engine jet plane.[4]

It was Winthrop's secular version of a city on a hill that his namesake, Puritan John Winthrop the elder, would surely have been proud of. John Winthrop the elder told his flock, as they headed to the Americas from England to found Massachusetts Bay Colony in 1630, that their new home would be a spiritual "city upon a hill," and he warned them that "the eyes of all people are upon us."[5] In Winthrop Rockefeller's case, as always, it was the eyes of the rest of the Rockefeller family that were upon him.

The move to Arkansas followed a third time in his life that Winthrop had failed to meet his family's expectations in New York. The first time was in his unsuccessful academic career, which culminated in his resignation from Yale University. His three older male siblings in the so-called brothers' generation of the family, John Davison Rockefeller 3rd (born 1906), Nelson Aldrich Rockefeller (1908), and Laurance Spelman Rockefeller (1910), together with his younger brother David Rockefeller (1915), all managed to navigate their way through school and to graduate from Ivy League colleges or universities. Winthrop (1912) was disappointingly and disapprovingly left the odd one out.[6]

Redemption came in the southwestern oil fields. Winthrop was the first family member to follow in the footsteps of his grandfather John D. Rockefeller Sr. (in family nomenclature and hereafter Senior) by going into the oil business where the family fortune had been made. Senior cofounded the Standard Oil Company in 1870 and built it into the world's first multinational corporation, becoming one of the richest men alive in the process.[7] Winthrop, who started out as a lowly roustabout laborer, earned the respect of his fellow workers and the acclaim of management. His efforts made up for his scholarly shortcomings and earned him a coveted place in the Rockefeller family office located in Room 5600 (which was, in fact, an entire floor of the building) in midtown Manhattan's 30 Rockefeller Plaza, where he joined his older brothers and his father John D. Rockefeller Jr. (in family nomenclature and hereafter Junior).[8]

The second time Winthrop failed to meet Rockefeller family expectations was in his business and civic career in New York prior to World War II. Winthrop returned from the oil fields with the idea of becoming a junior executive in the oil industry. He dabbled in banking for a while, but he found it deadly boring. He tried philanthropy and fundraising by cochairing the Greater New York Fund, but this met with mixed results. He then secured an appointment at Socony-Vacuum Oil Company in the Foreign Trade Department as liaison officer with the Near Eastern Development Company. Socony-Vacuum, formerly Standard Oil of New York, was one of the many derivatives of the Standard Oil Company that were formed after the US Supreme Court broke up its operations under antitrust laws in 1911. Socony later morphed into Mobil, which in 1999 was absorbed into ExxonMobil. Although Winthrop enjoyed his time at Socony, it did not ignite his passion in the same way that performing practical manual work with his hands in the oil fields had. Meanwhile, his brothers were well on the way to pursuing their lifelong vocations in philanthropy, politics, business, and finance. Winthrop struggled to secure himself a similar role in which to represent family interests.[9]

Redemption came in military service. Winthrop enrolled in a Citizens' Military Training Camp before joining the Army as a volunteer in early 1941. He crisscrossed the United States in training, rising through the ranks to major. In 1944, he was deployed overseas. Island-hopping with the Seventy-Seventh Infantry Division in the Pacific during World War II, Winthrop participated in the battles of Guam, Leyte, and Okinawa. It was a grueling sixteen months that involved many brushes with death, including surviving a Japanese kamikaze attack on his transport ship the USS *Henrico*. He returned a decorated war hero, the only one of the Rockefeller brothers to see active combat duty in service to his country. Again, it had been in the cut and thrust of the field—this time in the battlefield, rather than in the oil field—that Winthrop had thrived and proved himself adept at dealing with its workaday issues and concerns.[10]

The third time Winthrop failed to meet Rockefeller family expectations was in his marriage and family life after World War II. He returned from war the only bachelor among his brothers and the only one childless. With time to make up, he became a fixture in New York's postwar café society nightclub scene. He was linked with a string of female stars of stage and screen and frequently described in the press as America's most eligible bachelor. On Valentine's Day, February 14, 1948, Winthrop married actress and divorcee Barbara Paul Sears (in family nomenclature and hereafter Bobo) at an impromptu ceremony in Lake Worth, Florida. Bobo was pregnant with Winthrop's only child, Winthrop Paul Rockefeller (in family nomenclature and hereafter Win Paul). Within eighteen months, the couple separated, and protracted and acrimonious divorce proceedings followed. The sensationalist headlines alarmed the private and secretive Rockefellers. Winthrop and Bobo eventually arrived at a divorce settlement in 1954.[11]

By then, Winthrop had moved to Arkansas. The failure of his marriage prompted a good deal of soul-searching and reflection. For the third time in his life, Winthrop sought redemption. But this time, it was different. He craved a more permanent fix, rather than just a temporary escape. It was, he decided, time to finally take his destiny into his own hands and to define his own place in the Rockefeller family firmament. To do this, he once again returned to the field. This time, it was not to the oil field, nor to the battlefield, but to the fields of Winrock Farms. Although all three were very different sorts of propositions, they shared a common denominator. Whereas his brothers were contented pen-pushers with office jobs, happily pulling the strings and making decisions behind their desks at major organizations, Winthrop had always craved to work with his hands, to deal with practical matters, to grapple with issues face-to-face on a daily basis, and to constantly interact with and shape the environment around him. He lived his life, metaphorically, and often quite literally, in the field, with his boots planted firmly on the ground.[12]

The same central theme that profoundly shaped Winthrop's life as a New Yorker continued to dominate his life as an Arkansawyer: the ever-present tension between seeking to embrace and fulfil the high demands of being a member of the Rockefeller family and forever striving to step out of its shadow and to become his own person. In Arkansas, Winthrop found a place where he could continue to sow the seeds of the Rockefeller legacy, but one that would also allow him to grow them in his own independent and distinctive way.

Winrock Farms was symbolic of Winthrop's fresh start in Arkansas, but it was, like almost everything else he did there, at the same time deeply rooted in and informed by his New York Rockefeller past. The view from his new family homestead, built clinging to the side of the mountaintop, looked out on a vista of rolling hills and the meandering Arkansas River. It was not unlike, as more than one commentator cannily observed, the view from Senior's mansion Kykuit (derived from the Dutch words for "look out") in Pocantico Hills, Westchester County, New York, that also sat on a verdant plateau above the mighty Hudson River.[13] Two of the lakes at Winrock Farms were named after family members: Lake Abby, in honor of his mother, Abigail Greene Aldrich Rockefeller (in family nomenclature and hereafter Abby), and Lake Lucy, in honor of Abby's sister, Lucy Truman Aldrich, who was Winthrop's favorite aunt.[14] Even the very idea of building and owning a cattle farm had its origins in a visit to Latin America with his brother Nelson in 1937. On that trip, they toured Argentinian cattle ranches and returned besotted with the notion of running a shared enterprise together. They failed in attempts to convince their father to back them, but they continued to hold discussions about the project for the next decade. The plan never came to fruition. Winthrop separately realized his ambition with Winrock Farms, while Nelson owned ranches in Venezuela and Texas.[15] Nelson stocked his ranches with Santa Gertrudis cattle purchased from his brother.[16]

Something else Winthrop brought to Arkansas with him was his family's commitment to promoting better race relations. Winthrop's great-grandparents, Harvey Buel Spelman and Lucy Henry Spelman, were fervent abolitionists. Their home was part of the Underground Railroad that helped to assist in the escape of enslaved people from the South.[17] In 1884, the Atlanta Baptist Female Seminary was renamed Spelman Seminary in honor of Winthrop's grandmother Laura Celestia Spelman Rockefeller (in family nomenclature and hereafter Cettie) and her parents. Today, as Spelman College, it is the oldest private historically Black arts college for women in the United States.[18] Among Senior's earliest acts of philanthropy was giving money to a formerly enslaved Black man so that he could buy his wife's freedom.[19] Subsequent Rockefeller family philanthropy in the area focused mainly on Black education. Senior's General Education Board (GEB) built Black public schools and Junior's involvement with the United Negro College Fund supported Black colleges and universities.[20] Winthrop and his brothers continued family tradition by funding and supporting a number of civil rights organizations.[21]

Winthrop was particularly associated with the National Urban League (NUL). Established in 1910, and headquartered in New York, the NUL was dedicated to pursuing better living conditions and employment opportunities for Black people in America's cities.[22] Junior had been involved in the support and development of the organization since its early years.[23] Starting in 1940, Winthrop served on the NUL board of trustees for twenty-four years and played a leading role in promoting its activities. If there was one area in which Winthrop could stake a claim as the main spokesperson among the Rockefeller brothers before his move to Arkansas, it was in race relations.[24] One of the very few people who moved to Winrock Farms along with Winthrop from New York was his trusted assistant James "Jimmy" Hudson. Winthrop placed him in a position of authority as general superintendent, thereby bucking the southern racial mores that governed the state and laying down a marker for his future intentions.[25]

When Winthrop expanded and developed his own business, civic, philanthropic, and political interests in Arkansas, Rockefeller family influences always remained very much in evidence. It often appeared that Winthrop was trying to recreate his entire Rockefeller family heritage albeit on a far smaller scale. In 1913, Senior founded the Rockefeller Foundation to coordinate his pioneering and prodigious philanthropy.[26] In 1956, Winthrop set up the Rockwin Fund (today the Winthrop Rockefeller Foundation) to coordinate his extensive philanthropy in Arkansas.[27] In 1903, Senior founded the GEB to promote public education, especially in the South, where it aided in the construction of hundreds of public high schools.[28] In 1956, Winthrop's first major project though the Rockwin Fund was the construction of a model school district in Morrilton to advance public education.[29] In 1901, Senior founded the Rockefeller Institute for Medical Research (today Rockefeller University) in New York, a trailblazing biomedical research center. In 1909, he founded the Rockefeller Sanitary Commission for the Eradication of Hookworm Disease (RSC) that helped to virtually eradicate the malady, which was widespread in the South.[30] In 1955, Winthrop helped to fund and staff the Perry County Community Health Clinic, an experiment in providing locally based healthcare in rural communities.[31] In 1929, Winthrop's mother Abby, along with two other women, was instrumental in founding New York's Museum of Modern Art (MoMA).[32] In 1959, Winthrop and his second wife, Jeannette Edris, whom he married in 1956, played a pivotal role in launching a statewide capital campaign to substantially enlarge and expand the existing Museum of Fine Arts in Little Rock. This led to the creation of the renamed Arkansas Arts Center in the 1960s.[33]

Politicians could not long resist the opportunity to harness the influence of a Rockefeller in their midst. In 1955, Democratic governor Orval E. Faubus appointed Winthrop as head of the Arkansas Industrial Development

Corporation (AIDC). With an impoverished and faltering cotton economy, Arkansas was hemorrhaging population that went in search of industrial jobs elsewhere. With the zeal of a recent convert, Winthrop set about selling his newly adopted state to industrial leaders nationwide. Using his family name, contacts, and money, Winthrop compiled an impressive record, making him a popular figure in Arkansas. In early 1956, readers of the *Arkansas Democrat* newspaper voted him the state's "Man of the Year" for 1955. Over the following decade, Winthrop helped to attract ninety thousand new jobs and six hundred new plants. This added $270 million (equivalent to over $2.1 billion in 2020 dollars) to Arkansas's annual payroll; general state revenues increased by more than 50 percent; per capita income increased by $600 (equivalent to $4,849 in 2020 dollars); and around $100 million (equivalent to about $808 million in 2020 dollars) was spent in capital construction projects.[34]

Winthrop was by no means inexperienced in southern race relations, but nothing could have prepared him for the maelstrom that descended on Little Rock when the city found itself at the very heart of developments in a nascent civil rights movement. He had already set himself against the tide of massive resistance to the US Supreme Court's 1954 *Brown v. Board of Education* school desegregation decision by opposing the Arkansas General Assembly's plans to create an investigative State Sovereignty Commission. This was modeled on Virginia's State Sovereignty Commission that intimidated and harassed pro-civil rights groups. Winthrop condemned the move as "dangerous" and deemed the commission a potential "Arkansas gestapo."[35] Worse was to follow. On the eve of a desegregation plan being implemented at Little Rock's Central High School in September 1957, Gov. Faubus called out the Arkansas National Guard, preventing the attendance of Black students. This precipitated a constitutional crisis. After several weeks of standoff between state and federal authorities, Pres. Dwight D. Eisenhower sent in troops from the 101st Airborne Division to quell the white mob that had gathered at the school and to ensure the safe entry of nine Black students.[36] Winthrop was one of the main voices urging Faubus to show restraint. He pleaded with him for over two hours at the Governor's Mansion not to derail all the hard work that had been done in securing new industry and bettering the state's image and reputation. Faubus ignored him for the sake of political expediency and was rewarded by voters with a record-breaking six consecutive terms in office.[37]

The events surrounding the desegregation of Central High School gave Winthrop pause for thought. He became convinced that for Arkansas to truly move forward the state needed to tackle more than just its economic woes. It also needed to address other core concerns that had historically held back its progress: poor race relations, an entrenched one-party political system, and a failure to invest in its social and cultural infrastructure.[38]

Winthrop first turned his attention to laying the foundations for Arkansas's political transformation. He set up a campaign to revive two-party politics, which had been moribund in the state for almost a century.[39] In his landmark 1949 study *Southern Politics in State and Nation*, political scientist V. O. Key described Arkansas as the purest one-party Democratic state in the South.[40] As the campaign progressed, Winthrop became aware, as did those around him, that he was by far the best-equipped person to challenge the state's political stagnation.[41] Some advised him to run as a Democrat, as his nephew John Davison Rockefeller IV (in family nomenclature and hereafter Jay) later did when he moved to the Democratic state of West Virginia in 1964. Jay served as governor from 1977 to 1985, and as a US senator from 1985 to 2015. Following in Winthrop's footsteps by moving southward to a state with high poverty levels, Jay regularly sought his uncle's advice during visits to Winrock Farms.[42] Others told Winthrop to run as an independent. The bald fact was that Arkansas had not elected a Republican governor since Reconstruction. To all intents and purposes, the Republican Party hardly even existed in the state.[43]

Winthrop would hear none of it. Senior had been a northern abolitionist supporting Abraham Lincoln's Republican Party in the lead up to the Civil War.[44] Junior continued the Republican family tradition.[45] Winthrop's grandfather on his mother's side, Nelson W. Aldrich, was a Republican Party leader at the turn of the century, serving Rhode Island as a US representative from 1879 to 1881, and then as a US senator from 1881 to 1911.[46] Winthrop could not countenance abandoning family tradition, and he, too, was a lifelong Republican supporter. As he did so often throughout his life, Winthrop took the road less traveled. He managed to wrest control of the party apparatus from Arkansas's so-called "Post Office Republicans" that existed only to dispense federal patronage in the state when there was a Republican president. In 1961, Winthrop was elected Arkansas's Republican national committeeman. In 1964, he resigned as chair of the AIDC and three days later announced his candidacy for governor.[47]

In November 1964, Winthrop ran as a Republican against five-term incumbent Orval Faubus. Winthrop's platform was based on a sixteen-point "Statement of Beliefs" that echoed Junior's earlier ten-point "Rockefeller Credo," which he first delivered on New York City's WMCA radio in 1941.[48] Although defeated, Winthrop showed promising polling numbers. In 1966, Faubus stepped down as governor. Winthrop then ran against the state's leading segregationist, James D. Johnson, former head of the Associated White

Citizens' Councils of Arkansas, which had been in the vanguard of opposition to school desegregation. With help from dissatisfied young white progressive Democrats and Black and urban voters, Winthrop edged to victory. He became Arkansas's first Republican governor in ninety-four years and the second of the Rockefeller brothers' generation to win political office after Nelson was elected governor of New York in 1958.[49]

Two bruising years battling an overwhelmingly conservative Democratic-dominated Arkansas General Assembly—only three of the 135 legislators were Republican—in efforts to pass an agenda for reform won some limited concessions. Winthrop ran for a second term in 1968 and won again. He gamely fought the Democrats for a further two years, but again with varying results. Winthrop did manage to pass some signal legislation during his two terms in office, including Arkansas's first minimum-wage law and a Freedom of Information Act to make state government operations more transparent. He tackled the state's rampant illegal gambling and the fly-by-night insurance and securities sales companies that fleeced the state's citizens. Many of his efforts focused on trying to chart a path for an improved future by promoting more efficient government, building better race relations, spending more on education and social services, and beginning the massive task of overhauling Arkansas's archaic and decrepit criminal justice system.[50]

Winthrop often found himself having to combine the powers of his office with his own finances to initiate change. For example, in race relations, he attempted to establish a Governor's Council on Human Relations, but the Arkansas General Assembly refused to fund it. Winthrop then funded it himself and used it as a think tank to provide recommendations for appointments to state commissions. Winthrop made more Black appointments to state government positions than any previous Arkansas governor in the twentieth century. This included the appointment of William "Sonny" Walker as the first Black southern director of a state Office of Economic Opportunity (OEO), an agency created by national War on Poverty legislation. Walker also became the first Black gubernatorial cabinet member in the twentieth-century South.[51] After civil rights leader Dr. Martin Luther King Jr.'s assassination in 1968, Winthrop was the only southern governor to prominently participate in a memorial service. He made a very public statement of support by appearing as a speaker on the steps of the Arkansas State Capitol.[52] In race relations, as in several other areas he addressed, it was the tone, emphasis, and direction of government that changed. It was this, rather than an extensive record of legislative success, that defined his administrations.[53]

Ultimately, a great deal of Winthrop's tangible lasting political impact in the state lay in the transformation he brought about in the Arkansas Democratic Party. In the party's four years without a governor, a sea change took place. As in other parts of the South, a generation of New Democrats moved to the fore. These younger politicians were more aligned with the national Democratic Party's progressive politics than with the southern Democratic Party's old regional neo-Confederate allegiances. In 1970, one such candidate, Dale Bumpers, defeated Winthrop in his reelection bid.[54]

As a more familiar homegrown Arkansas Democrat rather than a northern Republican, Bumpers was more successful in passing his own reform legislation, in a program that very closely resembled the one advanced by Winthrop. There followed a succession of progressive Democratic politicians in Arkansas, with David Pryor succeeding Bumpers as governor, and then William "Bill" Jefferson Clinton succeeding Pryor. Clinton married state progressive politics with national progressive politics to win the White House for the Democratic Party in 1992 and then again in 1996.[55] Clinton readily acknowledged the important role that Winthrop's years in office played in paving his way to the presidency.[56] In a bittersweet farewell address to the legislature in 1970, Winthrop reflected, "When the history of the past four years is written, I hope the historian may think of me as something more than a political phenomenon, but as a catalyst who hopefully had served to excite in the hearts and minds of people a desire to shape our own destiny."[57] That he did, but he would not live to see its full fruits.

Winthrop's four years as governor came at a heavy personal cost. The stresses and strains led to a greater dependency on alcohol. His marriage to Jeannette crumbled. Soon after he ended his term as governor in 1971, the couple divorced amicably. The following year, Winthrop developed pancreatic and liver cancer, which took his life on February 22, 1973. He died in Palm Springs, California, where he had gone to escape the Arkansas winter. His ashes were returned and laid to rest in a memorial service held at his beloved Winrock Farms. Although he was born, raised, and lived most of his life as a New Yorker, Winthrop died an Arkansawyer.[58]

The extensive connections between Winthrop's life as a New York Rockefeller and his later life as an Arkansas Rockefeller have remained largely unexplored in an infuriatingly and often obstinately bifurcated historiography. All three books dedicated to solely examining Winthrop's life and achievements have been written from an Arkansas perspective. They steadfastly gloss over the importance of the events in his earlier New York life. The first of these books, John Ward's *The Arkansas Rockefeller* (1978), can be judged by its title. Ward was a journalist by training, as well as Winthrop's director of public relations from 1964 to 1971, and the director of Winthrop's successful 1968 reelection campaign for governor.[59] Hailed at the time by reviewer Francis Irby Gwaltney in the *Arkansas Gazette* newspaper as the "Best Book Written on a State Subject," Ward was especially singled out for praise because he, "doesn't concern himself with the Rockefeller who lived in that distant mystery called New York."[60] Ward devoted less than a page-and-a-half to Winthrop's New York life out of 206 pages in total.[61] This constituted a doubling-down on what Ward had earlier told a journalist during Winthrop's unsuccessful 1964 campaign for governor: "Anything that appears in print implying that Mr. Rockefeller is really a New Yorker transplanted into the state will damage us. Mr. Rockefeller is an Arkansan."[62] A second book written by Ward, *Winthrop Rockefeller, Philanthropist: A Life of Change* (2004), provides an inventory of Winthrop's philanthropic activities, principally in Arkansas.[63] The third book, written by Cathy Kunzinger Urwin, *Agenda for Reform: Winthrop Rockefeller as Governor of Arkansas, 1967–71* (1991), focuses upon Winthrop's two terms as governor.[64]

Accounts of Winthrop's life written from a New York perspective developed in two distinct stages. From 1938 to the mid-1970s, Winthrop was considered an integral part of the larger story of the brothers' generation of the Rockefeller family, alongside his male siblings. It was the *Saturday Evening Post* newspaper that launched this particular genre in 1938 when it published a major feature on "The Rockefeller Boys" that for the first time announced them to world with their own distinct collective identity.[65] In 1940, the brothers founded the Rockefeller Brothers Fund to coordinate their rapidly growing philanthropic activities, further consolidating them in the public mind as a singular cohesive unit.[66] In 1946, they formed Rockefeller Brothers Inc. to fund their joint business ventures.[67] Books were written on the topic of the Rockefeller brothers phenomenon from Joe Alex Morris's *Those Rockefeller Brothers: An Informal Biography of Five Extraordinary Young Men* (1953) to Alvin Moscow's *The Rockefeller Inheritance* (1977).[68]

Yet Moscow's book was the last to treat all five Rockefeller brothers with parity. In no small measure, this was due to the significant shifts that took place in the Rockefeller family's composition in the 1970s. Winthrop was the first of the brothers' generation to die.[69] His only sister, and the eldest of his siblings, Abigail Aldrich Rockefeller (in family nomenclature and hereafter Babs) was born in 1903 and died aged 72 in 1976 from cancer.[70] John died aged 72 in 1978 in a car accident.[71] Nelson died aged 70 in 1979 from a heart attack.[72] The two remaining brothers survived much longer into old age: Laurance died aged 94 in 2004, and David died aged 101 in 2017.[73] The deaths of the majority of the

The Rockefeller brothers in the 1950s. *Left to right:*
David, Laurance, John D. 3rd, Nelson, and Winthrop.
Winthrop Rockefeller Collection, UA Little Rock Center
for Arkansas History and Culture.

Rockefeller siblings in the 1970s began the process of turning the living legacy of the brothers' generation into history. During the same decade there was also a rising interest in the Rockefeller family as a whole, although this was mainly oriented toward providing a critique of American capitalism through one of the surnames that most singularly embodied it.[74] Combined, these developments produced new directions in approaches to documenting the history of the brothers' generation.

On the one hand, as the Arkansas books written about Winthrop testify, the literature moved toward individual profiles of the brothers. Nelson received the most attention, since he was the most publicly visible and therefore the most well-known of the brothers: he served as governor of New York from 1959 to 1973 and as vice president of the United States under Pres. Gerald R. Ford from 1974 to 1977. Numerous biographies and studies have assessed Nelson's life and career.[75] Accounts of the other brothers' lives have been relatively sparse by comparison. The closest thing John has to a biography is as part of a larger multigenerational study that includes Senior and Junior, written over two volumes by Rockefeller family historians John Ensor Harr and Peter J. Johnson.[76] Laurance is the subject of one book dedicated to examining his involvement with the conservation movement, written by academic Robin W. Winks.[77] David was the only brother to publish a memoir, currently the sole book-length commentary on his life.[78]

On the other hand, the Rockefeller brothers became subsumed into larger histories of the Rockefeller family. In these histories, the brothers, who had previously been treated as equals, now fared quite differently. Winthrop was swiftly marginalized and maligned. By the time of these histories, which appeared in the 1970s, he had long ago left New York and was but a dim memory in the minds of most of those writing about the East Coast–based Rockefeller family. It was therefore easy to blithely dismiss Winthrop and his contributions though crudely and clumsily drawn caricatures. The earliest and harshest example of this appears in journalist Ferdinand Lundberg's hostile, opinionated, and avowedly anti-elitist *The Rockefeller Syndrome* (1975), which was published just two years after Winthrop's death. Lundberg pilloried Winthrop as "the limper or lame duck of the Rockefeller brothers. . . . Widely regarded as the *schnook, schlemiel,* and *schlepper* of the family . . . he developed this way quite by family accident. He is a difficult case for the eugenicists to account for."[79] Elsewhere in the book, Lundberg describes Winthrop as "the odd man out in the family, the fumbler," "a misfit, full of self-doubt," and, "disorganized and adrift, a loser."[80] Lundberg concludes, "If anyone wants to weep for a Rockefeller, weep for Winthrop, the victim of childhood family undercurrents that left him a loser all the way, internally crippled."[81]

A book by historians Peter Collier and David Horowitz, *The Rockefellers: An American Dynasty* (1976), followed a year later and became one of the most widely read critiques of the Rockefeller family. The study carried more weight and legitimacy since it involved the cooperation of the so-called cousins' generation of the family, the collective name for the sons and daughters of the five brothers and Babs. Controversially, the book focused a great deal on the dissatisfaction and discontents that the cousins' expressed with certain aspects of their family's capitalist past. Many of these feelings reflected the same generational divides that were evident in wider American society at the time, no doubt amplified by the New Left politics of the two coauthors. If less bluntly than Lundberg, Collier and Horowitz still perfunctorily dismissed Winthrop as the "most troublesome son" of his generation, a "sad-eyed giant of a man," who "could [only] distinguish himself . . . by failure."[82]

Rockefeller family historians Harr and Johnson in *The Rockefeller Century: Three Generations of America's Greatest Family* (1988) did Winthrop few favors. The book was intended as a rebuttal to the criticisms about the family made by Collier and Horowitz and others. Yet even in the Harr and Johnson account, Winthrop is portrayed as "the 'black sheep,' unable to finish college, drifting from job to job and into an unfortunate first marriage, and engaged in a life-long struggle with alcohol." They were at least willing to concede that "he had moved to Arkansas, pulled himself together, and performed the notable service of becoming an honest and reform-oriented governor of a state not previously well-known for such leadership."[83] This analysis reflected Nelson biographer Joseph Persico's earlier conclusion that Winthrop's New York life represented "a disastrous first act as a Rockefeller."[84]

Books written since the 1980s that reference Winthrop's New York life have done little by way of original primary research to flesh out the story any further. Rather, they have relied largely upon rehashing the well-worn stories that already exist in the secondary literature. In creating this echo chamber, they have repeated many of the same errors that those works contain. A necessary task in the present book is to debunk the myths and to correct the inaccuracies that these studies have perpetuated, and to set the historical record straight.

In sum, the writings about Winthrop over the almost fifty years since his death leave us with a distinctly odd and imbalanced impression of his life overall. As the attention paid to Winthrop's New York life has diminished and he has been treated dismissively in Rockefeller family histories, the attention paid to his Arkansas life has been disproportionately expanded and moved front and center. This produces the effect, when seeking to understand Winthrop's life as a whole, of walking into the second act of a two-act play with only the vaguest of thumbnail sketches to explain what happened in the first act. Putting the two acts together and trying to make any sense of them is extremely difficult, if not impossible. The first act has far too little substance, and the second act therefore has far too little context.

This book has two main goals. Firstly, and foremost, it writes Winthrop back into the history of the Rockefeller family and recovers the lost details of his New York life. Secondly, it provides a solid foundation for a more searching and thorough reexamination of his Arkansas life. The time is ripe to do so. As part of my research, in 2015 I had the distinct pleasure and privilege of interviewing Winthrop's younger brother David, just a couple of years before his death. David was the last remaining member of the brothers' generation, with a direct memory of the events recounted in this book. He recalled Winthrop as "someone who in many ways was quite unique. And lived a very different life from the rest [of us]." David added, "I think in retrospect what he did during the war, and many of the other things that he did will be recognized as courageous, and responsible, and good. I would think that he will emerge much more favorably than he was for a time."[85] I wholeheartedly agree with this assessment. In writing this book, however, I do not seek to engage in hagiography, turning the previously presumed Rockefeller family sinner into a saint. This account is fully intended as a warts-and-all telling of Winthrop's New York years. Yet in contrast to other existing portraits, which have fixated solely on the warts, it seeks to paint a far more balanced, textured, nuanced, and complete picture.

In providing the most extensive account of Winthrop's New York life ever published, this book fills one of the largest lacunas in Rockefeller family history. It forces a reassessment of Winthrop's place in the Rockefeller family, and it provides a new perspective on his later Arkansas years. There was plenty of available material to accomplish this with. By far the most valuable primary source that my research uncovered was an extensive interview with Winthrop conducted by journalist David Camelon in the late 1940s.[86] Camelon was a staff writer at the *American Weekly*, a Sunday supplement in William Randolph Hearst's *New York Journal-American* newspaper.[87] The interview provided the basis for a manuscript titled "A Letter to My Son" that recounts the first thirty or so years of Winthrop's life.[88] The manuscript has hitherto been the main source used by historians, journalists, and others to examine Winthrop's New York years. In discovering the original and apparently long-forgotten source material for the manuscript, I found a treasure trove of firsthand testimony. The interview amounts to a much lengthier, unedited, and unredacted version of "A Letter to My Son," which provides for a far more comprehensive, detailed, and candid memoir.

My research gave much-needed clarity to the opaque origins of "A Letter to My Son." Following his return from World War II, Winthrop had the idea of editing a collection of letters that he had exchanged with his parents while in military service. He felt that the collection might document what he considered to be a very significant episode in his life.[89] In 1964, when he first ran for governor of Arkansas, Winthrop's key campaign document, "The Win Rockefeller Story," listed military service as his main achievement.[90] Initially, Winthrop thought about editing the letters and inserting footnotes to provide them with context. He then realized that the project required much more of substance than this, including some biographical background material. After the birth of Win Paul in September 1948, Winthrop believed that a memoir of his early life and wartime experiences was something that he could usefully pass on to his son for posterity.[91]

To that end, David Camelon was hired to conduct an interview with Winthrop and his two best Army friends, Dr. Graham G. Hawks and Frank Newell.[92] The journalist composed "A Letter to My Son" in the early 1950s based on these interviews. But according to John Ward, Camelon "did not finish the job."[93] Somewhat ironically, the manuscript ends at the beginning of World War II, omitting the very events that Winthrop was most eager to document. Exactly why this happened remains unclear, but three factors appear to be central. Firstly, Winthrop moved to Arkansas just as the project was getting off the ground, which no doubt distracted his attention from it. Secondly, one of the reasons that Winthrop purportedly wanted the manuscript written in the first place was to correct what he believed may have been Win Paul's mistaken picture of him, since his son was exclusively in Bobo's custody during the couple's tempestuous separation and divorce proceedings. Such a concern, however, turned out to be unwarranted, as will be discussed in the final chapter.[94] Thirdly, Camelon died in 1956.[95] Camelon's incomplete manuscript was eventually presented to Win Paul on his twenty-first birthday in 1969.[96]

At least in part, then, this book represents the fulfillment of an enterprise that Winthrop first embarked upon over seventy years ago: documenting his New York life, including his wartime experiences, using both the wartime letters to and from his parents and Camelon's interviews. In this book, I have deliberately eschewed referencing "A Letter to My Son," not because I think Camelon did a bad job, but because I wanted to get back as much as possible to Winthrop's original account of his own New York story. Although Winthrop left and returned to New York numerous times during these years, the city always remained his anchor and home base, and a place that was synonymous with the Rockefeller family name. New York defined the first two-thirds of Winthrop's life just as Arkansas defined its final third.

This book in fact has a much broader scope than the project Winthrop envisioned, covering as it does the entirety of his New York life, and drawing upon a wider range of sources. While Camelon's interview is an extremely valuable document, fortunately there is also a vast wealth of other material available to assist in verifying its contents and in contextualizing its stories, as well as charting other developments that the interview does not cover. The Winthrop Rockefeller Collection at UA Little Rock's Center for Arkansas

History and Culture contains over two thousand boxes of written and printed materials, along with film recordings, tape recordings, photographs, and other miscellaneous primary sources.[97] A good deal of this collection has never been used before, and I am certainly the first researcher who has ever deeply mined the areas that relate to Winthrop's New York life. Also valuable were the Winthrop Rockefeller Papers, part of the Office of the Messrs. Rockefeller Records at the Rockefeller Archive Center, along with other Rockefeller family manuscript collections held there.[98] In addition, I drew upon a wide range of further primary sources, including oral history interviews, newspapers, and magazines, and I conducted an exhaustive search of all relevant and available published secondary sources.[99]

In what follows, chapter 2 looks at Winthrop's early life from birth to the age of sixteen, between 1912 and 1928. Chapters 3 and 4 assess his education at the Loomis Institute in Windsor, Connecticut, and at Yale University, between 1928 and 1934. Chapter 5 sketches his experiences in the southwestern oil fields between 1934 and 1937. Chapter 6 outlines his attempts to build a business and civic career in New York between 1937 and 1941. Chapters 7 through 10 follow Winthrop's life during World War II, including his enlistment in the Army, his training and rise through the ranks, his deployment overseas, his experiences in combat, and his return to New York, between 1941 and 1946. Chapters 11 and 12 examine Winthrop's relationship with Bobo: how they met, married, became parents, separated, and divorced, and how Winthrop ended up moving to Arkansas, between 1946 and 1956. Winthrop's life was never uneventful or dull. "God," Alvin Moscow, journalist and author of a collective biography of the Rockefeller brothers, confessed to Winthrop's long-serving Arkansas secretary Jane Bartlett, "if I'd just met Winthrop first I would have written the book about him and not the five brothers."[100]

The Rockefeller family in 1915. *Front row*: Laurance Spelman Rockefeller, David Rockefeller, Winthrop Rockefeller, Nelson Aldrich Rockefeller. *Middle row*: Abigail "Babs" Aldrich Rockefeller, John D. Rockefeller Sr., Abigail Greene Aldrich Rockefeller, John D. Rockefeller 3rd. *Back row*: John D. Rockefeller Jr. *Winthrop Rockefeller Collection, UA Little Rock Center for Arkansas History and Culture.*

CHAPTER 2

Growing Up Rockefeller

WINTHROP ROCKEFELLER WAS BORN May 1, 1912, at 13 West Fifty-Fourth Street in Manhattan, New York City. His parents, Junior and Abby, were both thirty-eight at the time.[1] Their original intention was to name Winthrop after his uncle, Abby's brother, Winthrop Aldrich. But when Abby realized this meant her son's initials would spell out WAR, as a committed pacifist she elected to drop the Aldrich middle name.[2] The name *Winthrop* was derived from John Winthrop the younger, an early governor of Connecticut Colony. Family folklore has it that Winthrop Aldrich was almost named Roger Williams instead, after the Puritan preacher who founded Rhode Island Colony. With his mother agonizing over which of the two men she admired most, she finally decided to merge the two names into Winthrop Williams Aldrich. The choice underscored the Aldrich family's claims to New England ancestry and loyalty.[3] The Museum of Modern Art (MoMA) today occupies the land where Winthrop Rockefeller's birthplace once stood. The land was donated in 1937, following Abby's role along with two other women, Lillie P. Bliss and Mary Quinn Sullivan, in founding the museum that first opened in rented quarters in 1929.[4]

Winthrop was born into one of America's wealthiest and most powerful families. His grandfather, Senior, was the architect of the family fortune as a cofounder of the Standard Oil Company. The Rockefeller name became synonymous with the oil business. To some, Senior was a titan of American industry and capitalism, while to others he was the archetypal exploitative robber baron of America's Gilded Age.[5] Senior was seventy-two when Winthrop was born. By then, he had long retired from business and entered the second phase of his life as a philanthropist. The first mention of Winthrop in the *New York Times* is as a two-year-old infant at his grandmother Cettie's funeral, sitting on Senior's knee.[6]

Winthrop and his siblings had vivid and fond memories of their grandfather. Sprightly even into his later years (he died in 1937 aged ninety-seven), Senior regularly played hide-and-seek with the boys at his Kykuit home. One occasion in particular stood out in Winthrop's memory, since it led to an uncomfortable brush with death, the first in a number of such close encounters that all too frequently seemed to punctuate his childhood and later adult life. Senior was chasing a six- or seven-year-old Winthrop through some bushes. Winthrop was so caught up in the excitement that, focusing on his grandfather in pursuit behind him, he ran over a wall and plummeted headfirst down a ten-foot drop on the other side. Fortunately, the wall had an eight to ten-inch grass border between it and the hard gravel road below. It was here that Winthrop's head landed, while also narrowly missing an iron drain just inches away. As he so often did in such scrapes, Winthrop simply dusted himself off and continued on.[7]

Winthrop and his brothers watched Senior play golf, his grandfather's favorite outdoor pastime, on his Kykuit course. Card games were among Senior's favorite indoor pursuits, which he always played with family members after dinner. Senior spent around two hours sitting at the dinner table each evening, believing that it was unhealthy to rush meals. Playing cards, he said, aided in digestion. Senior's card game of choice was numerica, a form of solitaire that could incorporate as many players around the table as necessary. To provide an incentive to participate, Senior awarded the winner of each game a dime, with a nickel consolation prize to everyone else who took part. The dime was a staple unit of currency for Senior, and it became his calling card in introductions and encounters with many people. He gave away hundreds of thousands of dimes over the course of his life, telling each person who received one that if they kept it, they would never go broke. This was usually followed with advice about opening a savings account and other money management tips.[8]

As a child, Winthrop stayed with his grandfather occasionally at the Casements, Senior's Florida home in Ormond Beach. Winthrop remembered Senior being generally pleasant and easygoing, but it proved virtually impossible to get him to talk about his life and business experiences. When Winthrop later followed Senior into the oil business, he discussed his thoughts about the industry with his grandfather. One day, after listening to him for a while, Senior abruptly cut Winthrop short to remind him that the most important thing was the profit margin. Winthrop believed that until the very end of Senior's life, the bottom line always remained the bottom line.[9]

Winthrop's father, Junior, was Senior's only son, and the youngest of his five children. Establishing the family's patriarchal line of succession, Junior inherited the family name, its legacy, and most of its wealth from Senior. Much of Senior's transference of wealth to Junior occurred during Winthrop's childhood between 1917 and 1922 because of changing tax laws in the Progressive

Era. The Revenue Act of 1916 introduced the United States' first federal estate tax. When reformers realized that taxing inheritance money was leading to the transfer of wealth between generations before death, they pushed for a federal gift tax. The Revenue Act of 1924 instituted this, although it was repealed just two years later.[10] The estimated amount in total that Senior gifted to Junior was just under half a billion dollars (equivalent to over $193 billion in 2020 dollars), with an equal amount going to Senior's philanthropic foundations.[11] Senior kept back a tidy sum to see him through retirement, although at one point during the Great Depression in the 1930s, he was down to his last $7 million (equivalent to $134 million in 2020 dollars). "For grandfather," Winthrop explained, "that was being practically broke!"[12] Junior was a serious, dutiful, and obedient son, and the weight of shouldering the responsibility for the family fortune lay heavily upon him. Although Junior wanted to relieve Senior of his business burdens and responsibilities, he did not take to the cut and thrust of that world. Rather, Junior found his vocation as a dedicated steward of Senior's philanthropic interests.[13]

Winthrop had the greatest of admiration and respect for both his parents, but his relationship with his father was sometimes fraught. Junior tried to instill discipline into his children from an early age, shaped by the Victorian values and strict Baptist upbringing that was handed down to him from his parents. There were, according to Winthrop, three things that mattered the most to Junior about his children: fiscal accountability and abstinence from smoking and drinking.[14] Winthrop proved unsuccessful at meeting his father's expectations in any of these areas. "I was always so afraid that money would spoil my children," Junior reflected, "and I wanted them to know its values and not waste it or throw it away on things that weren't worthwhile."[15] Winthrop and Nelson were far too casual in their finances for his liking. Although Winthrop appreciated Junior's desire to convey money management lessons to his children, he felt that the ensuing conflict it created was not worth the stresses that it placed on family bonds. Winthrop became anxious about any encounter with Junior lest the topic of his accounts arose. On more than one occasion, Winthrop contemplated stealing so that he could set his financial affairs in order to placate his father's demands. But his ever-gnawing Rockefeller conscience prevented him from crossing that line.[16]

By contrast to Junior, Winthrop's mother, Abby, was the main source of warmth, affection, and fun for the children growing up.[17] She was the fourth of eleven children born to Rhode Island's Sen. Nelson Wilmarth Aldrich and Abigail Pearce Truman Chapman. Abby met Junior in 1894 at a friend's house in Providence. A protracted engagement followed, with an indecisive Junior wringing his hands over the big decision of matrimony. The couple finally married on October 9, 1901, with the ceremony held at the Aldrich family's summer home in Warwick Neck. The wedding was one of the major society events of the era, attended by over one thousand members of the American elite.[18]

A newspaper reporter once observed of the Rockefeller brothers that "their grandfather and father made them millionaires, but their mother made them men." Winthrop agreed.[19] Several people have testified to the close relationship between Winthrop and his mother. As Mary McLeod, one of Winthrop's advisors in his later philanthropy in Arkansas, observed, "That there was a great bond between him and his mother was obvious." Melinda Kendrew, a friend of Abby's, recalled, "[Abby] held him close to her heart.... She worried about him and felt very tender toward him."[20] In turn, Winthrop doted on his mother, writing to her on Mother's Day as a young man, "It seems strange to me that anyone would need to have any particular day set aside in which to remember his mother, but then . . . everybody couldn't have a mother like you."[21]

Yet between Junior and six children, Abby often found that the demands placed on her love and attention were outstripped by what she was able to supply. Junior remained passionately in love with Abby during their more than forty-six years of marriage, and he competed with the children over her.[22] Shortly after Winthrop's birth, Junior wrote his wife, "Five little people need you now, besides a man who needs you more than ever, and who wants a great deal more of you than he has been having."[23] As David later lamented, "Father expected Mother to be there for him when he needed her, and his needs in that regard were practically insatiable."[24] Winthrop, who struggled to find his place in the world more than any of the other children, and who arguably needed Abby's nurturing and support the most, suffered because of this.

Winthrop's difficulty in finding a niche for himself within the Rockefeller family was established early. The other children more quickly identified with and seemed to intuitively understand their respective roles. Babs was the only daughter in the brothers' generation and clearly felt that inherent sense of isolation growing up. Refusing to play the part of the dutiful daughter, she rebelled. Babs initially declined to give any of her allowance to charity as family tradition demanded, and she smoked and drank as soon as she became of age. In 1925, she married lawyer and banker David M. Milton. She had therefore already moved out of the family home before Winthrop was scarcely a teenager. John D. 3rd inherited the famous family name and its concomitant responsibilities. Groomed as Junior's successor from an early age, like his father, John could appear older than his years, and he was just as self-conscious and serious. He marshaled the other boys on Junior's behalf and later assumed his father's responsibility in stewarding the family's philanthropic interests. Nelson Aldrich inherited his maternal grandfather's name, although he frequently acted as if he were the one true Rockefeller heir. Supremely confident in his own abilities and sometimes overpowering in his exuberance, Nelson became the family politician. Laurance Spelman was named after his paternal grandmother. A wily and shrewd operator, Laurance established a tight-knit childhood alliance with Nelson that lasted a lifetime. The two were the closest friends of all the brothers. Laurance became the family's entrepreneur and businessman, and he continued Junior's interest in the area of conservation.[25] David, the youngest, was just as determined and single-minded as Nelson, but in a far quieter and more understated way. He became the financier and banker in the family, most notably serving as chair and CEO of Chase Manhattan Bank between 1969 and 1980.[26]

Birth order played an important role in shaping Rockefeller family dynamics. Babs's seniority was undermined by her gender, which excluded her from having anywhere near as much of a say in family affairs as her brothers. John sat atop the family hierarchy as the first-born son and possessor of the coveted name. Nelson relentlessly struggled to transcend his status as second son and to assert his credentials as leader of the pack. Laurance cozied up to Nelson without ever posing a threat to him. David, as the baby of the family, was relatively isolated from the rest, but as the youngest of the children he could at least rely on having more of his mother's attention than any of the others. Winthrop occupied a difficult position as the fifth child and the fourth brother. He desperately wanted to be viewed as one of the older boys and constantly looked to join Nelson and Laurance in their gang of two. They refused to have him. Rather, Nelson and Laurance bonded through their teasing and tormenting of Winthrop, asserting their authority over him by purposefully excluding him from their alliance. Winthrop might have formed his own compact with younger brother David, but he viewed that possibility as only confirming that he was one of the family's junior members.[27]

At times, Winthrop's bullying by his older brothers became particularly mean. Early in life, Winthrop developed a semi-chronic kidney condition. When he was twelve, this led to a serious episode of acute nephritis. He lost his appetite, he could no longer urinate, and his body began to swell up so alarmingly that his shirt barely fit him anymore. Winthrop's chaperone Miss Kline rushed him to hospital, where he was diagnosed and treated. He spent the next six weeks in hospital. After he pulled through, the underlying kidney condition also cleared up. Winthrop's cousin, Winthrop Williams Aldrich Jr. (the son of Abby's brother), had the same chronic kidney condition. He was not so fortunate. Aldrich Jr. died as a toddler aged four in 1921, just a few years before Winthrop fell ill. Nelson and Laurance taunted their younger brother that sharing the same name and the same condition with his cousin would lead to the same outcome.[28]

Nelson and Laurance also used a birthmark on Winthrop's right knee to rile him. They told him that it meant he had "Negro blood" and they nicknamed him "Beanflop nigger."[29] The casual use of the N-word by Nelson and Laurance speaks to the ubiquity of racism in all levels of American society in the early twentieth century.[30] Abby was appalled to hear her children using such language. "One of the greatest causes of evil in the world is race hatred or race prejudice; in other words the feeling of dislike that a person or a nation has against another person or nation without just reason, an unreasoning aversion," Abby chastised Nelson and Laurance. "It is to the everlasting disgrace of the United States that horrible lynchings and brutal race riots frequently occur in our midst."[31] Abby further complained about the older boys' treatment of Winthrop: "It seems so cruel to me that you big boys should make poor little Winthrop the goat all the time. I know that he is often trying but the only way to help Winthrop is by being kind to him. Abuse only makes him angry and worse, while for love and kind treatment he will do anything."[32] While Abby's intervention put a stop to the use of the offensive nickname, Nelson and Laurance fell back on the slightly less overtly racist term *cotton picker*. According to Winthrop, the name-calling continued for several years afterward.[33]

Winthrop did not always take his brothers' insults meekly. When things went too far, he could easily snap and lose his temper. On those occasions, one of his brothers had to sit on his head and the other on his feet until he calmed down. But Nelson and Laurance were not always successful in subduing their younger brother. Winthrop was big in size beyond his years, and he could stand up to them one-on-one. Nelson discovered this to his cost one Sunday morning before church when he and Winthrop were out playing seesaw. Nelson liked to sit on his end, lift Winthrop up in the air on the other end, and then quickly jump off, bringing Winthrop crashing painfully to the ground. Each time Nelson promised not to do it again, his overly trusting younger brother climbed back on, only to suffer a recurrence of the same fate. When he eventually grew tired of this, Winthrop grabbed a pitchfork, chased Nelson down with it, and stabbed him in the knee. Junior administered a spanking to both of them after church. Corporal punishment was not commonplace in the Rockefeller household. Abby spanked the children when they were younger, but the one Winthrop and Nelson received from Junior that day was remembered even more because it was such a rarity.[34]

Nelson never appeared phased by any of the sanctions imposed upon him for his misbehavior. When he was denied dessert one night for dumping paint powders on Winthrop's head, he cheerfully chewed a piece of gristle in defiance as he watched the other boys eat their ice cream.[35] Always endeavoring to look on the bright side, Winthrop later credited the encounters with his brothers as being helpful in learning to bring his temper under control as an adult.[36] There seems little doubt that the episodes also left lingering resentments and mental scars. Years after, a contrite and remorseful Nelson confessed to a friend, "I'm responsible for a lot of Winthrop's problems."[37] One of Nelson's biographers, Joseph Persico, maintains that "the scars from Nelson's childhood bullying . . . left Winthrop resentful and Nelson feeling guilty."[38] And yet, for all that, both Winthrop and Nelson remained joined by a sense of solidarity and comradeship as fellow Rockefeller brothers. Though their relationship may have been rocky over the years, it was cordial enough for them to work together and to cooperate with one another for the benefit of the family on any number of occasions as well.

A year after Winthrop was born, the family moved into their new home at 10 West Fifty-Fourth Street. At the time, it was the largest private residence in New York City. The nine-story building included a rooftop squash court, a playground, a gymnasium, and an infirmary. The hallway to the building was furnished in lavish English Chippendale and Louis Quinze antiques. A stream of visitors included royalty, clergy, educators, and medical pioneers. Polish virtuoso pianist Ignacy Jan Paderewski performed in the second-floor music room and former president Theodore Roosevelt called by to bounce Nelson on his knee and regale the family with stories.[39]

The Rockefellers' Manhattan residence was the hub of their weekday activities. The daily routine for the boys was an early start, a quick breakfast, and then morning prayers and bible study with Junior. This was strictly an all-male affair, with neither Abby nor Babs in attendance.[40] On April 17, 1927, just before turning fifteen, Winthrop, along with David, joined Junior's Park Avenue Baptist Church by profession of faith and baptism.[41] Despite a strict religious upbringing—or perhaps because of it—none of Junior's children shared their father's same devotion to the church. Winthrop always considered himself a man of faith, although he was convinced that his faith could flourish equally well outside of organized religion.[42] This later vexed his political advisers in Bible Belt Arkansas who felt that Winthrop's lack of church attendance might hurt his standing with the electorate. Winthrop refused to budge on the matter, even for the sake of appearances.[43]

School dominated the boys' early lives. John attended the traditional, elite Browning School in Manhattan, just as his father had. He later went to boarding school at the Loomis Institute in Windsor, Connecticut.[44] All of the other boys attended the Lincoln School, founded by the Rockefeller-funded General Education Board (GEB) in 1917, and the brainchild of GEB secretary Abraham Flexner.[45] Lincoln was conceived as a university laboratory school as part of the Teachers College at Columbia University, one of the premier centers for educational excellence in the country. Very much following the ideas of philosopher John Dewey, a Columbia University faculty member and the leading educator of the day, Lincoln stressed experiential learning through practical study rather than a traditional school curriculum.[46] Lincoln discarded the common mainstays of a liberal arts education, such as Latin and Greek, and replaced them with a science focus at its core. The emphasis was on concrete examples of life and learning, such as visits to farms and factories. Building on these real-world foundations, the teachers constructed a new and innovative curriculum that they hoped would replace the rote learning of traditional education with greater critical-thinking skills.[47]

The original building that housed the Lincoln School was part of what was formerly the Sulgrave Hotel on Park Avenue and East Sixty-Seventh Street, a prime piece of Manhattan real estate. In 1923, the school relocated to 425 West 123rd Street, at Amsterdam Avenue, in Morningside Heights, moving into a new and well-equipped facility. The six-story building contained two rooftop playgrounds, two gymnasiums, an indoor swimming pool, shop and studio equipment, a pottery room and kiln, and some of the most pedagogically advanced science laboratories in the country.[48] The change in location meant a much longer commute for the Rockefeller boys. Later, Nelson told Black voters in New York that he had "gone to school in Harlem."[49]

Following Junior's insistence on getting plenty of fresh air and exercise, each morning the boys strapped on their roller skates and darted up Fifth Avenue alongside Central Park. The younger brothers, Winthrop and David, generally ran out of steam around Seventy-Second Street, whereas Nelson and Laurance would make it to Ninety-Sixth Street. As each of them tired, one of the three Irish Concannon brothers, the family drivers, picked them up in the family's state-of-the-art Nash sedan to carry them the rest of the way.[50] Junior always hired a young student from the nearby Union Theological Seminary to collect the boys after school. Often, this was a French student, and this provided an opportunity for the boys to have extra language lessons. Winthrop was proud of his fluency.[51]

Lincoln perfectly suited Winthrop. He started kindergarten there in the first year of the school's operation in 1917. Never excelling as a traditional scholar, Winthrop relished the practical learning and hands-on experiences that the school offered. He enjoyed arts and crafts the most, particularly woodwork, where he made printing blocks for homemade Christmas cards. As a coeducational institution, Lincoln sought to transcend traditional gendered expectations. The boys learned to cook and sew, and the girls studied electrical engineering.[52] Lincoln also had some class, racial, and ethnic diversity, certainly more so than many other private schools in the city. Nevertheless, given the location of the school and its tuition fees, the students were predominantly upper-middle class and drawn mainly from business and professional families.[53]

In the fourth grade, Winthrop focused on farming, and especially cattle-rearing. One project, alongside classmate Walter Douglas, involved describing what silos were used for. Little did Winthrop know at the time just how directly relevant to his later life at Winrock Farms these lessons would be. Another assignment required keeping a food diary for a week, providing an insight into what the nine-year-old Winthrop typically consumed. For breakfast each morning, Winthrop had cereal with milk, sometimes supplemented with bacon and toast, and with an occasional egg. A typical lunch menu consisted of soup, turkey, cranberry sauce, potato, sweet potato, squash, cauliflower, ice cream, and cake. For supper, there was shredded wheat, beans, bacon, potato, and cream puffs. In between meals were snacks of milk, candy, cookies, and fruit, supplemented with the odd sandwich or two.[54] "Overweight" declared his ninth-grade physical examination.[55] Nelson and Laurance added "Pudgy" to their growing list of nicknames for their younger brother.[56] Winthrop remained self-conscious about his weight throughout the rest of his life, and its fluctuations often depended largely upon the stresses and circumstances he encountered.[57]

In the fifth grade, Winthrop played Mr. Pickles the Fishmonger in the class-play adaptation of Charles Dickens's children's story "The Magic Fish Bone."[58] Later that year, he and a classmate performed a skit based on Ben Fisher's popular comic strip *Mutt and Jeff*.[59] In the sixth grade, Winthrop was chosen to conduct a school assembly welcoming Adm. Richard E. Byrd to speak about his recent expedition to the North Pole, which Junior had partly funded. Winthrop believed the experience gave him confidence in his capacity for public speaking—a skill that he would use for the rest of his life.[60]

In the seventh grade, as class president, Winthrop drew up a compact signed by the school director and all the other students in his year to "abstain from the use of tobacco in any form" while they were students at Lincoln.[61] A couple of years later, when he was in the ninth grade, Junior drew up a similar agreement with Winthrop and his brothers, offering them a sum of $2,500 (equivalent to $37,135 in 2020 dollars) if they abstained from smoking until they turned twenty-one. Each was promised an additional $2,500 if they continued not to smoke until they turned twenty-five.[62] Winthrop accepted the challenge, but he failed to collect the reward.[63] Only Nelson and David received their checks.[64] In the tenth grade, Winthrop took on the role of Nitro Gliseriniski, an anarchist, in Ian Hay's play *The Crimson Cocoanut: An Absurdity in One Act.* The same year, he attended singing classes at David Mannes Music School, where he reportedly had "quite a good ear" but needed more "steadiness and concentration."[65]

Winthrop and his family spent most of their weekends at Abeyton Lodge, their country residence on Senior's Pocantico Hills estate. The drive up from Manhattan in the family's Crane-Simplex sedan took around ninety minutes.[66] Located just down the hill from Senior's Kykuit home, Abeyton Lodge was a country pile that served as an impressive corollary to the Rockefeller Manhattan mansion. The rambling home contained oak paneling and floors, a wide golden oak staircase, and a large oak table in the front hall. Many rooms, including the bedrooms, had fireplaces, with the living room fire always lit in cooler weather. The living room contained an entire wall of bookcases with glass doors that housed volumes of the classics, including works by Charles Dickens and Robert Louis Stevenson. A large landscape painting by the celebrated American artist George Innes hung on the wall. The long hallway between the living and dining rooms was lined with the heads of big-game animals in the style of the day, even though Junior was not a hunter. In the front hallway there was a stuffed emperor penguin, a present to Junior from one of Adm. Byrd's Antarctica expeditions, which Junior also helped to fund.[67]

When Winthrop was in his teens, Junior built a recreational facility called the Playhouse, close to Abeyton Lodge, that included a gymnasium, a squash court, a bowling alley, and an indoor pool.[68] When guests came over, Winthrop's job was to set up the pins for bowling.[69] Pocantico Hills offered possibilities for all sorts of outdoor activities year-round. In winter, there was skating and sledding; in spring, Winthrop collected sap to make maple sugar; in summer, there was swimming and fishing. During World War I, each of the boys had their own plot of garden to weed and tend. Encouraging entrepreneurship from an early age, Junior permitted them to sell their produce to the family household at the going rate. The boys also raised rabbits to sell to the Rockefeller Institute for Medical Research, with Nelson and Laurance the most successful at turning a profit from the venture. To confer further the values of responsibility and self-sufficiency in the boys—common themes than ran throughout their entire upbringing—each had their own pony, which they were expected to fully care for as they learned to ride it.[70] Winthrop's was named Beauty.[71] While participating in these activities, the boys were assigned chaperones to ensure their safety.[72]

Some of Winthrop's fondest memories in Pocantico Hills involved the various modes of transportation he employed to dart around his grandfather's 3,400-acre estate.[73] As a child, Winthrop rode his bicycle.[74] Later, the boys each had what they termed "red bugs." These mini motorized vehicles consisted of wooden slats with four wheels fastened to them, two seats on top, and a steering wheel at the front. Attached at the rear was a Smith Motor Wheel that propelled the contraption. In the winter, Bill Tripp, a mechanic from nearby Tarrytown, replaced the wheels with runners. This allowed the red bugs to traverse the snow and ice. Winthrop also had access to his father's vintage 1902 Baker electric car from an early age.[75] The Baker was a status symbol of the rich and famous. The King of Siam owned one, and there was one in the first-ever presidential White House fleet owned by William Howard Taft.[76] The vehicle traveled at twenty to twenty-five miles per hour on level ground, but it could only reach some twenty to thirty miles without recharging. At the age of fourteen, Winthrop was taught to drive a Ford Model T by Fred Rowe, another of the family's drivers.[77] Winthrop's passion for transportation remained throughout his life. In 1964, he founded the Museum of Automobiles on Petit Jean Mountain. The museum showcased Rockefeller family vehicles alongside a collection of cars he purchased from the James Melton Museum in Hypoluxo, Florida, in 1961.[78]

Winthrop spent a good deal of his time playing with the children of the employees on his grandfather's estate. This was one of the ways in which Winthrop gained a greater appreciation for those who lived in different circumstances from his family. "He tended to enjoy the company of people with a very different educational and social background," David remembered. Over the course of Winthrop's life, his circle of friends and acquaintances were drawn from a much wider and more diverse pool than those of his brothers.[79] Winthrop connected with the employees' children through community projects. One of them involved organizing a clean-up squad. Since Pocantico Hills was not an incorporated village, it had no street-cleaning department. Yet the highway that ran through it generated a considerable amount of trash from passing traffic. On Saturdays, Winthrop rode the Baker or his red bug into the village and joined with boys from the estate to pick up litter. Afterward, as a reward for their efforts, he treated them to a marshmallow or hot dog roast funded from his allowance. Winthrop continued to do this for two or three years. Company also came from classmates at the Lincoln School. The school had an overnight cabin on the Rockefeller property. Each weekend, different groups, such as the scouts, used the cabin for an all-day outing or overnight camping trip. The red bug allowed Winthrop to travel over and see who was around. On other weekends, children were invited to Abeyton Lodge to play.[80]

Summers each year were spent at the Eyrie, the family's retreat in Seal Harbor on Mount Desert Island, the largest island off the coast of Maine. Junior and Abby first visited there in 1908 and purchased the Eyrie in 1910. Built on a granite bluff, the Tudor-style cottage originally had 65 rooms. Junior quickly expanded this to 107 rooms, with 22 bathrooms, 44 fireplaces, and 2,280 windows.[81] The annual trek to the Eyrie began like clockwork on July 9, the day after the family celebrated Senior's birthday. Moving the Rockefeller household from Manhattan to Maine was quite an undertaking. David remembers weeks of lengthy preparations beforehand for the nearly three-months stay. On the day of departure, the family's luggage was loaded onto a truck along with ice chests containing pasteurized Walker-Gordon milk for the children to drink on the journey. This was all then transported to Penn Station and placed on a train. Junior, Abby, the six children, and the household staff, including a variety of maids, nurses, chaperones, tutors, and personal secretaries, as well as Junior's valet, took up an entire Pullman sleeping car. Junior had another car hooked onto the back of the train for the horses, ponies, and carriages that the family took with them from Abeyton Lodge. The sixteen-hour journey aboard the Bar Harbor Express started at around 5:00 p.m. Upon arrival the following morning, the entire Rockefeller entourage boarded the *Norumbega*, a side-wheeler ferry, for the four-hour voyage to Seal Harbor. They finally arrived at the Eyrie by mid-afternoon.[82]

Seal Harbor was just nine miles away from Bar Harbor, one of the most fashionable summer resorts on the East Coast. But according to David, Junior and Abby found Bar Harbor too overbearing for their liking, and they preferred the more sedate and conservative Seal Harbor. In his memoirs, David characterizes Bar Harbor as a place of "elaborate parties . . . bands playing on yachts . . . [and] dancing all night," where speedboats "carried guests back and forth," and the "champagne flowed for all ages." The Rockefeller existence at Seal Harbor was a far more low-key affair. There were no wild parties or dancing, and certainly no alcohol for the Prohibition-supporting Junior.[83]

The Rockefellers owned a thirty-six-foot racing sloop, called the *Jack Tar*, rather than a luxury yacht.[84] In the early years, the family hired an experienced captain to help them navigate through the treacherous waters. As they learned the ropes, family members took more responsibility for the sea-faring journeys. Quite purposefully, the Rockefellers did not have an engine on their boat, as other families did, since they believed it fostered a greater sense of independence. If all else failed, the fishermen on the island came to their aid. As the boys grew older and became more proficient sailors, they began to enter races. One of Winthrop's proudest achievements was placing third at age sixteen.[85]

The family dynamic at Seal Harbor was the same as in Manhattan and Pocantico Hills. The older boys, John, Nelson, and Laurance, played together, while Winthrop played mostly with the seven children of the family chauffer Valentine.[86] David remained isolated, spending his time with French tutors, various governesses, and Babs's friend the Russian aristocrat Regina DeParmant, who traveled along to keep his sister company.[87] Winthrop enjoyed shopping trips into town with the housekeeper Mrs. Scandage. He also hung around in the kitchen pestering the family cook Christine with endless questions about culinary matters. Winthrop's parents arranged for their children to take cooking classes over the summer months. Each Wednesday evening at the Eyrie, as in Manhattan, the boys oversaw dinner. This meant planning the meal, ordering the produce, cooking the food, doing the washing up, and putting away the cutlery and dishes.[88]

On Sundays, the boys accompanied Junior on walks to inspect the various road-building and park-planning projects that he was involved in at Seal Harbor.[89] Many of the properties that the Rockefellers owned on the island, along with the improvements that Junior made to them, were later turned over to the Acadia National Park. Private investment for the public good was one of the central tenets of the Rockefeller family, and something that became deeply ingrained into each of the boys from a young age. The boys worked with their father in various activities, such as cutting the limbs off trees to create picnic areas and pulling up stumps with the help of their ponies and a block and tackle. John, Nelson, and Laurance even built themselves a little log cabin in the woods. Winthrop, to his great disappointment, was not deemed old enough to participate.[90] The usual bullying inflicted upon Winthrop by his older brothers traveled along on the summer holidays. In later years, showing a guest around the Eyrie, Winthrop stopped and pointed to a tree. "That's where Nelson and Laurance used to kick me and tie me up and leave me," he told them plaintively.[91]

Competition among the boys extended to orchid hunting. A rare, tiny orchid, native to the Maine swamps, was a much-coveted prize. When the boys found orchid patches, each jealously guarded their own secret stash so that they could show off their haul to the others. One such discovery proved very much to Winthrop's detriment.[92] When he was twelve, Winthrop found a

Winthrop at the Eyrie in Seal Harbor, Maine, 1922.
Winthrop Rockefeller Collection, UA Little Rock Center for Arkansas History and Culture.

prime orchid patch while on a field trip with his tutor Mr. Sangrue. They loaded up their 1917 Dodge truck with over forty of the flowers.[93] Excited by the find, Winthrop headed home with his trophies. But when Winthrop and his tutor reached the top of a hill on the way back, the truck's accelerator got stuck. The car careered down the hill and plowed straight into a fence at the bottom. The force of the impact hurled Winthrop through the windscreen, over the fence, and into the field beyond it. The resulting gash on Winthrop's face from the shattered windscreen glass required ten stiches and left a permanent scar from his right temple to the top of his right ear.[94] Junior was out West on a trip with the older boys at the time, and he sent an anxious telegram of concern at the news of Winthrop's accident.[95] Winthrop's reply set Junior's mind at rest. He stoically reported that he was already patched up and on the mend.[96]

While he recuperated, following the doctor's orders to get plenty of rest, Winthrop took up the hobby of wood etching. He discovered that if he dismantled his flashlight lens, he could use it to focus the sun's rays to burn words into a piece of plywood. Winthrop's standout achievement was transcribing the first verse of Edgar Albert Guest's 1919 poem "It Couldn't Be Done." The stanza extolled the ability to attain the seemingly impossible through strength of will and determination alone.[97] The philosophy, and the piece of inscribed wood, followed Winthrop on his travels, eventually ending up in his Winrock Farms office in Arkansas.[98]

Another seasonal rite of passage for the boys was attendance at summer camps. Winthrop's first was at thirteen. It proved a traumatic experience. The problems began, Winthrop believed, with the fact that Laurance attended the first month at Camp Merryweather in North Belgrade, Maine, while Winthrop attended the second month. This meant that everyone at the camp had already forged friendships and were acclimatized to camp life, whereas Winthrop turned up as the disoriented new boy. He suffered from severe homesickness.[99] The letters he sent to family members were pitiful. Winthrop complained constantly about his weight loss, headaches, sore throat, sick stomach, broken dental braces, having to wash dishes, and the camp counselors' use of the paddle on him.[100] Family members urged the usual Rockefeller resolve in return.[101] The episode became the stuff of family folklore. A couple of years later, David's governess, Atta Albertson, still referred to the "awful memory" of the camp, telling Winthrop, "I am glad you had some summer camp, but hope you don't have any more. You served your term, didn't you?"[102] Even thirty years later, Winthrop vividly remembered it. He shared his experiences with his stepdaughter, Anne Bartley, when she was homesick while away at school.[103]

Family travels across the United States and the world while Winthrop was growing up provided him with yet another set of shaping experiences. An early memory was visiting the Hampton Institute (today Hampton University) in Virginia, an historically Black college that was founded just after the Civil War. On Easter 1923, the family drove down to the Hampton Institute via Washington, DC, and Mount Vernon.[104] While there, the Rockefellers lived on campus. They visited classes, and in the evenings they were invited to the guesthouse where they spoke with students. The Rockefeller boys were so moved by the stories they heard that each decided to sponsor a student from their allowance. It was not much, but, Winthrop felt, given the low tuition rate at Hampton, the relatively cheap cost of living, and the very modest backgrounds from which many of the students came, in many cases it was enough to make a difference.[105] Winthrop exchanged several letters with the students he sponsored, gaining an insight into their daily lives, hopes, and aspirations.[106]

Also influential in molding Winthrop's early understanding of race and ethnicity was the International House in New York. Junior and Abby, along with the Cleveland H. Dodge family, helped to found and fund the project. The main goal of International House was—and indeed still is—to extend a welcoming hand and a place to live for international students studying in New York. Winthrop met many students from a wide variety of different countries, cultures, and backgrounds there.[107]

Family trips further afield were, like the annual summer moves to Seal Harbor, meticulously planned. Lengthy itineraries were drawn up weeks beforehand. Each of the boys was assigned a particular role to ensure the smooth running of the operation. On several occasions, Winthrop was the designated luggage handler. The other boys paid the hotel bills and took care of sundry other details on the trip. Some journeys were by car, others by train, and yet still others by both, with a private car stowed on the train for excursions along the way. Friends and other families accompanied the Rockefellers on their travels, and it was not unusual to have twenty or more people in the party.[108]

Winthrop traveled extensively with his family. In 1925, Junior and Abby, along with Nelson, Laurance, Winthrop, and David, took a trip to Sulphur Springs, Texas.[109] In 1926, after first visiting Philadelphia and then the Hampton Institute, the family toured Virginia, including a stop in Colonial Williamsburg. While there, Junior was persuaded to fund a large restoration project of the entire town. This became a long-term commitment and an expensive endeavor, but one that, David said, "gave [Junior] as much pleasure as anything he did in the field of philanthropy during his lifetime."[110] In 1953, Winthrop become chair of the board of trustees at Colonial Williamsburg, a position that was among his most high-profile family commitments. It was also one of the few family responsibilities that he continued to maintain after his move to Arkansas.[111]

Later in 1926, the family took a two-month trip exploring the western states.[112] In 1927, Winthrop experienced his first travels outside of the United States when he joined David, Junior, and Abby on a trip to France. They visited Rheims Cathedral, the Palace of Fontainebleau, and the Palace of Versailles, all of which had benefited from funds provided by Junior for their renovation. Afterward, they toured the Loire Valley, Mont-Saint-Michel, and the coasts of Brittany and Normandy.[113] In 1928, Junior, Abby, and all five boys traveled around the Midwest's Great Lakes together.[114]

In the fall of 1928, Winthrop's life underwent a decisive change when Junior and Abby decided to transfer him from the Lincoln School to John's alma mater, the Loomis Institute, for the eleventh grade. Winthrop enjoyed the Lincoln School tremendously, but it had its drawbacks. Chief among them was a failure to foster the traditional academic skills required for admission into university. Junior and Abby concluded that Winthrop needed the discipline and focus offered by a more traditional boarding school for that task.[115] Nelson, Laurance, and David all later complained that the Lincoln School did not sufficiently equip them to succeed academically.[116] The decision to move Winthrop was a painful one for Junior. The Rockefeller-funded GEB had backed Lincoln as a model school, and Junior had given his personal endorsement to it by enrolling his own sons. Now he was forced to concede that such an education did not necessarily work for everyone.

By 1928, the Rockefeller family was growing up fast. Most of the children were well on the way to establishing their own lives outside the family home. Babs and her husband David M. Milton gave Junior and Abby their first grandchild, Abigail Rockefeller Milton, on April 27 that year.[117] In the fall, John entered his junior year at Princeton University in New Jersey, and Nelson entered his sophomore year at Dartmouth College in New Hampshire. Both majored in economics. Laurance joined John at Princeton as a freshman, where he majored in philosophy.[118] Only David was left at home, entering the ninth grade at the Lincoln School. He still had another four years to go before attending Harvard University as a freshman in the Class of 1936 to major in economics.[119] Attending the Loomis Institute was Winthrop's first stepping-stone toward independence and adulthood.

CHAPTER 3

The Loomis Institute

THE LOOMIS INSTITUTE was chartered in 1874 by the four sons and one daughter of Col. James Loomis and Abigail Sherwood Chaffee. The five siblings achieved success in their chosen vocations, but each shared the same family tragedy: all their children died before reaching adulthood. To provide educational opportunities for the children of others, they raised funds to open a school.[1] In 1912, the Loomis Institute board of trustees selected Nathaniel Horton Batchelder as the school's first headmaster. On September 24, 1914, it admitted its first students, with thirty-nine boys and thirteen girls.[2] The heart of the school's mission was "to foster a lifelong zeal for learning through a rigorous and diverse curriculum and to instill an abiding respect for others predicated on the egalitarian notion that neither religion, sex, geographical origin, nor financial standing will preclude a student from enrolling in the school." In 1926, a separate girls' school was set up in Windsor as the Chaffee School, leaving Loomis an all-boys' school. The two schools later merged again, in 1970, to form today's Loomis Chaffee School.[3]

Loomis was Junior's choice for John's preparatory education. As always, Junior was fastidious in his research. According to a later Loomis headmaster, Francis O. Grubbs, Junior sent out "a scout to study private schools to find one that had no frills, fostered the simple life, encouraged participation in the chores of everyday living, and would provide a first-class education surrounded by austerity and habits of vigor."[4] Loomis met those requirements. After a few years in operation, Batchelder recommended that Loomis should become a boarding school, and that it should represent a cross-section of society. Winthrop remembered there being a broad spectrum of scholarship and non-scholarship students, all of whom treated one another equally.[5]

Having made up his mind, Junior wrote to Batchelder to arrange for John's admission. But Batchelder initially turned down Junior's request since, he wrote, he did not want to "risk changing the character of the school" through showing "unfair discrimination against some other boy who did not have as many privileges as [Junior's] son." He underestimated Junior's resolve not to take no for an answer. Upon receipt of Batchelder's rejection letter, Junior drove to Windsor to personally plead the case for admitting John. Junior said that "he felt it grossly unfair discrimination of the worst kind to turn down a boy simply because his father was wealthy." Junior was persuasive enough to get Batchelder to relent, and John was enrolled at the school.[6] When Batchelder learned that Junior wanted to send another of his sons to Loomis, he was, he reported, delighted. True, it was late in the academic year and the school was already full, but, he said, he was always willing to "make adjustments for younger brothers and in special cases." Knowing Junior's aversion to any suggestion of special treatment, Batchelder assured him, "I am only doing for Winthrop what I have done in a number of cases before."[7]

Winthrop's stay at Loomis was geared toward the goal of making the necessary grades to get into college. Yet this was precisely the thing that he found the most difficult to do.[8] At the end of his three-year association with Winthrop, Batchelder tried to explain his pupil's academic shortcomings. He watched Winthrop's development closely and got to know him well, and his analysis provides some instructive observations.

Batchelder was convinced that Winthrop had "a physiological difficulty in some of his studies." He noted that Winthrop understood concepts far better when delivered orally than when presented in written form. In turn, Winthrop was a much more accomplished speaker than he was a writer. Batchelder's belief, constrained by the limitations of educational knowledge at the time, was that Winthrop's difficulty with written material was somehow connected to his left-handedness. Both Nelson and David were also left-handed. Following the practices of the day, Junior had tried to "correct" Nelson's left-handedness but with limited success. He did not bother to repeat such attempts with Winthrop and David.[9]

Although Batchelder misunderstood the cause, he may well have been on to something regarding the symptoms underlying Winthrop's poor academic performance. Later in life, Winthrop, Nelson, and David all appear to have been diagnosed with the learning disorder of dyslexia.[10] Dyslexia was not recognized as a learning disorder when the boys were in school, and it remains a complex condition that is still not fully understood today. We do know that it affects different people in different ways and to different degrees and that a common trait is a difficulty with reading and writing. Unquestionably, dyslexia should be considered when assessing Winthrop's lack of academic accomplishments.[11] "Dyslexia plagued him all his life," insists John Ward, Winthrop's Arkansas biographer and associate. "Give him a memorandum and he might or might not read it. If he did, it seemed to take forever, and most things he just didn't bother to read." At Winrock Farms, Winthrop instituted a reading program for his employees. He studied alongside them and still struggled to keep up.[12]

Batchelder felt that Winthrop's learning difficulties—whatever their cause—led him to turn away from his academic studies and made him inclined to direct his attention to other pursuits. One of the potential consequences of dyslexia is exactly this: an aversion to academic study and an embrace of other, more welcoming activities. Winthrop was clearly far more disposed to attend to matters outside the classroom than to those within it. As Batchelder put it, "A personal or moral problem, in his mind, needs immediate attention; time for study can be found later." Batchelder admired Winthrop's abilities beyond the classroom, including his maturity, his capacity for empathy, his enthusiasm, and his awareness of the world around him. Batchelder had known students like Winthrop in the past who, despite not being academically gifted, had gone on to use their other talents to become influential community leaders.[13]

Batchelder held no regrets about Winthrop's time spent at Loomis or his being pushed to achieve college-worthy grades. Winthrop himself was keen to attend college, and Batchelder felt he deserved the opportunity of trying to meet his goal. Moreover, Batchelder believed that without the goal of college admission Winthrop may have become even more disinterested in pursuing his academic studies. Batchelder expressed little worry about whether Winthrop would in fact attend college or not. There were, he pointed out, plenty of other options for a man of his talents, particularly given the very wide range of Rockefeller family opportunities that were open to him.[14]

Batchelder even had some very specific thoughts about what might prove most beneficial for Winthrop should he fail to gain admittance to college. He recommended that in such circumstances Winthrop "should spend the first half of the year in travel, or in work, perhaps in your [Junior's] office, or on one of your projects" to gain some practical experience. Batchelder was convinced that Winthrop would thrive in an environment where he had the opportunity to "meet a great variety of interesting people and to visit a great many interesting places." He signaled that he thought this preferable to Winthrop struggling on in academia, where he was plainly a fish out of water. It was elsewhere, Batchelder said, that Winthrop could best deploy his "extraordinary gifts."[15]

Batchelder's analysis turned out to be prescient, and Winthrop was undoubtedly on two very different tracks during his time at Loomis. One track lay inside the classroom and led to academic failure on a consistent basis. The other track led outside of the classroom, and it was here that Winthrop truly flourished: he cheered on the football team, joined the Political Club, advised freshmen, set up his own short-lived barber shop, chauffeured the school car, won election to student council, organized dances and orchestras, set up and ran a school endowment fund, helped to build tennis courts and an outdoor theater, and founded and ran a lunch shop. Winthrop's time at Loomis was the first indication that he was not able to fulfill his family's conventional expectations about who and what he should be. His path led in a very different direction, and most family members constantly struggled to understand or accept that fact.

Winthrop's first report at Loomis in fall 1928 set the general tone for the rest his studies there. It contained no grades above D—that is, no passing grades. Winthrop's tutor, David Newton, wrote to Junior to assure him that he would take matters into hand and arrange a study schedule and academic plan for the rest of the semester. The only redeeming factors in the report were decent marks for effort and punctuality, which at least indicated that Winthrop was attempting to engage in his studies.[16] Loomis alum John advised his younger brother, "If they see that you are doing your best they will be very decent even if you don't get onto things very well at first, but if they feel that you are loafing they won't have so much sympathy for you."[17]

Winthrop rarely let bad news about his grades get him down. He threw himself enthusiastically into extracurricular activities. Shortly after receiving his poor first report, he wrote excitedly to his parents about beating the Taft School 25–7 in football. It was Loomis's first victory over their state rivals in four years and only the second such victory in the history of the school. After the game, Winthrop went out with other new students to gather firewood. When supper was finished, they poured on gasoline and set the bonfire ablaze: "Then after the fire we got a big hay wagon and got the whole football team in it and the rest of the school got ropes and the like and pulled the wagon and all the way over to town where we cheered for about ten minutes and then the team went into the drug store and Mr. B[atchelder] treated them to anything they wanted to eat then we gave another cheer for the team and next for the town of Windsor." By the time the wagon was pulled back to school, Winthrop was dripping with sweat. All the students went back to the dormitory to sing songs, eat food, and listen to the double-touchdown-scoring team hero John Ferguson read poetry.[18]

Winthrop also became a member of the Political Club, winning entry with his treatise in support of Prohibition.[19] (This introduction to politics is not without irony; as governor of Arkansas, Winthrop would be responsible for a controversial bill that provided voters with a local option to permit the sale of mixed drinks.[20]) Junior was suitably impressed with his son at the time for gaining a place in the club and for following in his Prohibitionist footsteps.[21] Abby was equally encouraging and asked to read a copy of the treatise. At the same time, she took the opportunity to remind her son that his main priority should be raising his grades.[22] Winthrop heard regularly from the rest of the family, too, referring to the letters from his "very nice thoughtful brothers."[23] Typically, in these exchanges, John gave advice on academics, Nelson on sports, and Laurance on girls.[24]

Winthrop's second report at Loomis in November was worse than the first. Batchelder assured Junior that this was mainly due to Winthrop's "habits of work and his attention to detail." The headmaster placed the blame squarely on the Lincoln School, noting, "Winthrop has had until now the great advantage of a school that stresses creative effort. We try very hard not to stifle creation, but at the same time to achieve the obvious benefits of discipline." A plan was put in place for Winthrop to visit tutor David Newton in the evenings for additional supervised study. Batchelder remained confident that Winthrop could still enter college in 1930 as planned, but only if he went flat-out in his studies.[25]

Junior concurred with Batchelder's conclusions about this son's need to knuckle down with his schoolwork.[26] Yet he also made it clear that he did not appreciate Batchelder's implied criticism of Lincoln's experiential approach to education, something that evidently remained a sensitive topic. Junior demurred, "I fancy the real problem for the educator is to try to steer a middle course between the two [academic and experiential learning], and get what he can for his students from each."[27] Despite his spirited defense of Lincoln to Batchelder, Junior made a point of sending Winthrop's reports from Loomis, along with Batchelder's correspondence, to Lincoln's director, Dr. Jesse H. Newlon.[28] Junior, repeating Abby's earlier comments, advised Winthrop to cut down on the amount of time he spent on extracurricular activities and to focus more upon bringing up his grades.[29]

Winthrop's next report at the end of November showed little sign of improvement. Extra lessons in grammar were arranged three times a week with Mrs. Cole, a private tutor in Windsor.[30] Winthrop's final report in December still contained no passing grades.[31] David Newton advised that the extra grammar lessons were desperately needed and must continue. He also suggested further tweaks to Winthrop's study and class preparations. But overall, Newton was decidedly downbeat about Winthrop's chances of academic success. The most he could muster on a positive note was: "The picture isn't complete without mention of Win's constantly helpful attitude. He volunteered to manage the pouring of refreshments after the Christmas reading, a function I had threatened to abandon because it had become difficult with so many. Win organized his crew and all quite beautifully. I feel badly that he has to suffer as he must at present over his studies, but we shall come through."[32]

The latest reports about Winthrop's academic failings prompted a long talk between Junior and his son.[33] Again, this changed nothing. In the spring 1929 term, the failing grades continued unabated.[34] By April, Batchelder was resigned to advising Junior that Winthrop should complete an additional year at Loomis if he was to have any hope of entering college. He also recommended enrolling Winthrop at Long Lake Lodge summer camp in North Bridgeton, Maine, where Loomis French teacher Mr. Sharp was tutoring over the summer. Batchelder felt that this would help Winthrop catch up in his studies. Junior initially hesitated on the grounds that "boys who go there [summer camp] are behind in their work and therefore not a group that is particularly inspiring." He decided to send Arthur Woods, a former New York City police commissioner now employed as a trusted advisor in the Rockefeller family office, to personally inspect the camp on his behalf. Pending Woods's positive report, Junior agreed to float the idea of summer camp to Winthrop, so as to make it "easier to secure his acquiescence in the scheme and bring about his enthusiastic support of the program."[35]

When Junior broached the subject of attending summer camp with Winthrop, his son did not exactly jump at the idea given his previous traumatic experiences at Camp Merryweather.[36] Winthrop made a counterproposal to hire a private tutor, not least because he personally did not care very much for Mr. Sharp.[37] Junior urged Winthrop to discuss the matter further with Batchelder. In the meantime, Arthur Woods's report on the camp was encouraging and concluded, "The type of boy who goes to this school is above rather than below average."[38] After conferring with Batchelder, Winthrop agreed to attend the summer camp.[39] Junior and Abby enrolled Winthrop from July 9 to August 31.[40]

There was no doubt that Winthrop needed all the help he could get. His end-of-year report showed a cumulative total of fourteen fails and just eight passes.[41] Junior described his son's record as "disappointing." Never one to resist employing economic leverage to set his children on the right track, Junior noted Winthrop's recent request for a new car. He posed the question directly to his son: "I wonder whether you feel that the aggregate of your accomplishment at Loomis this past year as indicated in your reports is such to form a basis that would justify our considering a new car for your use"—especially, given the added expense incurred for Winthrop's attendance at summer camp to address those deficiencies. Junior said that he would keep an open mind on the matter, with a distinct eye on how Winthrop's academic studies progressed over the summer.[42]

Junior sent Winthrop's end-of-year report from Loomis to the Lincoln School.[43] "Winthrop's experience raises the most fundamental problem of method, a problem that has been on my mind constantly since coming to Lincoln School, and especially since I have come to know the school intimately," replied Lincoln's director, Dr. Jesse H. Newlon. He pondered, "How can the values for which this school has been most noted be secured without sacrifice of giving the individual the thorough-going intellectual training, including the building of habits of industry, of accuracy of thought and work, which certainly are essential factors for which every school should stand?" Newlon's answer to his own rhetorical question was less than convincing: "We may not succeed in the Lincoln School, but I wanted you to know that we are keenly conscious of the problem and are doing the very best that we can to meet the challenge."[44]

Winthrop's summer at Long Lake Lodge was much better than his previous experience at Camp Merryweather. He threw himself committedly into a daily schedule: waking at 6:30 a.m. for a swim in the lake; breakfast at 7:00 a.m.; English lessons with Mr. Wollingate at 8:00 a.m.; French with Mr. Sharp at 11:00 a.m.; and then lunch at 12:30 p.m. The afternoons and evenings were free for recreation.[45] When Winthrop started back at Loomis in fall 1929, there was a slight improvement, with C and D grades replacing the earlier E and F grades in his class reports.[46] Batchelder meanwhile worked feverishly in finding a way to get Winthrop into his desired college choice of Yale.[47]

Throughout his academic woes, Winthrop remained popular with the other students at Loomis. Early in the fall 1929 term, he was selected by the student council to act as an adviser to new students at the school.[48] Enterprising as ever, Winthrop set up his own barbershop. The cuts were cheap but of poor quality, and the business quickly folded on that basis.[49] Winthrop was also one of the few students whom Batchelder trusted to drive the school car.[50] A notable assignment that term was to collect Dr. Robert Russa Moton, principal of the Tuskegee Institute in Alabama, from the train station. Moton succeeded the renowned Black educator Booker T. Washington as principal at Tuskegee; in turn, he had become one of the leading Black educators in the United States. Moton visited Loomis as chair of a campaign being run by Tuskegee to foster greater interracial cooperation. At the station, Winthrop quickly grabbed Moton's bags, loaded them in the car, and chauffeured him to the school. This did not escape Moton's attention. When he later visited Loomis alum Robert F.

Duncan, the vice president of the John Price Jones Corporation, a fundraising consultancy firm in New York, Duncan noted, "Dr. Moton was visibly moved by this experience. It seems that the mere thought of a son of one of America's richest families carrying the bag of and acting as chauffeur for a black man was almost more than the leader of that race could contemplate without strong emotion. The school made a tremendous impression on him." Dr. Moton certainly did not receive the same treatment in Alabama, where Winthrop's actions would have contravened the strict racial hierarchy.[51]

Winthrop's grades began to slip again toward the end of the fall 1929 term.[52] Though disappointed, Junior now appeared far more concerned about the state of his son's finances. He calculated that Winthrop had spent $18.10 (equivalent to $272 in 2020 dollars) on food, which he considered "a little extravagant." Winthrop was a regular eater at Ed Prouty's drugstore and Ira Hemphill's café in Windsor, among many other establishments.[53] He had also spent $11.65 (equivalent to $175 in 2020 dollars) on taxi fares, not including the $9.75 spent on a single fare when Winthrop absent-mindedly handed the taxi driver a $10 bill rather than a $1 bill. Junior had plenty of questions about these indiscretions: Why wasn't Winthrop riding the bus or streetcar? Why didn't he get up in time for breakfast? And why didn't he attend supper on Sunday evenings, which he had already paid for at the school? "These comments are made in view of the fact that you are considerably over-running your allowance," warned Junior. "This is not an interesting letter, but I am sure you will agree it is important from both our points of view."[54]

Junior's mood lightened somewhat at the news that Winthrop had been elected to the student council at Loomis in spring 1930. He offered his son "hearty congratulations" and continued, "For a boy to win so conspicuous an evidence of the confidence of his fellows is indeed a high honor. You are worthy of the honor, I well know, and I am confident that you will acquit yourself of the responsibility which attaches to it with fullest credit."[55] The election to student council came with the added benefit that Winthrop became a personal advisee of Batchelder. The headmaster opened his home to Winthrop for study sessions.[56]

Winthrop's class reports in March returned to mostly C and D grades.[57] Junior was pleased at this tentative progress, telling Batchelder, "This is most gratifying and only shows what Winthrop can do when he puts himself wholeheartedly to the task."[58] As was always the case in the Rockefeller family, applied effort and success reaped rewards. Junior informed Winthrop that he intended to raise his allowance to $1,500 per year (equivalent to $22,411 in 2020 dollars) starting on his birthday.[59] John wrote soon after to notify Winthrop that an

Winthrop as a teenager at the Loomis Institute, ca.
1930. *Winthrop Rockefeller Collection, UA Little Rock
Center for Arkansas History and Culture.*

order had been placed for a new Ford, according to Winthrop's requested specifications: a dark-blue touring car with six red wheels, two on the side, with a truck rack to the rear.[60]

Yet just as things were beginning to perk up in his studies, Winthrop found himself in trouble outside of the classroom. He was serving on his class's end-of-year dance committee, and part of the job involved hiring an orchestra for the event. A couple of the other students on the committee knew the names of two or three orchestras in nearby Hartford. One evening they all decided to drive into town and listen to them. They hired a car and set out on a pass that was valid until midnight. While in Hartford, they met two or three other Loomis students who were out on passes until 10:00 p.m. Since Winthrop's party finished listening to the orchestras earlier than planned, they agreed to drive the students with 10:00 p.m. passes back to school before dropping off the car. When one of the students returned to Loomis, he casually mentioned that Winthrop had given him a ride home. That slip of the tongue had far-reaching consequences.[61]

It was a strict school policy that students, even those with licenses, could not drive cars without permission. Winthrop had thought nothing of it, since he was allowed to drive the school car on a regular basis. The school did not view the matter the same way. Winthrop's English teacher spearheaded the prosecution and demanded that Winthrop resign from student council immediately for having committed such an egregious crime. Winthrop had little choice in the matter, even though he felt it was a harsh judgment that he never forgave his teacher for. He did at least make a swift return to the student council when his peers reelected him in the fall 1930 term.[62]

Junior was not so forgiving. "The idea of knocking about Hartford, going to different places where dance music was to be heard, does not appeal to me as a very desirable thing to do as a rule," he informed Winthrop. "If you all knew that driving the car without Mr. Batchelder's consent was against the rules, it seems a little strange that none of you happened to think of it. I am wondering what time you got home that night. It must have been pretty late." As far as Junior was concerned, the moral of the story came down to this: "It is hard to be dropped from the council; on the other hand, the whole episode will probably be very helpful in toning up the morale of the school, by making it evident that rules are rules, whoever breaks them, and that all boys are treated alike and without favoritism."[63]

Being forced to resign from the student council meant that Winthrop's second year at Loomis ended under something of a cloud. His academic work did not improve any either, with a steady preponderance of C and D grades.[64]

Winthrop also sat college entrance exams, which likewise did not go at all well. Batchelder reported being disappointed with them, and he recommended an intensive period of preparatory classes before Winthrop sat more college entrance exams in the fall.[65] Over the summer, Winthrop attended the wedding of Nelson to Mary Todhunter Clark (in family nomenclature and hereafter, Tod), and afterward accompanied the family on another a trip out West.[66] In August, he enrolled at the Roxbury School in Cheshire, Connecticut, for a month of intensive study.[67] Roxbury was more of a cramming school than the relaxed summer camp atmosphere of the previous year. Winthrop found himself in very different company this time. He studied alongside several coal miners who were being tutored to pass college entrance exams so that they could take up football scholarships. Most of them were headed to Columbia University, and one went on to be an outstanding player for the City College of New York.[68]

Winthrop once again committed himself to a rigorous schedule. At 8:00 a.m. he had English class, followed by French and history. After lunch, it was back to history again, and then after a brief respite for exercise, even more history. After supper, it was trigonometry until bedtime.[69] The strict regimen succeeded in steadily improving Winthrop's grades.[70] The September 1930 college entrance exams produced far better scores than the ones he had sat earlier in the year, "a very admirable result of his summer tutoring," Batchelder concluded.[71] Junior echoed Batchelder's praise, telling Winthrop, "We are still rejoicing with you in the good marks you got in your examinations."[72]

Yet distractions elsewhere again appeared to undermine Winthrop's incipient academic progress. This time it was his involvement with a school endowment fund. Winthrop came up with the idea of launching a campaign among students at Loomis to follow the previous year's fundraising drive among friends and alumni. Near the end of the 1929–30 school year, Winthrop discussed the idea with Batchelder, who was naturally enthusiastic about raising school revenues. After drawing up a plan, Winthrop presented it to his fellow students at the school's daily assembly. They readily expressed support. Winthrop set up the endowment fund and became its first president, taking on responsibilities for planning and directing its activities. The initial idea was for students to earn money over the summer from either working a job or running their own campaign.[73] Together with his fellow endowment fund committee members, Winthrop ambitiously looked to raise $2,500 (equivalent to $37,351 in 2020 dollars) over the summer.[74]

The drive yielded a far more modest $400–$500 (equivalent to $5,976–$7,470 in 2020 dollars). Unperturbed by the shortfall, the endowment committee used the money raised to start a mid-morning, late afternoon, and evening snack bar at Loomis. Over the course of the year, the snack bar raised $2,000 (equivalent to $29,881 in 2020 dollars). It became an institution at the school and, after Winthrop's departure, received its own dedicated room in a new dormitory supplied with chairs, tables, a refrigerator, and a sink. Winthrop suggested that students donate not only their money but, just as importantly, their time and labor in service to the school. This led to the construction of tennis courts and, with a little help from the school carpenter, a small outdoor theater too.[75] Although Winthrop took great pride in these achievements and received many plaudits for his success, the role also had its drawbacks. One of them was bookkeeping, which had never been one of Winthrop's strong suits. More importantly, the endowment fund got in the way of Winthrop's academic studies.[76]

Winthrop's academic progress at Roxbury was to a large extent due to an enforced period of focus on his studies with few other distractions allowed to get in the way. Batchelder and Junior were adamant that Winthrop should learn from this, and they recommended that he tenaciously guard against becoming overburdened with extracurricular activities during his final year at Loomis. Batchelder confided to Junior that he feared the endowment was becoming this very type of distraction.[77] Junior renewed his caution to Winthrop about taking on too much responsibility.[78] Winthrop's adviser for fall 1930, Known Mills, reported that Winthrop had subsequently "talked over his situation with me and explained how he has reduced the time spent on extra-curricular activities in order to improve his work on his studies."[79] If that was true, it did not appear to make much difference. The same steady diet of C and D grades continued.[80]

As Winthrop started his final term at Loomis in spring 1931, the push to get him into Yale intensified. Junior dangled a carrot by raising his allowance to $1,650 per year (equivalent to $26,336 in 2020 dollars).[81] He also brandished a stick in the form of a rhetorical question: "In view of all that is at stake in connection with your winter's work, namely, the question of whether you pass the examinations for Yale this spring or fail, have you not come to the point where you cannot afford to delay another day adopting the policy of making your studies your first and only concern from now until the end of the school year?" This came with both a warning and an added dollop of guilt for good measure: "I feel further that such failure would have a very depressing and unfortunate effect upon you, not to speak of the humiliation it would be to your family and friends. . . . I am writing very seriously and very earnestly."[82]

Other family members also piled on the pressure in hopes of eliciting some positive response. John wrote, "If you should slip up on your college boards the family would be terribly disappointed, and also it will be a little hard for you to explain when people ask you why you didn't go to college." He added, "Excuse this little fight talk but I do think it would be rather sad if you should slip up on making college when there is no reason in the world why you should not get in when the rest of us were able to."[83] Nelson additionally proffered, "We hear varying reports about you that come in every now and then from which I gather you have lost interest in examinations and feel that they indicate little, if anything. We are all hoping this will prove to be true, for we just got a new office boy down here and I am afraid there wouldn't be any position for you for four or five years. . . . Don't bother to answer this as we all know that you are straining to the utmost to get into Yale next year. I sure hope you do as I think you will make a great mistake not to go to college."[84] Neither the encouragement, nor the dire warnings, nor the attempt at humor, seemed to have any impact whatsoever.[85]

Winthrop's parents attended their son's commencement ceremony at Loomis on June 6, 1931, staying overnight with the Batchelders on campus.[86] Mr. Batchelder told Junior and Abby that Winthrop had graduated in the bottom fortieth percentile of private-school pupils, "i.e., 6 out of 10 are better than he."[87] Still, if Winthrop had not been a star academic performer at Loomis, his all-around contribution to the school certainly made a long-lasting impression. This was duly rewarded. Winthrop graduated with the school's most prestigious award, the "Industry, Loyalty and Manliness" prize. Even John was jealous of that achievement.[88]

"Thank fortune," wrote Abby to her sister Lucy, upon Winthrop's graduation from Loomis. "I am now hoping . . . that he can pass his examinations for Yale."[89] Winthrop's Aunt Lucy did not seem quite so concerned. Alone among family members, she appeared to support Batchelder's view that Winthrop was destined to pursue a different path. "I think [he] is a wonder," she wrote of Winthrop. "[A]nd [I] don't think it makes one bit of difference whether he goes to college or not. If he doesn't go he won't miss it in the least. He will always be the center of the stage some where and when he is with the other boys they wont [sic] talk about their college experiences they will be trying to keep up with him. He is so alive and eager."[90]

In early July, Batchelder reported that the college board results were in. Though Winthrop's scores were by no means outstanding, Batchelder told him that, "Yale has repeatedly taken Loomis boys with such slight failures, and I have hopes for you."[91] Abby was similarly upbeat, noting to Lucy, "I think [Yale] President [James Rowland] Angell is very anxious to have him come there. He likes Winthrop and I also think would like to have a member of the family go to Yale." She quickly added, "Not that we would like to ask for any special favors or concessions on his behalf, because we wouldn't."[92] Junior was more guarded, writing, "Until we hear the result of Winthrop's examinations, it is hardly worth while for us to try to make plans, for we are still hoping the result may be favorable."[93] August finally brought the news they were all eagerly waiting for: Winthrop had made it into Yale by the skin of his teeth, and he was admitted to the Class of 1935.[94]

Winthrop's acceptance into Yale was a mixed blessing. Headmaster Batchelder's and Aunt Lucy's respective assessments of him were both insightful. They recognized a truth about Winthrop's qualities and talents that his immediate family members all seemingly refused to accept: Winthrop was no scholar.[95] Rather, he possessed an abundance of enthusiasm, energy, and sheer joie de vivre. Ever since his time at the Lincoln School, he had delighted in throwing himself into practical problems and tackling them, gaining hands-on experience, and interacting and engaging with other people and the world around him. In this context, college represented a stifling ivory cage, not an alluring ivory tower. Yet Winthrop's nagging sense of Rockefeller responsibility and duty, which had been hardwired into him from an early age, trumped all these concerns. Going to Yale was not about doing what he wanted to do; it was about doing what his family expected him to do. For now, fulfilling those expectations seemed more important to him than asking the more fundamental question about what he wanted to achieve with the rest of his life.

CHAPTER 4   Yale University

YALE UNIVERSITY REPRESENTED a lofty ambition for someone with such an undistinguished academic track record as Winthrop's. Founded in 1701 as Collegiate School to educate Congregational ministers, Yale is the third-oldest institution of higher education in the United States. In 1716, the school moved to New Haven, Connecticut, and two years later it was renamed Yale College after its largest benefactor, Elihu Yale. By the time of the American Revolution, Yale was beginning to move beyond its religious focus to teach the humanities and sciences. In the nineteenth century, it began to incorporate graduate and professional instruction. Yale awarded the first doctorate in the United States in 1861 and became a university in 1887. Over the course of the twentieth century, Yale continued to expand in size and scope as one of the nation's leading universities. When Winthrop entered Yale in fall 1931, James R. Angell had been president for over a decade. Angell was a former acting president at the University of Chicago, an institution that Senior played an instrumental role in founding in 1890. As president of Yale, Angell proved adept at gaining funds from the Rockefeller Foundation, including a $1 million (equivalent to $15 million in 2020 dollars) endowment to form a Nursing School in 1929.[1]

Winthrop's stay at Yale was not a success. Inside the classroom, his grades were even worse than at Loomis. Outside the classroom, without mentorship from figures like Batchelder, and without communal projects to keep him engaged, Winthrop found other activities to fill his time. Principally, these were smoking, drinking, and socializing. In turn, these pursuits, among other things, had a catastrophic impact on Winthrop's finances. Needless to say, such developments rang alarm bells for Junior and other family members. Then a glimmer of hope arrived when John arranged for his younger brother to spend the summer of 1933 working in the oil industry. The work world was a revelation to Winthrop. Here was a place where he could throw himself back into more constructive and productive pursuits without the albatross of failing grades constantly hanging around his neck. This environment, Winthrop concluded, was far more appealing and much more conducive to his success than staying in academia.

Winthrop's intended major at Yale was history, although he found art and architecture the most enjoyable among his classes.[2] Regardless, within six weeks of starting, Winthrop was already in academic trouble. Percy T. Walden, Dean of Freshmen, wrote to tell Winthrop that his grades were "unsatisfactory, and place you on disqualification. A similar record at the time of the December report would place you on 'General Warning.' " Walden added, "This letter is written to warn you that you are not meeting Yale's standards. You are already deficient in the background of your Freshman courses, which will make the work that comes later more difficult to master. . . . It is imperative, therefore, in order to establish yourself in good standing in the Class, that you make a most determined effort to improve the quality of your work and that you do this without delay."[3]

A copy of the letter went to Junior, who heard further from Winthrop's English instructor and student counselor Samuel B. Hemmingway. Presumably unaware of Winthrop's previous academic difficulties, Hemmingway optimistically offered, "He is so obviously intelligent and co-operative that I can not believe that he will find it impossible to pull his grades up to a satisfactory level."[4] Of course, Junior had seen and heard it all before. He warned Hemmingway about his son's inclination to neglect his studies at the expense of other matters that he found more pressing.[5] Batchelder's glowing report to Winthrop about how well all the other boys in his year at Loomis were doing in college did not help ease the pressure any. Upon discovering Winthrop's predicament at Yale, Batchelder advised, "Start a vigorous regime of study and find a tutor for your really difficult subjects. You *can't* flunk out!"[6]

Winthrop begged to differ. His end-of-term grades revealed one borderline pass and a long string of fails.[7] At the beginning of spring 1932, Walden wrote a stiff letter to Winthrop informing him that his performance was unsatisfactory, that he had been placed on a General Warning, and that his grades were so under par that his case would have to be considered by the Committee on Rules. He was in imminent danger of being dropped from the Class of 1935.[8] Junior, who was once again copied into the correspondence, replied that his son's situation was "most distressing to Mrs. Rockefeller and [himself]." He restated the perceived problem that Winthrop "finds life and folks so thrillingly interesting outside of the classroom that it is a question of whether he is going to be able to make himself do the work necessary in order to carry on at Yale."[9]

Walden advised Winthrop to drop his advanced French class for an easier intermediate class. In an echo of Batchelder's earlier comments, Walden noted Hemmingway's concern that Winthrop appeared "confused, especially in extracting information from the written page," and wondered if there was a "connection between the boy's slow reading and his left-handedness." Again, this observation about reading difficulties is consistent with a diagnosis of dyslexia.[10]

Further reports from Hemmingway about his son's lackadaisical approach to his studies prompted Junior to send John to Yale to find out what was going on.[11] John's discovery that Winthrop was being detained in the college infirmary for a sinus infection helped to rein in Junior's ire. Junior explained his son's predicament to Hemmingway.[12] Abby wrote to Winthrop with some motherly practical health advice, imploring him to wear a hat to avoid further sinusitis attacks in the future.[13]

Winthrop's mid-term exams and his end-of-term finals evidenced no improvement in academic performance.[14] By the conclusion of the school year, the scales even appeared to be falling from Junior's eyes. He openly questioned if Winthrop staying in college was serving any useful purpose at all. Revisiting Batchelder's earlier advice, Junior pondered "whether it might not be better for Winthrop not to return to college but to take up some active, vigorous work for someone other than his father, where he would be held to his task and would have to stand or fall on his own performance." Junior informed Hemmingway that he had discussed the matter with Winthrop and that his son also thought this might be the best course of action. Both Winthrop and Junior were adamant that he should not walk away from Yale having failed, but that he should fight for his place in the sophomore year through completing make-up exams before making any final decision.[15]

Hemmingway wrote back from his summer vacation at Taymouth Castle in Scotland, confirming that Winthrop needed to pass English and complete his work in biology by the end of September 1932 to stay in college. He suggested that before then Winthrop should seek out a tutor in New Haven for another round of intensive study. Hemmingway agreed that if Winthrop was not fully committed to college, it would be a waste of time for him to continue just for the sake of it.[16]

Over the summer of 1932, starting on July 10, Winthrop spent six weeks at Camp Winona in Denmark, Maine, as a camp counselor. The nature of his departure for camp underscored Winthrop's growing devil-may-care attitude. Almost two weeks after he left home, his parents had still not heard from him, which drove them to distraction. Junior began a long and indignant letter, expressing his fears about the dangers of kidnapping and condemning Winthrop's thoughtlessness about his parents' feelings. Yet before Junior finished writing the letter, Winthrop telephoned from camp to let his parents know that all was well. After the phone call, Junior finished and mailed the letter anyway, adding a warning not to let a similar situation arise again.[17]

With the panic over, Winthrop enjoyed his summer as a camp counselor. Camp director Philip Cobb, a former Loomis teacher, ran the operation along with his two brothers. The Cobb boys' parents had established the camp some twenty-five years earlier. It was through the Loomis connection that Winthrop was invited to work there, although he did so for the fun of it, since it was not a paid position. Winthrop was in his element mentoring the boys at the camp and undertaking practical activities with them. He also believed that his former experiences of being bullied by his brothers and by counselors at Camp Merryweather allowed him to better understand his charges and their concerns.[18] Philip Cobb agreed, feeling that Winthrop had "contributed more to Winona [than] any new counselor that we have had." As a bonus, the camp delivered a pleasurable and entirely unexpected opportunity to rehearse with the Rockettes, the precision dancers who went on to form the famous chorus line at Radio City Music Hall when it opened later that year. Seven Rockettes were living in vacation cottages nearby the camp, and in the evenings they taught Winthrop and other camp counselors some of their routines.[19]

Toward the end of summer there were two exciting pieces of family news. Firstly, David was admitted to the Harvard Class of 1936.[20] Secondly, John set a date to marry Vassar graduate Blanchette Ferry Hooker.[21] Winthrop returned from camp on August 27, spent a couple of days at home with his parents, and then traveled to New Haven to receive tutoring from Richard Brooks for his end-of-summer examinations. In an apparent change of heart, Winthrop told Junior that he was determined not only to win reinstatement but to continue in college for at least another year.[22] Winthrop received eighteen hours of tutoring from Brooks, but to no avail. He failed all his exams.[23]

Junior anxiously wrote to Yale president Angell to clarify what would happen next, since it appeared that Winthrop had gone AWOL again. Junior was resigned to Winthrop being thrown out of Yale and wanted to assure Angell that he did not expect his son to receive preferential treatment.[24] Quite why, then, under these circumstances, Winthrop was still promoted to the sophomore class remains something of a mystery. Dean of Freshmen Walden hinted that Winthrop's earlier hospitalization had been considered as an extenuating circumstance.[25] Angell's letter of reply to Junior read, "We want very much to keep [Winthrop] and we hope that he will not make this impossible."[26] Being a Rockefeller often meant receiving preferential treatment whether it was solicited or not. For whatever reason, Winthrop was permitted to return to Yale in fall 1932.[27]

Winthrop lived alone during his freshman year. In his sophomore year, he became much more involved in campus life, which was not always a good thing. Winthrop and a group of friends decided to "pack an entry" by selecting adjacent rooms together in a dormitory entryway so that they could all live next to one another. Winthrop roomed with his Loomis friend Joe Johnson, who was on the Yale football team. A particularly memorable character in the dormitory was Bowen Charlton "Sonny" Tufts III. Tufts, the son of a well-known Boston banking family, was in the habit of going out, getting drunk, and practicing his operatic scales in the courtyard at three in the morning. This brought a hail of bottles in his direction from the others, which they kept ready by their bedsides for such occasions.[28] Tufts went on to make a living as a star of stage and screen, and as an opera singer.[29] Years later, when Winthrop returned from World War II in 1945, his second night back in the United States was spent with Tufts out on the town in Los Angeles.[30] One of Winthrop's best friends in his sophomore year was George Henry. Winthrop and Henry often went into New Haven with their friendly neighborhood cab driver Buck, who hung out with them in town while they played cards, smoked, and drank.[31]

Winthrop began smoking the summer before he entered Yale as a freshman and drinking once he started college. Given his family's teetotalism, he had never tasted alcohol before. He quickly fell in with a crowd who thought it was amusing to ply him with drinks and to watch him become deathly ill because of his low tolerance levels. To Winthrop's eternal regret, he was soon able to hold his drink as well as they could.[32] Exactly when and how drinking began to seriously impact Winthrop has been subject to different interpretations. Historians Peter Collier and David Horowitz, citing a "close friend," conclude that Winthrop was "pretty much a confirmed alcoholic by the time he was thirty-five."[33] David Rockefeller maintained that by the time of his death his brother was a "chronic alcoholic." He added, "I think he was the only member of the family who tended to drink more alcohol more frequently. That was not in the best interest of his health. And that was something that I think he couldn't, he came not to be able to do without. I think alcohol was to a large extent part of his difficulties."[34]

According to journalist Alvin Moscow, however, Winthrop was more of a cyclical drinker who could, to some degree, maintain a control over his alcohol intake, including sustained periods of abstinence. As with his yo-yoing weight gain and loss, stresses and circumstances were triggers. "If I could only solve a problem or two which I have, I could cut out this stuff completely," Winthrop once told friends. The more burned out he felt, the more he drank. This was particularly telling after he assumed his duties as governor of Arkansas in 1967, when his use of alcohol was regularly called into question and subject to greater public scrutiny.[35] Winthrop's drinking added to the perception of a lack of self-control and self-discipline in the eyes of his family and others. Yet with the benefit of modern science, we now know that alcoholism is an addiction and a disease rather than an indication of personal failings.[36]

Not only did Winthrop's newfound socializing fail to improve his academic grades, but it did little for the state of his finances. A forewarning of this came in fall 1932 as preparations took place for John's forthcoming nuptials. Winthrop, along with his other brothers, was an usher at the wedding. Nelson took charge of buying John a silver cigarette and cigar box as a gift. He requested a sample signature from each brother to engrave on the box, along with a $5 contribution (equivalent to $88 in 2020 dollars) to cover the cost of the purchase.[37] "Thank you very much for sending your signature," wrote Nelson to Winthrop a couple of weeks later. "How about the $5?!"[38]

When the end-of-year reckoning came, things were far worse than Junior or anyone else could ever have imagined. In addition to spending all his annual $1,800 (equivalent to $31,682 in 2020 dollars) allowance, Winthrop had accumulated an extra $1,885.22 (equivalent to $33,182 in 2020 dollars) in unpaid bills, more than doubling his permitted expenses for the year. This prompted a stern talk with Junior, who agreed to make Winthrop a loan to cover his debts. In addition, Junior raised Winthrop's allowance in 1933 to $2,400 (equivalent to $47,079 in 2020 dollars) based on a mutually agreed budget and with the "strict understanding that there will be no more bail outs."[39] The increase came with an itemized list of areas for reduction in spending, including "breakfasts at your club, fewer taxicabs, unnecessary travel, excessive smoking, careful buying of clothes at bargain sales when possible, etc." To provide an incentive, Junior offered to cancel two dollars of Winthrop's loan for every dollar that he applied to it from his allowance.[40] Shortly after, Winthrop sent a check to Junior, cut from the new loan, to cover a previous loan from the year before.[41] Winthrop also reduced the deficit on loans that he had received from his mother and his sister.[42]

Winthrop was left in no doubt about Junior's determination to hold him to account in his future financial affairs. In early February, Junior brought his son's attention to dentist bills that Winthrop had incurred over the New Year's holiday. On December 30, Winthrop was fifteen minutes late for a one-hour appointment, and on January 3 he was half an hour late for a one-hour appointment. Junior said that Winthrop owed him a quarter of the $25 (equivalent to $490 in 2020 dollars) per hour charge for the first late appointment, a sum of $6.25 (equivalent to $123 in 2020 dollars), and a half of the $25 per hour charge for the second late appointment, a sum of $12.50 (equivalent to $245 in 2020 dollars), coming to a total of $18.75 (equivalent to $368 in 2020 dollars). Under their agreement, Junior was happy to pay for Winthrop's medical expenses, but he was not willing to pay for Winthrop's tardiness. He let his son know so in no uncertain terms.[43] When Winthrop did not reply within a week, Junior wrote him again pressing for payment.[44]

On May 1, 1933, Winthrop turned twenty-one. Junior and Abby could not be with him on the day, but his father wrote in advance to wish him well and to dispense some life advice: "I know that you have high ambitions for yourself; I know that you want to make the most of your life and your opportunities; and I know that more and more the problems of how to accomplish these ends are in your thoughts. How eager I am to be of help to you in these and all other ways, it would be difficult for you to overestimate," Junior communicated. "At the same time, with you and with all the other children, I am anxious not to interfere with your freedom of action or your choice of those fields of useful service which appeal most particularly to you and which you may feel that you can make your life count most largely. Let us talk of these matters any time you so desire." The letter came with a check for an undisclosed amount.[45]

Winthrop took his father up on the offer. "What is going to be my life work?" he asked Junior. "My interest in 'people' has made me think that I could be a useful citizen in politics or some public service. On the other hand my pleasure in 'developing things' makes me wonder whether I could not be happier and of more use to you in helping relieve some of your burdens by going into business."[46] By way of reply, a noncommittal Junior wrote, "It is difficult to give a categorical answer." He acknowledged that it was indeed tricky to make up one's mind about one's future at such a young age. Politics and public service were good choices. But business experience was considerably useful in those careers too.[47]

Winthrop's future came into sharper focus over the summer of 1933 in discussions about how he could most productively spend his time between academic years at Yale. The debate initiated a tug-of-war between his older brothers over Winthrop's best interests. On the one side were Nelson and Laurance with, as always, Nelson the chief instigator. Nelson made an appointment for his younger brother to meet with Hugh Robertson of Todd, Robertson and Todd Engineering Consultants at their Graybar Building offices on the thirtieth floor at 420 Lexington Avenue. The firm was working on the construction of the Rockefeller Center, a massive midtown Manhattan development project funded by Junior. Robertson had come up with a few different opportunities that might interest Winthrop.[48]

On the other side was John, who wrote, "I feel quite strongly that you would find some form of industrial relations position not only exceedingly interesting at the moment, but also quite helpful as a background for anything which you may later do in politics."[49] John came up with an idea, in conjunction with a triumvirate of experts from Standard Oil of New Jersey—C. J. Hicks, H. C. Pierce, and T. H. A. Tiedemann—for Winthrop to spend the summer in the oil industry. According to the plan they devised, over a period of three months Winthrop would spend time at refineries in New Jersey before moving to Humble Oil Company, a Standard Oil of New Jersey subsidiary based in Houston, Texas, and finally to Colonial Beacon Oil Company, another Standard Oil of New Jersey subsidiary based in Boston, Massachusetts. This, John said, would give Winthrop "a pretty good picture of the oil business."[50]

John quickly followed up with another letter the very next day to impress upon his younger brother that his suggestion was a "really serious proposition" that involved taking on "a twenty-four hour a day job." It demanded a full workday followed by a good deal of socializing afterward to meet people and to make contacts in the industry. "It would be a wonderfully interesting and valuable experience I feel if you were to go at it as a real job and not as a summer vacation," John advised. "Unless you feel that you would want quite definitely to avail yourself of the opportunities which these interesting and worthwhile contacts would afford, I should not for a minute be in favor of the tentative plan as presented."[51]

As might be expected, Nelson was none too pleased by John's attempt to railroad the plans that he and Laurance had already drawn up. "Johnny showed me the letter he wrote you and I thought it was very interesting indeed," Nelson told Winthrop. "Larry and I differ with Johnny fundamentally on what we think would be the most interesting and helpful way for you to spend the summer. I suppose it is just a matter of opinion and each of us is judging more or less from his own personal experience." Nelson went on to restate the case for his own proposition and added that working in New York would give Winthrop the extra benefit of being able to spend more time with the rest of the family over the summer.[52]

Winthrop finally concluded that John's proposal was the most appealing. The sociology classes Winthrop had taken at Yale earlier that year piqued his interest in industrial relations and helped to clinch the deal. The decision attracted a good deal of media attention, as Winthrop was the first Rockefeller to work in the oil business since the retirement of his illustrious grandfather.[53]

Whereas Senior had exited the oil industry at the very top, Winthrop started out on the very bottom rung of the ladder. On June 19, he caught a bus to New Jersey and began his stay in a $4.50 (equivalent to $88 in 2020 dollars) a week room at the YMCA with other Standard Oil of New Jersey employees. He worked in the personnel department at the Bayonne Refinery, which was located adjacent to Staten Island.[54] On July 16, Winthrop drove his 1931 model Ford on the short hop over to the other side of Newark Bay for employment at the Bayview Refinery in Elizabeth, New Jersey.[55] Before Winthrop moved on to the Texas portion of his summer, he held a party in Pocantico Hills for the new oil industry friends he had made in the New Jersey refineries.[56]

After spending some time in New York, on July 24 Winthrop flew to Houston, where he stayed in the more resplendent surroundings of the Hotel Lamar while working at the Humble Oil Company.[57] On August 19, he flew to Fort Worth amid a good deal of drama. Winthrop was accompanied on the trip by two armed bodyguards, and he had two federal agents ready to meet him at the airport.[58] A rumor that members of the Chicago mob were in town to orchestrate a kidnapping prompted the escorts. FBI director J. Edgar Hoover personally investigated the matter. He concluded that the whole thing was a complete fabrication.[59] Winthrop was in Fort Worth to visit Yale classmate W. H. Slay Jr. for dinner before flying back to the East Coast the following day.[60] After spending the weekend in New York, Winthrop traveled to the Colonial Beacon Oil Company in Boston for the last leg of his oil-industry sojourn.[61]

While Winthrop was in Boston, the press had a field day at his expense. Winthrop placed a wager with a friend that after work he could visit Hull Bay to enjoy a swim, then go to nearby Cohasset to dine with recent debutante Miss Martha Chapin, and then still catch the 8:35 p.m. express train to Manhattan from Trinity Place Station in Rochester. All went as planned until soon after Winthrop left Cohasset. While he was passing through the town of Hingham, the engine of his car died. In his haste, he had forgotten to fuel up. "Rockefeller's Grandson Runs Out of Gasoline," snickered the *New York Times*. The ever-enterprising Winthrop waved down some fellow motorists, went to a nearby filling station, procured some gasoline, and made it to Trinity Place Station with only thirty-five seconds to spare.[62]

Despite the motoring snafu, overall Winthrop's first foray into the oil business was a resounding success. Glowing reports about Winthrop's activities arrived from all the places he worked. "I want you to know that we enjoyed

Winthrop (*on the right*) with R. S. Mason, Joseph
Bagley, and an unidentified man, at the Bayonne
Refinery in New Jersey on his summer vacation
from Yale University, ca. June–July 1933. *Winthrop
Rockefeller Collection, UA Little Rock Center for
Arkansas History and Culture.*

Winthrop's visit with us. It was most constructive in many ways. His fine per-
sonality, his direct questions, and eagerness to acquire knowledge made a
splendid impression on everyone in our organization who had the pleasure
to contact him," wrote Robert L. Blaffer, president and treasurer of Humble
Oil Company, to Junior. "He really was an ambassador of good will. We sincerely hope that we will have the pleasure of another visit from him."[63] Junior
replied that, "The experience was a thrilling one to Winthrop, and educative
and inspiring to a high degree."[64]

Winthrop was exposed to a good deal of media attention for the first time, ranging from a possible kidnapping attempt to a vehicle breakdown, and he had taken it all in his stride. Junior had nothing but praise for his son: "Our unanimous opinion was that you handled the situation with extraordinary wisdom, tact and good nature. We all wished we might have done as well in your place."[65] Indeed, Junior was so pleased that he wrote Winthrop a check for $400 (equivalent to $7,847 in 2020 dollars), which was more than enough cover his expenses over the summer months.[66] After a difficult year, it was surely a relief to be back in his father's good books again.

With the excitement and adventure of summer over, returning to Yale in fall 1933 was an exceptionally deflating prospect.[67] Winthrop's mind was now very much elsewhere than on campus. Junior did not know the half of it when he wrote, "The contrast between the kaleidoscopic life which you have been leading this summer and the prolonged concentration on studies which the past weeks have involved, must have been at the very least pretty striking."[68]

Winthrop's academic performance at Yale in his sophomore year had remained lousy. On top of his previous failures, he also failed English and classics. "The whole situation looks pretty black to me," Hollon A. Farr, officer for the Class of 1935, told him. The odds were very much stacked against Winthrop. To make it into the junior class, he needed to pass make-up exams in English and classics with a minimum grade of 75. If he made between 74 and 60 in the two exams, he would be placed on disqualification for half a year, as in the previous fall term. If he passed one and failed the other, he would be demoted to the Class of 1936, with only an outside chance of earning his place back into the Class of 1935. If he failed both exams, he would come up before the Committee of Rules with the distinct possibility of being dropped from college altogether.[69]

Winthrop failed both exams badly, scoring 45 in English and 37 in classics.[70] The results meant that by rights he should have been automatically dropped from Yale. Dean Clarence W. Mendel reported to Junior that he instead intended to restore Winthrop to a lower class. Winthrop was moved into the Class of 1936 to repeat his sophomore year. But Mendel made it clear that Winthrop was fast running out of options. This was his last chance.[71]

Yale president Angell backed Mendel's assessment of the situation. He agreed that Winthrop should be offered one final opportunity to make good.[72] But as Angell explained to Junior, "I feel quite clear that it would not be in the interests of his morale, and indeed the College rules I fear could not possibly be stretched, to extend the period of probation."[73] Junior appeared surprisingly unfazed by these developments. Possibly, this was due to Winthrop's travels over the summer, which may well have persuaded Junior that there were indeed other viable alternatives outside of academia that his son could successfully pursue. Junior sent an uncharacteristically comforting telegram to Winthrop, saying, "Never mind about the failures old man. There is no use in crying over spilt milk. I am with you sympathetically and whole-heartedly in whatever lies ahead. Let us keep in close touch. Love, Father."[74]

Winthrop, as always, appeared oblivious to the seriousness of his situation. He was filled with his usual misplaced optimism about his studies. Winthrop reported that he was busy with fraternity calling and rushing. In terms of his academic performance, "I will give you the story as I see it," he informed Junior. Winthrop said the real problem was a lack of time to study for his exams. All the cramming made him "sick from nervous exhaustion." He felt that this was because of "poor management on my part, rather than lack of effort." Winthrop recalled his earlier wood etching of the Edgar Albert Guest stanza and believed that just like the boy in the poem he could turn things around and succeed. This time he was confident it would all be different: "I have been exercising hard every day and trying to get a good nights [sic] rest with the result that I have been losing weight, getting in better shape physically and feeling much happiness mentally. I hope to surprise you and myself by bringing into circulation a new Winnie that we will all be proud of."[75]

Yet things did not improve much for Winthrop in fall 1933, which he spent rooming with New Yorker John Shawcross.[76] Winthrop barely made a passing grade of 80 in his Nineteenth- and Twentieth-Century Art class, and he squeaked a passing grade of 75 in his American Society class. But he failed International Relations, History in Contemporary Europe, and Contemporary Political Theory. This meant over half of his work was still deemed unsatisfactory. Dean Mendel advised Junior that there was no way back: "I am sure that his Class Officer would . . . [advise] him to resign at this time putting it to him just as strongly as he could." In the very best-case scenario, Winthrop might hope to make it through to the end of the year, but there was little likelihood that he could—or indeed would—be permitted to progress any further than that.[77]

Over the Christmas break, Winthrop had minor surgery to remove a pilonidal cyst that had troubled him since the summer.[78] A period of enforced bedridden rest and recuperation gave him time to consider his position and to talk things over further with Junior.[79] Junior informed Angell that in these conversations they had both come to the same conclusion: it was time for Winthrop to withdraw voluntarily from college.[80] Angell was regretful about the situation, but resigned to the outcome: "I can have no real doubt that it is wise for the boy to withdraw, and, if he can find an outlet for his energies and interests in a business position, I feel sure this is the wise thing to do."[81] Junior also informed Dean Mendel of the decision.[82] On February 5, 1934, Winthrop officially resigned from Yale.[83]

One final loose end about Winthrop's college career needs tying. Rockefeller family historians John Ensor Harr and Peter J. Johnson assert that "Winthrop was thrown out [of Yale] . . . [for] being caught taking a shower with a lady in his campus room."[84] The yarn has since taken on a life of its own, and it has been repeated in several other works.[85] However, there is little documented evidence to verify it. Burrowing deep into the footnotes of their book *The Rockefeller Century*, one finds the source cited by Harr and Johnson for the story is "a staff aide [at Winrock Farms] who asked to remain unidentified." The aide claimed that it was Winthrop who had told him the tale about his Yale dismissal.[86]

There are quite a few issues with this account. The fact that the details come from an unidentified source make them impossible to check. Even if we do accept that Winthrop did indeed discuss the alleged incident with the aide, there is no real context to understand the circumstances surrounding the conversation. It may well be that Winthrop was simply trying to hide his embarrassment about the truth of his academic failures or that it was instead—maybe even as well as—a fit of braggadocio designed to impress his employee. In the final analysis, there is little by way of corroborating evidence to back the claim up.[87]

The one tiniest tangential shred of possible supporting information comes in a newspaper account published soon after Winthrop left Yale, claiming that he was engaged to a young woman named Betty Shallcross. Writing to his cousin Faith Rockefeller, who inquired about the story, John replied that it was "entirely made up," although he noted that Winthrop had known the woman in question "for some time." John further pointed out that Shallcross's mother had denied the rumor.[88]

There is by contrast a copious and incontrovertible amount of evidence to show that Winthrop was failing academically in his studies for many years. Extensive documentation exists outlining Winthrop's exchanges with his family about these failings, its consequences, his preparations to leave Yale, and the arrangements that had already been put in place as an alternative to his college education. The shower story can therefore be comfortably dismissed as just another salacious tidbit of gossip that has been mistaken for an historical fact. This has no doubt been colored by the ever-present black sheep label that perpetually haunts the telling of Winthrop's story in the Rockefeller family literature. But Winthrop did not get thrown out of Yale because of a romantic liaison. He resigned because all possible academic options to stay had finally run out. The focus of Winthrop's education now shifted from Yale to what turned out to be the far more congenial surroundings of the southwestern oil fields.

CHAPTER 5

An Education in Oil

WINTHROP'S THREE YEARS SPENT in the southwestern oil fields offered an elegant solution to the ongoing conundrum of striking a balance between who and what Winthrop wanted to be and what the rest of the Rockefeller family expected of him.

From the family's perspective, Winthrop's interest in the oil industry opened a career pathway. The opportunity to reconnect the Rockefeller name with its dynastic origins in oil was appealing, as was Winthrop's willingness to start on the ground floor, to gain hands-on experience, and to make his own way in the world. Winthrop's eagerness and desire to mix with people from different backgrounds particularly suited him to the role. Quite possibly, the family also believed that the excursion into the oil fields would satiate Winthrop's wanderlust and thirst for adventure, allowing him to get that out of his system before he buckled down to the more serious business of life in the family office. Their goal was to see Winthrop in a boardroom setting where he could oversee and manage the family's interests alongside his brothers. Winthrop, they believed, could be their representative in the oil industry.[1]

From Winthrop's perspective, he was entirely agreeable with most of what his family had in mind, except, crucially, for the final outcome and destination. What Winthrop discovered in the oil fields was not a means to an end, but an end in itself. He loved the life there: the people, the freedom, the excitement, and the adventure of being on the frontlines of the industry. They were, he later reflected, some of the happiest days of his life. The very different ways that Winthrop and the rest of the family viewed the purpose of his time in the oil fields only delayed the final reckoning over his future. For the moment, however, it was a blessed relief for both parties to see Winthrop finally garnering rave reviews about his work.[2]

Junior gave plenty of thought as to how Winthrop's time in the oil fields could be useful both in terms of his son's career aspirations and in terms of his son's personal growth and moral reform. If Junior was going to cut Winthrop loose to stand on his own two feet, it would still be within a carefully controlled and managed environment. Winthrop's plan of work was put together by Junior in close consultation with Walter Clark Teagle, president of Standard Oil of New Jersey, and William Stamps Farish II, who had recently moved from the Humble Oil Company in Texas to become chair of the board of Standard Oil of New Jersey. The plan involved Winthrop learning the oil business at Humble by moving through every stage of production from the oil field to the oil refinery. Firstly, he would work at an easy pace as an assistant on a geophysical crew; secondly, as a "roustabout" general laborer; thirdly, as a "roughneck" on an oil rig; fourthly, in manufacturing; fifthly, in sales; and finally, in an oil refinery. After this, he would move on to the boardroom level for executive training.[3]

Junior held strong opinions about what Winthrop would—and would not—get up to outside of work. He was adamant that Winthrop was not going into the oil fields to party. Management at Humble was instructed not to entertain his son to any extent, so that he could experience life there on an equal basis with the other working men. Neither was Winthrop going to the oil fields to casually flit around. Junior decided against paying for a vehicle for Winthrop's use, since the company already provided his transportation to and from work.[4] Junior also felt that Winthrop's stay in the oil fields should be low-key and that he should not make any headlines or attract any unwanted attention. He was there to learn the ropes in the oil industry, not to become a media story.[5]

Most important of all, Winthrop was not going to spend his time boozing in the oil fields with the other men. Junior was already concerned enough about his son's drinking that he made Winthrop an offer similar to his earlier smoking abstinence agreement. Junior wrote, "It seemed to me that for you to drink anything, even beer, was just working against every effort to develop will-power and to build up inhibitions, both of which you agreed with me it is so important for you to develop." Therefore, "If you should decide not to drink anything for a period of at least a year, and should feel that it would help you to live up to that decision, I would be quite willing to agree to give you a thousand dollars [equivalent to $19,468 in 2020 dollars] at the end of the year if you have not taken anything to drink during that period."[6] Winthrop mulled over the sobriety-for-cash offer for more than a month before finally agreeing to it.[7] He ultimately viewed the decision in very practical terms: given the many inherent dangers lurking in the oil fields, he felt that it was best if he kept his wits about him at all times.[8]

In February 1934, just two weeks after resigning from Yale, Winthrop was ready to set off on his second, and this time longer, excursion into the oil indus-try in the Southwest. "Everything is in readiness," Junior reported to Senior, "and he goes with high hopes and enthusiasm."[9] On February 20, Winthrop arrived in Houston to begin work at Humble.[10] Alongside him for the duration, to provide him with company and for safety reasons, was William "Bill" Alton, one of Nelson's best friends from the Lincoln School and Dartmouth. Alton, a year older than Winthrop, had been hired by Junior and Abby on occasion in the past to provide their son with company during summers at the Eyrie.[11] In his youth, Alton was a top Eagle Scout in New York, and at Dartmouth he was runner-up in the intercollegiate welterweight boxing competition. The family believed that he was a good influence on Winthrop.[12] The kidnap scare the last time Winthrop was in Texas led J. Edgar Hoover to suggest that he should not return there alone. Hoover also insisted that both Winthrop and Alton should be armed, just in case they were called upon to defend themselves. Neither of them ever used their weapons.[13] In solidarity with Winthrop, Alton also took a pledge not to drink.[14]

On the first stage of their education in the oil industry, Winthrop and Alton were assigned to Bellville, around seventy miles northwest of Houston, to work on a geophysical crew. Winthrop was still recovering from his surgery over the Christmas holidays, and the assignment was intended as an easygoing introduction to work in the oil fields.[15] The two men lived in Eagle Lake, since all available accommodations in Bellville were full. This meant riding sixty-five miles into work each morning.[16] For the first month, Winthrop was in a con-stant state of exhaustion. Small wonder, since, he reported, "It has taken me longer to get used to the climate and this business of getting up at six in the morning than I had expected. If anyone had told me more than two months ago that I would be seeing the sun rise every morning by now I wouldn't have believed it possible." The weather conditions were variable: when it rained, the red and black clay soil made things heavy going, but there were also enough sunny days for Winthrop to quickly develop a tan.[17]

Nineteen people worked on the geophysical crew.[18] Most of them were young college men hopeful of climbing the company ladder.[19] Management at Humble's head office first chose an area for the crew to work in. Next, the head of the crew picked various locations within the area and secured permissions to drill. The drilling outfit was then sent in to drill shot-point holes of between 30 and 150 feet deep. Winthrop and Alton were the ones who filled the shot-point holes with dynamite before adding water to confine the blast into the ground as much as possible.[20]

A few weeks later, Winthrop and Alton moved on to the next stage in the process, working as assistants in the instrument truck. The truck was set up around 2,400 feet away from the shot-point holes that were filled with dynamite and water. Winthrop and Alton had to drive instruments called graphones into the ground near the blast point. When the dynamite exploded, the graphones submitted radio and photographic information back to the truck. Based on this information, experts analyzing the readings were able to determine if subsoil irregularities existed. The irregularities indicated if oil was present. Only then was the decision made about whether to drill for oil or not.[21]

Winthrop sent his parents a map of Texas so that they could follow his travels. This was gratefully received: East Coast people to the bone, their geographic knowledge of the Southwest region was limited.[22] For the generation of the Rockefellers with virtually no direct involvement in the oil industry, it was a vicarious thrill to reconnect to the roots of the family fortune. As Abby put it, "I frankly confess I am very ignorant of how oil is found or produced or refined, and I suspect even your father doesn't know very much about it, so as you progress through the company, if you would be good enough to write us about your work, we will learn a lot about the oil business by the time you arrive at the top."[23] Winthrop's parents were not the only ones following his exploits with interest. Having read his brother's reports from the field, Nelson wrote, "You must be having a wonderful time out there and I certainly envy you for the experience which you are getting."[24]

The practical work undertaken by Winthrop and Alton in the field was accompanied by written homework set by Wallace E. Pratt, Humble's chief geologist.[25] This included the production of such page-turning reports as "Torsion Balance as Used in Geophysical Prospecting and the Magnetometer as Used for Geological Prospecting" and "Surface Geologic Work in the Marathon Basin, Brewster County, Texas."[26] No doubt getting wind of Winthrop's academic performance in the past, Pratt after a while asked Winthrop and Alton to submit separate reports to make sure that each of them individually was doing their own written work.[27]

Winthrop's three months with the geophysical crew involved a meandering journey across West Texas that finally strayed just over the state line at Hobbs, New Mexico.[28] During that time, Winthrop had an opportunity to familiarize himself with all the various duties involved.[29] In late April, Winthrop was in McCamey, Texas. Demonstrating that life in the oil fields was not all work and no play, he spent Friday night out at a nightclub with Alton and fellow worker Frank Michaux. Driving back at dawn, Winthrop relished the natural beauty of his surroundings: the dark clouds that turned purple at sunrise and the glittering lights and flares from the oil derricks that dotted the landscape.

McCamey was in cattle and sheep country and plagued with coyotes. Men were out hunting them all the time. The custom was to hang each coyote they killed on a fencepost as a symbolic warning to others to stay away. Winthrop counted more than a dozen coyote carcasses. There were plenty of snakes too. "We killed a four foot rattler this morning," Winthrop recorded. "I am saving the rattles as a souvenir."[30]

On June 6, Winthrop and Alton began the second stage of their education in the oil industry by working in the production department as "roustabouts," the oil-field term for a general laborer. They were initially stationed in Luling, Texas, a small town of around one thousand people located fifty miles south of Austin and sixty miles northeast of San Antonio. The operation there was already well-established and producing three thousand barrels of oil a day.[31] Winthrop and Alton decided to forgo lodging in a boarding house in favor of living with the rest of the men in a company bunkhouse.[32] Being a roustabout was "the lowliest and dirtiest job in the whole industry," Winthrop reported. "You can't imagine how hot a day really can be until you have spent several of them on a business end of a shovel, or some other tool, for eight hours without having any shade from the sun." At the end of each day, Winthrop came home covered in grease from head to toe.[33] His shirt was so caked with salt from sweat that he could stand it up stiff in the corner of his room every night. A change of clothes was a luxury that came at most twice a week.[34]

The work was dangerous too, with heavy machinery that crushed many a hand and cut off many a finger. One of the biggest dangers was working on the floor level of an oil rig, since any number of objects could accidentally plummet from above. A particular hazard was the metal cable used to hoist materials upward. Eventually, the cable wore out. If someone pulled too hard on it while it was weak, the whole thing broke and came tumbling down onto the derrick floor. Precisely that happened to Winthrop one day, although fortunately he was wearing his hard hat and he only caught a glancing, albeit stinging blow on the shoulder.[35]

The federal government offered some relief when the New Deal agency the National Recovery Administration limited the working week to thirty-six hours rather than the regular forty to forty-eight hours. In practical terms, this meant Winthrop and Alton rotating between a five-day week and a four-day week. The two men pooled funds to buy themselves a small, cheap Plymouth car. On the short weekends, after a five-day week, they drove to San Antonio, where they stayed with Rockefeller family friend and World War I flying ace Edgar Gardner Tobin. Tobin ran an aerial mapping firm that played an important role in surveying Texas and in aiding the development of the oil industry there.[36]

Winthrop (*third from right*) working as a roustabout laborer in the Luling, Texas, oil fields, ca. June–July 1934. *Winthrop Rockefeller Collection, UA Little Rock Center for Arkansas History and Culture.*

On the longer weekends, after a four-day week, they drove to Houston, where they stayed in the home of William Stamps Farish II. Farish rented his house out to his sister and her husband, Jim Winston. The Winstons let Winthrop and Alton use a room as their base in the city. Winthrop spent a portion of each weekend in Houston with David B. Harris, the head of industrial relations at Humble. This allowed Winthrop to gain a greater insight into that aspect of company operations. Alton showed no interest at all and sat out those meetings. He later had a hard time living this down when he was appointed assistant director of employee relations at the Rockefeller Center.[37]

Winthrop relayed to Junior that he was enjoying Texas tremendously, especially the friendliness and hospitality of the people. At the same time, he confessed that he missed home. Of course, he had grown up a good deal since his days as a twelve-year-old at Camp Merryweather, but still, he said, "Every day I realize more clearly that one doesn't begin to appreciate how fortunate we really are not only in a worldly sense but also in the sense of friendship and loved ones until we get away from it all for a while."[38] Despite this smidgen of homesickness, family friend C. E. Shaw reported to Abby that "Winthrop says that this work in the field is far more interesting than the highly technical geological, geophysical work which they previously had, and he seems to be getting a lot of real satisfaction out of working with the men, for which we are all very happy."[39]

Another thing that Winthrop gained a new appreciation for was the value of money. When he started work, Winthrop decided to receive the same rate of pay as the other men and to live solely off his earnings without any assistance from other family members. He discovered that the $117 (equivalent to $2,278 in 2020 dollars) per month earned by a roustabout did not stretch very far. "Quite frankly I don't see how these boys with big families ever get by. They all have radios, electronic refrigerators, and cars. Most of them are in the stock plan as well as the insurance plan which means quite a deduction of their pay check each time, and then they all spend anywhere [sic] from 10 to 30 dollars a month on gas, so what I want to know is what do they use to buy the necessities of life with[?]" Winthrop wrote. "Of course most of them have a garden and a Cow but even then—I know for my self that by pay day I don't usually have too big of a balance left, and I am only one. Things look brighter though, we are getting a three-cent hourly raise starting to-morrow—Oh boy Oh Boy."[40]

Without doubt one of the things that Winthrop relished most about working in the oil fields was the wide variety of different people he encountered. As he reported home to his parents, "Some of these old oil men [are] certainly characters!!"[41] Winthrop met more than his fair share of them. In Luling, there was Claude Adams, who worked the pumps on the rig. Each morning, Claude had an assortment of questions for Winthrop: How many siblings did he have? Where did he live? What did he normally do? One morning, Claude asked how many cars Winthrop's family had. Winthrop deflected the question by saying quite a few, but that he didn't know exactly. On another occasion, Claude asked him outright how much his family was worth. Winthrop told him that he'd never gone without, but that he'd never really asked about the full amount either. Winthrop's answers always appeared to satisfy Claude's burning curiosity.[42]

Someone else with questions was the gang pusher—essentially, the foreman on the job—named Ross. Even more direct and assertive than Claude, he came right out and accused Winthrop of being a company spy. Winthrop patiently explained to Ross that he was there simply to learn the oil industry from the ground up. He reasoned with him, would Humble really send a spy into the oil fields named Rockefeller? Ross scratched his head and eventually conceded that perhaps not.[43] Junior was always tickled at receiving the stories his son sent home: "Your analyses of the characters of the different people whom you are meeting and working with is very penetrating. How much you are learning about human nature!"[44]

There were other times when the eagle-eyed Junior could read too much into Winthrop's letters. In one missive back home, Winthrop wrote about attending a weekend barbecue and beer party in San Antonio: "Unfortunately I had an upset stomach and was not drinking, so I found myself out of place and as a result went home rather early." By way of reply, Junior noted his own and Abby's different interpretations of what that line meant. "[Abby] takes it to mean that was the way in which you avoided drinking," wrote Junior. "On the other hand, it seemed to me that you were taking that means of advising us that you were no longer on the water wagon."[45] Winthrop swiftly reassured his parents that all was well and that he was still sober. For that matter, Winthrop said, he did not care for the barbecue either, describing it as "tough meat" in a "peppery sauce."[46] After the next such party, he remarked, "Even with a strong stomach I couldn't bring myself to eat [it]."[47]

In August 1934, Winthrop took a brief pause from the oil fields to return home for groomsman duties at Laurance's wedding to Mary Billings French in Woodstock, Vermont. Nelson was best man.[48] When he returned to Texas in October, Winthrop and Alton graduated from roustabouts to the third stage of their education in the oil industry as "roughnecks." *Roughneck* was the term used for oil rig workers. Winthrop and Alton were assigned to a wildcat crew that speculatively drilled for new oil reserves on the O'Connor Family Ranch just outside Victoria, Texas, around 120 miles southeast of San Antonio.[49] The two men lived in an old white house in Victoria that belonged to boarding lady Mrs. Beckham.[50]

The drilling area the crew worked on was heavy going, and the closer they inched to the Gulf Coast the marshier and soggier it got. When it rained, it was impossible to reach the site by car. The men had to get out the four-team mule wagon for the last six-mile, hour-long slog. These intervals provided an oppor- tunity for Winthrop to chat with his fellow workers. As usual, they were wary about having a Rockefeller in their midst, and they never knew quite what to make of him. They always tested him by sending him for left-handed monkey wrenches, buckets of steam, or skyhooks. Winthrop soon became wise to most of these ruses. The crew in Victoria finally broke him on a conversation about fraternities. The men described a handshake that Winthrop had to perform that ended up with him in a contorted shape and his face pressed close to his posterior. He innocently asked what he should do next, when back came the obvious reply.[51]

The next destination for Winthrop and Alton, in November, was on a drilling crew in the Roanoke oil field, six miles northwest of Jennings, Louisiana, around halfway between Lake Charles and Lafayette.[52] They lodged at Mrs. Inez Daugherty's Ardennes Hotel.[53] On weekends, they continued to drive back to Houston, although it was now a four-hundred-mile trek. They were young and eager, and so it did not bother them in the slightest. After finishing work at 4:00 p.m., they set off in the car, arrived in Houston, and went straight out to party, staying up all night long without thinking twice about it.[54]

The conditions in the oil field at Jennings were just as bad as they had been in Victoria, if not worse. Winter was arriving, and the Roanoke oil well was slap-bang in the middle of a rice field that was knee high in water. One day, Winthrop worked in a pit with mud up to his waist for four hours. It was the coldest he had ever been. To warm up, he went back to the hotel and lay in a warm bath. He was still cold. He then got into bed and wrapped himself in blankets. He was still cold. Finally, he took a big gulp of apricot brandy. Only that managed to warm him up.[55] Winthrop clearly believed that the tipple was for medicinal purposes only. He went on to collect his $1,000 sobriety check from Junior the following year.[56]

Just before Christmas, a delegation from Chase Bank visited. This included Winthrop's uncle Winthrop Aldrich, who was president and chair of the board, and Nelson, who was at the bank on an apprenticeship. While in Houston, the Chase delegation drove to Jennings to see the drilling rig where Winthrop worked. The occasion offered an opportunity for Winthrop to take another break from the oil fields as he joined the touring party for a few days. After attending a banquet in Houston, Winthrop found dates for himself and Nelson, and they all went out dancing. "When we got home," Winthrop related to his parents, "even though it was late, Nel and I had a very delightful heart to heart chat which I hope meant as much to Nel as it did to me. It just charged me with a new fire and ambition to go out and do even better than I have been trying to do all along."[57]

Nelson was suitably impressed by the progress that his younger brother was making, telling him, "You certainly have gone a long way since I last saw you. I want to tell you that as a member of the family I am mighty proud of you. From all sides I got reports of the fine work and wonderful impression you were making."[58] Nelson's visit did, however, bring out further pangs of homesickness.[59] Winthrop felt his distance from the rest of the family even more keenly at Christmas, not least because 1934 was the first yuletide gathering in

Pocantico Hills that he had ever missed. Junior was understanding about his son's absence, writing, "You are maintaining most worthily the family name and are bringing added credit and goodwill to it; therefore, our hearts are filled with inexpressible gratitude."[60] Winthrop sent Junior a box of Texas grapefruit as a present.[61] Writing to Laurance early in the New Year, Winthrop reported that he and Alton had thoroughly enjoyed their Christmas break. Texas was fast becoming a home away from home: "You know I think that it [sic] pretty lucky that I was raised in New York for if I hadn't I think that I would like this Texas country about as well as anything that I have seen outside of New York for a steady diet."[62]

Appropriately enough, it was during his time in the oil fields that Winthrop made his fortune, although under quite different circumstances to his grandfather. Winthrop's was inherited wealth rather than that of a self-made man. In December 1934, Junior set up what became known as the 1934 Trusts, which were the main vehicle for transferring the Rockefeller family's vast wealth down the generations. Junior was reticent about doing this, since he believed his children were not yet mature enough for the responsibility.[63] Eighteen months earlier, all six siblings had sent a collective letter to Junior pleading for increased allowances and greater economic independence. They diplomatically complained about their father's draconian approach when it came to their financial relationships.[64] Pres. Franklin D. Roosevelt's changes in tax policies during the Great Depression, which meant far steeper estate- and gift-tax rates, finally forced Junior's hand. Initially, Junior created trusts for the older siblings, Babs, John, and Nelson, that were higher than those for Laurance, Winthrop, and David. In 1935, when Congress approved more hikes in estate- and gift-tax rates, he equalized all the trusts at $16 million (equivalent to about $307 million in 2020 dollars).[65]

Yet in his inimitable fashion, Junior still sought to exercise control over how they could access the money. A board of trustees was appointed to oversee the 1934 Trusts. The trustees determined how much of the annual interest the brothers should receive until they turned thirty. Until then, any extra balance was distributed as charitable gifts to specified recipients. Even after turning thirty, the brothers could only access the annual interest from the trust. They needed express permission from the trustees to invade the capital. The 1934 Trusts were also generation-skipping in the sense that although the brothers benefited from them, they did not own them. Upon their death, the deeds specified that the trusts should be divided between their legitimate offspring. When those offspring died, the trust was terminated, and the tax-free proceeds were divided equally between their surviving children. The 1934 Trusts only represented the beginning, rather than the end, of the family wealth transfer. More money was added to them over time, enough of an incentive to keep Junior's children still towing the family line. Although the immediate impact of the new trust on Winthrop was negligible, it assured both his and his family's security for many years to come.[66]

Toward the end of January 1935, Winthrop was laid low with a cold and stayed in Houston with Harry Weiss, the vice president of Humble, and his family. In early February, Winthrop and Alton transferred from Jennings to Raccoon Bend, Texas, just seven miles outside of Bellville, where they had previously been based. There they stayed at Mrs. M. B. Duncan's boardinghouse. The move caught the attention of the press, which for the first time in almost a year reported on Winthrop's work in the oil fields.[67]

When Winthrop and Alton arrived in Raccoon Bend, the drilling crew was between wells, so the two were put to work digging a new well for three days. The first two days were spent laying lines and digging ditches. The final day involved working on a "cellar gang," which meant digging the foundations for the drilling rig. Four people, including Winthrop and Alton, dug a hole eleven by eleven feet wide and six and a-half feet deep. They started at 8:00 a.m. and finished at 2:00 p.m., with an hour off for lunch. Winthrop had never worked so hard in his life.[68] By the noon lunch break, he was too exhausted to climb out of the hole. He told the rest of the men that he would eat his lunch down there to stay out of the wind and cold. One of the men tossed Winthrop's lunch to him, though none of them seemed to buy his excuse. Later, Winthrop learned that the cellar gang had come within fifteen minutes of the record for digging a hole of that size, and that the others were secretly pushing him to see how fast and for how long he could go on the job.[69]

Also in February, Junior and Abby visited Winthrop, making the forty-eight-hour road journey from Ormond Beach, Florida, where they had been visiting Senior.[70] Winthrop arranged a program of meetings and entertainment for his parents that gave them a thorough overview of life in the oil fields.[71] He was overjoyed that his parents had taken the time to visit him, writing to tell them, "Such a trip has been one of my most frequent dreams and the realization of these dreams gave me truly a great thrill."[72]

On a brief visit back to New York shortly after, Junior paid Winthrop the $1,000 he promised for his yearlong sobriety.[73] To all appearances a reformed character, Winthrop told Junior, "The first thing that I intend to do [with the money] is clear up that loan that I have outstanding with you."[74] Junior expressed his pleasure by raising Winthrop's annual allowance to $3,000 (equivalent to $57,531 in 2020 dollars) effective April 1.[75] Two days later, Winthrop duly received a speeding ticket in Houston and was handed a $10 (equivalent to $192 in 2020 dollars) fine.[76]

Winthrop and Alton were transferred to Houston on a permanent basis in March to begin the fourth stage of their education in the oil industry in manufacturing.[77] They were there for almost two years, living in apartment 12 at 302 Portland Street.[78] While spending a more settled and extended period of time in the city, Winthrop had his first adult experience of dealing with southern race relations. The series of events began when two local women from Rice Institute (today Rice University) in Houston were at the Portland Street apartment for dinner. Both women had taken a sociology course with an eminent professor at Rice who was considered a leading authority in the field. As the evening's conversation unfolded, Winthrop asked the women what the professor had to say about "the Negro problem" in his lectures. They looked at him puzzled: What Negro problem? Winthrop could hardly believe his ears that the topic was not covered in classes.[79]

The exchange whetted Winthrop's appetite for a rendezvous with the professor. Harry Weiss helped to arrange the meeting. When Winthrop confronted the academic for not addressing race relations in his classes, he just laughed it off. Winthrop insisted that they should have dinner one evening to more thoroughly interrogate the topic. The professor invited Winthrop to his home. Over dinner, the professor explained that he avoided using the term "problem" since it suggested conflict, and that Houston did not want to give any impression of racial conflict in the city. Winthrop was again taken aback by this response. He concluded that he was not going to get anywhere discussing the subject with the professor any further.[80]

There soon arose an opportunity for Winthrop to become even more directly involved in race relations in Houston. Winthrop and Alton hired a Black maid to clean their apartment. Friends thought it exorbitant that they paid her as much as $10 per week.[81] Winthrop was raised to know better. As Abby contended to her sister Lucy just a couple of years before, "Negro servants should be given wages that are commensurate with their services. . . . They should be treated not only with kindness, but with consideration for their ability."[82] One day, the maid called Winthrop to say that she had a bad pain in her side that she thought was appendicitis. She had called her doctor, who was ready to operate. Winthrop told her that he would help her in any way that he could, including arranging for her to have treatment at the Hermann Hospital, which was Houston's finest. The maid told him thank you but no. She was going to the Houston Negro Hospital at 3204 Ennis Street to see a Black physician,

Dr. Joseph G. Gathings. She was determined to stay loyal to the hospital and its physicians because of a strong sense of race pride and solidarity.[83]

The episode made Winthrop think more attentively about how he could help to improve race relations in Houston. He spent three or four afternoons with his maid's physician, seeking to understand the issues involved. Gathings was a University of Wisconsin alum who had also undertaken graduate work at Howard University in Washington, DC.[84] The two men discussed the high rates of venereal disease in Houston's Black population. They felt that addressing this concern as a public-health issue could win interest and funding from both Black and white communities. Winthrop agreed to seek outside assistance to develop the idea further. He first contacted the Rockefeller Foundation, but it was already committed to a policy of only funding a limited number of centers of excellence for Black medical facilities.[85] The Rockefeller Foundation pointed Winthrop to the Julius Rosenwald Fund in Chicago, which had more of a track record in specifically funding Black-oriented projects.[86] Winthrop contacted Dr. Midian Othello Bousfield, the director of the Negro Health Division at the Rosenwald Fund, who agreed to visit Houston.[87]

Bousfield was undoubtedly one of the leading figures in his field. Born in Tipton, Missouri, in 1885, he received degrees from the University of Kansas in 1907 and the Northwestern University Medical School in 1909. After completing his residency at Freedmen's Hospital in Washington, DC, which was affiliated with the Howard University School of Medicine, he became one of the first Black doctors appointed to Kansas City Municipal Hospital. In 1912, he moved to Chicago, setting up a private practice and joining the staff at Provident Hospital, the first Black-owned and Black-operated hospital established in the United States. In 1919, Bousfield was one of the incorporators of the Black insurance company Liberty Life Insurance, where he served as medical director and president. When the company merged with others to form the Supreme Life Insurance Company ten years later, he served as medical director and vice president. Bousfield's experience led to his appointment as chair of the public health committee of the National Negro Insurance Association. He accepted the position at the Rosenwald Fund in 1935. There, he pursued an ambitious agenda that included training Black public-health personnel, establishing scholarships for Black nurses and physicians, and influencing public opinion about Black health needs.[88]

It was only when Winthrop went to the train station to collect the doctor that he discovered Bousfield was Black. Demonstrating Winthrop's own ignorance and naivete, and how much he had yet to learn in the area of race relations, this came as something of a surprise to him. Winthrop drove Bousfield to the home of the Black doctor whom he would stay with while in Houston. On parting, Winthrop told Bousfield that he had planned a luncheon at the Houston Club the following day with several influential white people in the community. This produced an awkward silence. Both men knew full well that a Black person sitting down to eat food with whites under such circumstances was a breach of the strict racial segregation demanded in the city.[89]

To spare Winthrop's evident blushes, Bousfield, who was no doubt all too familiar with handling such excruciating situations, told him that he was unable to attend because he had other plans, but that he could join them after lunch. It was just the sort of painful dance that Black and white people so often had to perform to accommodate what Winthrop felt were the blatantly absurd requirements of southern racial etiquette. Winthrop was mortified at the embarrassing situation he had placed Bousfield in, while at the same time humbled and grateful that the physician had diffused the situation for them both.[90]

The luncheon took place the following day, with Winthrop's acquaintance, the Rice professor, in attendance. At twenty-five years old, Winthrop was by far the youngest person in the group. After the luncheon, Winthrop outlined the circumstances that had brought Bousfield to the city. Bousfield then gave his presentation, explaining that the Houston Negro Hospital could be used more effectively to tackle community health issues. But as with other such Rosenwald-funded projects, this required the cooperation of the city's health department to ensure the sustainability of the program. This in turn meant appointing at least one or two Black doctors to the health department. At the time, Houston had never had a Black doctor serve in that capacity. The Rosenwald Fund was prepared to invest $40,000 (equivalent to $767,087 in 2020 dollars) to get the program started.[91]

Winthrop believed that it was a perfectly reasonable presentation and proposal. Yet no sooner had Bousfield sat down than the Rice professor stood up and declared that Houston would never accept handouts from a Black person. Although the others balked at the professor's rudeness, they appeared to share his sentiments. Nothing happened as a result of Bousfield's visit. Winthrop had to come to terms with the fact that he was not going to be in Houston long enough to achieve anything of substance.[92] The episode certainly provided Winthrop with valuable insight into the difficulties in dealing with southern race relations. It was an issue that he would return to many times throughout the rest of his life.[93]

Entering the fifth and penultimate stage of their education in the oil industry soon after, Winthrop and Alton set off on an extensive field trip to find out more about the sales side of the business. Accompanying them were brothers Dan and Malcolm Monroe, both of whom were old hands in the sales game. The Monroe brothers had started as youngsters, strapping five-gallon cans of petroleum onto their backs and selling door-to-door, before working for the Waters-Pierce Oil Company. When the company became part of Humble, Dan Monroe was appointed head of retail sales, while his brother Malcolm was appointed head of bulk sales. Even before they set off on the trip, each brother approached Winthrop separately and badmouthed the driving capabilities of the other, imploring him not to let his sibling anywhere near the wheel. The two brothers were always at one another's throats, although woe betide anyone who said a bad word to one about the other.[94]

The trip covered 2,400 miles in just eleven days. To placate both brothers, Winthrop drove the entire journey. It was a hard-drinking tour that ended Winthrop's sobriety pledge. He reckoned they drank a quart of whiskey for every 100 miles they traveled. The brothers had only one rule: no alcohol before eleven in the morning unless someone else was buying. Everywhere they went, each customer wanted to sit down, have a drink, and talk. Sometimes whole communities gathered for their visit. As well as the drinking, both brothers were keen on early 6:00 a.m. starts on the road, although Winthrop usually managed to stall them until at least 8:00 a.m. There were also hunting expeditions that took place in the freezing-cold woods before the start of the workday. Winthrop believed that the Monroe brothers were deliberately trying to wear the two younger men out. If so, their plan backfired: both older men needed three days in bed to recover when they returned.[95]

On the sixth and final stage of their education in the oil industry, Winthrop and Alton spent time at the massive Baytown Refinery, just outside Houston. There was so much to learn about the different processes in an oil refinery that a short stay could not do full justice to its complexity. Winthrop and Alton quickly skipped around from one place to another, trying to take in as much as they possibly could.[96] By the end of 1936, the two were approaching the completion of their mutual journey in the oil industry. Junior began to consider, along with Messrs. Teagle and Farish, what Winthrop's next steps should be. Winthrop expressed a desire to first take a short vacation before moving on. Junior approved. From the end of 1936 into the beginning of 1937, Winthrop holidayed in Mexico.[97] He then resigned from Humble, formally ending his association with the company.[98]

Winthrop's time in the Southwest's oil industry was a resounding success. He acquitted himself well, won praise from colleagues, and earned newfound respect from family members. The testimonies were glowing. "It must be said that Winthrop holds the affection and respect of all with whom he comes into contact. He is just as much at home in the ditch, on the derrick floor or in the field, as he is in the offices and homes of the executives, and he makes friends with all in both groups with equal facility," wrote David B. Harris to Junior. "The men with whom he has labored in the oil fields are his staunchest and most loyal friends. They call him 'Rock' and 'Rocky' and they are for him 100%. He has earned their good will and respect by his sincere democracy and his constant endeavor to do more work than anyone else in his gang. . . . Winthrop is a splendid representative of the family, and he is doing much to perpetuate your good name."[99]

A pleased Nelson wrote, "You know that I'm a strong believer in the family and when I see one member pulling on his oar the way you were doing it certainly does my heart good. I am mighty proud of you Win, you've certainly done a swell job and I know enough about what you were up against both inside and out to appreciate the stuff it took to come out on top. You have a combination of qualities that no other member of the family has and with the use you're making of them now there is no telling how far you may go."[100] Junior was similarly overjoyed: "Your decision to accept the opening there offered seemed to me a wise one at the time and subsequent events have only confirmed that belief. . . . It is not so difficult to make a good impression for a short time, but much more difficult to continue to keep one's standards high to convert temporary good impressions into permanent ones. That this is what you are doing . . . amply justif[ies] the gratifying comments that come to us about you, [and] gives Mama and me great happiness."[101]

As Wallace E. Pratt summed up the three years to Junior, "It is as though Winthrop had been in school—in oil."[102] Having graduated from the oil fields, Winthrop was now ready to begin the next stage of his career as a junior executive working in the Rockefeller family office.

CHAPTER 6

Entering the Family Business

THERE WAS NO GREATER accolade and demonstration of confidence in Winthrop than Junior officially appointing his son to a place in the family office on January 29, 1937. Winthrop's starting salary was $1,800 (equivalent to $33,040 in 2020 dollars) per year. "You have finished, with credit to yourself and the family, your three years of service with the Humble Company," wrote Junior. "From now on I would like to have you feel, as I do, that whatever you do is done as a member of the office family in our common interest and for our common benefit." He continued, "The boys are happy as I am to have you thus definitely a part of the office. We feel, as we want you to feel, that you are serving our common interests as really and as effectively while on these various trips as though you were in the office currently. It makes me very happy to thus have a fourth of my splendid sons directly associated with me in business." Junior concluded: "I have complete confidence in you and know that you will pull your weight in the boat, that you will at all times and in all ways, to the best of your ability, maintain the family honor and its high business standards and that you will continue, as you have in the past three years, to bring added credit to the family name."[1]

The next few years of Winthrop's life did not fully live up to this exalted billing. Back from the oil fields, he struggled to find focus, direction, and purpose. He tried his hand at several activities, none of which particularly helped him to discover his own distinctive place in the family. He traveled to the West Coast to further his training in the oil industry. He took a business trip with Nelson to Latin America. He enrolled in a junior executive training program at Chase Bank. He co-led a campaign for the Greater New York Fund. He helped to form and promote the organization Air Youth of America in a joint venture with Laurance. He took a job in the Foreign Trade Department of Socony-Vacuum Oil Company and traveled to the Middle East and Europe during the early years of World War II. He joined the board of trustees of the civil rights organization the National Urban League. Yet if all of this provided

Winthrop with valuable experience, nothing enthused him quite like his time in the southwestern oil fields had done. With his motivation waning, he was in danger of going adrift once more, as he had previously been at Yale. His saving grace was World War II, which provided him with an opportunity to return to the same sort of environment that he had encountered in the oil fields. Winthrop's time back in New York was relatively brief, before he set out the next big adventure of his life as a soldier.

When Winthrop flew to Los Angeles on February 2, 1937, with John A. Brown, president of Socony, and then on to San Francisco to meet Kenneth R. Kingsbury, president of Standard Oil of California, they were his first official business trips as a newly minted member of the Rockefeller family office.[2] Befitting his newfound status, in San Francisco Winthrop stayed at the luxury Mark Hopkins Hotel, a far cry from the boardinghouses of the oil fields.[3] In a whistle-stop tour of the West Coast, Winthrop was based in San Francisco from February 12 through 26, spending a couple of nights at the Biltmore Hotel, Los Angeles, and a night at the Olympic Hotel, Seattle, on short hop business trips during his stay. For much of the final month of his visit from February 26 through March 22, he was based at the Ambassador Hotel in Los Angeles.[4] There was plenty of time to enjoy some leisure excursions along the way. On the weekend of February 20 and 21, Winthrop went skiing at Lake Tahoe with Ralph K. Davies, one of the directors of Standard Oil of California.[5] Winthrop reported home, "In spite of several good falls I must admit that I am now another ski enthusiast. The weekend could not have been more delightful, and I found Lake Tahoe even more beautiful than in the summer."[6]

Junior, Abby, and the rest of the family followed Winthrop's exploits out West with interest. The media attention it grabbed led Junior to observe, "It looks as though you would soon qualify as the No. 1 publicity member of the family."[7] On March 2, Winthrop sent Abby and Junior a telegram telling them that he was sad to leave San Francisco but was quickly adapting to life in Los Angeles. He had already attended a cocktail party at the house of John A. Brown; had lunch with Frank Vanderlips, a former president of National City Bank of New York, a former assistant secretary to the US Treasury, and, along with Winthrop's grandfather Sen. Nelson W. Aldrich, one of the founders of the Federal Reserve System; spent a day at the races; taken in some of the Hollywood sights; and even made it into the Standard Oil of California office.[8] Junior, always keen to keep his son focused on the business at hand, responded: "Evidently when you come out East, you will have seen a good deal more than just the oil business of the Coast. . . . I hope you are keeping well and not being swamped with social activities and that you are getting all that you had hoped out of your interesting experiences."[9]

Over the weekend of March 13 and 14, Winthrop was out skiing again, this time in Yosemite National Park.[10] Yet although Winthrop certainly enjoyed himself on his jaunt out West, he remained very much dedicated to studying the oil industry. The trip provided him with an overview of Standard Oil of California's operations. "Each of the departments has been considered in as much detail as time allowed, and I believe Winthrop has had an interesting and instructive experience. In this connection, I think it not amiss to comment briefly upon the individual himself and the impression he has made upon our people here," wrote director Ralph K. Davies to company president Kenneth R. Kingsbury. "A frank and open manner and naturalness have quickly excited the admiration of all with whom he has come into contact. He has been liked and spoken of repeatedly in the most friendly and complimentary terms. Further, he has displayed a stability and maturity quite beyond his years. It seems to us his father may well be proud of such representation."[11]

Winthrop traveled back to New York at the end of March to prepare for a two-month-long trip to Latin America with Nelson. In 1934, taking the advice of Rockefeller family attorney and trusted counsel Thomas M. Debevoise, Nelson went to Chase Bank on an apprenticeship. While there, he became interested in the foreign department and the role that it played in managing the relationship between oil companies and international politics. Joseph Rovensky, head of Chase Bank's foreign department, acted as Nelson's mentor. In 1935, Nelson traveled to Europe, following up on contacts that Rovensky had shared with him. All the talk in the oil industry at the time was about the discovery of the Lake Maracaibo oil fields in Venezuela that had rapidly made the country second only to the United States in oil production. Standard Oil of New Jersey owned the largest share in the Venezuelan oil fields. Its subsidiary, the Creole Petroleum Company, was the largest single producer. Nelson successfully persuaded Junior to allow him to trade some Standard Oil shares for shares in the Creole Petroleum Company. The investment was enough to make Nelson a significant shareholder and to get him on the board of directors.[12]

In December 1935, Venezuela's president, Juan Vicente Gomez, died. Gomez was compliant with foreign interests looking to control Venezuelan oil, and he had allegedly grown rich on the back of the deals that he had struck, even as the country remained mired in poverty. Gomez was replaced by Pres. Eleazar Lopez Contreras and a new government that was far less sympathetic to foreign oil companies. There were also wider concerns in the United States

about the rise of left-wing governments in Latin America and their potential impact on American business interests. Winthrop and Nelson, the two
Rockefeller brothers most interested in the oil industry, decided to explore
firsthand the conditions that existed in the region.[13]

Accompanying Winthrop and Nelson on their trip were Nelson's wife,
Tod; Tod's cousin Eleanor Clark; Joseph Rovensky; Jay E. Crane, treasurer of
Standard Oil of New Jersey; and a Chilean interpreter.[14] The journey proved
even more of a whirlwind than Winthrop's West Coast travels. For both
Winthrop and Nelson, it was their first visit to Latin America. Since Nelson
was traveling there to learn the oil business, Winthrop told his brother jok-
ingly, "It was obvious that he better have somebody competent along with
him to tell him what the hell he was seeing." The party set off in Sikorsky flying
boats from New York on Sunday, March 28, 1937, arriving in Miami the following day.[15] They then traveled to Barranquilla, Colombia, and to Maracaibo,
Venezuela. Beginning on Thursday April 1, both by plane and by boat, they
visited the Maracaibo Basin oil fields, the Dutch-owned island of Aruba,
and Venezuela's capital city of Caracas.[16] While in Caracas, Nelson met with
President Contreras, his cabinet, and the governors of four Venezuelan states.[17]
The party next toured the oil fields in eastern Venezuela. On Sunday, April 11,
they departed from Caripito and flew to Port of Spain, the capital of Trinidad
and Tobago, where they spent the day before traveling to Belém, Brazil.[18] "To
tell you what we have done in the past two weeks would fill a small book,"
wrote an out of breath Winthrop to his parents. "It really does not seem possible that we could have done so much."[19] The next few days were spent in Brazil
visiting Recife and Rio de Janeiro. On Friday, April 23, the traveling party flew
from Rio to Montevideo, the capital of Uruguay, where they caught a steam-
boat to Buenos Aires, the capital of Argentina.[20]

While in Buenos Aires, Winthrop and the others toured the area's old
estates and spent a couple of days with a well-known rancher. Winthrop and
Nelson were both taken by the romance of cattle ranching, and they came back
to the United States determined to run their own operation as a joint enterprise.[21] After a week based in Buenos Aires, they flew to Santiago, the capital of
Chile, and then on to Arica.[22] Winthrop reported that he enjoyed Chile more
than any other country on the trip.[23] Next was Bolivia, with a visit to La Paz
before catching a train to Guaqui, where they boarded a steamship crossing
Lake Titicaca overnight. They arrived in Puno, Peru, the following day. From
there, it was a train ride to Juliaca, and a flight to Peru's capital city of Lima,
arriving on the afternoon of Saturday, May 15.[24]

Up to that point, everything had gone smoothly. Then, on May 21, the

On tour in Latin America, ca. April–May, 1937. *Left to right*: Eleanor Clark, Nelson Rockefeller, Jay E. Crane, Mary Todhunter Rockefeller, Winthrop, Joseph Rovensky, and an unidentified Chilean interpreter. *Winthrop Rockefeller Collection, UA Little Rock Center for Arkansas History and Culture.*

Pan-American-Grace Airways plane they flew out of Lima on had to make a forced landing just a few minutes after taking off when one of its motors failed. The plane crashed into a wire fence, but thankfully no one was injured. It was Winthrop's first of several close encounters involving airplanes that occurred throughout his life.[25] Winthrop appeared unperturbed by the whole affair. "There was no real danger right up until the end because the plane was an amphibian and we were flying along the coast. The motor held up until about two minutes before we landed. When it did finally burn out the vibration was pretty severe and caused some anxiety but the pilot landed the plane well," he calmly explained to a friend. "Due to the fact that we had the one motor on landing the pilot was unable to use the brakes so we ran over the end of the field, through a fence, over a irrigation ditch and into a corn field without any serious damage to the plane or passengers and only slightly shaken nerves."[26] No sooner had they recovered from the shock of the plane crash than news from home set them reeling once again. On May 23, Senior passed away at the Casements in Ormond Beach. Winthrop and Nelson immediately abandoned their trip and hurried back to Pocantico Hills for the funeral.[27]

For Nelson, the trip with Winthrop was a defining experience that sparked a lifelong interest in Latin America. After returning home, he immediately began learning Spanish at Berlitz Corporation. He then set about trying to convince the oil industry that it needed to become far better attuned to local conditions in Latin America. This, he argued, was essential in laying the groundwork for continued American business success in the region. Nelson urged oil companies to take down the barbed-wire fences that isolated their compounds, to encourage their executives to learn the local language and culture, and to introduce public-health initiatives. In 1940, Nelson formed the Venezuelan Development Company (VDC) with $3 million (equivalent to about $55 million in 2020 dollars) in initial capital, a third of which came directly from the Rockefeller family, a third from Venezuelan investors, and a third from the oil business.[28] The VDC's first major project was the construction of the Hotel Avila in Caracas. This followed a chance remark made by President Contreras to Nelson that the capital city lacked a luxury hotel. The hotel opened in 1942 with 114 rooms, including a fourteen-room apartment house, a ten-room residence, and a seven-room annex for staff quarters.[29]

Around the same time that the VDC was formed, Nelson assembled a group of experts to draw up a framework for the future of American policy in Latin America.[30] In August 1940, Pres. Franklin D. Roosevelt appointed Nelson as Coordinator of Inter-American Affairs in the Office of Inter-American Affairs (OIAA). The OIAA took a two-pronged approach to Latin America, spending almost equally between public-relations propaganda and food and health programs.[31] In 1944, Nelson was appointed assistant secretary of state for Latin America. The following year, he helped negotiate the Act of Chapultepec, which established an early Cold War mutual security agreement with a number of Latin American countries. In 1946, now outside of government, Nelson formed the American International Association for Economic Development (AIA). The AIA established community centers, waged nutritional education campaigns, ran farm training programs, and taught home economics courses.[32] In one commentator's words, Nelson became "the best-known American in all of Latin America."[33] Not everyone has viewed Nelson's involvement in Latin American affairs as being entirely benign and benevolent. Some see his motives as being driven by capitalist imperialism, and he has stood accused of unwelcome interference in the region's politics.[34]

Another legacy of the Latin American trip were efforts by Nelson and Winthrop to purchase a family ranch in Texas adjacent to the famous King Ranch in Kingsville, around fifty miles southwest of Corpus Christi toward the Mexican border. Winthrop was still smitten by Texas, and both Winthrop and Nelson were enthralled by the cattle ranches that they had seen in Argentina. Nelson penned a joint representation of their case to Junior. He argued that a Texas ranch would be a welcome place for rest and relaxation, that many family friends had residences there, and that it offered bountiful opportunities to network and make new contacts. Nelson continued, "I have felt that it was wiser not to hasten bringing this matter to your attention because I was afraid that it might be just an enthusiastic burst on my part following our delightful trip. However, as time goes on, both Winthrop and I find ourselves more anxious than ever to go ahead and buy this property." The proposed purchase never did go through, although Winthrop and Nelson continued to pursue the idea for the next decade.[35] Winthrop would of course eventually fulfill his ambition, not in Texas, but in neighboring Arkansas, where he built Winrock Farms after moving to the state.[36] Nelson owned ranches in Venezuela and bought land next to the King Ranch in Texas.[37]

After attending his grandfather's funeral on May 25, Winthrop thought hard about his next steps in the oil business. According to the plan that Junior, Teagle, and Farish had earlier drawn up, Winthrop was due to spend some time in the Midwest and then in Europe. But on the Latin America trip, Winthrop spoke with Joseph Rovensky at length. Rovensky convinced him that some banking experience would be beneficial for a future business career. Junior was agreeable to the idea. Through Rovensky, Winthrop learned that Chase Bank was planning to take on a small number of interns to train in the basics of banking. Winthrop wrote his uncle, Winthrop Aldrich, president and chair of the board at Chase Bank, to inquire about vacancies on the program.[38] His uncle was happy to oblige.[39]

As Winthrop prepared to start on the junior executive program at Chase Bank on September 13, he moved into his first independent New York apartment on West Fifty-Fifth Street. To assist him in his new home life, he sought the services of someone who could cook and more generally manage his domestic affairs. Charles C. Huitt, president of Dunbar National Bank in Harlem, which Junior helped to found in 1928, offered his assistance in the matter. The bank's management and staff were all Black, and the bank had a predominantly Black clientele. Huitt said that he knew a James "Jimmy" Hudson, a twenty-nine-year-old who lived at 408 West 150th Street, who might fit the bill.[40] Hudson was from Virginia, where he had attended St. Paul's Normal and Industrial School in Lawrenceville before gaining a bachelor's degree in science at Wilberforce University in Ohio. After graduation, he worked at New York's Grand Central Station, the Pennsylvania Railroad, and at various other places on the East Coast as a waiter. During the 1930s, with jobs scarce because of the Great Depression, Hudson worked in Harlem at the Thirty-Second Precinct Police Department as a civilian investigator. One of his jobs was to solicit funds from merchants and businesses to provide recreational opportunities for Black youths. It was in this capacity that he knew Huitt. When Huitt asked him if he was interested in a new job, Hudson pounced on the opportunity.[41]

Huitt informed Winthrop that Hudson was "single, an Episcopalian, and feels competent to handle the work that you have in mind with the proviso that he does not claim to be a chef for fancy dishes." Hudson also came highly recommended by the Dunbar National Bank doorman. The doorman had known Hudson for nine years and testified, "He is absolutely honest and worthy of your confidence."[42] Winthrop formally interviewed Hudson in the family office at 30 Rockefeller Plaza. Afterward, he took him downstairs for a more informal chat and bought him an ice cream soda. Happy with what he heard, Winthrop hired him as his "assistant" on the spot. Hudson gave his two weeks' notice at the precinct before beginning work for his new employer.[43]

Winthrop reported back to Huitt, "We talked over my housekeeping problems and he decided to accept the position. From what little I have seen of him he seems like a fine young fellow and I am happy to have him working for me."[44] To make up for his professed limitation in culinary matters, Winthrop taught Hudson how to cook. Winthrop was a dab hand at whipping up tasty sauces and soups, as well as an expert on roasting chickens.[45] Hudson proved an exceptionally good hire who stayed with Winthrop for the best part of the next twenty-three years. He was one of the very few people from New York who accompanied Winthrop on his move to Arkansas. To this day, there is a Jimmy Hudson Drive named after him at Winrock Farms on Petit Jean Mountain. Soon after taking the new job with Winthrop, Hudson married his fiancé, Hortense, and the couple moved into the Dunbar Apartments in Harlem. The apartments were built with the help of Junior's funding and the Hudsons managed to secure a rental place there with a little help from the Rockefeller family's redoubtable office fixer Robert W. Gumbel.[46]

In October and November, Winthrop took an overseas trip to Europe and the Middle East to explore the oil industry there.[47] At the beginning of 1938, an opportunity arose for him to work with the Greater New York Fund (GNYF).

The fund was part of a new effort to raise money for charities in the city. In the past, much of this fundraising had taken place along strictly sectarian lines, with separate campaigns in the Protestant, Catholic, and Jewish communities. Due to the ravages of the Great Depression, the need for such funds had risen to $85 million (equivalent to $1.5 billion in 2020 dollars) a year, but there was a shortfall of $10 million (equivalent to over $178 million in 2020 dollars) in giving. The GNYF was an attempt to make that money up through extending solicitations to corporations and employee groups.[48] Junior was one of the New York civic leaders who helped to establish the fund, which became a precursor to the United Way.[49]

Chairing the drive was James T. Blaine, president of Marine Midland Bank, who had been active in the city for a number of years as a civic leader in philanthropy. Blaine secured an agreement from some 450 different agencies to coordinate their charitable efforts through the GNYF. Reflecting the previously sectarian nature of such drives in New York, Paul Felix "Piggy" Warburg, scion of a German-Jewish banking family, was appointed vice chair to represent Jewish philanthropies. John S. Burke, chief executive of the B. Altman & Company department store chain, was appointed vice chair to represent Catholic philanthropies. This left an empty vice chair position open to represent Protestant philanthropies. The other vice chairs felt that a Rockefeller would be the perfect fit for the job. Nelson was the first choice, but he declined, and instead pointed them toward his younger brother. Winthrop was delighted to accept. The opportunity opened the door to making business contacts in New York, and the Chase Bank training program was not working out. Banking, Winthrop discovered, bored him to death.[50]

Winthrop paused his studies at Chase Bank for six months at the beginning of 1938. The GNYF hired the John Price Jones Corporation, the leading experts in fundraising in the city, as their professional consultants. Yet it was not long before Winthrop was the one left holding the baby for the project. Blaine had to travel to Europe on a business trip. Warburg's father passed away, and his son spent a couple of months in Honolulu grieving. Burke, according to Winthrop, proved of little practical help. Winthrop maintained that although he was listed as only one of the vice chairs, he pretty much ran the campaign single-handed.[51]

It was quite a responsibility to rest on the shoulders of a raw twenty-six-year-old recruit fresh out of the oil fields. Winthrop decided to use the campaign to improve his speaking skills, delivering over 120 speeches in the following months. The opportunity also afforded him experience in a boardroom setting and in making executive decisions. Early on, the search for an appropriate campaign slogan slowed the campaign's progress. Winthrop suggested quite a few of them. John Price Jones, the head of the consulting firm, and the leading guru in the fundraising world at the time, pooh-poohed each and every one. This quickly wore thin. Winthrop reared up on Price, telling him that he expected more effort on his part. Winthrop insisted that if Price did not like any of his ideas, then he had better come up with some of his own, because that was what he was being paid to do. Price was not used to being spoken to in that way. But a clearing of the air proved beneficial, since it won Winthrop the respect of Price and the rest of the team. Now everyone knew where they stood, and the campaign moved forward all the more effectively for it.[52]

When Winthrop did receive a hand from his fellow team members, it was not always for the best. Winthrop believed that Blaine made a tactical error early in the campaign when he asserted that the GNYF reserved the right to solicit all corporations under $1 million (equivalent to $17.8 million in 2020 dollars) in valuation. Very few corporations in New York met that criterion. It fell to Winthrop to confront Blaine about what he had done. He told Blaine that if he did not straighten the situation out, it would make the campaign untenable. With Winthrop's help, Blaine corrected the misstep.[53] In the end, the GNYF proved something of a disappointment, raising only $4.4 million (equivalent to $78.5 million in 2020 dollars) of its ambitious $10 million target.[54] The following year, when John A. Brown, president of Socony, chaired the campaign, Winthrop was his executive assistant. This gave him more leeway to manage things in the way that he wanted to.[55] But the result was even worse the second time around, with the GNYF raising only $3.2 million (equivalent to $57.1 million in 2020 dollars).[56]

Although the numbers were disappointing, the experience proved beneficial. Jimmy Hudson, who worked on the campaign, believed that Winthrop's involvement with the GNYF significantly raised his profile in the city, not least in New York's Black community, where it was Hudson's job to help Winthrop mobilize support. Hudson did this by tapping into New York's Black colleges, sororities, and fraternities. He arranged a cocktail party in Smalls Paradise, a Black-owned nightclub in Harlem, so that Winthrop could address the movers and shakers in the Black community. The campaign in Harlem climaxed with a baseball game at Yankee Stadium, starring Satchel Paige and other players from the Black baseball leagues. The experience further nurtured Winthrop's burgeoning interest in race relations.[57] In 1940, Winthrop joined the board of trustees of the National Urban League.[58]

In a separate development, in late 1938, along with Laurance, Winthrop became involved in founding and promoting Air Youth of America. The

Winthrop addresses a Greater New York Fund rally
in front of midtown Manhattan's General Post Office
Building (today the James A. Farley Building), June
1940. *Winthrop Rockefeller Collection, UA Little Rock
Center for Arkansas History and Culture.*

organization sought to train young people for careers in aviation. Winthrop devoted a considerable amount of time and energy to the project over the next few years. The organization eventually merged with the National Aeronautic Association in December 1941.[59]

At the beginning of 1939, having finally completed his Chase Bank training program, Winthrop started working for Socony. His position was in the Foreign Trade Department with a focus on the Middle East. Winthrop was assigned as Socony's liaison officer with the Near Eastern Development Company (NEDC). The NEDC was formed after World War I, when disagreements arose about who should manage the lucrative Mosul oil field in Iraq, previously under German occupation. The Iraq Petroleum Company was formed with a joint ownership between Britain, France, the Netherlands, and the United States. American interests were represented through the NEDC, with a number of oil companies jointly participating. Gradually, Socony and Standard Oil of New Jersey bought out all of the other companies until they each shared a 50 percent stake. When Winthrop came on board, the immediate issue he faced was how to increase pipeline facilities. He worked closely with the British director of the NEDC, Stuart Morgan, on drawing up a proposal. Morgan suggested that Winthrop should visit the Middle East to address the pipeline issue firsthand.[60]

At the end of September 1939, Winthrop embarked upon a three-month trip to Europe and the Middle East. Germany had invaded Poland on September 1, and the outbreak of World War II formed an historic backdrop to the journey. There was certainly no difficulty in booking an eastward passage across the Atlantic, with most Americans looking to travel back home in the opposite direction. Only twenty-five passengers traveled with Winthrop in first class. Winthrop's traveling companion was Robert Stewart, the manager of Socony's operations in Egypt. Their first port of call was Italy. The two disembarked in Naples and visited Rome, Florence, and Venice, before catching a boat across the Mediterranean Sea to Alexandria, Egypt. The boat was crowded with people heading back home to Africa. Winthrop and Stewart spent some time in the Egyptian oil fields before traveling to Iran, where they visited the Abadan oil fields and refinery.[61]

Next on the itinerary was Bahrain, followed by a trip across the Arabian Peninsula, where the California-Arabian Standard Oil Company was in the infant stages of its drilling operations. In 1944, the company was renamed the Arabian American Oil Company, known as Aramco, and in 1988 it became the Saudi Arabian Oil Company, known as Saudi Aramco.[62] Winthrop and Stewart completed their tour at the Iraq Petroleum Company development in Qatar.[63]

Drilling for oil in Qatar had only just begun the previous year, and the first strike did not occur until January 1940.[64]

While visiting Qatar, Winthrop and Stewart attended a lunch meeting at the home of a local sheikh. A group of men gathered around for conversation before a six-foot copper tray was brought out with food piled on it. A six-inch foundation of rice was topped with a feast of three full-size roasted sheep, garnished with a number of roasted chickens. Winthrop declined silverware and followed local custom by eating with his hands. Much to Winthrop's relief, the sheikh did not offer him the prime delicacy of a sheep's eyeball to eat. At the end of the meal came the customary gifts. Firstly, there were Persian rugs. Winthrop tried to explain that they were traveling light, and that they could not possibly carry the huge rugs around with them. Such protestations did no good, however, and Winthrop was forced to relent and accept them. Secondly, out came the treasure chest, from which the sheikh plucked three button-shaped pearls and presented them to Winthrop.[65]

Next, they got down to business. Winthrop and Stewart wanted the sheikh to sign a contract to allow the construction of a pipeline. They explained to him that the money had been deposited into his account in the Bank of Bahrain. Winthrop gained an insight into how business was conducted in the Middle East when the sheikh refused to sign the contract until all the money owed to him was presented in cash. A compromise was finally struck. The sheikh sent his financial adviser to the bank to personally count every rupee. Only when his financial adviser had verified the amount would the sheikh sign the contract. Having secured the agreement, Winthrop and Stewart headed back to the Iraq oil fields, where they stayed at an Iraq Petroleum Company camp near Kirkuk.[66]

Afterward, Winthrop continued on alone to Turkey, where he traveled from the capital city of Ankara to Istanbul, and then on to Bucharest, the capital city of Romania. While there he earned an audience with King Carol II. The two men met for forty-five minutes in an informal setting, although Winthrop did not find the king, who spoke fluent English, very forthcoming in response to his questions. At his next destination, the Hungarian capital city of Budapest, Winthrop found prime minister Pál Teleki far more engaging. With a Socony representative acting as their interpreter, the two men spoke very frankly about the war situation and the ominous prospect of a German invasion of Hungary. Winthrop returned to the United States over Christmas 1939 and submitted a report of his overseas travels to Socony. In the new year, he grew increasingly concerned, as did many other American citizens, about his country's preparedness for war. Winthrop had witnessed developments in

Europe, and he wanted to do something to raise public awareness about what was happening there.[67]

The Citizens' Military Training Camps (CMTC) afforded Winthrop the opportunity to do just that. The CMTC was rooted in the Plattsburgh Movement of 1915 and 1916, when forty thousand men, drawn mainly from America's upper class, volunteered to attend summer military training as part of the Preparedness Movement to strengthen the nation's readiness for World War I. The most famous of these camps was based in Plattsburgh in upstate New York. In the National Defense Act of 1920, Congress authorized the expansion of the camps as a compromise after rejecting the idea of universal military training. The camps were run every year from 1921 to 1940, and they trained an estimated four hundred thousand men in total. In contrast to National Guard and Organized Reserve training, CMTC allowed male citizens to obtain basic military training without the obligation of a call-up for active duty. Participants in the camps were able to receive a reserve commission as a second lieutenant upon the completion of four consecutive summers of courses. The camps focused on physical fitness, marching, and shooting skills. A number of high-profile figures participated in the camps, including two future presidents, Harry S. Truman and Ronald Reagan. Winthrop joined the Plattsburgh camp in the final year of CMTC operations before it was superseded by the introduction of the draft, after which the federal government took over the job of military training. Winthrop was among the most well-known of the last crop of Plattsburgh recruits.[68]

On June 25, 1940, the New York Times reported that 1,933 men in New York City had applied for an available 250 places at the Plattsburgh camp, with another 250 places reserved for men from upstate New York, New Jersey, and Delaware. Final approval for selection lay in the hands of Lt. Gen. Hugh Aloysius Drum, commander of the Second Corps Area. The Times noted, "Applicants came from every walk of life—business, professional and labor— and the selections will be made solely on a basis of military and educational background and civic leadership indicative of ability to lead men." Winthrop grabbed an application form and hurried down to the Federal Building at 90 Church Street for his medical exam. He told a Times reporter, "All of us do a lot of talking about American institutions and blessings, but we can't appreciate them very much unless we offer ourselves to defend them."[69]

On June 29, Drum, along with Col. Julian Ochs Adler, civilian adviser to the secretary of war, released a list of eight hundred men accepted for the Business and Professional Men's Training Camp at Plattsburgh. The number of recruits was expanded to accommodate demand. The Military Training Camps

Association successfully used the large number of applications to press for the establishment of further training camps that year.[70] In all, eight camps opened in July 1940, with three thousand trainees.[71] Joining Winthrop among the notable enrollees accepted into Plattsburgh were Newbold Morris, president of the New York City Council, and Judge Robert P. Patterson, who sat on the US Court of Appeals for the Second Circuit.[72] By the end of the year, Patterson was serving as President Roosevelt's undersecretary of war and playing a vital role in mobilizing the United States' armed forces nationwide.[73] One story has it that he was on dreaded Kitchen Police (KP) duty at the camp alongside Winthrop when he received the news of his promotion to Cabinet rank.[74]

The Plattsburgh camp opened on July 5. Unlike many of the other men who caught special trains up from New York City, Winthrop elected to drive there. He arrived in Plattsburgh bright and early at 6:00 a.m. By 10:00 a.m., he was through the processing line before everyone else had arrived. In an early lesson that being first on the spot in the Army was not always the best policy, First Sgt. Hubert Williams of Company D, Twenty-Sixth Infantry, to which Winthrop was assigned, enlisted his first KP recruit. Dressed in denim overalls, Winthrop wolfed down his lunch of frankfurters, sauerkraut, and mashed potatoes, and then prepared to wait on the rest of the company. Still retaining his rookie trainee enthusiasm, Winthrop told the press, "You ought to put a plug in for the non-commissioned officers. They've been swell—in the processing, the trouble they're going to in arranging tents and in tipping you off to things." Col. James I. Muir, camp commander at Plattsburgh, and commander of the Twenty-Sixth Infantry, told reporters that, while trainees would not be "put through an endurance contest or dance marathon," training was nevertheless being taken seriously. The next afternoon the trainees were formally inducted in a ceremony featuring addresses from Lt. Gen. Drum and Col. Adler.[75]

Junior was pleased by Winthrop's early, positive reports from the camp, telling his son, "We are very proud to have the family name thus splendidly represented in this patriotic movement and feel increasingly the wisdom of the action you took so promptly and wholly on your own initiative."[76] Only a matter of days after Winthrop enrolled at the camp, David's engagement to Margaret "Peggy" McGrath was announced in the press.[77] Laurance was heard to quip, "Well, now that we've got Dave lined up and Winnie in uniform, we've got the whole family in order."[78] David's wedding took place on September 7 and left Winthrop as the only unmarried sibling of the brothers' generation.[79]

Life at Plattsburgh was no picnic. Reveille was at 5:45 each morning and marked the beginning a twelve-hour day filled with exercises and instruction. Yet neither was it the full-on experience of Army life that Winthrop later encountered. The trainees took weekends off, and Winthrop usually drove home to play golf and visit friends. At times, he complained that Plattsburgh was too much for show and that not everyone took the training seriously enough.[80] Other more seasoned recruits admitted that Plattsburgh "gave them little but the ABC of modern war."[81] Still, Winthrop's time at Plattsburgh did have distinct advantages, one of which was getting him into better physical shape. He also made some important connections at the camp. Winthrop was elected as a member of the Committee of Twenty-One to represent the trainees' views with the camp's military leadership. In that capacity, Winthrop got to know Lt. Gen. Drum, thereby gaining a useful mentor and contact.[82]

It was not long until Winthrop entered the full rigors of Army life. On September 16, Congress passed the Selective Training and Service Act of 1940, which required all men between the ages of twenty-one and thirty-five to register on the draft rolls for military service. Over the course of the following month, sixteen million men registered.[83] This included all of the Rockefeller brothers. Winthrop drew the highest number of 8,812 out of approximately 9,000 men entered into the local draft, making him the least likely to serve. Nelson, meanwhile, drew the lowest number of 87, making him the most likely to serve. Winthrop used the disparity to return some of the teasing he had received from Nelson during their childhood. When the five brothers sat down to discuss the matter more seriously, Winthrop told the others that he felt strongly it was his responsibility to represent the family on the front lines in the forthcoming conflict, not least because he was the only one still single. He next sought Lt. Gen. Drum's advice about the best course of action to take. Drum confirmed Winthrop's thinking that he should volunteer as a private in the Army. Winthrop told Drum that if it all possible he would like to rejoin the Twenty-Sixth Infantry at Plattsburgh.[84]

In the final months of 1940, Winthrop and his brothers incorporated the Rockefeller Brothers Fund (RBF), a partnership agreement to coordinate their philanthropic contributions and activities. The RBF became a powerhouse in the philanthropic world after World War II and consolidated the Rockefeller brothers' standing as an influential collective force.[85] But there was a war to fight first. Upon Abby's urging him to do so, David later followed in Winthrop's footsteps and enlisted as a private in the Army in March 1942. He rose to the rank of captain and served in North Africa and France in Army intelligence.[86] John and Laurance both joined the Navy. John, a lieutenant commander, initially served in the Bureau of Naval Personnel as a recruiter and administrator for the American Red Cross, before transferring to a staff role. Laurance, a lieutenant, worked with aircraft plants to expedite wartime production, drawing upon his interests and experience in the aviation industry. Nelson worked in government, principally as Coordinator of Inter-American Affairs in the OIAA.[87]

Winthrop's intention to volunteer was leaked to the press at the beginning of 1941. He told reporters that he did not intend to enlist before January 15, since he was busy getting his personal affairs in order and all the necessary military formalities done and dusted first.[88] On Monday, January 21, 1941, Winthrop was one of eleven volunteers among a total of thirty-one men in Manhattan Draft Board 20 who were told to report for duty the following morning.[89] The next five and a half years of Winthrop's life would be dedicated to military service.

CHAPTER 7 # Mobilizing for War

VOLUNTEERING FOR MILITARY SERVICE allowed Winthrop to revisit the same possibilities that the southwestern oil fields had previously offered: starting on the ground floor, gaining hands-on experience, and making his own way in the world. In the process, he continued to broaden his horizons, meet new people, and make new friends, while encountering freedom, excitement, and adventure on the front lines of history. In doing so, he once more received high praise from family members and colleagues for his endeavors. For their part, the Rockefeller family was able to point to one of their own doing their duty on behalf of the country and shouldering responsibility for defending the nation. In this way, who and what Winthrop wanted to be, and what the rest of the family expected of him, came back into an agreeable alignment.

On Tuesday morning, January 22, 1941, Winthrop stepped out of his West Fifty-Fifth Street apartment at 6:55 a.m. and into a media scrimmage waiting on the sidewalk to capture the story of a Rockefeller enrolling in the Army.[1] Wearing a gray hat and blue coat, and lugging a heavy brown suitcase, Winthrop hurriedly flashed a grin for the cameras and stepped into a taxicab. The press followed him downtown to the Manhattan Draft Board 20 offices at 125 West Forty-Sixth Street, where photographers snapped shots of Winthrop shaking hands with Charles T. Stone, the local draft board chair. Winthrop also fielded questions from reporters. What did he expect to be called in the Army? "Hey, you," Winthrop replied. How much money was he carrying with him? "Just pocket change," he responded. Winthrop was instructed to lead a group of thirty other men down to the induction center at the Seventy-First Regiment Armory on Park Avenue and Thirty-Fourth Street. He strode out with the other inductees clutching their free subway passes.[2]

The men caught the subway from Forty-Seventh Street and Sixth Avenue to Thirty-Fourth Street, and then walked from Sixth Avenue to Park Avenue. Winthrop led the line, accompanied by three newsreel trucks and photographers' flashlights popping at every step along the way. By the time he got to the

Armory, he was visibly perspiring. "It wasn't the heat of the exercise," the *New York Times* explained, "but the embarrassment at receiving so much attention, and besides he was half blind from the flashbulbs." Reporters continued to pepper him with questions. Winthrop's only audible reply was, "This is pretty good experience for me." Walter D. Shackleton, head of the local Selective Service Administration's information department, introduced Winthrop to Maj. Edward Joseph, who was in command at the induction center.

By 10:00 a.m. Winthrop had passed all of the required tests and answered a number of induction questions, one of which revealed that his weekly salary at Socony was $88 (equivalent to $1,604 in 2020 dollars), a juicy tidbit that reporters lapped up. By 10:17 a.m., Winthrop was Private Rockefeller, serial no. 32,002,756. Next came a wait until it was time to walk down to Penn Station and catch the train to Fort Dix, New Jersey. Winthrop found a worn leather chair in the officer's supply room and slumped into it. The press still swarmed around him. He did not join the other men for a free lunch at a nearby restaurant, perhaps to give them some peace and quiet from the media spotlight. Instead, he ate a couple of sandwiches and drank a glass of milk in the Armory.[3]

After lunch, the men started out to Penn Station. Winthrop figured that he would take advantage of the media presence. He asked a newsreel man traveling in a car alongside him to transport his suitcase down to the station. The move soon misfired. A few minutes later, a corporal approached the now empty-handed Winthrop with a big sack of mail to take to Fort Dix. Winthrop flung the mailbag over his shoulder and discovered that it was even heavier than the suitcase. As the media men scoffed at him, a watching policeman came to Winthrop's aid. He told the reporters to give the new soldier a break. They agreed to transport the mailbag down to the station for him too.[4] The enlistees arrived at Penn Station at 2:00 p.m. with the next departure to Fort Dix leaving at 2:15 p.m.[5] Upon arrival at Fort Dix, there were more reporters waiting with yet more questions, and still more photographers wanting more photographs.[6] A fellow inductee who spoke to the press about "Mr. Rockefeller" was sharply corrected by a major who barked "he's Private Rockefeller from now on."[7] Winthrop turned in that night at 10:45 p.m., sleeping in a tent with five other soldiers.[8]

Winthrop won applause from the rest of the family for the way that he had conducted himself. Nelson wrote first: "Congratulations on the way in which you handled a difficult situation yesterday. I have heard nothing but the most enthusiastic comments from all sides. The four of us are proud to be your partners."[9] John followed later with, "I have heard nothing but the most favorable comments on all sides. . . . Certainly you deserve to get pleasure and satisfaction out of it all as by volunteering you have done something which is of tremendous value both to the country and the family."[10] Laurance added, "We are all tremendously grateful for the job you are doing for your country, your family, and I hope, and believe, yourself. The publicity in connection with your departure was most gratifying and I hope more of an ordeal than you will ever have to face in the Army for some time to come."[11] Finally, Junior noted, "We continue to hear so many favorable expressions about your having volunteered."[12]

The praise was not wholly universal. A syndicated piece that appeared in a number of newspapers nationwide asked, "Is not young Rockefeller an American? Have we not decided that all eligible Americans should render military service to their country?" It declared, "There should be nothing remarkable about the fact that a singularly fortunate young American decided to accept, casually and good-humoredly, his plain duty. It would be a bad day for the country if this perfectly normal thing should become regarded as a phenomenon."[13]

There followed another hectic few days of Winthrop being bounced around the military bureaucracy before he reached his desired destination. Most certainly, that place was not Fort Dix, which was cold, muddy, and miserable.[14] On Wednesday, January 23, Winthrop's first full day there, the media still followed his every move. He arrived for reveille at 5:45 a.m. and had breakfast. "I couldn't name it, Hash of some sort, I suppose," he told reporters, about what was later revealed to have been creamed beef on toast. He then marched along in the mud for processing and received his uniform. That afternoon, he attended lectures about "Articles of War" and "Customs of the Service."[15]

The next day, Winthrop was transferred to Fort Jay on Governor's Island, New York, to join the 518th Military Police Battalion. The transfer baffled him. Although the assignment was an honor—the Military Police required a height of over six feet, and an advanced level of education, both of which Winthrop possessed—he did not want to be an MP.[16] All became clear after spending only three hours there. Winthrop was told to gather his belongings: he was going to Camp Plattsburgh, which was now a full-fledged Army training camp. Lt. Gen. Drum had granted Winthrop's assignment request. Because of Army rules and regulations, Winthrop first had to accept an assignment in Drum's jurisdiction before he could be transferred to Plattsburgh. With much relief, Winthrop caught the train to Plattsburgh, where he joined the Army's First Division, Twenty-Sixth Infantry Regiment (hereafter Twenty-Sixth), in the heavy weapons outfit of Company M.[17] His platoon was a machine-gun unit.[18]

Upon arrival at Plattsburgh, Winthrop had time to catch his breath and report back to his parents, writing them the first of many letters during his military service. Winthrop's parents relished learning the details of their son's life in the Army, just as they had done with his dispatches from the oil fields. Winthrop revealed that he expected to be on the move again within a month or two. By that time, he hoped to have transitioned beyond the rookie stage. He was scheduled to start a new recruit course on January 28. The barracks at Plattsburgh were chronically overcrowded at almost double the intended capacity. Between sixty and seventy men slept in double-decker bunk beds in each building.[19] His pay was $20 (equivalent to $365 in 2020 dollars) a month.[20] Socony topped up that amount to his regular $88 per week pay for one year, as it did for other enlisted employees.[21]

Winthrop informed his parents, "All my old friends up here from last summer have given me a very hearty welcome." To the new recruits, he remained an object of curiosity. "They all hang around my bed to such an extent that I can hardly do anything about getting established," Winthrop wrote. "And last night when I went up to watch the dance for a while so many gathered around that one of the 'non-coms' came over thinking that such a gathering could mean nothing but a fight." But, he continued, "it is all very friendly and I trust will pass away quickly." Finishing the letter in fine spirits, he reported, "I am well, happy and looking forward with pleasure to the days of training that lie ahead."[22] Quarantine for a measles outbreak in the barracks, followed by a head cold, set Winthrop back a week in training. By mid-February, he had graduated. This came with its own drawbacks, since he was now eligible for KP, guard duty, and other grunt work.[23]

On February 28, Winthrop and the Twenty-Sixth traveled to Fort Devens in Ayer, Massachusetts, just outside Boston, where all fifteen thousand men of the First Division were being gathered together. The night before, Winthrop wrote his parents that he was dreading it. The journey was due to start at 4:30 a.m. and last twelve to fourteen hours. A total of 150 trucks stood by to transport the men, and Winthrop was one of the designated relief drivers. His assigned truck was entirely open except for a canvas overhead. The temperature at Camp Plattsburgh the day before departure was a chilly 10 degrees Fahrenheit. Winthrop was confident that the hand warmers his mother had sent him would be put to good use.[24] It was zero degrees when the convoy set off for Fort Devens, and the water in Winthrop's canteen was frozen solid.[25]

When he got there, Winthrop discovered that conditions at Fort Devens were even worse than they had been at Fort Dix. The First Division's Sixteenth and Eighteenth Infantry Regiments arrived earliest. By the time the Twenty-Sixth turned up, the regular Army barracks space had run out. Winthrop's

Company M was assigned to an old New Deal Civilian Conservation Corps barracks with tar-paper walls. The cold was reminiscent of his days working on the drilling rigs. Each night, one soldier stayed awake to keep the two pot-bellied stoves in the middle of the room burning. To make matters worse, Winthrop was located on the top bunk bed against the outer wall nearest to the door, one of the draftiest spots in the barracks. He slept in a knitted woolen balaclava helmet. Further inviting ridicule, Winthrop also wore pajamas to bed, while all the other men slept in their long johns. The ensuing catcalls did not bother him in the slightest: the pajamas served their purpose and kept him warm.[26]

The freezing temperatures, along with the snow, meant that much of the training took place indoors. In one break in the weather, Winthrop was able to go outside for some machine gun target practice. He did rather well for himself, scoring 175 out of a possible 200. This ranked him fifth out of more than forty participants and entitled him to wear a marksman's medal.[27] Lt. Gen. Drum confirmed Winthrop's progress to Junior: "He's doing more than well. He missed expert with the machine gun by 9 points; is one of the selected privates attending N.C.O.'s [Non-Commissioned Officer's] school and made 93% on the last examination; has applied for and been recommended for the 10 series in the extension course, being qualified therefore; neither asks for nor receives any special consideration nor favors. The rest of the men of M company think he's 'swell,' and he is not, and has not been, the subject of any publicity."[28]

As always, Winthrop found some time for play in between all of the hard work. He reported that he had "found some good but rough and tumble friends among the ranks of [his] fellow privates."[29] These included Italian Americans Tony Pugleisie, Jimmy Lopresto, Frankie LaScala, and Lou Caffaro. Danish American Bob Bondorff rounded out the group. After acquiring a new car, Winthrop began to travel out of the barracks every weeknight, taking select friends along with him. A distinct obstacle they faced was finding an establishment nearby that would entertain regular soldiers and that was not restricted to "officers only." They discovered the Mohawk Tavern, run by a Romanian woman called Jenny, which served the requisite good food and drink. At noon every Saturday, Winthrop and two or three friends traveled to New York to meet their respective dates. On Sunday morning, they all met up at Winthrop's West Fifty-Fifth Street apartment for breakfast. Later they visited one of his favorite nightspots, such as the El Morocco, the Stork Club, or the 21 Club. Winthrop got a kick out of introducing his new Army friends to his regular New York pals. Though it could often be touch and go, they always managed to make it back to Fort Devens for reveille at 6:00 on Monday morning.[30]

Meanwhile, training continued, and Winthrop was getting into much better physical shape. He claimed to have shed twenty-four pounds in his first four months in the Army, and he attributed much of that to slinging machine guns around.[31] Winthrop also acquired a new boss when the Twenty-Sixth made headlines in appointing the fifty-three-year-old Col. Theodore Roosevelt Jr., son of the former American president, as its commanding officer. Roosevelt Jr. left his civilian job as vice president of publishing house Doubleday, Doran and Company to take up the position, reprising the same role of commanding officer that he had performed during World War I. The *Time* magazine story announcing his appointment noted that Winthrop was the "26th's most famed enlisted man."[32] One day, Roosevelt Jr. invited Winthrop to lunch. Winthrop used the opportunity to issue a few complaints about the way things were being run. Roosevelt Jr. listened carefully before completely ignoring his advice.[33] At the end of May, after serving the mandatory four months minimum required in service, Winthrop was promoted to private first class.[34]

In July, it was Junior who was in the spotlight when he read out his ten-point "Rockefeller Credo" on New York City's WMCA radio as part of his participation in a fund-raising campaign for the United Service Organizations (USO).[35] Richard W. Lawrence, New York City USO chair, introduced Junior as "one of the 200,000 parents of the young men from New York who are now wearing the country's uniform." Junior continued this theme in his address, finding a "common basis" with the radio audience: "Each of us [is] the parent of a son who is in the defense forces of our country. I am proud, as you are, that my son, like yours, is serving his country in this important field." The much-lauded address was reported on the front page of the *New York Times*.[36] Junior later affirmed his sentiments to Winthrop in their private correspondence, writing, "You will never know how proud I am to be your father and to have had the opportunity of speaking as I did to other parents about their sons and mine."[37]

Following his promotion to corporal, on July 22 Winthrop accompanied the Twenty-Sixth to the Carolinas for landing maneuvers. They were joined there by the First Division's Sixteenth and Eighteenth Infantry Regiments, and the Fourth, the Ninety-Fourth, and the Ninety-Seventh Field Artillery Battalions. It was rumored that the nine thousand Army men would meet up with six thousand members of the Marine Corps at another destination.[38] Exactly where remained a secret, although the scuttlebutt suggested Puerto Rico.[39] From Fort Devens, the port of embarkation was the Army base at Fifty-Eighth Street and First Avenue in Brooklyn. This gave Winthrop the opportunity to meet up with Robert W. Gumbel from the Rockefeller family office, who passed along a new bible to Winthrop from his parents, as his existing copy had gone missing. Delays in Brooklyn meant that Winthrop spent several more hours there than anticipated, and his parents later rued the opportunity not to have delivered the gift themselves.[40]

After finally boarding, the soldiers were packed tight into the cargo hold. Quick thinking meant that Winthrop managed to secure himself a spot close to a porthole so that he had enough light to do some reading on the journey. He planned to catch up on family history with Allen Nevins's biography of Senior.[41] While at sea, Winthrop learned that the rumored Puerto Rico maneuvers were canceled.[42] A few days later, he discovered that the Twenty-Sixth was being joined by the Navy, the Marines, and the Air Corps for a mock invasion of the North Carolina coast. Winthrop reported, "From what we have seen of the mainland so far, I think that the mosquitoes will finish off what is left of the boys after that last three weeks on this tub." To occupy himself, Winthrop grew a moustache, something that became a variously appearing and disappearing feature throughout the war. He wrote his parents, "It is a protest at having been taken out on a two week trip and then trapped for five. It is developing into quite a protest."[43]

In one brief interlude during the maneuvers, the soldiers were allowed to grab a quick shore leave in Charleston, South Carolina. Winthrop took the opportunity to rent a hotel room and take a bath. Generous to a fault, he extended an invitation to his fellow soldiers to visit and do the same. The offer proved a popular one. By 9:00 a.m. there were already twelve to fifteen soldiers in Winthrop's room. By 10:00 a.m. it was clear that the line was going to last all day. He sent out the bellboy to procure a washtub, some ice, and a few crates of beer. Winthrop also rented another couple of rooms to accommodate the demand. In all, he counted seventy-two soldiers that attended the impromptu bathing party.[44]

On August 14, the First Division troops were back in Brooklyn. Trains awaited to transport them to Fort Devens.[45] A *Time* magazine reporter spotted Winthrop in Manhattan on a furlough the following week, reporting on his "full-blown mustache" and impertinently asking him for tips about how to stay rich in the Army. Winthrop told him, "The best investment I ever made was not learning how to play craps or poker."[46] Winthrop also managed a rare short stay in Pocantico Hills, which was a tonic for his parents.[47] More good news was forthcoming shortly after, when Winthrop was promoted to sergeant.[48] Junior wrote: "How proud and happy it makes Mamma and me it would be difficult for you to realize. Each day you are not only maintaining the reputation of the whole family, but adding to it by the quiet, upright, efficient way in which you are bearing yourself as a soldier."[49]

A month later, Winthrop's growing reputation in the military was rewarded with an appointment to Officer Candidate School (OCS) at Fort Benning, Georgia. Winthrop was training there when on December 7 the Japanese attack on Pearl Harbor occurred, leading to the United States's official entry into World War II.[50] On January 24, 1942, the *New York Times* announced that Winthrop had been promoted to second lieutenant. He was now a commissioned officer.[51] Nelson wrote on behalf of the other brothers: "How proud we all are of your new promotion as second lieutenant and the record you have made at officer's training camp. You certainly have won an awful lot of credit for the family and we are all indebted to you."[52]

Winthrop spent the next eight months at Fort Benning as a machine-gun instructor, his most settled period of time while enrolled in the Army. He even bought an off-base residence at 2413 Willard Street in Columbus, his second independent home after his New York apartment.[53] Winthrop also made a new friend in William "Bill" Sylvan, whom he hired to assist him with his affairs in the Rockefeller family office after the war. Although Winthrop appeared happy enough, an opportunity to move elsewhere made him think more intently about his future career in the Army. Plans were mooted to open an OCS training camp based in Scotland or England to train officers overseas. Winthrop was offered a place as head of the weapons section.[54]

The offer of a new position prompted Winthrop, while on a short leave pass, to discuss his future with Nelson as the two drove up to Pocantico Hills one weekend. Nelson encouraged his younger brother to press for a Washington, DC, desk job like he, John, and Laurance all had. This provoked an outburst of anger from Winthrop. He felt that Nelson's comments indicated the rest of the family thought Winthrop's contribution as a soldier was less important than what his brothers were doing for the war effort. Winthrop was convinced that the exact opposite was true, and he told Nelson so in no uncertain terms. In a rarity, his brother sat stunned and at a loss for words. The exchange only underscored the very different sense of priorities and values that existed between Winthrop and other family members.[55]

Despite the disagreement, Winthrop did have a favor to ask of his brother. When there was a delay in the plan to open an overseas OCS training camp, Winthrop became restless and still wanted to move forward in his Army career. He sought Nelson's assistance in finding a good division to serve in for the rest of the war. The next time Nelson saw Gen. George C. Marshall, chief of staff of the Army under President Roosevelt, he approached him with a request for help. Impressed by Nelson's entreaty that his brother get into rather than out of a combat division, Marshall immediately picked up the telephone and ordered Winthrop's transfer to Fort Jackson, South Carolina, to join the Seventy-Seventh Infantry Division (hereafter Seventy-Seventh). The division was Winthrop's home for the rest of the war.[56]

The Seventy-Seventh became the first of three reactivated reserve divisions during World War II in March 1942.[57] Originally organized at Camp Upton, New York, in September 1917, the division's insignia was a golden Statue of Liberty set against a blue background. In World War I, the Seventy-Seventh "called itself the 'Metropolitan' Division because its personnel came almost entirely from the sidewalks of New York," according to its official history. "It was the aggregation of about 23,000 Manhattan taxi drivers, Bronx tailors, Brooklyn factory hands, Wall Street executives, with a generous sprinkling of professional men from the entire city."[58] Similarly, the distinct New York character of the division remained intact during World War II, when it was known as the "Statue of Liberty Division."[59] Winthrop arrived at Fort Jackson on August 26, 1942.[60] He was assigned to the 305th Infantry Regiment (hereafter 305th) as commander of Company H over 161 men.[61] The company was plunged straight into the deep end with one of the Seventy-Seventh's legendary endurance exercises, a twenty-five-mile march.[62]

Another new assignment meant making yet more new friends. Winthrop met two people at Fort Jackson who he remained in close contact with throughout the war and for the rest of his life. The first was Frank Newell. An insurance broker from Little Rock, Arkansas, Newell was one of Winthrop's students at Fort Benning, although the two men had only known one another in passing there. At Fort Jackson, Newell was initially assigned to Winthrop's company for about a week, long enough for Winthrop to rib him for evermore that he had taught him everything he knew about the Army.[63] Winthrop's mother Abby was particularly fond of Newell. Later in the war, when he was posted overseas, Abby sent him a number of books and presents. When Winthrop took his Army friends back to Pocantico Hills, Newell was always seated next to Abby at the dinner table.[64] Abby described him as "very clever. . . . He had read everything in the world. I liked him because he was interested in Russian literature."[65]

The second was Dr. Graham G. Hawks, who even Newell conceded was Winthrop's closest friend in the Army.[66] A medical doctor and a New Yorker, Hawks was a 1935 graduate of Colgate University and a 1940 graduate of the New York University School of Medicine.[67] His grandfather, Byron Hawks, had worked as a gardener and superintendent on the estate of Senior's brother, William Avery Rockefeller Jr., near Kykuit. When Winthrop and Hawks were assigned to the same company at Fort Jackson, Hawks told Winthrop about their family connections and the two became fast friends.[68] They lodged together throughout the war.[69]

In November, the Seventy-Seventh transitioned from smaller training exercises to coordinating large-scale operations. In the rain and snow, Winthrop took part in long overnight marches and slept on the ground in the field.[70] There was a welcome pause in maneuvers over the Christmas holiday season. Winthrop joined the celebrations by evoking his grandfather's memory and giving each of the 161 men in his company not a dime, as had been Senior's practice, but a silver dollar each, allowing for inflation.[71] The 1922 silver dollars were supplied by his friend Bill Sylvan's father Joe, who co-owned a jewelry store in Columbia, South Carolina, with his brother Gustaf "Gus" Sylvan. Winthrop had a card printed to accompany the coin explaining its family origins and meaning. His charges were not so sentimental. The next morning, one of his men proudly showed him a set of ten silver dollars he had won in a poker game the night before.[72] Each of the soldiers in Winthrop's company also received a scarf, a sweater, and pair of wristlets from Pocantico Hills, all hand-knitted by Abby and her friends to help boost troop morale.[73] In addition, Abby sent each of the men a comb and nail file set.[74]

Early in 1943, a communication from home highlighted the ever-widening gap between Winthrop's life as a soldier and the Rockefeller family and its affairs back in New York. Junior decided that it was no longer practical for Winthrop to retain his formal association with the family office while he was serving in the Army. The relationship was officially terminated, with an intention to revisit the matter again after the war.[75]

Frank Newell believed that the temporary severance had a significant impact on Winthrop's increasing sense of isolation from the rest of the family. This isolation was evident in two different ways. The first was in business matters, where Newell felt that Winthrop was not happy about his lack of integration into the family's financial affairs. The second was in his personal relationship with his parents and his brothers. Winthrop was the last brother to marry and the last to have a child. Newell felt that Rockefeller family bonds noticeably strengthened with the addition of spouses and grandchildren in a way that made Winthrop feel left out. In particular, Newell remembered Abby proudly showing him family photographs of her children and grandchildren. He noted that there was always a blank left in the album next to Winthrop. Newell wondered what kind of psychological effect this must have had on his friend.[76]

January 25 brought the more cheering news that Winthrop had been promoted to the rank of captain. This came just as the Seventy-Seventh was about to begin a large-scale war-games exercise in Many, Louisiana. The place was not far from where Winthrop had earlier spent time in the oil fields. There was a new job to mark the occasion too, as Winthrop became the regimental supply officer, known by the designation of S-4. Newell took credit for getting Winthrop the assignment. While Winthrop was away on a visit to his parents, there were numerous supply problems at Fort Jackson. Newell told the regimental commander that the solution to the problem was his friend Rockefeller, whose family always appeared to keep themselves pretty well supplied. And so, upon his return, Winthrop became S-4.[77] The S-4 was responsible for supplying food, clothing, ammunition, ordnance, and pretty much everything and anything else that the regiment needed in terms of procurement.[78] "I might add," wrote Winthrop to a friend, telling her about the new role, "that the table of organization calls for a Major in this particular job."[79] Winthrop already had his sights set on his next promotion.[80]

On January 27, the Seventy-Seventh arrived in Louisiana.[81] It took three to four days to get all the men relocated there aboard fifty-six trains, and it was Winthrop's first big test as a supply officer.[82] For the next two months, the soldiers entered into maneuvers under the direction of Maj. Gen. Daniel I. Sultan, the commanding general of the Eighth Corps of the Third Army. The training exercise pitched the Seventy-Seventh against the Ninetieth Motorized Division, another reservist division. At the end of March, the troops bivouacked on the outskirts of Camp Polk near Leesville, Louisiana, for some well-earned rest, reequipping, and reorganization, as they awaited news of their next destination.[83]

During the training exercise in March, a photograph of Winthrop appeared in the *New York Times* alongside Pvt. Frank Morris captioned, "Cleaning equipment while in the field with the Third Army in Louisiana."[84] Junior did not at first recognize his own son and he only did a double take after a friend sent him a copy of the newspaper. The photograph, Junior reported, "almost made Mamma and me weep. You look so sad. Apparently you were not conscious of being photographed but were meditating on all the sorrows of the world. You also look very thin."[85] Winthrop telephoned his parents soon after to reassure them that all was well and to let them know that he would soon be moving to a new destination.[86]

In early April, Winthrop and the Seventy-Seventh traded the cold, damp Louisiana swamps for the hot, arid Arizona desert.[87] The soldiers traveled in relative luxury on Pullman cars from Louisiana to Arizona, but what greeted them there was anything but the high life. The desert oasis of Camp Hyder was little more than a railroad water stop halfway between Phoenix and Yuma.[88] Once the soldiers arrived, there was a period of acclimatization, with firing-range exercises and infiltration courses. Then came a steady diet of day and night marches. On May 27, the Seventy-Seventh had a change in leadership when Maj. Gen. Roscoe B. Woodruff left to take command of the Seventh Corps in England. Maj. Gen. Andrew D. Bruce assumed command of the division and remained in charge until the end of the war.[89]

Much of June and July was spent on large-scale desert maneuvers in Arizona and neighboring California under the direction of the Ninth Corps. The Seventy-Seventh, along with the Seventh Armored Division, the Fourth Cavalry, and a number of Tank Destroyer Battalions, took on the Eighth Motorized Division in war games.[90] Around ninety thousand men participated.[91] "This was a maneuver of supply and movement. The emphasis was on ammunition, water, gasoline, and rations," reports the Seventy-Seventh's history. "For the troops it meant only scorching, dusty, endless miles of marching or riding; it meant temperatures of 130 degrees and no shade, and never quite enough water." Tired and weary, the soldiers of the Seventy-Seventh finally returned to Camp Hyder at the end of July. They were disappointed to learn that rather than moving on to a new location as expected, they were going to remain in the desert for another two months.[92] During the maneuvers, the division surgeon estimated that each man lost an average of ten to twenty pounds in weight.[93] Frank Newell believed Winthrop lost closer to twenty to thirty pounds.[94]

Winthrop did everything he could as supply officer to make life as comfortable as possible for his regiment. Providing showers was a particularly notable achievement. At the camp, there was just one shower area shared by seventeen thousand men, and it was located about a mile away from where the 305th was stationed. Winthrop discovered a well close by and procured the machinery from Phoenix to drill down far enough to provide the troops with their own private shower area.[95] "The morale of the outfit registered a ten-point climb," notes the 305th's history. "There was nothing in the world like a cool shower to hit the spot after a day's work in the hot sun. We almost felt like civilians again."[96]

Meeting the men's recreational needs was always an important part of Winthrop's role as S-4. He ran a truck convoy to get soldiers from Camp Hyder to Phoenix and back over the weekends on a 240-mile round trip. The trucks also kept a steady supply of ice cream and beer running into the camp. The Army occasionally granted furloughs to travel home, but since most of the men lived on the East Coast, the train fare was beyond their means. Winthrop dug deep into his own pockets to supply a pool of money for the fares. Yet not even Winthrop's pockets were deep enough to finance all the soldiers. When

Winthrop loaned out the money, he made it clear that it was the responsibility of each person to pay him back so that he, in turn, could loan it out again to others to pay their fares with. The appeal to altruism worked: Winthrop was pleasantly surprised at how many reimbursements he received.[97]

In August, Winthrop took a forty-eight-hour pass to visit his sister Babs in Reno, Nevada. Babs was there to establish residence for a quick divorce from her husband, David Milton, after eighteen years of marriage. She was swamped by journalists on arrival. Winthrop decided to make the thousand-mile round trip from Camp Hyder to Reno to lend his support. "It was a crazy, illogical and wasteful thing to do," writes journalist Alvin Moscow, "and she loved him, her kid brother, for it."[98] Abby O'Neil, Babs's daughter, recalls, "Win and my mother were very close. . . . They used to sit up for hours, talking together." The two "reminisced over old times and the demands and expectations of being who they were—Rockefellers." Babs admitted that she had been relieved at shedding the dreaded family surname when she married. Unlike the grand ambitions demanded of her brothers, all she had ever wanted was a settled home life and her own friends. She had not found that in her marriage to Milton. Her husband was "sweet and kind" but "addicted . . . to gambling in investments." This obsession kept him away from home, sometimes for weeks on end. Junior predictably did not approve of Babs's divorce, which was the first among his children. He liked her husband, and he remained a friend and mentor to Milton throughout the divorce proceedings and afterward.[99]

At the beginning of September, Winthrop gained an appointment to the Command and General Staff School at Fort Leavenworth, Kansas, to receive training for promotion to the rank of major.[100] He drove his Oldsmobile from Camp Hyder to Fort Leavenworth in what was a bumpy ride. Winthrop reported "having four flats (blow outs at that) on the way."[101] To keep him company, he picked up a hitchhiker who rode with him for some seven hundred miles of the journey to Denver.[102] In Denver, Winthrop stayed over and took a three-day rest.[103] He arrived at Fort Leavenworth on the afternoon of Sunday, September 5, for nine weeks of intensive training.[104] Despite the positive reports about Fort Leavenworth to his parents, Winthrop confided to Laurance that he felt the place was overrated.[105] As a practical-minded person, he believed that the training was done too much by the book and was far too abstracted from the day-to-day realities of Army life.[106]

In November, on completion of his training at Fort Leavenworth, Winthrop rejoined the Seventy-Seventh.[107] The division had moved from Camp Hyder a month after Winthrop departed. From there, the soldiers were split up into different locations for training, with the division headquarters

Winthrop in uniform at the Command and General
Staff School, Fort Leavenworth, Kansas, September
1943. *Winthrop Rockefeller Collection, UA Little Rock
Center for Arkansas History and Culture.*

established at Camp Pickett, Virginia. On a three-week rotation, Seventy-
Seventh soldiers moved between the West Virginia Training Area near Elkins
for mountain exercises, Indiantown Gap Military Reservation in Pennsylvania
for marksmanship and combat exercises, and Camp Bradford, Virginia, and the
Solomon Islands, Maryland, for amphibious exercises.[108] Winthrop was first
sent to Elkins for mountain training. At night, he slept in four to five inches of

snow rolled up in just a couple of blankets. He tried to use an Army issue sleeping bag, but it was too small and formfitting for his comfort. Winthrop woke up in the middle of the night with a claustrophobia attack and tore his way out.[109]

After two weeks, Winthrop was sent to Camp Pickett, and then finally to Camp Bradford for amphibious training. Winthrop, Newell, Hawks, and another friend, Chuck Borson, decided to rent a hotel room to share together in Virginia Beach rather than staying in the camp's Quonset huts. Everyone knew that deployment overseas was fast approaching, and they wanted to take as much time as possible to experience home comforts before the inevitable day came. Winthrop had a letter of introduction to a Navy man, Ross McNeil, in Virginia Beach. He and his friends visited McNeil in the evenings, sitting around drinking whiskey and reflecting on their experiences in the military.[110]

At the beginning of 1944, Winthrop received news of his promotion to major.[111] Congratulations poured in once more, and Junior noted one letter in particular from "Mr. Forbes of Forbes Magazine," who wrote, "Back from a brief sojourn in Florida, I am delighted to read of Winthrop's new promotion, to the rank of Major. He proved to the American people that he could 'take it' by starting as a private, asking no favors whatsoever."[112] Soon after, Abby and Junior visited Winthrop, making the journey down from Bassett Hall, their home in Colonial Williamsburg.[113] "It was the first [visit] that they had been able to make since I have been in the service and I hardly need to say that I was thrilled!" Winthrop reported. "I arranged for them to meet quite a cross section of the outfit from the general on down to a group of my sergeants—all in all it was quite a time and I only hope that they enjoyed it half as much as we enjoyed having them."[114]

In March, the news arrived that the Seventy-Seventh was moving to Camp Stoneman in Pittsburgh, California, in preparation for an overseas combat assignment. For a supply officer, mobilizing a regiment for war was a huge and complex task. The small details mattered too: Winthrop sent one of his sergeant mechanics into Richmond to procure the parts for a refrigerator big enough to house three or four crates of beer. It supplied the men with cold beverages throughout the war. In addition, he obtained some cases of whiskey, along with razors, fountain pens, and cigarette lighters.[115]

Shortly after arriving at Camp Stoneman, Winthrop went into San Francisco for a final three-day supply-officer shopping trip.[116] He reported, "[I] worked like a dog during the day, but when night came I had a lot of fun playing with the several friends that I have out there and most of whom I had not seen since I was out there in 1937."[117] Winthrop also took the opportunity to check into the Mark Hopkins Hotel again, where he enjoyed a final few days of luxury. Still thinking of the troops, Winthrop returned to camp with a film projector and an electric generator. The colonel gave him permission to make the purchases if they came out of Winthrop's own pocket. It proved a good investment, both in terms of the soldiers' entertainment and morale, and in providing Winthrop with electric lighting throughout the war rather than having to rely on the standard issue Coleman lantern.[118] Winthrop also procured mosquito netting, chicken wire, watches, pens, pencils, twenty-one radios, and various other odds and ends.[119]

On Saturday morning, March 25, Camp Stoneman was bathed in warm California spring sunshine with a cool breeze wafting in from the Pacific as the soldiers of the Seventy-Seventh prepared to set off on the short trip to San Francisco, their transfer point for the journey overseas. Wearing woolens, leggings, combat packs, and steel helmets, and with their rifles slung over their shoulders, they marched through Pittsburgh to steamboats waiting to carry them down the Sacramento River.[120] At the riverside they passed under signs that read "Through These Portals Pass the Best Damn Soldiers in the World!" and "The Army Ground Forces Trained You, the Services of Supply Equipped You, the Air Force Watches Over You. Now it's up to You." As the steamboats pulled away from the shore, the band struck up "The Sidewalks of New York" and "Over There."[121]

It took three hours to travel the thirty-four miles to San Francisco. The steamboats pulled into the docks, and the soldiers disembarked, listening to the roster call and reclaiming their duffel bags. Nurses from the Red Cross passed out coffee, doughnuts, tomato juice, and cookies.[122] Half an hour later, the men of the 305th boarded the USS *General William M. Black*, a 600-foot, 15,000-ton vessel, that would take them to their overseas destination. Winthrop staggered on board carrying 150 pounds of gear on his back. He could only just about make it through the hatchway without assistance.[123] With everyone and everything squeezed in tight, and all final preparations made, the USS *Black* set sail the next morning at seven, passing under the Golden Gate Bridge and out into the great wide Pacific Ocean.[124]

In his final letter to Abby and Junior before deployment, Winthrop wrote, "Often I have wondered just exactly what would be my emotional reaction to the day that we finally take off for parts unknown—would I be nervous? would I be excited? would I be sad? or just what would be the reaction?" He discovered, "I am glad to say that I experienced none of these feelings. It just turned out to be another day of duty in the Army with the usual number of new and interesting problems. . . . Makes me begin to think that I really must be getting an old soldier after all these years."[125]

Hawaii and the Battle of Guam

WORLD WAR II in the Pacific can be divided into two distinct phases. The first, a defensive phase from 1941 to 1943, began in the years after the bombing of Pearl Harbor when Japanese forces advanced, capturing island after island and placing an unprepared United States and its allies very much on the back foot. The second, an offensive phase from 1944 to 1945, marked a turning point in the war when US forces led an island-hopping advance to push the Japanese forces into retreat to mainland Japan.[1]

By the time the Seventy-Seventh set sail from San Francisco, the second, offensive phase of the war was already well underway. Two thrusts forward in the early months of 1944 turned the tide. In the Admiralty Islands, two hundred miles to the north of New Guinea, US forces under Gen. Douglas MacArthur, the supreme commander of the South West Pacific Area, successfully invaded Los Negros Island and Manus Island, gaining strategic airfields and a significant harbor. The maneuver brought US forces to within seven hundred miles of the main Japanese naval base on Truk Island. Meanwhile, in the Marshall Islands, located between Hawaii and the Philippines in the central Pacific Ocean, US forces under Adm. Chester W. Nimitz, commander in chief of the Pacific Ocean Areas, captured the island atolls of Kwajalein and Eniwetok. This brought the Pacific Fleet to within seven hundred miles of Truk and to within one thousand miles of the Mariana Islands. The Marianas contained airfields close enough to launch strikes against the Japanese mainland.[2] It was in preparation for the Mariana Islands campaign that Winthrop and the Seventy-Seventh were deployed overseas.[3]

For security reasons, the USS *Black*'s final destination of Honolulu, Hawaii, was only announced to the soldiers after they were at sea for several days.[4] The voyage took a week in total. Winthrop remembered a lot of seasickness among the troops at first, but he put this down to plain nerves. With around fifteen hundred men traveling in cramped conditions, it was tough going. Poor ventilation and basic sanitary conditions only added to the stench.[5] At 8:00 a.m.

on April 1, 1944, Hawaii came into sight and preparations for unloading got underway. The USS *Black* sailed past the famous landmarks of the Diamond Head Crater, Waikiki Beach, and the Royal Hawaiian Hotel before pulling into Honolulu's busy harbor and docking at the base of the Aloha Tower. The band struck up to the tune of "Aloha Oe" as the soldiers disembarked. Members of the advance detachment, including Maj. Gen. Andrew Bruce, were there to greet them.[6]

Not long after arrival, Winthrop bumped into family friend Frank C. Atherton, a business executive and philanthropist based in Hawaii. The two spent several hours chatting. A recurring motif in Winthrop's overseas wartime service was the astonishing number of friends and acquaintances he crossed paths with from back home. These provided him with welcome reminders of civilian life and, on many occasions, valuable contacts. As Abby noted, "It must make an awful lot of difference to know people in the communities in which you are stationed."[7] Atherton told his nephew Herbert M. Richards, who was about to travel from Honolulu to San Francisco, to let Winthrop's parents know that their son had arrived safely. When he arrived in the United States, Richards's letter brought the first news to the Rockefeller family that Winthrop was now based in Hawaii.[8] Soon after receiving Richards's letter, Abby received another from Dr. Graham G. Hawks, assuring her that Winthrop was "enjoying good health and is kept busy enough to stay out of trouble." Abby and Hawks's wife, Margery, had already begun meeting at Kykuit to compare notes on the letters that they each received from the front lines and to provide mutual support for one another. These meetings continued throughout the course of the war.[9] When Winthrop wrote his parents, he told them about his arrival in Hawaii, and he assured them that all was well "except for mosquitoes."[10]

The Seventy-Seventh's various components were sent from Honolulu to different encampments on the island of Oahu, with the 305th accompanying the Seventh Antiaircraft Artillery Battalion to Camp Pali in the eastern foothills of the Koʻolau Range. The eight-mile ride from Honolulu to Camp Pali meant traversing the Pali Pass (Nuʻuanu Pali), a windward section of the range.[11] "Every time I cross it, I must marvel at the beauty of what one sees below," wrote Winthrop. "In the near view is a charming valley or plane [*sic*] which is bounded by a very irregular coast line, which forms itself into many intimate coves and bays. Outside the shore line are the famous breakers of the island accentuating the vivid colors of the ocean."[12]

Camp Pali's natural beauty needed a little more working on.[13] The first task was to dig drainage ditches. Unusually heavy rainfall meant the camp was covered with sticky, red mud. The rain, accompanied by tropical humid heat, was a near-constant feature of weather conditions during the 305th's time in the Pacific. Next came the task of clearing the land using "machetes, trench knives, bayonets, and every other sharp instrument upon which we could get our hands to remove the tall grass and bush around our area."[14] Winthrop persuaded the bulldozer drivers to create a ballpark. This was named Woodward Field in memory of J. Henry Woodward, a fellow officer and friend of Winthrop's who had been killed in a jeep accident while the Seventy-Seventh was moving to Indiantown Gap. With the camp established, combat training began at the Unit Jungle Training Center. This involved navigating jungle terrain while under fire, crossing streams on rope bridges, learning how to survive on fruits and other native edibles, and training in hand-to-hand combat.[15]

Winthrop shared his tent with Hawks and Al Rennick. Rennick was from Washington, Missouri, and was the camp's resident joker. Another person Winthrop became close friends with at Camp Pali was Lt. Col. James "Jim" Landrum from Mississippi, a West Point graduate and the commander of the 305th's First Battalion. Winthrop already knew Landrum from their training together at Fort Leavenworth.[16] Making new friends helped ease somewhat the wrench of Winthrop's enforced separation from Frank Newell. Upon arrival in Hawaii, a Twenty-Fourth Corps was created out of the Seventy-Seventh. Col. Cecil W. Nist, executive officer of the 305th, was appointed as the G-2 intelligence officer in the corps. Nist personally requested Newell as his assistant. The request crossed the desk of Gen. Crump Garby, the Twenty-Fourth Corps chief of staff. Garby was impressed with Newell's credentials and by the fact that he was a fellow Arkansawyer. Garby hailed from Harrison in the northern part of the state. Denying Nist's request, Garby appointed Newell as his own assistant.[17] Although Winthrop still found time to hook up with Newell on Oahu occasionally, the Twenty-Fourth Corps ultimately stayed there longer than the Seventy-Seventh before heading out to war.[18]

The mood was palpably beginning to change among the soldiers who knew that Hawaii was their last stopping point before actually entering into combat. Anxiety about the imminent introduction to the front lines always hung over the camp. Winthrop definitely detected the increased sense of urgency among the officers. To help prepare the men, the Army sent experienced combat veterans who were being transferred from the front lines to talk about their experiences. Winthrop was struck by the matter-of-fact way they spoke, something that he would better understand and similarly adopt as the war progressed. The gist of their message was that you either caught a bullet or you didn't, and that if you didn't then it was no worse than regular training practice. Winthrop found the frank and candid sessions oddly comforting and they helped him get to grips with the grim realities that lay ahead.[19]

Hawaii offered a last opportunity for some much-needed recreation that Winthrop and the other men keenly exploited. Winthrop traveled to Honolulu every weekend. Often on these trips he met up with Bill Turner, the head of Standard Oil of Hawaii. Turner and his wife invited Winthrop to their parties, and they allowed him to stay over at their house on Saturday evenings when he was on leave from camp.[20] Sometimes he took Newell along with him and they hit the beach and went swimming.[21] On May 1, Winthrop traveled to Honolulu on a twenty-four-hour pass to celebrate his thirty-second birthday with Newell, Hawks, Landrum, and the Turners. Newell was accompanied by a Red Cross nurse that he knew from Little Rock. She brought a number of friends based on the island along with her. They all went out to a local night spot for dinner and dancing.[22] Unfortunately, the party did not last very long. Alcohol was only served until 7:00 p.m. on the island, and a curfew followed at 10:00 p.m.[23] As in other places in the Pacific, and indeed other places around the world, the Rockefeller name opened doors in Hawaii. One evening, Winthrop and his commanding officer were invited to dinner with the Castle family, one of the most preeminent families on the island whose roots stretched back to the founding of the kingdom.[24]

Back in the United States, on May 31 Junior gave a nationwide radio address in support of the United Negro College Fund. Abby brought this to Winthrop's attention since, "I know that both you and David have the deepest sympathy with the Negroes and understanding of their problems." Winthrop congratulated his father on the speech, telling him, "I have frequently said in the past, and I repeat now, that the relationship of White and Negro races will be one of the greatest post war problems that will have to be faced by the leaders of this country."[25] Abby replied, "I am so glad you have written so sympathetically and interestingly of Papa's work in helping the Negro colleges and universities. He was enormously pleased to hear about this and I am sure will write you about it. He has had one or two disagreeable letters asking if he is trying to be the second 'Eleanor.' "[26] This was in reference to First Lady Eleanor Roosevelt, who had become one of the leading white public figures in the United States advocating for civil rights on the home front.[27]

To keep himself occupied, a pet project of Winthrop's at Camp Pali was the construction of an officers' club. This came in handy, since there was little else by way of entertainment in the evenings at the camp. Winthrop enlisted some of the engineers to assist him in exchange for an extra beer or two at the end of the day. Everything for the construction of the club, inside and out, had to be plundered or improvised since there were precious few spare materials lying around.[28] At the grand opening on June 3, Winthrop's date was the secretary of Harold Kainalu Long Castle.[29]

On June 13, as news of impending orders to relocate began to circulate around the camp—the Mariana Islands campaign began just two days later on June 15 with the invasion of Saipan—Winthrop brought all of his friends on the island together for one last time at the club. "One of the mess sergeants assures me that he will prepare a splendid dinner, our band leader has promised me some dance music," Winthrop wrote a friend, "and I have decided to break out a little of my hoarded scotch so I feel that we have most of the ingredients for fun, no?"[30] By all accounts the event went well, with Junior noting knowingly, "You are certainly in your element getting up to an affair of this kind."[31] Winthrop continued to show a fond interest in the officers' club. He took charge of the gardening and landscaping right up until his departure from the island.[32] Winthrop was heartbroken to leave it behind: "I only hope that the next group coming in will take enough interest in it to keep the lawn trimmed and I believe that in several months time they will have a lovely place."[33]

The final call to arms arrived in late June. At Fort Leavenworth, Winthrop was taught that it took ninety days to load and mobilize a division for war. In Hawaii, the Seventy-Seventh had five days, working around the clock.[34] On July 1, the 305th was aboard one of five ships that set sail from Honolulu zigzagging west at seventeen knots to avoid enemy torpedoes. "There was a very nasty war on," reports the Seventy-Seventh's history, "and they were sailing right into the midst of it."[35] Rumor had it that the soldiers were heading to the Mariana Islands, but where exactly remained a mystery. The military plan was to take the three principal islands of Saipan, Tinian, and Guam in quick succession. The Second Marine Division and the Fourth Marine Division were assigned to Saipan and Tinian, while the Third Marine Division was assigned to Guam. The Army's Twenty-Seventh Division was aboard ships as a floating reserve, and the Seventy-Seventh formed the land-based reserve force in Hawaii.[36] The Saipan campaign began on June 15 and things did not go as planned. The US forces underestimated the number of Japanese troops on the island and encountered far greater resistance and more casualties than anticipated. The Guam campaign, initially slated to begin on June 18, was postponed indefinitely. The Twenty-Seventh Division was sent to Saipan to provide reinforcements. The fighting in Saipan continued as the Seventy-Seventh departed Hawaii.[37]

After setting sail, Winthrop whiled away the time on his typewriter, catching up with correspondence.[38] He found the voyages between destinations in the Pacific to be generally pleasant and relaxing times. "All continues well!" Winthrop wrote his parents. "The only thing that I am afraid of now is that I will be spoiled by this life at sea. Each morning I get up for an eight o'clock breakfast after which I take care of the daily chores. Lunch is a little early, but that gives us that much more of an afternoon for reading or letter writing until my daily exercise hour. At about four o'clock Jim Landrum and I go up on deck and throw medicine ball and run in place to get a good work out, shower and then it is just about dinner time." The evenings were "not so exciting, but pleasant." Winthrop's ritual was to "watch the sun set and enjoy the lovely soft evening air and then go below for several hours of pleasant conversation or more reading and letter writing." He concluded, "I know that to read this schedule does not sound particularly enticing, but the sheer luxury of the contrast to our normal life is so wonderful that I just purr with contentment. Of course, I'll have to admit that one does not have any great privacy on this kind of a cruise, but that is incidental in the eyes of a man with over three and a half years' service."[39]

The first port of call for the Seventy-Seventh was Eniwetok, an island atoll that provided a good harbor and a useful refueling point. There, the Seventy-Seventh learned that Saipan had finally been declared secure on July 9 and that they would now be assisting in the invasion of Guam.[40] Guam had been a Spanish colonial possession for four centuries until it became a territory of the United States under the terms of the Treaty of Paris in 1898 following the Spanish-American War. The island was an important strategic base for the United States in the Pacific as home to a Navy Yard and Marine Corps barracks.[41] Just three days after the attack on Pearl Harbor, on December 10, 1941, a Japanese force that outnumbered the Americans stationed there by ten to one quickly overran and captured the island. Guam was the first Pacific territory belonging to the United States captured by the Japanese, and it was also destined to be the first one recovered. The largest island in the Marianas, Guam was thirty-four miles long from its northernmost to its southernmost tip and varied from five to nine miles wide east to west. One hundred miles south of Saipan, Guam had a more equatorial climate that was hot and humid. A predominantly jungle terrain of dense forests and thick underbrush covered the island. In the wet season—which began in July—it rained incessantly. The Orote Peninsula, jutting out several miles from Guam's southwestern coast, contained an airfield that was the main target for the US forces.[42]

The Army's experience in Saipan informed military strategy in Guam. Taking more precautions this time, the landings there were preceded by the longest bombardment of the Pacific War. This was intended to thoroughly weaken the island's defenses before an invasion was launched. Warships and aircraft pounded the island for almost two weeks. The tactic was effective but time-consuming, and the speed with which the war began to unfold afterward meant there was no repeat of this in future campaigns. The Third Marine Division and the First Marine Provisional Brigade began landings on July 2. Casualties were significantly smaller than in Saipan because of the advance bombing campaign.[43]

The Seventy-Seventh left Eniwetok on July 17 and arrived in Guam early on July 21, almost three weeks after the first Marine landings. Initially, the Marines unflatteringly referred to the volunteers and drafted men of the 305th as "the old bastards" because of their higher-than-average age. By the end of the campaign, the Marines dubbed them the "305th Marines."[44] The Seventy-Seventh's ships sat three miles offshore upon arrival, with soldiers witnessing the explosions and gunfire on the island. Winthrop went back to his typewriting while keeping abreast of the latest developments. It was not until later that night at 10:00 p.m. that the order to land south of the Orote Peninsula came.[45]

The Seventy-Seventh soldiers advanced from the ship at midnight aboard landing craft but soon hit a coral reef around one thousand yards from the beach. They jumped overboard and made the rest of the journey on foot, wading through the sea. Bright phosphorous flares illuminated the night sky every two to three minutes. Both the US and Japanese forces used them to detect each other's movements. Winthrop did not feel in any immediate danger from enemy fire since he knew he was beyond machine gun range. Far more precarious was wading through the sea on the coral reef. The earlier shelling of the island meant that the reef was pockmarked with deep craters from explosions. Loaded down with all of his gear and waist deep in the water, Winthrop made his way toward the shore, followed closely by his sergeant major. Although Winthrop tried to move ahead in a straight line, he drifted to the right. Suddenly, behind him, he heard a cry: "Help, help, help, I'm drowning." The sergeant major disappeared underwater into a bomb crater. Winthrop went back and fished him out.[46]

The sergeant major lost all of his gear. Winthrop tried to calm him down while struggling to keep his own nerve. The two men attempted to wade toward the shore again. Soon after, the sergeant major fell into another bomb crater, and once more became stranded beneath the waves. Winthrop went back to pull him out. This time, Winthrop's entire uniform and equipment were soaking wet, and they became a hindering dead weight. He was pulled into the forty-to-fifty-foot round crater too. Winthrop began to panic. His helmet fell forward on his face, and he started to inhale sea water. He thought he was about to drown. Winthrop then steadied his nerves, came to his senses, and inflated his life belt, which provided enough buoyancy to lift the two men back to the surface. They staggered onto the coral reef and made it ashore.[47] Reports about Winthrop saving the sergeant major's life appeared in the United States through headlines in the *New York Times* and the *Tarrytown Daily News*.[48]

Winthrop and the sergeant major drifted so much in the sea that they arrived on shore at the edge of the beach perimeter in what was virtually no-man's-land. The beach was strewn with bodies. It appeared that half of them were dead and the other half sleeping. The only way to tell the difference, Winthrop macabrely noted, was that the alive ones yelled when they were stepped on. The two men found the beach master, who advised them that they should stay put rather than follow orders to head inland. There was heavy sniper fire ahead. Winthrop phoned Marine headquarters and was instructed to stay on the beach. He found a foxhole—a small pit used by soldiers for cover—and occupied it along with the sergeant major.[49] "There was nothing left to do but have one good drink, quickly followed by several others," Winthrop wrote later.[50]

Together with his ordeal in getting ashore, the drink quickly put the sergeant major to sleep. Winthrop was still flooded with adrenaline and stayed awake the rest of the night. He was left wondering where the rest of the twenty or so other soldiers in their landing craft were. The 305th's commanding officer, Col. Vincent J. Tanzola, who was aboard with them, could not swim. He was helped ashore by Capt. Eugene H. Rennick on a rubber raft they found floating at sea. The two made it to the beach an hour after Winthrop and the sergeant major. Communications officer Capt. Carmedy found his way to Winthrop's foxhole and spent the night there. Come daylight, the men were able to regroup on the beach and received orders to move forward. The 305th inched up the island alongside the Marines for the next two to three days.[51]

It took twenty days in total between the 305th landing in Guam on July 21 and the island being declared secure on August 10. During that time there was fierce fighting, although Winthrop was largely removed from it.[52] In Winthrop's recollection of events, "once we got the troops ashore there was no organized resistance."[53] Meanwhile, the Tinian campaign, which began on July 24, was completed within a week. The US forces now held control of all the Mariana Islands.[54]

The exchange of letters between Winthrop and his parents reveals that the weather in Guam was as much an obstacle as the Japanese forces: "Writing from my fox-hole on the island of Guam . . . everything has gone beautifully. . . . Rainy season makes supply job difficult. . . . I find Guam a lovely spot. . . .

Once again it is a combination of mountains, a beautiful ocean and of course rich tropical growth."[55] To fortify himself, Winthrop took the B-1 vitamins he had brought with him. "I can't say enough for them!" he exclaimed. "It was my experience that if I took them three times a day plus a salt tablet with each I could get along splendidly regardless of how much or how little bulk I was able to get to ward off the actual pangs of hunger."[56]

Junior responded, "Your letter brings to us another vivid picture of conditions on your island. We can fairly see the roads so deep with mud. . . . How wise you have been to take vitamins during your most strenuous days and how fortunate it is that they carried you through so well!"[57] Abby wrote with words of comfort and inspiration, telling Winthrop, "One of my favorite quotations from the Bible . . . [is] 'What doth the Lord require of thee, but to do justly, to love kindness and to walk humbly in the sight of the Lord.' If any of us can accomplish this, we are certainly prepared to meet life with faith and courage."[58] Winthrop later had this scripture from Micah 6:8 inscribed on a plaque and installed outside his home on Petit Jean Mountain in Arkansas.

As hostilities concluded, the 305th was sent to a hillside rest area to await their next assignment. Not knowing exactly how long this would take, Winthrop sought to make his immediate surroundings as comfortable as possible. He observed that the indigenous native islanders, the Chamorro, built their homes out of palm logs and branches. Winthrop liked the look of them. Fortunately, Winthrop knew Maj. Gen. Henry L. Larsen, the commanding general on the island. Larsen was an old friend of Winthrop's uncle, Ezra Parmalee Prentice, who was married to Junior's sister Alta. Winthrop persuaded Larsen to let him hire five Chamorros to build a house. He reasoned that this would provide employment and support the local economy.[59]

Within a week, Winthrop and Hawks moved out of their tent and into their new home. "To think of you now as living in your own villa on this far-away island amid surroundings so utterly foreign is also truly a strain on the imagination," wrote Junior. "How like you to dig in, so to speak, in so comfortable and sensible a way."[60] Winthrop's new ten-by-fourteen-foot abode offered two separate sleeping areas in the back and two office areas in the front. He even found some Army surplus mosquito netting to put in the windows. The rats proved more troublesome. Winthrop and Hawks took turns emptying the traps, which caught three or four of the creatures each night.[61] The structure was conveniently located near the electric generator, which meant that it was supplied with abundant lighting.[62]

The rest of the company appreciated the items that Winthrop had procured in San Francisco too. "We owe a vote of thanks to Major Rockefeller for his foresight and generosity in bringing to this island, for our use, an electric generator and a motion-picture projector," reads one history of the 305th. "The Navy and Marines loaned us films. The movies we saw were not the latest issue by far but they were the greatest morale booster we had at this time."[63] Around six weeks later, orders came to up sticks and move. Winthrop was devastated to leave his new home behind. The 305th decamped and moved to a new base on the Orote Peninsula.[64]

Before leaving, Winthrop sent Abby and Junior photographs of himself proudly standing in front of his palm-tree hut. The images revealed that he was now growing a beard to accompany his moustache, something that provoked much comment. "They amuse me enormously because all of our married life your father seems to have had a hankering to revert to a beard much to my grief, because I never felt any enthusiasm about being kissed by a beard or even a moustache," Abby confided. "One of the snapshots really is very good of you, I think. You look very American and look yourself but in the others you look to me very French and not at all like yourself. All the photographs suggest to me that you are very much thinner and I think they show that you have experienced a great deal."[65]

An uncommonly jocular Junior giggled, "Is your beard the type that is common in Guam or is it an invention of your own? It looks like such a beard as the French students used to wear. As it grows, are you going to turn it into fantastic shapes like the boxwood pieces in the sunken gardens at Pocantico or is that a matter you haven't yet decided?" More earnestly, he added, "We are delighted to have the pictures, beard or no beard, and to see the same twinkle in your eye that is so typical and that indicates that nothing in the hard life you are leading has gotten you down or can get you down."[66]

Winthrop's new campground on the Orote Peninsula was not quite so convivial. The soldiers hacked out a clearing in the jungle and discovered that the land underneath it was mainly exposed coral. This was far from ideal for pitching a tent on. Winthrop ventured into nearby Sumay, a small town that was little more than a collection of buildings, or rather it had been, since most of it was flattened in the conflict. The only structure left standing was the remains of an old church located under a coral cliff. Winthrop decided to pitch his tent there.[67] He invited Hawks over to bunk with him again, but when he arrived, Hawks discovered a large, unexploded bombshell partially blocking the tent entrance. He refused to occupy the tent until Winthrop called in the bomb disposal unit to take it away.[68]

The unexploded bomb was not the only danger on the new site. Since the coral cliff provided good material for rebuilding roads, there was constant drilling

Winthrop stands outside his Chamorro-built palm
log and branch residence in Guam, October 1944.
*Winthrop Rockefeller Collection, UA Little Rock Center
for Arkansas History and Culture.*

Winthrop with his "French student" beard in Guam, October 1944. *Winthrop Rockefeller Collection, UA Little Rock Center for Arkansas History and Culture.*

nearby. Later a steam shovel was placed right next to the tent. Lacking in choices for other desirable spots, the two men decided to stick it out despite the din. The Army then began to use dynamite to dislodge the coral. Usually, a five-minute warning was given before the blasting commenced. One day, after a short one-minute warning, the dynamite exploded with Winthrop still in the tent taking a telephone call. All of a sudden, a huge chunk of coral ripped through the tent roof and thudded into the ground, just missing Winthrop's head along the way. Yet another test for the new dwelling came when a typhoon swept through the island one night. As the gusts were about to blow the entire tent away, Winthrop leapt out of bed from underneath his mosquito net and, stark naked—it was too warm for pajamas in the Pacific—held the tent down by hand for thirty to forty minutes while Hawks pretended to sleep.[69]

At the new encampment, the troops started getting equipment and supplies ready for their next move. Aside from that, it was a simply a matter of grabbing some much-needed rest and relaxation. Winthrop's movie projector continued to come in handy in the evenings, and every now and then the USO sponsored some live entertainment to break up the monotony. The most memorable of these occasions was the arrival of Betty Hutton.[70] Hutton was an actress, comedian, dancer, and signer, and at the time one of Hollywood's rising young female stars. In 1942, she featured alongside Paramount Studios' number-one female star, Dorothy Lamour, and William Holden, in the film *The Fleet's In*. In 1943, she featured alongside Victor Moore in the film musical *Star Spangled Rhythm* and costarred with Bob Hope in *Let's Face It*. Her big break came early in 1944 with the release of *The Miracle of Morgan's Creek*, when she costarred with Eddie Bracken in Paramount's highest-grossing film that year. She later starred as Annie Oakley alongside Howard Keel in what became her best-known role on the silver screen in the 1950 film *Annie Get Your Gun*.[71]

Hutton played two shows in Guam, one for the Marines, based on the east side of the island, and one for the Seventy-Seventh, based on the west side of the island. Winthrop managed to see both shows thanks to his extensive network of connections. This time it was courtesy of Robert "Bob" Kriendler, whose family owned the 21 Club, one of the Manhattan hotspots that Winthrop frequented. Kriendler was in the Third Marines, and he invited Winthrop and his friends over to the much better-equipped Marine base, which had, Winthrop reported, "one of the most attractive officer's clubs I've ever seen in my life."[72] The Marines put on quite a spread for Hutton and her entourage. Another New Yorker, George Percy, the senior partner in one of the city's leading brokerage banking firms, organized a fishing party that caught fresh lobster. Everything was perfect except that now, Winthrop, having already made Hutton's acquaintance, was the person in charge of entertaining her the night afterward in the Seventy-Seventh's far less salubrious surroundings.[73]

Hutton's stage at the Seventy-Seventh's camp was a boxing ring, and there was no place for a dressing room and no planned after-show hospitality. Winthrop immediately busied himself putting up a hospital tent to accommodate Hutton, gathering some chairs together, and generally tidying up the mess.[74] A true professional, Hutton did not seem to mind the conditions, and the show went on.[75] "The show itself was nothing very formidable," reported an underwhelmed Winthrop, "but it did offer a pleasant interlude."[76] Abby commented, "Although I do not know Betty Hutton or who she is, I am sure she is a most charming and attractive person." Junior expressed pleasure that his work with the USO at home was directly benefiting his son and the troops overseas.[77]

Shortly after the Betty Hutton concert, the Seventy-Seventh received new orders. The initial plan was for the division to join the Twenty-Fourth Corps in an assault on the island of Yap and the island atoll of Ulithi in the western Caroline Islands. When this failed to materialize, the Twenty-Fourth Corps was assigned to an assault on the Philippine island of Leyte, along with the Seventh and Ninety-Sixth Divisions. The Seventy-Seventh was held in reserve.[78] An armada of over seven hundred US ships arrived in Leyte Gulf on October 19 and 20 to clear mines and to install navigation lights to guide the invasion forces. When Gen. MacArthur landed ashore on October 20, it was a moment of personal triumph for him. MacArthur was forced to flee the Philippines in ignominy in 1942 as Japanese forces closed in and took the island country. Standing on the beach in Leyte, MacArthur declared, "People of the Philippines, I have returned. . . . Rally to me."[79] The Japanese fleet arrived four days later. Between October 24 and 26, the US and Japanese fleets fought the largest naval battle of World War II, and by some estimates the largest naval battle ever. The US fleet prevailed.[80]

On October 29, confident of a swift victory, Gen. MacArthur indicated that the Seventy-Seventh would not be needed.[81] The division was ordered to Nouméa, the capital city of New Caledonia, for rest and relaxation. New Caledonia was a French territory in the Coral Sea between Australia and Fiji, about 2,700 miles south of Guam. "The island was wild with French women, whiskey . . . all matter of delights" was the word among the troops, reported Winthrop. "And that did a great deal for the morale and anticipation."[82] There was first the task of loading everything back onto the ships. As with the previous exercise, although the Army textbooks said the process should take ninety days, it was once again completed in five days at full tilt.[83]

Winthrop was in such a hurry that he almost left Guam without his jeep. Through Bob Kriendler, Winthrop met Col. Pete Barron, the adjutant general for the island command. Among his duties, Barron was in charge of the island command officers' club, which ranked up there in quality with the Marines' club. The command club contained the messing facilities for all of the island command and all of the Red Cross nurses. It was an invitation-only place, and Winthrop visited half a dozen times or so thanks to Barron's friendship. On one of those visits, Winthrop met Paul Smith, a Marine and editor of the *San Francisco Chronicle*, and the two became friends.[84]

A night or two before the Seventy-Seventh was due to set off from Guam, Winthrop traveled to the club with his trusted jeep driver Jim Rogers to say goodbye to Smith and some other friends. Upon arrival, Winthrop told Rogers to go grab dinner and catch a movie, and they could rendezvous for the return journey later. When Rogers arrived at Barron's tent at 9:30 p.m., he informed Winthrop that their jeep had disappeared. Barron told Winthrop to call the general, who in turn told Winthrop that this was a common occurrence. Soldiers walked up to the club to watch a movie. It was a two-mile trek back to camp, so they grabbed any spare jeep they could find and then abandoned it. In the morning, the vehicles were rounded up and returned to their rightful owners. Barron loaned Winthrop his jeep to get back that night. Thankfully, Winthrop's own vehicle was recovered before his ship departed.[85]

The Seventy-Seventh set sail aboard the USS *Leonard Wood* for New Caledonia on November 3.[86] Winthrop got out his typewriter and started to catch up on letters. On November 10, the Seventy-Seventh received new orders. Gen. MacArthur decided that the division would be needed in Leyte after all. Taking the island had proved much more difficult than expected.[87] The USS *Wood* immediately changed course.[88] Along the way to Leyte, on November 17, the Seventy-Seventh stopped off on the small island of Manus, a naval resupply base in the South Pacific just north of Papua New Guinea in the Admiralty Islands.[89] Hawks joked that Winthrop could not possibly find anyone he knew in such a small and remote place. Within an hour, Winthrop ran into a former classmate from Loomis and Yale. There was an officers' club in Manus that put all those Winthrop had previously encountered to shame. The bar was approximately 100 to 150 feet long. Beer was served all day, and from 6:00 to 10:00 p.m. there was whiskey too. With such plentiful amounts of alcohol available—a relative rarity in the armed forces—few demonstrated any restraint. Closing time at 10:00 p.m. was quite a sight. Many of the officers made it back onto ships, although not necessarily the same ships that they had arrived on. The coxswains crisscrossed the harbor all night trying to match up the right officers with the right vessels.[90]

On November 19, the 305th set sail for Leyte. Winthrop went back to letter writing. Straight after breakfast every morning, he sat down at his typewriter and started pounding away at the keys. The incessant clattering noise drove Hawks to distraction. He reported that Winthrop wrote eighty-one letters on the circuitous voyage from Guam to Leyte.[91] Approaching almost three weeks on the waves, Winthrop complained, "By this time I am beginning to feel like the ancient mariner, we have been at sea so long."[92]

The journey from Manus to the Philippines took only four days. On Thanksgiving Day, November 23, 1944, the Seventy-Seventh landed at Tarragona Beach on the east coast of Leyte.[93] The 305th began establishing a beachhead.[94] "We still are on the sea shore and I have never seen such a bathing beach in my life unless it is around Daytona Florida," Winthrop wrote to a friend soon after. "I have been taking full advantage of it and just loving it."[95] The respite was all too brief. Soon, Winthrop and the Seventy-Seventh would be fully immersed in combat duty in their second campaign of the Pacific War.

Winthrop in Leyte, the Philippines, ca. November
1944–March 1945. *Winthrop Rockefeller Collection,
UA Little Rock Center for Arkansas History and Culture.*

The Battles of Leyte and Okinawa

THERE WERE CONSTANT REMINDERS that despite the natural beauty of his surroundings at Tarragona Beach, Winthrop was in a war zone. Not long after arrival, he witnessed an aerial dogfight between a Japanese Mitsubishi A6M Zero and three American P-38 Lightnings that took place offshore. With the Lightnings in pursuit, the Zero flew toward one of the command ships, which were easy to pick out since they were more heavily equipped with radio and radar equipment. The Zero suddenly plunged toward the ship in a kamikaze attack, a suicide mission in which the pilot used the plane as a weapon to plow into the target. The maneuver was increasingly used during the final years of the war in the Pacific, a reflection of Japan's growing desperation and fear of defeat. The Lightnings did just enough to deviate the Zero's course. It crashed into the water only thirty feet away from the command ship.[1]

Air raids on the beach were a common occurrence. Winthrop was sharing his tent with Hawks and Al Rennick, and each time the siren went off, his bunkmates dived into a nearby foxhole. Winthrop grew tired of all the drills and complacently began to ignore them. But when a hundred-pound bomb exploded close to his tent one night, it was enough to wake him up. He hurriedly jumped out of bed and performed a naked streak across the sand before diving into the foxhole with his two friends. Another night during the campaign, three Japanese planes came in so low and in such a casual manner that everyone mistook them for US aircraft. They landed on the beach carrying a group of Japanese intelligence officers. Without any resistance, the officers ran into the surrounding jungle for cover. Belatedly realizing what was happening, patrols were mobilized to pursue them. Soldiers eventually found them sleeping in an abandoned shack.[2]

While on the beachhead at Tarragona, a unit of Black soldiers operating amphibious supply vehicles was attached to the 305th.[3] The US military was under a strict segregation policy during World War II with separate white and Black units.[4] A few days later, two white officers from Georgia complained to

Winthrop that the new unit's Black sergeant was not following orders quickly enough for their liking. Winthrop called the sergeant in for an explanation. The sergeant admitted that he had been conducting an important task and that he had therefore delayed obeying an order. Winthrop told him that it was essential to follow orders immediately. Yet, shouldering some of the blame himself, Winthrop told the sergeant in front of the white officers that he was partly at fault for not making this clear at the outset. At that, Winthrop let the matter rest. The two white officers left angry since the Black sergeant had not been disciplined for his disobedience. Winthrop feared repercussions over the incident, although none came: "They knew that I was going to back up the new unit just as if it had been a white unit or any other unit. And from that time on, we never had one unpleasant word or one unpleasant experience."[5]

Orders soon arrived for the Seventy-Seventh to make an assault landing near the city of Ormoc, located on Leyte's northwest coast. The date was set for December 7, the third anniversary of Pearl Harbor. Leyte was in the inner ring of the large islands at the center of the Philippines. Measuring 110 miles from its northern to its southern tip, it has been compared in shape to a human torso with short legs, a thin waist, a wide chest, and with a wing off the right western shoulder. Below the waist, the southern part of the island was mountainous and remote. This area was unoccupied. Most of the combat occurred in the northern portion of land above it. The US forces entered Leyte on the northeast coast and spread out across the low, flat land to the north and west. To the southwest was a mountain chain that rose abruptly from the plain to roughly 3,000 to 4,000 feet. Over the mountains lay a strategic valley corridor between Ormoc Bay, south of the island's western wing, and Carigara Bay to the north. The wing itself was covered in a mixture of hills, dense forests, rocky ridges, and cultivated land.[6] The near-constant torrential rain hampered attempts by US forces to take the island, and the campaign there proved more protracted than first anticipated. This led to the call-up of the Seventy-Seventh reserve.[7]

Before the assault landing, Winthrop and Jim Landrum went to visit their old friend Frank Newell. Newell had been in the Philippines with the Twenty-Fourth Corps for some time already, and he had few cheery words for his comrades. He told them that the Ormoc landings were nothing short of a suicide mission.[8] But things did not turn out as bleakly as Newell forecast. On December 7, the 305th sailed south from Tarragona Beach, through the Surigao Strait, and north to a beach four miles southeast of Ormoc in the Ipil region. They landed virtually unopposed. The regiment set off on foot toward Ormoc.[9] As usual, Winthrop reported, "the rain has been dreadful," and he developed a cold and fever on the very first day of the campaign.[10]

The rain continued the following day. That night, the 305th decided to take shelter at an abandoned sugar refinery mill in a small town nearby.[11] Winthrop cautioned against sheltering in the building itself since it was too much of an obvious target. Instead, the men dug foxholes in the yard outside. Winthrop put up a shelter over his foxhole in a vain attempt to stay dry. The heavens opened, and the rain began to pour down even harder. The deluge was so intense that the water table began to rise, and the foxhole flooded twelve to sixteen inches deep. Winthrop tried bailing the water out with his helmet, but it made little difference. In the end, he simply gave up, laid back, and slept in the puddle, making sure to keep his head well above the tidemark. Despite the conditions, Winthrop's cold soon disappeared. "But it still rains," he complained, "every night—all night!"[12]

While in the Ipil region, Winthrop encountered a close call. He was down on the beach checking supplies and talking with the quartermasters. When he was done, he jumped in his jeep with Jim Rogers, and the two drove off. They had not traveled but seventy-five yards when a Japanese plane flew overhead and dropped a bomb exactly where the jeep had just been parked. Winthrop and Rogers were close enough to the blast that the debris fell on top of them. The bomb killed thirteen men.[13]

The Seventy-Seventh captured Ormoc on December 10, although the 305th were in reserve and so did not see much of the combat.[14] On December 11, the 305th began to push north out of the city and into the Ormoc Valley. The Japanese Imabori Detachment guarded the valley entrance.[15] The 305th referred to the Japanese mountaintop stronghold, which was a stone house reinforced with concrete, as the Alamo. The Japanese were dug in deep, and a three-day siege unfolded that produced a high number of casualties. From an abandoned house nearby, Winthrop witnessed events while sitting on the balcony. The Japanese troops launched what the US forces referred to as a "banzai attack," essentially an on-foot land-based version of a kamikaze attack. Winthrop watched as over one hundred troops charged headlong into the US lines, seeking to inflict as many casualties as possible before being killed. On the first day alone, Winthrop counted three separate waves of such attacks. All the while, the bombardment of the mountaintop stronghold continued.[16]

On December 14, the position was finally captured. A couple of days later, so, too, was the town of Cogon, and the nearby road junction to the main Ormoc Valley highway. On December 17, the 305th traveled up Highway 2 toward Valencia, seven miles to the north. Encountering resistance, they only made it halfway on the first day. On the second day, they arrived at their destination, along with the 306th and 307th Infantry Regiments.[17]

Winthrop cooked up a memorable meal on the first night in Valencia to lift his and his friends' spirits. He spent several hours constructing an intricate wood-burning oven out of bricks, scrap iron, and any other materials he could find to hand. Winthrop poured three cans of baked beans into a pot before adding some bacon and, as a substitute for molasses, his secret ingredient of half a dozen butterscotch lifesavers.[18] Soon the aroma began to circulate around the camp, but there was not enough to serve everyone. A select group of Winthrop, Hawks, and Col. Tanzola got to sample what passed as a cordon bleu dish in the field.[19] When Hawks returned home from the war, he drew a map of his and Winthrop's exploits in the Pacific. He later had this converted into a large oil painting, which he then presented to his friend. Today, the painting hangs in a re-creation of Winthrop's Winrock Farms office at the Winthrop Rockefeller Institute on Petit Jean Mountain. A striking illustration on the map, out of the many things that the two experienced during the war, is the memory of "Winthrop's Bean Feast" in Leyte.[20]

The 305th next headed into the western Ormoc Valley and the hills bordering the Camotes Sea. Their assignment was to capture the coastal town of Palompon, home to around seven thousand civilians and the main port of entry into Leyte for the Japanese forces. The campaign proved hard going. The Japanese destroyed bridges in the area and offered increasingly organized resistance. Getting bogged down in the hills, Maj. Gen. Bruce decided to launch an amphibious operation to take Palompon by sea.[21] Jim Landrum led the sea assault, while the 305th and other troops continued to advance from the opposite direction by land.[22] The 305th took the small town of Matag-ob, where it set up camp as a base for the final push toward Palompon.[23]

On Christmas Day, December 25, 1944, the island of Leyte was declared secure. Although this provided some timely seasonal propaganda for the citizens back home, the purported victory was a misrepresentation of the situation on the ground. As Winthrop wrote his parents, "Regardless of what the press say, the battle is still very much on for us!"[24] To keep up appearances, it was decreed by no less than Gen. MacArthur himself that every American soldier in Leyte should receive a celebratory Christmas dinner with turkey and all the trimmings. The practical logistics of doing this were far from straightforward. It meant getting full Christmas dinners some twenty-five miles from Ormoc to Matag-ob in large thermos cans that were not properly sealed. On the way, dirty rainwater from the canvas-covered convoy trucks that transported them leaked in. When the meals finally arrived, taking eight hours on a road made treacherous by the rain and Japanese soldiers, they were served up into the men's helmets and eaten by hand. Most of the men had jettisoned their mess kits due to the added weight a long time ago. Given that the troops used their helmets for everything from a wash basin to a makeshift toilet facility while in a foxhole, they made far from ideal food receptacles.[25]

Hawks exploded at the idea of having the men eat meals delivered in such poor shape and in such unsanitary conditions. He implored Winthrop and Col. Tanzola to put a stop to the madness. Both tried, but the orders came back from the very top that all the men must eat their Christmas dinners. Afterward, around 90 percent of the command officers suffered from dysentery, including Tanzola. Winthrop was one of the lucky 10 percent.[26] A few days later a consignment of hamburgers arrived under similar conditions. This time, Tanzola, who was still green around the gills from Christmas dinner, agreed that the food could not be served. He lied and told headquarters that it had been accidentally destroyed in transit.[27]

The 305th arrived in Palompon on January 1, 1945.[28] Jim Landrum's amphibious operation was a success, and the land-based forces encountered little resistance. Yet the cost of actually making it to Palompon was a heavy one.[29] In all, between December 7 and 25, the 305th saw 112 men killed in action, 43 men die from wounds, and 385 men wounded. These numbers paled in comparison to Japanese casualties, with a reported 4,381 Japanese soldiers dead.[30] Anywhere between 3,000 to 4,000 more had fled into the surrounding rural areas. They began conducting a guerrilla warfare that lasted for months. Reinforcements from the nearby island of Luzon, which the Japanese forces continued to hold, only added to their numbers.[31]

On the first day in Palompon, Winthrop found himself in a dicey position with his own soldiers. Keeping supply trucks running between Palompon and Division Headquarters in Ormoc was an arduous task. Winthrop quickly understood the need for a constant turnaround in traffic. He ordered two trucks to travel to Ormoc, spend the night there, pick up supplies, and return the following morning. Both trucks were ambushed on the journey. In the first truck, the assistant driver was killed, while the driver, Mitchell, survived. In the second truck, the assistant driver, Taylor, had three fingers shot off his right hand, while the driver, Berger, was shot in the leg and chest. The two men managed to drive away, but they later had to abandon their damaged vehicle around two miles from Matag-ob. After a mile of trying to walk into town, Berger, who was losing blood rapidly, collapsed. Taylor, in none-too-good a shape himself, carried Berger the rest of the way. The next day, Mitchell was back in Palompon and blaming Winthrop for sending out the trucks so late in the day and directly into an ambush.[32]

Winthrop started to encounter the silent treatment from the men, but he stood firm in his resolve. The day after his return to camp, Mitchell and several other soldiers visited the wounded Taylor and Berger in Matag-ob. Mitchell once more began blaming Winthrop for what had happened. Berger, however, blamed the drivers and assistant drivers, including himself, for having dallied around for two hours rather than setting off straight away. Berger's interjection quickly reversed the situation. The soldier's honesty helped to restore Winthrop's authority. Winthrop was eternally grateful to Berger for speaking up. After the war, Winthrop put Berger in touch with his contacts at Socony, who helped him to secure a service station in the New York Life Insurance development in Fresh Meadows, Queens. Back in Palompon, Winthrop doubled down on the necessity of speeding up the supply chain. He proposed to keep the trucks rolling all through the night as well as during the daytime. To demonstrate that he was fully prepared to do anything that he asked of his men, Winthrop personally led the first convoy with his own jeep at the head of it.[33]

Winthrop served as the main military liaison with the local population in Palompon.[34] The role kept him constantly occupied, since the town had been almost entirely demolished during the campaign. Winthrop reported that he was "working on an average of at least fourteen hours a day, seven days a week" to get things back in order. It was about the "busiest that I have . . . been in the service."[35] This took a physical toll. Winthrop rapidly lost weight and dropped from a thirty-six-inch to a thirty-four-inch waist.[36] Nevertheless, he found the work fulfilling and rewarding. As he wrote, "I have enjoyed working with the local people. It is indeed surprising to find so many interesting and intelligent people in such an out-of-the-way place." The locals were certainly appreciative of Winthrop's efforts. Many invited him into their homes to share meals. One family even named their son after him. Winthrop attended the christening of the newest Palompon resident, Winthrop Pastor.[37]

Among the many people that Winthrop made an impression on in Palompon was Monserrat S. Del Gallego, a nurse in a civilian hospital. After the war, Del Gallego felt compelled to write about Winthrop's service to the town. She told of how Winthrop had brought food to sick patients; how he had led volunteers in reconstructing destroyed homes; how he had waited up all night on the beach to escort an amphibious medical emergency evacuation; how he had worked around the clock to help treat burns victims by bringing plasma and other medical supplies from the military hospital; and how he had taken personal responsibility to sign off on leaving behind military blankets for the local population to use. As Winthrop was about to leave Palompon, Del Gallego and a group of other nurses treated Winthrop and Hawks to a freshly caught shrimp dinner by way of thanks. In parting, Winthrop gave Del Gallego his silver Cartier pen as a gift. "We stood there on the beach with lumps in our throats," wrote Del Gallego, "too poor for words to express our gratitude and thanks for such unselfishness and kindness—no words for such greatness of heart as Winthrop Rockefeller's."[38]

Winthrop's work in Palompon did not go unnoticed by his superiors. He was decorated with a Bronze Star Medal for meritorious service in a combat zone. In a memo notifying him of the award, Col. Tanzola wrote, "The personal satisfaction derived from this commendation stems from your spontaneous zeal, realistic approach, and determined, constructive deeds to alleviate the sufferings of an oppressed people. The people, themselves, voiced to me their high regard for your accomplishments in their behalf."[39]

Winthrop spent just over a month in Palompon. In February, the 305th relocated back to Tarragona Beach.[40] With feelings of weariness and exhaustion, Winthrop's mind began to wander beyond his immediate surroundings and circumstances. He became interested in reviving an opportunity that he had previously discussed with Ralph K. Davies, a Standard Oil of California director, when he was stationed at Camp Pickett in Virginia. The two had met up in Richmond and spoken about the prospect of Winthrop taking up a government job with the Petroleum Administration for War in London. The agency, established by a presidential executive order in December 1942, had oversight of the wartime petroleum industry. This included supervision in the areas of conservation, research, and development, as well as resource allocation and shipment. Winthrop dismissed the idea at the time, but while in Leyte he wrote to Davies to express an interest in further exploring the position.[41]

In a letter to Junior, Winthrop weighed the pros and cons of accepting such an offer. On the one hand, he had vowed not to leave the Seventy-Seventh until it had seen combat. But now he was a veteran of two campaigns. There seemed little prospect of further career advancement in the military. The new posting overseas might enhance his standing in the oil industry after the war. Living in London would certainly broaden his horizons and further increase his network of contacts. "In short," Winthrop concluded, "I can imagine nothing that I would like better than to get back to civilization where one could regain a certain amount of perspective." On the other hand, Winthrop was wracked with doubt: Was he qualified for the position? Would the job really help him advance in the oil industry? Would leaving the war now defeat the purpose of his having joined the Army in the first place? Winthrop decided to solicit his father's advice on the matter. Since Winthrop felt that time was too short for a prolonged back and forth, particularly given how long it took to exchange letters between the front lines and back home, he authorized Junior to make a final decision for him. Winthrop told Junior, "You may rest assured that I will be thoroughly satisfied with your decision whichever way it goes— and of course I will be awaiting news of the decision eagerly."[42]

Ralph K. Davies meanwhile separately wrote to Junior about the proposed job of "Petroleum Attaché in London." He explained that Winthrop would be "in brief, the U.S. Petroleum Administration in the United Kingdom," the main person who dealt with government and industry leaders. Davies believed that Winthrop was qualified on the basis of his "varied experiences in oil, his personal prestige, and his native abilities generally."[43] Davies also sent a letter to Winthrop that contained similar details, explaining that a Mr. Meyer from Socony was currently holding the position, but that the company wished to bring him back to the United States. Davies explained that Winthrop would serve in uniform while performing his duties; that the appointment would require approval from the State Department, although Davies assured him "that he wouldn't have any trouble there"; and that the Army would have to agree to reassign Winthrop to his new role, which, again, Davies did not believe would present too much of a problem.[44]

But before Winthrop had the chance to write to Junior about the newly revealed details, his father had already declined the offer. Junior sent a telegram to Davies that read, "Deeply appreciate the proposal contained in your letter February 12th and its implications. On the ground of his duty to his country and to himself, I am regretfully compelled to decline your proposal on my son's behalf. Please accept his and his father's thanks for your thought."[45] It was a momentous decision, and Junior wrote his son a long letter of explanation outlining his reasons for it. Junior, having consulted with Abby, and also with trusted advisors in the Rockefeller family office, concluded that the position was too much responsibility and not a good fit. "I know that you will come out of the war with an experience, a record and a public recognition that will mean everything to you in life after and that will add untold credit to the family name," wrote Junior. "I am confident, moreover, that your return to the oil industry will be so much better that the time will not be lost and your final position will be such as to more than justify the delay in attaining it." He added, "How much I appreciate the confidence in me which you have shown by leaving to my best judgment this important decision, it would be hard for you to understand."[46] Abby wrote her son, "[It] has been really very agonizing for us to have to decide what was right and best for you."[47]

When Winthrop showed his father's letter to Frank Newell, Newell's jaw visibly dropped. He could hardly believe what he read. Newell told Winthrop that in his shoes he would have swum home to take the job immediately.[48] On the face of it, Winthrop appeared remarkably forgiving of his parents' decision not to relieve him from duty on the front lines. He wrote them, "I will never be able to tell you how much I appreciate the time and careful attention that you gave the whole matter and I must say that after following your reasoning though to the end, there could have been no other answer and I am convinced that as time goes on I will be increasingly happy about it. In short I am in one hundred per cent agreement about the outcome."[49]

With that, the subject was dropped, and it was apparently never broached again. Winthrop's willingness to leave his fate in the hands of his parents demonstrated his deep faith and trust in them. The burden on his parents to make the decision was no doubt immense. Rather than removing their son from harm's way to a much safer posting, the Rockefeller family's steadfast commitment to duty and honor firmly held sway. The following months would prove among some of the most harrowing and dangerous of the war for Winthrop. He could very easily have not survived them. If the worst had happened, the decision by his parents would surely have taken on a very different complexion, and one that they would have found it incredibly difficult to live with. Mercifully for Winthrop, and his parents, that was not an eventuality that any of them ever had to face.

The longer-term impact of the decision on Winthrop's relationship with his parents is much more difficult to decipher. Though in full accordance with them at the time, the months ahead provided plenty of opportunities for reflection and brooding on what might have been. Toward the end of the war, Winthrop became noticeably more assertive in voicing his intentions about what he wanted to do when he returned home. After the war and back in New York, Winthrop exercised more autonomy and paid far less heed to his parents' advice and counsel. In that sense, the episode may well have been a pivotal turning-point in Winthrop's relationship with his father and mother, convincing him of the need to assert his independence more and to seize control of his own destiny.

The six weeks spent on Tarragona Beach were meant for rest, relaxation, and recuperation. But after three grueling months in Leyte, Winthrop was physically spent. "I do not wonder that you have found yourself utterly tired out after all you have been through," wrote Junior. "Nothing but rest and then more rest will correct such a situation. After all, being so tired means that the reservoir of surplus strength has been drained to the bottom and the pressure reduced to zero."[50] Yet Winthrop was already too far gone. An initial heavy cold quickly developed into bronchial pneumonia, which in turn led to hospitalization.[51] Winthrop sent his parents a photograph of himself in his hospital bed and reported that he was being treated with sulfa drugs that upset his stomach. He wrote them, "Please don't worry about me because everything is well in hand and I am quite willing to convalesce long enough to really feel myself before going back to duty."[52]

This was an overly optimistic assessment, since not long after, Winthrop became jaundiced with an attack of "infectious hepatitis." Known more commonly today as hepatitis A, the viral disease of the liver thrives in unsanitary conditions. Winthrop wrote, "I guess that the old saying that it 'never rains but it pours' is about right. Now I can look forward to a couple or three weeks of rest and careful diet."[53] As Winthrop lay in his hospital bed, he reflected upon what he was going to do after the war. "I will have to settle down a bit. . . . Dull thought, isn't it?" he wrote a friend, and confessed that, "These years that I have spent in the Army are beginning to pile up on me."[54] March 25, 1945, marked the one-year anniversary of Winthrop's departure from San Francisco. "In many ways it has seemed an eternity," he mused, "but then again it has passed faster than I would have dared hope."[55] At the end of March, Winthrop was beginning to perk up considerably, and, having previously lost weight, he reported that he was rapidly improving and ravenously hungry: "My comeback has been nothing short of a miracle. I bet I must have gained back at least ten of the pounds that I lost in the last week or so."[56]

Winthrop needed every ounce of his newfound strength in the days ahead. No sooner had he escaped his hospital bed than he was on the move again. With the United States in the process of securing all of the Philippines and the strategic volcano island of Iwo Jima, the push toward the Japanese mainland continued apace. The Seventy-Seventh left Leyte without Winthrop and sailed to Kerama Retto, a small group of islands around a thousand miles to the north. The islands offered a perfect base for ships and aircraft in a planned assault on Okinawa, just fifteen miles to the east. Stretching from northeast to southwest, Okinawa was a thin and craggy island, sixty-five miles long and between two to ten miles across. It was located right in the middle of the Ryukyu Islands, which straggled from Japan to Taiwan, dividing the East China Sea and the Philippine Sea. Some 340 miles south of Kyushu, Japan's southernmost home island, Okinawa provided a strategic stronghold for tightening a blockade on Japanese shipping and for air bases to support a ground invasion. The Seventy-Seventh arrived at Kerama Retto on March 26, and within five days it had taken control of the poorly defended islands.[57] The assault on Okinawa began on Easter Sunday, April 1, with the Seventy-Seventh in reserve.[58] On the early evening of April 2, with Winthrop now having rejoined the regiment from Leyte, the 305th set sail from Kerama Retto aboard the USS *Henrico*.[59] The plan was to head 350 miles south into the Philippine Sea to avoid Japanese air activity during the Okinawa hostilities.[60]

Normally, Winthrop would have been in his room tapping away on his typewriter and catching up with letter-writing for the duration of the journey. But he was still recovering from illness, and with the impending prospect of returning to combat duty playing on his mind, he opted to play cards in the wardroom with one of the warrant officers, a man named Reeves. They played double Canfield, a game that usually involved buying cards for $52 (equivalent to $751 in 2020 dollars) and selling them back to the house for $5 (equivalent to $72 in 2020 dollars). On soldier's pay, this translated into 52 cents (equivalent to $8 in 2020 dollars) and 5 cents (equivalent to 72 cents in 2020), respectively. As a married man with a family, Reeves had to carefully limit his losses. There was a gentlemen's agreement between the two that if one player lost more than $1.50 (equivalent to $22 in 2020 dollars) over four or five hands, then the other had the right to demand another five games to make the money back. This time Winthrop found himself on a $3 to $4 losing streak. He insisted that they play on.[61]

It was around 7:10 p.m. and less than sixteen miles into the journey when the card game was abruptly halted by a twin-engine Japanese aircraft carrying two five-hundred-pound bombs. The plane slammed into the captain's quarters in a kamikaze attack. There was no warning, no sirens, and apparently no defensive fire. The blast seemed to come out of nowhere.[62] Winthrop believed this was due to the attack taking place at dusk, with the plane flying in low from the west and remaining undetected. Almost all the senior Navy and Army officers on board, who were gathered in the captain's quarters, were killed instantly. This included the 305th commanding officer, Col. Vincent Tanzola.[63] A fireball caused by a flash explosion of gasoline traveled down the stairs and into the wardroom directly below. Winthrop was holding up his cards facing the door, and his hands caught the full impact of the flames. His head was turned down a little, which helped to shield his face, but it still received burns. Winthrop's carefully cultivated and sculpted moustache was scorched beyond recognition.[64]

There were around thirty men in the wardroom as panic and confusion broke out. All the lights went out, but it was far from dark since the room was ablaze. The men tried to get their bearings and conduct an orderly evacuation. When he arrived up on deck still in shock, Winthrop realized he had accidentally burst one of the blisters that had formed on the back of his hands. It now had virtually no skin left on it. With the amount of adrenaline pumping through his body, he hardly even noticed the pain.[65]

As he began to assess the situation, Winthrop realized that the ship had an eleven-degree list. He worried that it was sinking. In fact, in a piece of quick thinking, the ship's executive officer, Lt. W. D. Craig, purposefully flooded the hold so that the gasoline, explosives, and ammunition stored there would not catch fire and blow the vessel up. The USS *Henrico* was, however, immobilized. In the attack, one of the two engines from the Japanese plane tore through the funnel of the ship, ripping out all of the steam pipes and water lines before crashing into the engine room. The practice in the Navy was to never stop a convoy, but rather to leave incapacitated ships behind. Halting the fleet only provided stationary targets that invited more attacks. Two destroyers were sent back to aid the USS *Henrico*, dousing it with water to keep it cool and to stop the flames from spreading. On deck, the men managed to get the auxiliary water pumps working and brought the fire under control. Winthrop bumped into Hawks, who was busy administering medical care to the injured. Hawks greased and wrapped Winthrop's hands and gave him a morphine tablet that knocked him out until the morning.[66]

Hawks's routine had changed that evening too. While Winthrop went to play cards, Hawks visited with Lt. Craig just to the rear of the wardroom. Hawks recalled a sudden deafening explosion followed by flames and a feeling of suffocation. The room shattered into pieces, and he ended up buried beneath a sink. When Hawks and Lt. Craig crawled out from under the wreckage, Hawks saw a gaping hole, caused by one of the plane's bombs, going all the way down through the decks to the waterline. There was a good deal of fire, smoke, and confusion. The two men made their way to the stern of the ship. Hawks lost his shoes along the way, and when he surfaced on deck, dazed and confused, he stood there in tattered socks. It was not long before his physician's instincts kicked in and he started to attend to the wounded.[67]

When Winthrop awoke on deck the next morning, the men were beginning to line up the bodies of those killed. There were 98 dead and a further 150 wounded.[68] The second of the plane's bombs had traveled all the way through the ship and exploded with a delayed fuse as it was about to exit through the keel, causing considerable damage to the lower decks. The explosion took place just two compartments away from the sleeping quarters of Winthrop and Hawks. Had they been in there at the time, they would have both been killed instantly. Some of the worst injuries were to the men standing on deck, since the force of the blast from below shattered the bones in their lower body. As one of the two senior regimental officers left alive on the ship—the other being Hawks, who was still occupied with his medical duties—Winthrop toured the vessel to check for damage and to see how the other men were faring. His friend Jim Landrum later arrived as the relieving officer.[69]

With Landrum in charge, the evacuation of the wounded began. Small boats ferried injured men from the USS *Henrico* to the hospital ship the USS *Solace*, which transported them to military hospitals in Guam.[70] Winthrop, who was among the wounded, parted from Hawks, who stayed on board the USS *Henrico* until the following day, when the remaining men were transferred to the USS *Sarasota*. Hawks stood on the bridge and waved goodbye to Winthrop as he left for Guam. It was the last the two would see of each other until after the war.[71]

If Winthrop was physically scarred, Hawks's psychological wounds were less visible but no less real.[72] Winthrop later discovered that Hawks suffered constantly from insomnia after the ordeal. Capt. Lee P. Cothran was Hawks's cabin mate aboard the USS *Sarasota*. Cothran recalled that every time he awoke, Hawks was on the top bunk above him puffing on a cigarette. He believed that Hawks did not get more than two hours of sleep over the course of each twenty-four-hour day. Hawks went back to work, but he continued to suffer from physical and mental exhaustion. One day, when he was due to travel to one of the battalion stations in Okinawa, he did not feel up to it. Capt. Don Sheff, the company commander of the medical collecting company, volunteered to go in his place. On the way, Sheff's jeep hit a landmine, and he was killed. It was, Winthrop believed, the final straw for Hawks, who now also carried the guilt of Sheff's death on his shoulders. Eventually, Hawks was honorably discharged from the Army and sent back to the United States, displaying symptoms of what today would be referred to as post-traumatic stress disorder.[73]

Aboard the USS *Solace*, Winthrop was bearing up despite his injuries. He had a shower, and one of the corps men shaved off what remained of his moustache. He then climbed into a clean bed and received medical attention. The ship's doctor recommended bursting the big painful blisters that had formed on Winthrop's hands from the third-degree burns. Next, he applied petroleum jelly and pressure bandages. Winthrop was given sulfa drugs and penicillin to fight any potential infection. The procedure appeared to work, although plasma from the burns on his hands continually seeped into the bandages and soaked them wet. Winthrop needed both plasma and blood transfusions while on board. The pain in Winthrop's hands continued, but he found that holding them above his head helped to ease the throbbing. His facial injuries were less troublesome, and they were treated with petroleum jelly without the need for bandages. For his first two days on board the USS *Solace*, Winthrop stayed in bed and rested. On the third day, he got up to check on the other men and discovered that, all things considered, they appeared to be in fine spirits.[74]

The USS *Solace* arrived in Guam at Apra Harbor, where the injured were transferred to military hospitals on Navy buses. Winthrop was taken to the 373rd Station Hospital. Not for the first time, his Rockefeller family connections proved helpful. Dr. Thomas M. Rivers, the medical director of the Rockefeller Institute Hospital in New York, where the Naval Medical Research Unit No. 2 (NAMRU 2) was originally based, had recently relocated with the unit to Guam. Rivers immediately recognized Winthrop's name on the casualty list, and he was at his bedside within two hours of Winthrop's landing.[75]

First making sure that Winthrop received proper medical attention, Rivers next wrote a letter to Abby and Junior informing them about the situation. Rivers reported, "No part of his body except his face and hands are involved. His face is practically well now and there will be no scarring. His hands were somewhat more badly damaged." But the prognosis was good: "The doctors think that he will be here several weeks before going back to active duty. . . . He is in wonderful spirits and there is no need whatsoever for you to worry."[76] Winthrop had scribbled a letter in pencil to his parents while aboard the USS *Solace* with great difficulty due to his bandaged hands, telling them, "Hoping against hope that you haven't received one of *those* telegrams from the War Dept." He feared that they would be informed about his injuries without any further specific details, which would cause them to worry.[77] Rivers's letter arrived first. Abby and Junior were understandably alarmed to learn that their son was wounded, but they were nonetheless extremely relieved to know that he was now safe and in good hands.[78]

The 373rd Station Hospital where Winthrop was treated for his wounds was housed in Quonset huts. As the only field-grade officer, Winthrop snagged one of the two private rooms available. He missed out on some of the fun and camaraderie that the other officers enjoyed on the main ward, but he did manage to get some much-needed peace and quiet for recovery in his own room.[79] Yet Winthrop was never entirely lonely. Plenty of friends dropped by to visit him. The Third Marine gang, who he knew from his previous stay in Guam, all arrived one afternoon with a picnic hamper. There were many more such visits, which were always accompanied by a bottle of whiskey or other gifts to cheer him up.[80] While he was still laid up, reports of the kamikaze attack, and the injuries Winthrop had sustained, began to leak out in the press in the United States.[81]

Rivers continued to drop by to check up on Winthrop, reporting to Junior that his son had lost four or five pounds. He said that he was going to try to get Winthrop transferred to his NAMRU 2 facility where, he believed, he could "put some weight back on him."[82] Rivers's transfer request was successful. On

Winthrop (*reclining*) hospitalized in Guam after the kamikaze attack on his ship the USS *Henrico*, smoking a cigar with bandaged hands alongside friends from the Third Marines. Robert "Bob" Kriendler from Manhattan's 21 Club sits to his immediate right. April 1945. *Winthrop Rockefeller Collection, UA Little Rock Center for Arkansas History and Culture.*

the afternoon of April 23, three weeks after Winthrop had received his burns, Rivers personally relocated him from the 373rd Station Hospital to NAMRU 2. By that time, the burns on Winthrop's face had completely healed, and the heavy bandages were gone from his almost-healed hands. Rivers put Winthrop up in a private room in his own personal quarters and loaned him a jeep. Almost straight away, Winthrop was off driving around the island and visiting with friends. "He looks much better than he did when I first saw him," reported Rivers to Junior. "He informed me last night that he had gained 6 pounds. I am going to feed him well while he is here with me, and I hope to put many more pounds on him."[83] Winthrop presented a similarly rosy picture to his parents, although he noted that the new skin on his hands was still "mighty tender and nicks easily." He estimated that it would take another two weeks to toughen it up enough for him to return to duty.[84]

Staying at Rivers's home was one of the happiest times that Winthrop experienced overseas during the war. Stray letters finally caught up with him, and he spent three to four days reading through over three hundred of them. More friends popped out of the woodwork, including Mary Jean Kempner, who was assigned to Guam as *Vogue* magazine's overseas war correspondent.[85] "Every day I continue to run into more and more people that I know!" Winthrop reported home excitedly, estimating that in all he ran into twenty-five to twenty-eight people in Guam that he had known in civilian life.[86] The day before his thirty-third birthday, Winthrop went to the beach with some friends for a picnic. On the day itself, May 1, 1945, Rivers had his cooks bake a special birthday cake for him.[87] As he began to recover, despite the wonderful time he was having, Winthrop found his nagging Rockefeller conscience calling him back to duty. He started to talk with Rivers and others about returning to the 305th.[88] Rivers remained cautious about the prospect, noting that the rapid succession of pneumonia, hepatitis, and the flash burns that Winthrop had received "must have been a considerable shock to his whole physical and mental setup." Rivers did concede, "He is young, in good shape and has shown a remarkable ability to bounce back to normal."[89]

Not long after Winthrop's birthday celebrations, on May 8 the Allied Forces in Europe accepted the unconditional surrender of Nazi Germany as the war there officially came to an end. Victory in Europe (V-E) Day provided an indication that World War II was slowly but surely drawing to a close. With his recent experiences of home comforts in Guam and news about the conclusion of hostilities in Europe, Winthrop's mind increasingly began to focus on the prospect of returning back to civilian life in New York. It was a difficult and trying time: the end seemed tantalizingly close, but there was still plenty of work to do in bringing the war to a conclusion in the Pacific. A long and circuitous road home lay ahead. In the first instance, Winthrop was destined to head in the opposite direction, back to the front lines.

CHAPTER 10   From Soldier to Civilian

WINTHROP'S SECOND STAY in Guam brought him closer back to civilian life than any time since he had left the United States. It was just the boost he needed. As he wrote a friend, "The weeks here with Dr. Rivers have really been wonderful! I can't begin to count all the friends that I have out here and it has been such fun being with them. I have been out for dinner about every night and have loved every minute of it. Just think, with all my good living I have gained 16–18 pounds!" The whole experience made it difficult to leave and return to a soldier's life again: "I will be more than grateful for this little extra reserve in the months to come as I know the going is going to be pretty rough! It is taking all my best will power to tear myself away and start back tomorrow! This pleasant soft living has substantially reduced my ardor for the field life, if I ever had any."[1]

While revitalizing Winthrop physically, the period of convalesce weakened his mental preparedness for war. He found it difficult to muster any enthusiasm for what lay ahead. "Frankly, at this point, I don't find myself in any great rush, but suppose that that is rather understandable," wrote Winthrop to his parents on his day of departure.[2] Dr. Rivers likewise noted that Winthrop was "not enthusiastic about going back to the front. . . . [He] has a large number of friends here on the island and all of them hated to see him leave."[3] Before departing, Winthrop sent his Purple Heart, which he was awarded for being wounded in service, home to his parents for safekeeping.[4]

On May 17, 1945, Winthrop set off from Guam to return to war.[5] He did manage to cheer himself up on the plane ride from Guam to Okinawa, a trick that he had learned to master from his previous experiences in the military. This was aided by a four-day layover on the way, where he bumped into yet more friends.[6] Once he returned to active duty on May 23, there was little time to dwell on the recent past.[7] A new job with new responsibilities greeted him. He moved from the 305th staff as S-4 to the Seventy-Seventh staff as G-1, where he was in charge of personnel and morale. "This job calls for a Lt. Colonel

Winthrop in Guam getting ready to return to war,
May 1945. *Winthrop Rockefeller Collection, UA Little
Rock Center for Arkansas History and Culture.*

soooo—" wrote Winthrop, eyeing his next promotion. He welcomed the fresh
challenge, which he hoped would provide him with renewed motivation.[8]
Winthrop enjoyed the assignment, "because it is dealing with people—[his]
hobby—and anything that one can do in the Army to make life any easier for
the poor GI gives one a big lift." Still, it was hard and demanding work that
involved logging an average of fourteen to sixteen hours a day.[9]

In mid-June, Frank Newell, whom Winthrop met up with once again in Okinawa, wrote to Abby thanking her for the books that she had recently sent him, and provided an update on her son in return. "Win is still somewhat thinner than normal, but it is a healthful, hard leanness. His face is quite full and has excellent color," Newell observed. "He's as busy as a man can be, learning a new job and doing it while it's running at full capacity at the same time."[10] Winthrop told his parents, "It's papers, papers everywhere and hardly a moment to think."[11] Things only got busier when organized resistance ended in Okinawa on June 22.[12] Winthrop reported, "The past several weeks have been just about the busiest that I have had since I can remember, with the possible exception of the days in Palompon."[13]

As the end of the war drew ever nearer, the all-too-apparent differences between how Winthrop wanted to live his life and how his parents wanted him to live his life were increasingly laid bare. When Winthrop wrote enthusiastically about heading home through a recently introduced points system in the military, Junior did not appear quite so keen to add up the numbers. He emphasized the importance of Winthrop seeing his job in the Army through to the end. This brought an uncharacteristically testy reply from his son. "Father, your reaction was that I would stay as long at the front as I needed. True, but I would like to add that after a year in a position to see men of all ranks and grades get killed without even shaking the continuity of the whole, I would be a very conceited man indeed to think that I was, or am, indispensable," Winthrop asserted. "I don't feel any embarrassment nor any hesitancy as far as accepting my release when my turn comes is concerned."[14]

In the same letter to his parents, Winthrop also had some uncharacteristically terse words for his mother. Abby had begun to write about her expectations for her son's life after his return from war. "The experience that you have had in the Army will make you a most useful citizen. Of course you will have to forgive a mother's pride, but I feel that if you come back ready to concentrate, you will have a great future before you," she told Winthrop. "You are much needed not only in public life but in the business life of the community. I am very eager to see you take your place in the business world. I know that you can do it but you will have to sacrifice some things to carry on—I won't say what things."[15] As if unable to contain herself on the latter point, in her next letter Abby wrote even more directly, "That great contribution to Society which I mentioned in my last letter—and when I say society, I don't mean 'café.' " This seems an unmistakable reference to Winthrop's fondness for New York's nightlife, known colloquially at the time as "café society."[16]

The remark clearly rankled Winthrop. "And Mother, you are very kindly projecting me into my new role as a civilian—my taking my place in and serving society. I think that I hardly need point out that these are matters which have occupied considerable of my thinking over the past months," he replied. "In your last, you added the word 'café' after society. I realize full well that the job ahead of me is a serious one and when I undertake it, it will be on that basis, but I might add that before I undertake it I plan to make up for some of the 'playing' that I have missed as a soldier. As a matter of fact my plan calls for a month's vacation for each year that I have been in the service. I realize that this may be an ambitious program, but I'm sure going to try to hold out for it."[17]

Somewhat taken aback by Winthrop's unusually barbed comments, his parents responded in very different ways. Junior immediately went on the defensive. "What I said was not intended to imply that you ought to stay, but rather that irrespective of points I felt sure you would do what you thought was your duty. Not for a moment would I presume to suggest what your duty should be. Every one of us must decide that question for himself," he advised. "My purpose was merely to give evidence of my complete confidence in your sense of duty, hence the rightness of whatever decision you might make, whether it be to stay or to return. I hope I make myself clear."[18]

Abby was entirely contrite and apologetic. "Winthrop dearest, two minutes after I'd sent the letter in which I ended up my last paragraph with the reference to 'Café' society, I wished I might have snatched it back out of the mail. Every time I try to be funny, something unpleasant happens. I don't want you to feel I was trying to preach to you or rub in the fact that the world needs you," she explained. "I do want you to have a good time when you come back and certainly hope it works out that you will be able to take just as much time and get just as much rest and relaxation as you justly deserve." Having said all that, Abby could not seem to resist pushing her luck by further raising the prospect of marriage. "I was going to add I hope you will take time to consider matrimony, but perhaps you will think that is in a class with my remark about café society."[19]

No doubt adding to Winthrop's testiness were the stresses and strains of being overworked. This led to another descent into illness. The symptoms of jaundice returned, and Winthrop was yet again diagnosed with hepatitis. The last thing he wanted was to go back into an Army hospital, so he struggled on. Two weeks later, the Seventy-Seventh transferred from Okinawa back to the Philippines, this time to the island of Cebu. Winthrop could still not shake off his illness. A week after arriving in Cebu, he succumbed to the inevitable: "Finally after dragging around for about five weeks looking miserable and yellow, they up and sent me to the hospital."[20] Winthrop was in his hospital bed when, on August 15, 1945, Japan surrendered and the war in the Pacific officially ended.[21]

" 'Cease Fire'!!" exclaimed Winthrop to his parents. "The command that we have all been waiting and praying for all these months and years has finally been given."[22] Junior and Abby were every bit as elated as their son at the news, which they heard while at the Eyrie in Seal Harbor. Church bells and sirens rang out there to mark the occasion. Junior wrote Winthrop, "Thank God the fighting is over. What a wonderful moment this is in the history of the world. What it means to millions of parents like ourselves and to tens of millions of men like yourself who have given themselves so unreservedly and so unselfishly to the service of their country during these past years!"[23]

Nelson provided further encouraging words for Winthrop, writing that he had met with Gen. George C. Marshall, who "spoke in very simple and direct terms of the outstanding job you have done during the war, and of his respect for you personally. As far as I am concerned, you could have received no greater tribute." Nelson wrote that Marshall was particularly impressed by Winthrop's "courage and ability [in the face of] hazards and constant danger! It is a record that will long be remembered and will always reflect credit on . . . the family." Nelson concluded, "All of us will be awaiting your return, and none of us will ever forget what you have been through and the way in which you have conducted yourself. It will be wonderful to have you back! We have missed you and are very proud of you."[24]

On August 22, a week after Japan's surrender, Winthrop was informed that he was going back to the United States. Patients who needed longer-term convalescence were being evacuated to free up resources for those who needed more immediate medical attention.[25] The doctors believed a period of rest, better food, and a change of climate, would all make the world of difference to Winthrop's condition.[26] Winthrop set sail on September 6.[27] Once his hospital ship escaped the tropical heat, he quickly began to feel better. He enjoyed an uneventful, pleasant, and relaxing journey home.[28]

When the hospital ship docked in San Pedro, Los Angeles, on Friday, September 22, Winthrop and the other men on board were taken to Camp Hahn, sixty miles outside of the city. The men were told that they were free to do as they wished, so long as they returned back to camp in two days' time. "I can assure you that I lost no time in getting on in to LA and truly it was heaven!" reported Winthrop. Like the rest of the men who had spent time overseas, he could not wait to experience the freedoms of civilian life: "Just think, a room and bath all to your self. . . . And almost as good, you could walk into a restaurant and order the things that you like to eat." On his first night in Los Angeles, after phoning his parents, Winthrop met up with a friend from Standard Oil of California for a quiet meal.[29]

On the second night, he called up Sonny Tufts, his old friend from Yale. Due to a college football injury, Tufts had not been in military service during the war. The shortage of young male lead actors in Hollywood worked to his advantage. In 1943, Tufts played a Marine in the romantic drama *So Proudly We Hail!* starring Claudette Colbert, Paulette Goddard, and Veronica Lake. It was a critically acclaimed role that earned him the label "Find of 1943." In 1944, he featured in *Government Girl*, starring Olivia de Havilland, for which he was declared a "Star of Tomorrow." The same year, he shared the billing with Bing Crosby and Betty Hutton in the musical comedy *Here Come the Waves*.[30] Winthrop and Tufts set out to party: "About midnight we joined forces with Bing Crosby and several others and really went to town."[31] Among the people in Crosby's crew was Joan Caulfield, a model and aspiring Hollywood actress who starred with Tufts and Veronica Lake in the 1946 film *Miss Susie Slagle's*.[32]

When Winthrop had phoned his parents after arriving in Los Angeles, they informed him that he was going to be transferred to the Rockefeller Institute for Medical Research in New York. Dr. Charles L. Hoagland, an expert on liver diseases, would be his physician.[33] Junior and Abby personally visited with Hoagland, who told them he felt that Winthrop should be placed under special medical care to prevent further reoccurrences of hepatitis. They then contacted Nelson to see if he could help get his younger brother transferred. Nelson, who was good friends with US surgeon general Norman T. Kirk, said that he would give him a call. Separately, Hoagland wrote to Kirk, telling him that he would "be greatly interested in having Winthrop Rockefeller as patient for special study."[34]

Winthrop first had to transfer between military hospitals Camp Hahn and Halloran General Hospital in Staten Island before he could be admitted to the Rockefeller Institute.[35] The journey was something of an unexpected trek, though not an entirely unpleasant one. Winthrop traveled via the Air Evac Service. Flying eight hours a day, it was expected to take three days to travel from the West Coast to the East Coast, hopping between various Air Force hospitals to drop off and collect other patients along the way. With added weather conditions and engine troubles, it took five days in all. As always, Winthrop made the most of the situation. "We had two perfectly swell pilots and a flight nurse who had also just gotten back from a stretch overseas and then on top of that we had two student nurses who were also good kids," Winthrop wrote. "Each night we would put up at some Air base hospital and always the local personnel would insist that we use their officers club and mess if we were so inclined. At each place they were nicer than the last."[36]

When he reached the Rockefeller Institute, Winthrop was granted the weekend off to visit his family. He reported, "Mother and Father were wild with joy and excitement at the safe return of their wandering son from the Pacific."[37] The same weekend, the family received news that David was about to return home from the war in Europe. John had already been discharged from the Navy, and Laurance was expected to follow him by the end of the month. Nelson had already left the State Department. Winthrop remarked, "It is looking like the entire Rockefeller family will be unemployed most any day now, with the possible exception of this one. . . . That's life for you, first in and last out."[38]

When Winthrop returned to the Rockefeller Institute on Sunday evening, October 1, he was given a thorough medical examination. He weighed just 170 pounds and looked tired and drawn. The doctors discovered a malfunctioning liver, but no permanent damage done.[39] Hoagland believed that Winthrop had never fully recovered from his initial bout of hepatitis in Leyte.[40] During the first week under Hoagland's care, Winthrop took things easy while a number of friends and well-wishers dropped by to visit and provide him with company. By the second week, he was already beginning to put on weight, and he quickly regained twenty pounds. In turn, this stimulated the recovery of his liver. He was allowed out for a few hours in the afternoon, then for meals, and then for longer excursions.[41]

The down time in hospital gave Winthrop an opportunity to think about what to do next. Reading the newspapers, he became interested in the topic of veterans' readjustment to civilian life after the war. The doctors at the Rockefeller Institute told him to take things easy, but they were happy enough for him to do some light work. Winthrop began to explore ways in which he might combine his interest in veterans' readjustment and the doctors' advice. He wrote to some of his contacts in Washington, DC, including Rockefeller family friend Anna M. Rosenberg, who had previously worked on issues of demobilization for Pres. Franklin D. Roosevelt. Winthrop sketched out a potential project that involved taking a six-month trip across the United States to compile a nationwide survey on veterans' readjustment problems. This met with an enthusiastic response.[42] In November 1945, Winthrop's former KP duty comrade from Camp Plattsburgh, the now–secretary of war Robert P. Patterson, approved the plan.[43]

In January 1946, Winthrop began a nationwide tour of the United States to work on his report. The trip reunited him with Jimmy Hudson. After

Winthrop's induction into the Army in January 1941, Hudson worked for Winthrop's brother David in New York and then for Nelson in Washington, DC. In 1942, Hudson decided to relocate to Philadelphia. His wife's family lived there, and he wanted to have her settled before he left for war. With a letter of introduction from Nelson, Hudson landed a job at the Bendix Aviation Corporation. After working there for a year, in March 1943 he was drafted into the Coast Guard, where he worked aboard the USS *Hunter Liggett* ferrying troops back and forth from the United States to Saipan, Guam, and other locations in the Pacific. He may well have been the only person who did not bump into Winthrop on his travels overseas. Hudson was discharged from the Coast Guard in December 1945, having risen to the rank of petty officer.[44]

Even before Hudson ended his service, Winthrop was in touch with him about his latest project. Hudson's assignment was to seek out the views of Black veterans. Just a week after getting back to civilian life, Hudson set off with Winthrop on a six-month, eighteen-thousand-mile journey across the United States.[45] Winthrop spoke to local officials in hundreds of towns, meeting with chambers of commerce, civic groups, and journalists to solicit their opinions about veterans' readjustment needs.[46] While on the road in February, Winthrop received his final promotion to the rank of lieutenant colonel.[47] After completing his "Report on Veterans' Readjustment," he was officially discharged from the Army on June 30.[48]

Winthrop left the military with a Bronze Service Arrowhead Medal for his participation in the assault landing in Ipil; a Bronze Star Medal for his meritorious service in helping to rebuild Palompon; a Purple Heart for his wounds sustained in the kamikaze attack on the USS *Henrico*; and an Oak Leaf Cluster for his services as G-1 in Okinawa and Cebu. He also received an American Defense Ribbon, an American Theater Ribbon, an Asiatic Pacific Theater Ribbon, a Philippine Liberation Ribbon, and a Victory Ribbon.[49] "Five and one-half years is a long time," reflected Winthrop, "but it has been an experience, which, in retrospect, I would not trade for the world."[50]

The veterans' readjustment report was submitted to Secretary of War Patterson on July 18. It revealed that Winthrop was not impressed with the way that veterans were being eased back into civilian life. "I felt that the G.I. Bill was an effort to buy off the veterans with cash but without really giving them a helping hand," Winthrop said. "Not even giving them a college education could do the job without doing something else."[51] Winthrop proposed a far more comprehensive approach to veterans' resettlement.[52] But when Patterson responded to the report, he wrote, "I gave careful thought to the possibility of releasing it to the public but decided against such action, largely because so many of the matters covered relate to, or are the responsibility of, other government agencies." Patterson said that he would forward the report to those agencies for action.[53]

In effect, the report was shelved. In the six months since Winthrop began his project, the federal government's agenda and priorities had changed, rapid demobilization was underway, and the emphasis was now very much on getting back to normal as quickly as possible. Winthrop was disappointed that his efforts were being summarily dismissed, but he was resigned to the report's fate.[54] The report was finally made public on December 5, although by that time, Winthrop had already turned his attention to other matters.[55] An inquiry about the report in early 1947 met with the reply from Winthrop that, "Following my survey on Veterans' Readjustment for Secretary of War Patterson, I spent several months attempting to initiate certain programs to assist veterans, and regret to have to report that I found myself doing nothing but running up a series of blind alleys."[56]

Something that Winthrop did take it upon himself to do in the area of veterans' affairs was to set up a memorial trust for Col. Tanzola, his 305th commanding officer. With the funds, Winthrop hired two floors of the Breslin Hotel in Manhattan to provide accommodation and assistance for relocating war veterans. The Seventy-Seventh commander, Maj. Gen. Bruce, congratulated Winthrop, telling him, "I think this is a wonderful thing. In fact, I think that sort of action is far superior to a lot of monuments and plaques. My own World War I division spent over $100,000 on a monument in Washington that I think very few people know is there. I would very much prefer to see money like that go into something practical."[57] Winthrop continued his association with the armed forces through an appointment to the Officers' Reserve Corps.[58]

In September 1946, Winthrop fully turned his attention to returning to civilian life in New York. The first step was to set up a new home. Jimmy Hudson was placed in charge of overseeing renovations for Winthrop's penthouse apartment atop 770 Park Avenue, located in the building next to Winthrop's parents' apartment at 740 Park Avenue.[59] In March 1947, the guests who attended Winthrop's housewarming appeared to have a thoroughly enjoyable time. Winthrop related to Frank Newell the hallmarks of a good party: "The hour at which people left, the dent in my cellar . . . [and] the damage to furniture and carpets."[60] Winthrop tried to persuade Newell to join him in New York. "There's no way," Newell told him. His old Army friend was happily settled back in Little Rock, and he vowed, presciently, "I'll see you living in Arkansas long before you ever see me working in New York."[61]

On September 16, Winthrop returned to work at Socony.[62] Rather than going back to the Foreign Trade Department, he was assigned a position in the Foreign Producing Department.[63] As head of the Industrial Relations Division, he was in charge of coordinating industrial, public, and governmental relations.[64] He found the new role, and the mundanity of returning to desk-bound office work, singularly uninspiring.[65]

Far more stimulating were Winthrop's public commitments. On September 22, Winthrop attended a Brothers Meeting in Pocantico Hills, one of many such formal meetings held between the brothers to discuss their individual and mutual interests in the postwar era. In outlining his plans, Winthrop stated that his principal interest was in the National Urban League (NUL) and race relations. Winthrop had been appointed as a board member of the NUL in 1940, and he intended to resume his duties with new gusto. His work on the veterans' readjustment report alerted him to the plight of returning Black soldiers and the conditions that existed in Black communities. Declaring that the NUL was the "best national negro organization which is not communist dominated"—a reflection of the largely unfounded Cold War fears that were being attached to postwar Black struggles for freedom and equality—Winthrop suggested increasing its financial support from Rockefeller Brothers Fund.[66]

Winthrop considered his association with the NUL his "most interesting outside activity" and declared, "My ability to work with the group is a constant source of pleasure."[67] He became one of the most recognizable faces of the NUL in New York and nationwide, boosted by a string of high-profile appointments and speaking engagements. In 1943, Winthrop was elected to serve on the NUL National Committee.[68] In 1946, he delivered the opening address at the NUL's annual conference in Saint Louis.[69] In 1948, he was the plenary speaker at the NUL's annual conference in Detroit.[70] In 1951, he was the NUL's principal speaker at a career conference held at Bethune-Cookman College in Daytona Beach, Florida.[71] In 1952, he addressed the NUL's annual conference in Cleveland.[72] In 1953, he addressed the NUL's annual luncheon in Pittsburgh.[73]

Alongside the speaking engagements, Winthrop worked hard on fundraising. In 1947, he took on the job as chair of the NUL's Corporation Gifts Committee, which formed part of the organization's annual campaign.[74] Winthrop wrote letters of solicitation to a wide range of public figures.[75] In 1950, Winthrop became chair of the NUL's newly established Commerce and Industry Council.[76] In this capacity, he further used his family influence and connections to benefit the organization. Winthrop tapped Socony for donations and encouraged his employers to hire more Black workers.[77] In August 1948, Winthrop coordinated a party for the Urban League Guild, along with

Guild chair Mollie Moon, at the Rainbow Room in the Rockefeller Center. The event hosted 350 people.[78] The following month he helped put together a charity art exhibition.[79]

Winthrop also made his own significant financial contributions to the NUL.[80] His largest and single most important gift came in December 1952 when he transferred 1,800 shares in Standard Oil of California stock valued at $105,187.50 (equivalent to about $1 million in 2020 dollars) to the NUL to purchase a new headquarters.[81] The NUL used the money to buy a five-story structure at 14 East Forty-Eighth Street.[82] Having a Rockefeller prominently associated with the NUL's work was a boon in all respects. Lester B. Granger, the NUL national executive secretary, wrote, "Merely your identification with such a cause as ours is a big contribution because it encourages the recruitment of many white and Negro Americans who will not join a movement until they are assured that it is 'accepted.' "[83] Winthrop responded, "You know full well that I am that independent kind of person that puts out when he enjoys what he is doing."[84]

Winthrop did not view his remit in race relations as solely restricted to the NUL. In a revealing 1948 interview with Lillian Scott, a journalist at the *Chicago Defender*, which was one of the nation's leading Black newspapers, Winthrop indicated that he considered himself the Rockefeller family's official spokesperson on the topic. "I happen to be the member of the family who devotes the major portion of free time to race relations," he told Scott. "If you had gone to see my father, or Nelson, for instance, on this subject, they would have referred you to me." Meeting in his Socony office in lower Manhattan, Winthrop explained, "[The company] has employed Negroes for many, many years. Our effort now is to move some of them along to jobs more commensurate with their training and ability."[85]

Winthrop told Scott about his family's longstanding interest in race relations. His own involvement, he said, was first developed on trips that he had taken to Hampton Institute. Winthrop also shared his experiences with racism in the Army during World War II and talked about how his report on veterans' readjustment had recommended eliminating segregation from the armed services and other governmental agencies. Scott came away from the interview with the impression that "Winthrop Rockefeller is a very intelligent, sincere young man who accident of birth has given privilege beyond imagination. That he has accepted the concurrent responsibilities to his time is only to his credit."[86]

Winthrop was recognized and rewarded for his work. In December 1948, the Harlem Mobilization Committee of the Urban League held an appreciation dinner for him.[87] At the beginning of 1949, just a few months after his front-page interview with Scott, the *Chicago Defender* listed Winthrop among seventeen people included on its 1948 "honor roll of democracy." Other notables on the list included Pres. Harry S. Truman for his support of civil rights; Eleanor Roosevelt for her work in drawing up the Universal Declaration of Human Rights; Sen. Hubert Humphrey for his support of civil rights at the Democratic National Convention; and Dr. Ralph Bunche for his peacemaking work in the Middle East as United Nations Mediator. Winthrop was cited for his "work with the National Urban League which has fostered the spirit of Fair Employment Practices in American Industry."[88]

The *New York Times* carried the story about Winthrop's inclusion on the list, transmitting the accolade to an even wider audience.[89] It certainly caught Nelson's attention. He wrote to Winthrop, "I read in the Sunday TIMES that you had been named by the CHICAGO DEFENDER to its 'honor roll of democracy.' This is just a note to tell you how wonderful I think it is—you are certainly doing a grand job. Congratulations!"[90]

Alongside the NUL and race relations, Winthrop developed a portfolio of other public service interests. These came in three main areas. Firstly, there was healthcare. In 1949, Winthrop became chair of the board of trustees at the New York University–Bellevue Medical Center, and he was elected to the board of trustees of the National Fund for Medical Education. The following year, he became a member of the board of hospitals of New York City.[91] Secondly, there was education. In 1947, Winthrop was elected to the board of trustees of the Public Education Association; in 1951, he was elected to the board of trustees of the Loomis Institute; and in 1952, he was elected as a member of the New York University Council, its governing body.[92]

Thirdly, there were activities related to Rockefeller family interests. In 1945, Winthrop was elected to the board of trustees of Industrial Relations Counselors Inc., a consulting firm founded by Junior in 1926.[93] In 1951, he became chair of the Housing Corporation at the International Basic Economy Corporation (IBEC). Nelson founded IBEC in 1947 as a conduit for using money from private business to fund projects in less-developed nations.[94] In 1953, Winthrop became chair of the board of trustees at Colonial Williamsburg.[95] In addition, Winthrop served as a director and secretary of the Rockefeller Brothers Inc., sat on the board of trustees for the Rockefeller Brothers Fund, served as a director of Rockefeller Center Inc., and served as a director of Williamsburg Restoration Inc.[96]

Although busy with professional, civic, philanthropic, and family duties, Winthrop did not neglect his promise to live his postwar social life to the full. As one reporter wryly put it, Winthrop's unofficial role in the family was as the

Rockefeller who "handled all the night life."[97] Winthrop was a fixture on the nightclub circuit in Manhattan at venues such as El Morocco, the 21 Club, the Stork Club, Toots Shor's Restaurant, and the Copacabana.[98] David recalled that the "very fashionable" 21 Club became "almost [Winthrop's] second home."[99]

The press frequently described Winthrop as the "most eligible bachelor in America." The gossip columns reported a string of alleged romantic interests that included actress, singer, and dancer Virginia Catherine "Ginger" Rogers; actress Rose Joan Blondell; and singer and actress Virginia Ellen "Ginny" Simms.[100] "He was," David remembered, "attractive to the ladies."[101] The most mentioned, and apparently Winthrop's most serious flame, was actress, singer, and Broadway star Mary Martin. But according to publicist Tex McCrary, a friend of Winthrop's and a rival for the affections of Martin, "It was decided that no Rockefeller should marry a woman who was famous for singing 'My Heart Belongs to Daddy' in a mink coat."[102]

This was precisely the café society crowd that Abby worried would consume Winthrop upon his return home. Having been chastised once for making this point to her son, she largely appeased Winthrop's dalliances and put them down to him "finding [him]self" after the war. Abby simply expressed happiness that her son had "so many friends." As she confided to her sister Lucy, "I think Winthrop is still going through a stage that is the aftermath of the war in which he is a little bit afraid that the family will try to manage him."[103] Junior, meanwhile, quietly fumed at his son's indiscretions and apparently avoided the topic altogether. Winthrop seemed not to care either way. "After all," he pointed out, "I was a bachelor in my thirties, with six years in the Army to make up, so what did they expect!" Indeed, Winthrop secretly appeared to get a kick out of knowing that his family, and particularly his married brothers with children, were left to live vicariously through him.[104] While it lasted, Winthrop enjoyed the good times. His footloose and fancy-free days were numbered. Ahead lay his biggest challenge since the war: becoming a husband and a father.

CHAPTER 11

Husband and Father

ON MARCH 26, 1947, Winthrop held an intimate dinner party for close friends at his new 770 Park Avenue penthouse apartment. Philip Broun, whom Winthrop knew from his Houston days in the oil business, brought along some wild duck to cook. The guest list also included George Henry, Winthrop's old friend from Yale, and his wife; Walter Clark Teagle Jr., the son of the former Standard Oil of New Jersey president and chair of the board, and his wife; actress Whitney Bourne and her husband, Arthur Osgood Choate Jr.; and Mary Jean Kempner, the *Vogue* reporter whom Winthrop had met up with in Guam during the war. The final guest at the dinner party was Barbara Sears, more popularly known to everyone by her nickname "Bobo." Bobo's presence at the dinner party is one of the first mentions of her in Winthrop's correspondence. The future Mrs. Winthrop Rockefeller exerted more of an influence than anyone or anything else in his life over the next several years.[1]

The blue-eyed, blonde-haired, and pale-complexioned Bobo was raised in a very different world from Winthrop's. She was born Jievute Paulekiute on September 6, 1916, in a modest four-room house, one of thirty-two identical row houses in the mining community of Noblestown, Pennsylvania. Her parents, coal miner Julius Paulekiute, and his wife Eva—Jievute was a translation of "Little Eva"—were Lithuanian immigrants. A year later, Bobo's sister, Isabel, was born. When Bobo was four, her parents decided to escape the Pennsylvania mines. They returned to Lithuania and purchased a family farm. A few years later, having failed to prosper, they moved back to the United States, this time trying their luck in Chicago. Julius worked as a railroad fireman, and the family lived in a small flat in the stockyards district.[2]

When Bobo was seven, her father abandoned the family. Bobo did not see or hear from him again for another twenty-four years, and then only after her marriage to Winthrop. To support herself and her two daughters, Bobo's mother worked as a sweeper in the stockyards and later as a seamstress in a mattress factory. It was around the same time that Bobo went through the first of her many name changes, becoming Eva Paul to make it easier for teachers and parents at Englewood High School to pronounce. Outside of school, Bobo spent her time swimming in Lake Michigan off the rocky and dangerous Thirty-Third Street embankment and playing as the only girl on the local baseball team.[3]

Bobo's life then took another turn. Her mother formally divorced Julius and married Lithuanian carpenter Peter Neveckas. The newlyweds and the two girls moved to a farm in Lowell, Indiana, fifty miles southeast of Chicago, where Bobo helped out with the day-to-day chores. Bobo graduated from Lowell High School in 1933. That summer, without her knowledge, a classmate entered her photograph in a Miss Lithuania contest. Bobo made the finals, and the family scraped together $12 (equivalent to $235 in 2020 dollars) for some new clothes. The investment paid off when Bobo was crowned the winner at Chicago's Century of Progress Exhibition. Bobo decided to stay in Chicago, working as a waitress in a confectionary for $7 (equivalent to $137 in 2020 dollars) a week. She saved enough money to enroll at Northwestern University in 1935 for a year and half, while simultaneously launching a modeling career by posing for mail order catalogs. Bobo later graduated to full-page shots in *Vogue* and *Vanity Fair*.[4]

At nineteen, Bobo quit the modeling world and moved to New York to work as a cosmetics saleswoman. There she fell in with a show-business crowd, began taking acting lessons, and signed on with an agent. A few small roles came her way including a summer stock part in the George S. Kaufman and Moss Hart play *You Can't Take It with You*, but money was tight. Bobo began selling off her clothes to pay the rent.[5] She finally caught a break in landing the role of Pearl in a stage adaptation of Erskine Caldwell's popular novel *Tobacco Road*. She performed in the play with a touring company in 1939. While on tour, Bobo met Mary Elizabeth Sears at a Boston cocktail party. Mary introduced Bobo to her brother, the Harvard-educated Richard Sears Jr. After a whirlwind romance, Sears proposed to Bobo on Christmas Eve 1940, and the couple married on February 10, 1941, in Washington, DC.[6]

The wedding brought the Lithuanian coal miner's daughter into the wealthy and influential Sears family, which was a fixture in the traditional upper class of "Boston Brahmins." Bobo began mixing with Boston's social elite and soon made it onto the Social Register. During World War II, Bobo and Richard moved to Washington, DC, where he worked on the staff of the National Resources Planning Board. They later moved to New York, and then, when Richard entered the Navy, to a small house in Quonset, Rhode Island.

The couple also maintained a town house on historic Beacon Street in Boston, which they visited occasionally.[7]

When Richard left for war in the Pacific, Bobo resumed her acting career. One day, she received a call from a Broadway producer and rushed down to Manhattan to audition for a part. But the producer said that he was expecting a "Negro actress." He suggested Bobo change her name from Eva Paul to prevent any future mix-ups. On the advice of her father-in-law, Richard Sears Sr., she changed her name to Barbara Sears. One account has it that it was Sears Sr. who also subsequently came up with the nickname of Bobo, an Americanization of the French beaux-beaux, literally meaning beautiful-beautiful. The name stuck with her for the rest of her life. Bobo moved to Hollywood, and her association with a high-profile Boston family gained her attention and won over notable Tinseltown admirers. These included actress Ethel Barrymore and actor and singer Walter Huston, who was the father of acclaimed director, screenwriter, and actor John Huston, and the grandfather of acclaimed actress and director Anjelica Huston. Bobo played in a number of films, most of them westerns, but none of them were hits. At the behest of her mother-in-law, Susan Sears, who did not approve of the movies and theater as a vocation for her daughter-in-law, Bobo moved back to Boston.[8]

At the end of the war, Richard Sears Jr. pursued a career as a diplomat, becoming third secretary at the US Embassy in Paris. Bobo sailed to France to join him. She enjoyed postwar Paris, mixing with European royalty and the Parisian jet set while studying French and world politics and attending United Nations sessions. But Bobo's relationship with her husband began to unravel. She wanted to move from their plush hotel residence into a more permanent home and raise a family. Richard was a career man who enjoyed the high life. Bobo returned to New York to consider her options. It was there, one night at a dinner party thrown by socialite Mary Elizabeth "Liz" Whitney, that she was first introduced to Winthrop.[9]

The meeting was far from love at first sight. On a hot, sultry Manhattan evening in August 1946, Winthrop removed his jacket and his "shirt stuck to him damply, and I thought of him as hulking," recalled Bobo. Winthrop thought Bobo "glum and moody." The next morning, Bobo headed back to Paris to tell Richard that their marriage was over. The couple parted amicably, with Bobo moving to Nevada to establish residency for a divorce, which was finally granted on October 18, 1947, in Carson City.[10] Bobo remained on good terms with her in-laws. Susan Sears called her "a very nice, sweet, beautiful girl" and explained, "My son just couldn't get along with her. There was the war and Richard's foreign service. He was here, there and everywhere and I suppose that made for unrest." The divorce came with no settlement or alimony, since Bobo sought none. In later years, feeling slightly less charitable about events upon reflection, Susan Sears sniped, "Of course, Barbara didn't take any money; she had spent it all."[11]

Bobo did take a couple of things from the marriage. The first was another new name, which she legally changed to Barbara Paul Sears after her divorce.[12] The second was a rent-free apartment in Manhattan from the Sears family's property portfolio. The fourth-floor walkup at 921 Third Avenue between Fifty-Fifth and Fifty-Sixth Streets was run down and had not been lived in for twenty years.[13] There were garbage cans in the hallway, the elevated subway line roared by the window, and a large sign on the outside of the building on the second floor read "Home of La Contento Cigars," advertising a long-defunct business. Bobo moved in with her sister, Isabel, and the two began to renovate and furnish the flat. She took a magazine job as a fashion expert and Isabel worked as a chemist in Bound Brook, New Jersey.[14]

The apartment was an unlikely spot for soirees with the sort of wealthy friends that Bobo had made, but they did not seem to mind the mess, and it fast became a hub of activity. Guests were roped into participating in the repairs. One night, Bobo calculated that there was at least half a million dollars' worth of labor busy sprucing the place up. That amount increased significantly once Winthrop became a regular visitor. The dour pre-divorce Bobo he had once known was now a vivacious, attractive, and single woman. Bobo remembered the exact occasion that their friendship blossomed into romance. The overhead light in her bathroom burned out and Winthrop offered to assist. She bought a new bulb and held the flashlight while he replaced it. Bobo determined this qualified him as a potential husband. The two grew closer and started dating. They went out on dinner dances and Winthrop showered her with flowers, candy, and jewelry. She was even invited to attend Rockefeller family gatherings.[15] Although Winthrop did not appear to be the marrying kind to his friends, this did not prevent press speculation about the couple.[16] As early as July 30, 1947, the first rumors about Winthrop and Bobo tying the knot appeared in the press through Igor Cassini's syndicated Cholly Knickerbocker gossip column.[17]

The question about the couple's impending nuptials—or not—came to a head in dramatic fashion in late October 1947, barely a week after Bobo's divorce from Richard Sears Jr. was finalized. On Sunday, October 26, a Swedish plane flying from Istanbul to Rome crashed near Athens, killing forty-two people on board. The following day, Laurance received a call from Winthrop's secretary, Thelma Van Orden. She told him that Marion Davies, the well-known star of stage and screen, and the long-term mistress of newspaper magnate William Randolph Hearst, had earlier called Winthrop's apartment and spoken to his cook. Davies demanded to know if Winthrop had just married Bobo, and if the two had been killed in the plane crash. Bobo's sister, Isabel, had confided to friends, including Davies, that Bobo had traveled to Europe to meet Winthrop with the intention of marrying him in secret after her divorce. Isabel was expecting a cable to confirm the good news when she heard reports about the airplane crash. She was convinced that the two American fatalities—a Mr. Werner and a Mr. Rush, whose initials spelled "WR"—were in fact Winthrop and her sister traveling under aliases.[18]

A frantic Isabel called Davies, who used Hearst's newspaper contacts to try to find out the truth. They were about to involve Walter Winchell, the well-connected newspaper gossip columnist and radio broadcaster, when the Rockefeller family stepped in to prevent a full-scale blow-up of the story. Laurance immediately got in touch with Rockefeller public relations man Frank Jamieson. Jamieson rushed over to Laurance's flat. He picked up David, who was at the hospital with his expectant wife, Peggy, along the way. The three called several newspapers and the Swedish airline, trying to gather information. They also called the George V Hotel in Paris, the last known whereabouts of Winthrop, learning that he had left for Italy on October 24. Next, they called Paul Orvis, the manager of overseas personnel at Socony, who assured them that Winthrop could not possibly have been on board the plane. Although Orvis did not know Winthrop's exact location, he was certain that Winthrop was only on vacation rather than dead. Finally, they reached the State Department, which confirmed that the two Americans who were on board the plane were in fact actually called Mr. Werner and Mr. Rush.[19]

Laurance then sought to provide assurances to all interested parties that everything was fine. Newspaper headlines were avoided, although the episode did set the gossip columns buzzing even more intensely about an imminent marriage between Winthrop and Bobo. When Laurance finally caught up with Winthrop, he calmly explained to his brother that recent events might provide some useful lessons for the future. "As, if and when you should get married, Frank Jamieson is very anxious to get a cable in advance giving the important facts so that the society columns for once can beat the gossip columns which he feels he can do if he has the information first," Laurance informed Winthrop. "Any additional information to the individuals above mentioned"—a reference to Isabel, Marion Davies, and others on the gossip grapevine—"will quite obviously be distributed in no time at all."[20]

If Winthrop was listening to Laurance, then he most definitely did not follow his advice, as the events that followed clearly demonstrate. In February 1948, Bobo learned that Winthrop was secretly dating actress Patricia Dane, the former wife of bandleader Tommy Dorsey, behind her back. Bobo stormed out of New York to visit friends in Lake Worth, Florida. It took Winthrop three days to track her down, after which he immediately set off in pursuit.[21] On the morning of February 7, Winthrop boarded Eastern Airlines flight 661, which arrived at New York's LaGuardia Airport from Boston.[22] Laurance was the main shareholder in Eastern Airlines.[23] At LaGuardia, another forty-two passengers joined the eighteen people already on board. After a nineteen-minute delay, the plane took off at 10:07 a.m., bound for West Palm Beach, with its final destination Miami, Florida.[24]

At 1:09 p.m., the new four-engine propeller-driven Lockheed Constellation Model 649 ran into trouble 155 miles southeast of Brunswick, Georgia.[25] The number three engine exploded, and part of the jettisoned propeller ripped through the plane's fuselage in the galley area, instantly killing twenty-six-year-old flight attendant G. P. Foltz. At 1:20 p.m., the Coast Guard received a radio report that the plane would have to ditch at sea. Search-and-rescue planes from the Air Force, Navy, and Coast Guard were immediately dispatched. Among the six-person crew on board the Lockheed plane was Henry T. "Dick" Merrill, the chief pilot at Eastern Airlines and a veteran commercial flier. Merrill had been in Boston attending a hearing about an earlier accident, and he was riding in the cockpit as the check pilot along with Capt. W. E. Johnson and First Officer N. H. Turner. Merrill took over the flight when it ran into trouble, convincing Capt. Johnson that the plane did not need to ditch after all. Merrill subsequently landed the plane on an abandoned Navy airfield strip in Bunnell, Florida, about four miles from Daytona Beach. Some passengers suffered minor injuries when they panicked and hurriedly leapt out of the plane onto the asphalt landing strip below. Eastern Airlines dispatched a DC-4 and a DC-3 to shuttle the passengers on to their respective destinations as an investigation into the incident got underway.[26]

"It seems to me that you are developing a habit of getting yourself reported killed erroneously," joked Frank Newell, after the panic was over. He added, on a more serious note, "Let's just rejoice that the outcome was as merciful as it was."[27] Laurance kept Junior and Abby, who were in Arizona, updated minute-by-minute with the unfolding drama. Each winter, Winthrop's parents had begun to escape the New York cold with a stay at their favorite small inn in Tucson.[28]

According to Bobo, Winthrop's brush with death brought the two of them closer together, mended her hurt feelings, and prompted Winthrop to propose marriage. She accepted on the spot.[29] There may well have been another good reason to get married: Rockefeller family historians John Ensor Harr and Peter J. Johnson insist that Bobo was pregnant with Winthrop's only offspring, Win Paul, who was born seven months later.[30] On February 10, Winthrop and Bobo drove sixty miles from Palm Beach to Okeechobee to apply for a marriage license. They hoped that by traveling to the remote location no one would find out about their plans.[31] County judge T. W. Conley filled out the paperwork with them.[32]

The first person to discover the news was the unlikely figure of Bryant Bowden, editor of the weekly *Okeechobee News*, who often stopped by the courthouse to find out tidbits of information. Under Florida law, it was a requirement to post the names of the betrothed for three full days before the ceremony. There on the bulletin board were the names of Winthrop Rockefeller and Barbara Paul Sears. Bowden cursed his luck, since the *Okeechobee News* was not due out for another two days. He would miss his scoop. Then Bowden realized that he could at least be the one to break the news to the rest of the world. As Okeechobee correspondent for the Associated Press, he phoned in the story to the Jacksonville office. That lit the media fuse, and soon everyone knew about the planned wedding.[33] Bobo instantly became "the Cinderella Girl" who had captured "one of New York's most eligible bachelors." Winthrop was cast as her "Prince Charming."[34]

Winthrop and Bobo telephoned Junior and Abby to tell them about the forthcoming marriage. "I can't say we were entirely surprised," Abby wrote David and Peggy, who were holidaying in Venezuela. "Both your father and I had felt that probably Winthrop's recent, harrowing experience and miraculous escape would bring things to a head." Suggesting that developments were not quite so spontaneous, Winthrop informed his father that he had taken a ring with him on the trip to Florida. Abby asked to speak to "Barbara (I refuse to call her Bobo)" who told Abby that, "although she had been married once before she was so moved that she and Winthrop were far from very calm."[35] Neither set of parents attended the wedding. Junior and Abby remained in Tucson. Bobo's mother and stepfather were reportedly "making a batch of Lithuanian cheese on their Indiana farm," although "both announced that they were happy."[36]

The press wasted no time at all in tracking down Bobo's estranged sixty-year-old father, now going by the name of Julius Paulekas. He was photographed at a Washington, Pennsylvania, coal mine waving his hands with two thumbs tucked under his galluses.[37] "I am happy my little daughter is now a millionaire," he sobbed. "I am poor, will be poor, and will die poor."[38] The news came as a surprise to Winthrop, since Bobo had told him that her late father was a titled landowner in Lithuania. "I didn't care who her people were," Winthrop told friends afterward. "I loved her; it didn't matter."[39] Susan Sears, Bobo's former mother-in-law, was gracious in her comments to the press about the marriage. Abby wrote to her expressing the Rockefeller family's "warm appreciation of your generous attitude."[40] Sears responded, "I appreciate more than I can say your writing to me. . . . I sincerely trust you and your young people will find happiness in your new relationship."[41]

The wedding was set for the afternoon of Friday, February 13, at the Lake Worth estate of Winston Frederick Churchill Guest and his wife Lucy Douglas "C. Z." Guest, the friends Bobo had gone to visit in Florida. Winston Guest's father was Frederick E. Guest, a British politician and the cousin of former British Prime Minister Winston Churchill. His mother was Amy Phipps, the daughter of American industrialist and philanthropist Henry Phipps Jr. After his parents separated, Winston Guest was raised in the United States by his mother. He found fame as a polo player in the US national team that won the International Polo Cup in 1930, 1936, and 1939.[42]

Nothing ever seemed to go smoothly for Winthrop and Bobo. The couple had to delay the ceremony. For entirely practical reasons, choosing Friday the thirteenth for a wedding proved a bad idea. Florida law required three full days starting from midnight on the day of applying for a marriage license before the marriage could take place.[43] Because of this oversight, unconventionally the wedding reception was held in the afternoon before the midnight ceremony. The fifty guests in attendance at the reception contained a number of Palm Beach winter residents, including the former King Edward VIII of the United Kingdom, then Duke of Windsor after his 1936 abdication from the throne, and his American wife, Wallis Simpson, Duchess of Windsor.[44] Other notables included Woolworth Donahue, an heir to the Woolworth chain store empire; Manuela Mercedes Hudson Vanderbilt, the former wife of Alfred Gwynne Vanderbilt Jr., who was a descendent of Gilded Age shipping and railroad magnate Cornelius Vanderbilt; and society restaurateur "Prince" Mike Romanoff.[45] Laurance and Nelson hurried down from New York to represent the Rockefeller family.[46]

Winthrop and Bobo were married at 12:14 a.m. on the more romantic February 14, Valentine's Day, in a room filled with snapdragons, gladioli, and tulips. Rev. Winslow S. Drummond conducted the Presbyterian ceremony. Bobo wore a pink linen dress and matching shoes for the traditional something old; host Lucy Guest's handkerchief for something borrowed; and a blue orchid as part of her white orchid wedding bouquet for something blue. Winthrop

Winthrop and Barbara Paul Rockefeller at their wedding in Lake Worth, Florida, February 1948. *Winthrop Rockefeller Collection, UA Little Rock Center for Arkansas History and Culture.*

wore a tan gabardine suit, white shirt, and striped necktie. Bobo's ring was a one-and-a-half carat, square-cut diamond set in platinum. Winthrop sported a plain platinum band. The couple exchanged vows, with Bobo notably omitting the traditional promise to obey her husband. The ceremony took place in the Guests' lake house before a small and intimate audience of Winthrop's brother Laurance, who was best man; Bobo's sister, Isabel, who was maid of honor;

Winston and Lucy Guest; and Lucy Guest's brother, Alexander L. Cochrane Jr. At the conclusion of the ceremony, the newly married Rockefellers kissed, and the wedding party enjoyed a champagne toast.[47] Afterward, a choir on the lawn outside performed a selection of Negro spirituals.[48]

Winthrop and Bobo spent the night at the Palm Beach Biltmore Hotel. The following morning, they were up for a leisurely breakfast at nine, viewing and approving official pictures of their wedding ceremony to release to the press. Laurance called by to take them to the Guests' home in the afternoon.[49] Later, the newlyweds traveled to a secluded island off the Florida coast for a ten-day honeymoon. It was, in Bobo's memory, the happiest time they spent together as a married couple.[50]

Upon her return to New York, Bobo sent Junior and Abby a telegram thanking them for the, "warm welcome into the family circle which [she had] already learned to love."[51] As was often the case, Junior's pleasure was expressed through a financial reward: three months after the wedding he added $6.1 million (equivalent to $66.9 million in 2020 dollars) to Winthrop's 1934 Trust. The following year, Winthrop, along with his four brothers, each received fifteen thousand shares of Junior's Chase National Bank stock, worth of over half a million dollars. Nevertheless, given the relatively unsettled nature of Winthrop's life, he still remained well behind his brothers in terms of family inheritance. Junior remained fundamentally unconvinced about his ability to handle money matters.[52]

Her return to New York after the honeymoon gave Bobo a better sense of what life was like as a Rockefeller. Everything was accompanied by a whirl of media attention, cocktail parties, benefits, and charity events.[53] She hardly had time to find her feet before she was thrown into the midst of a traumatic Rockefeller family bereavement. On Friday, April 2, Junior and Abby returned to Pocantico Hills from Tucson.[54] That weekend there was a big family reunion at Kykuit, with all the Rockefellers' children, their spouses, their in-laws, and their eighteen grandchildren in attendance. The one notable absentee was Bobo, who was feeling under the weather and holed up in Manhattan.[55]

On Sunday evening, David drove Abby down to the 740 Park Avenue apartment with his six-month-old daughter Margaret sat on her lap. Before entering her own apartment building, Abby made a point of stopping by next door to greet Bobo for the first time since the wedding. Early the next morning, April 5, 1948, Abby woke up feeling ill. A doctor was called, and as he was examining her, she died of a heart attack at the age of seventy-three. It was a sudden and devastating loss. Junior was absolutely distraught and ordered Abby's cremation the very same day. A memorial service was later held at Riverside

Church on May 23. Abby's ashes were scattered in Pocantico Hills on June 20.[56] In her death, as in her life, Junior's feelings about Abby apparently drowned out those of the children. Winthrop does not appear to have documented his reaction to his mother's passing, although given his closeness to her it must surely have had a profound impact on him.

Just a couple of weeks later, Winthrop and Bobo delivered the news to Junior that his nineteenth grandchild was due later that year.[57] Junior wrote Winthrop, "That you were married while Mamma was still with us was the crowning joy of her life; it makes me very happy." His only regret was that Abby could not be present for the birth of the newest family member.[58] The news about the pregnancy was breaking to the public when Winthrop and Bobo attended a 305th reunion dinner dance and testimonial held for Winthrop at the Hotel Roosevelt on Saturday evening, May 8.[59] Entertainers Dean Martin and Jerry Lewis interrupted their run at the Copacabana to perform at the event.[60] The occasion came with a good deal of pressure. It was one of Bobo's first major functions in Manhattan as Winthrop's wife; the news of their pregnancy had just been announced; and it was one of Junior's and the family's earliest society events after Abby's death. Afterward, Junior sent words of congratulations and encouragement to Bobo, telling her, "I thought you, Barbara, were charming throughout the evening, perfectly at ease, and know how much your presence added to the satisfaction and happiness of everyone at dinner. I was proud of you as I know Winthrop was."[61]

Yet despite the happy façade in public, in private things were not going well. Bobo endured a difficult pregnancy that was beset with fatigue and illness. Winthrop reported to his Army friend Bill Sylvan that Bobo "was a little laid low for a month or so" in May.[62] Sylvan offered the condolence that "these things are not easy for the gals."[63] Bobo developed colds, heart palpitations, and felt generally unwell.[64] Added to this were the newfound pressures of being part of the Rockefeller family and the responsibilities that came with it. Taken together, this took a toll on Bobo and her relationship with Winthrop. "I wouldn't have minded the parties and those other affairs," Bobo said, "but I soon discovered I was going to have a baby. It seemed we could never get an evening to ourselves." Bobo was constantly in the limelight and Winthrop was slow to abandon his bachelor ways. He still went out at nights with his friends, entertained them at his home, and regularly traveled away on business trips.[65]

Rockefeller family historians Harr and Johnson claim that the "marriage was marked by stormy fights and drinking bouts."[66] Arriving back at LaGuardia Airport from a business trip to San Francisco in June, Winthrop was forced to deny to the press that he and Bobo were about to separate. He labeled such rumors as "preposterous."[67] With a newborn about to enter the picture, even more pressure was placed on the marriage. "Maybe it shouldn't have happened so soon," Bobo later ruminated. "When a man has been a bachelor for 36 years, perhaps he should have more time to get used to being a husband before he becomes a father."[68]

At 8:10 p.m., on Friday, September 17, 1948, Win Paul was born at the Polyclinic Hospital, 345 West Fiftieth Street, Manhattan, weighing five pounds and four ounces. He was delivered by Dr. Edward Denman, who was assisted by Winthrop's old Army friend Dr. Graham G. Hawks.[69] Reports mentioned that the baby was born prematurely, but there was little speculation in the press surrounding the proximity of the birth date to his parents' wedding.[70]

The initially frail Win Paul fast developed a healthy appetite. Winthrop and Bobo had planned to hire a nurse recommended by Nelson and his wife, Tod, to help out. But Bobo decided that she wanted to "really know the baby and have some responsibility outside of an occasional bottle feeding." Even if it "would keep us from going out or entertaining during the time," she continued, "but I don't believe I will want to go."[71] For his part, Winthrop, Bobo said, greeted "his heir . . . with heart-warming enthusiasm and paternal pride." She hoped that Win Paul could bring them closer together as a family.[72]

At the end of September, they all began their new life together at 770 Park Avenue. Junior was delighted to have them back home and close by, telling Bobo, "I feel less lonely now that you and your family are near me again." He added, "I think constantly of how happy Mrs. Rockefeller is with her new grandchild and what joy your deep interest in and continuous brooding thought about the baby would give her. She loved babies above everything."[73] Winthrop was giddy with excitement at having Bobo and Win Paul home. "On arrival Winnie made a quick inspection of the premises and has found them quite satisfactory and has evidenced his confidence in the management by quickly settling down, dividing his time it seems to me about equally between eating and sleeping, with only enough to sharpen his appetite and prevent us from forgetting he is here," Winthrop wrote a friend. "The net result has been marvelous, as he already exceeded his birth weight by one pound and even allowing for my obvious prejudice is getting cuter every day. Barbara is of course staying pretty close to home but has made a terrific comeback and seems in good health and excellent spirits."[74]

Two weeks later, Winthrop provided an update, with both Bobo and Win Paul "continuing to improve quite apace." Bobo "really seemed quite herself again," and Winthrop swore that Win Paul had "grown an inch since he has been home"—although he had some doubts about this, because "no one with-

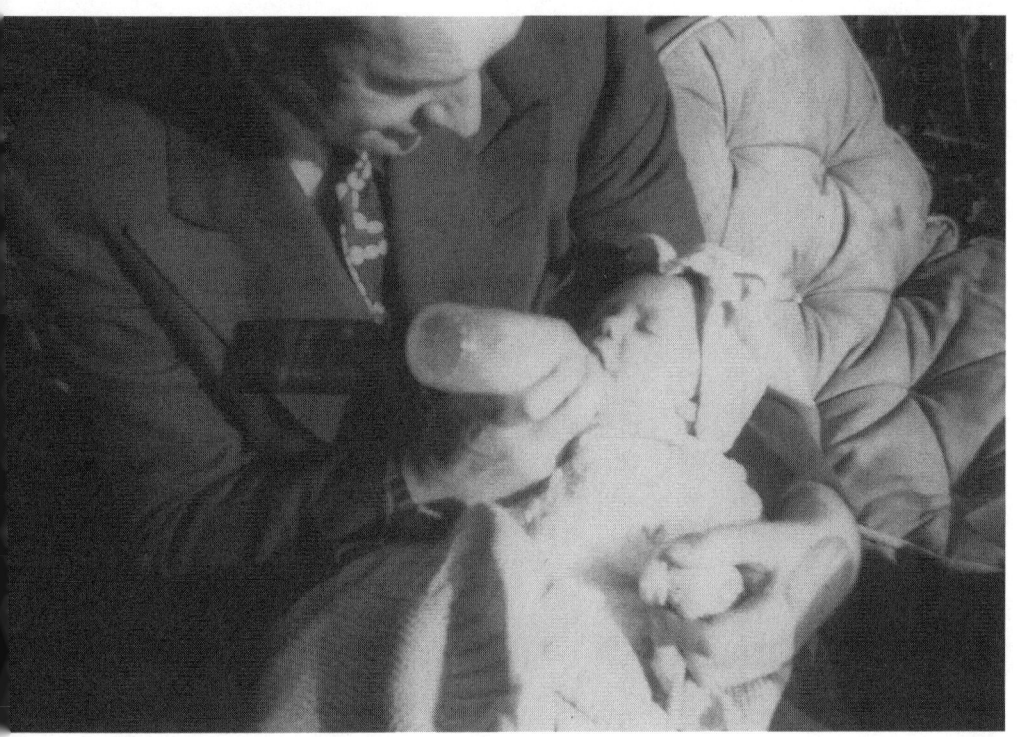

Winthrop, a future Arkansas governor, bottle feeds
his son, Winthrop Paul Rockefeller, a future Arkansas
lieutenant governor, ca. September–October 1948.
*Winthrop Rockefeller Collection, UA Little Rock Center
for Arkansas History and Culture.*

out a straight jacket can hold him still long enough to take measurements." Win Paul continued to put on weight, passing the seven-pound mark.[75] By November, all still appeared well, with Winthrop boasting to the Batchelders at Loomis, "I do not feel that I am taking parental license when I state that he is a truly handsome little fellow." Bobo was "making splendid progress in the return to her normal vivacious self."[76] In December, Winthrop wrote Bill Sylvan that Win Paul continued to grow "like a weed—almost 5 inches in length, and weighs nearly 12 pounds, and is now beginning to be quite responsive."[77]

Yet as 1949 began, the initial joyful months of parenthood gave way to the regular grind of routine once more. In January, Winthrop traveled to the Colombian capital, Bogota, on a business trip.[78] Upon his return, he was elected as the first chair of the board at the New York University–Bellevue Medical Center, a $32.7 million (equivalent to $348.7 million in 2020 dollars) construction project on Manhattan's East Side, just south of the United Nations.[79] Nelson wrote to congratulate him, telling Winthrop, "It's wonderful of you to take this on, and I know you will do a really swell job. All the family are very proud of the things you're doing."[80] In February, Bill Sylvan moved to New York to assist Winthrop with his business and civic affairs.[81] The same month, Winthrop and Bobo traveled to Montego Bay, Jamaica, for a two-week vacation.[82] Junior visited Win Paul while the couple were away. "I never saw a healthier, finer looking child. His cheeks are fat and rosy. He already gives promise of being a large man and a fine and strong one. He is a perfect darling and I am sure he and I will be great friends," he reported. "Of course, he told me that he had missed his parents but was very reasonable about their absence. He realizes that they have had a difficult year and that he has been partly the cause and that the rest and change together was good for them both."[83]

Illness continued to plague Bobo. In April, she was back in hospital for a check-up. Winthrop warned Junior that a letter was on its way to him from Bobo which had been written "in a moment of depression" and that she did not want him "to take [it] too seriously."[84] The contents of the letter remain shrouded in mystery. Bobo later conjectured about her condition, "Acute sinusitis, anemia and, I guess, just nerves."[85] On April 7, with Bobo still in hospital, Junior and Winthrop dined together. "The problems which you are facing are difficult in the extreme. The courage, the wisdom, the love and the self-control with which you are facing them command my deepest admiration and respect. I never was prouder of you," wrote Junior in an ominous tone the day after. "These are difficult days for you; you can only live them one at a time doing the best you can as each day passes. Wisdom and strength will be given to you for each succeeding day. You have been faced with countless impossible situations in these past years, in each instance you have solved the problem and worked your way through the difficulties, as you will in the present situation."[86]

No sooner had Bobo arrived home than Winthrop was off to Texas for a couple of weeks on a business trip.[87] Winthrop confided to his friend Clara Schiller, "Since our return from Montego Bay, life has really been more than busy. . . . Poor Barbara has continued to suffer from low metabolism with the result that she finally went to hospital for a three weeks stay which seemed to do her much good but did add confusion to my already confused life."[88]

There is little detailed record about what transpired over the following two-and-a-half months, but things clearly went from bad to worse. On July 15, Junior sent Winthrop the contact details of Timothy N. Pfeiffer at the legal practice of Milbank, Tweed, Hope and Hadley, the Rockefeller family law-yer who eventually handled Winthrop's separation and divorce.[89] In contrast to his reaction to Babs's earlier experience, Junior appeared swiftly resigned to the breakup of Winthrop's marriage.[90] Four days later, Junior followed up with a telegram to Winthrop that read, "I am thinking of you as you face the decisions of this week and am back of you to the end whatever the outcome. Love, Father."[91] In early August, Bobo was hospitalized with appendicitis.[92] On September 1, she sailed with David and Peggy for a vacation to Paris while Winthrop was away on yet another work trip in the United States. On September 6, Winthrop traveled to Europe to join his wife.[93] Win Paul was left behind again, and his parents missed his first birthday.[94] Winthrop spent two weeks with Bobo in Paris but attempts to rekindle their fast-fading relationship did not go well.[95]

By October, relations between Winthrop and Bobo were being discussed openly at Brothers Meetings, where the situation was euphemistically referred to as "Winthrop's problem."[96] Then, in Winthrop's version of events, on December 1 the couple entered into a ninety-day trial separation agreement.[97] Bobo said that Winthrop simply walked out and left. She and Win Paul moved to Pocantico Hills.[98] Winthrop retreated to Colonial Williamsburg.[99] There was little in the news headlines to indicate that any of this was happening, aided no doubt by the couple's handy media contacts. Marion Davies and William Randolph Hearst sent a telegram to Winthrop telling him that they had requested their outlets to go easy on them.[100] Winthrop wired back, "You are indeed most understanding folks."[101] At the December Brothers Meeting, Winthrop reported on recent developments in his personal life.[102] Neither Winthrop nor Bobo, nor indeed anyone else, ever made these events public. "This has not been an easy Christmas for you," wrote Junior to Winthrop, as 1950 approached. "You have, however, carried on like a good soldier and have made your father proud of you."[103] Yet if anyone thought that the ordeal would be over any time soon, they were very much mistaken. Over the next four years, Bobo dug in her heels, determined that she was not going to leave the Rockefeller family quickly, quietly, or cheaply.

Separation, Divorce, and Arkansas

CHAPTER 12

AT THE BROTHERS MEETING in January 1950, what had previously been referred to as "Winthrop's problem" now officially became "Winthrop's separation."[1] For the most part, the story still remained out of the press headlines. Bobo gave a tactfully handled interview to journalist John Watson from the William Randolph Hearst–owned *New York Journal-American*, and Winthrop wrote to Marion Davies, "I do so hope that now with this initial hurdle crossed the story will stay as dead as it rightly deserves, and that there will be nothing to attract further attention."[2] Davies replied with the reassurance that she would do her best to keep the story out of the newspapers.[3] True to her word, she wrote to Paul Schoenstein, editor of the *New York Journal-American*, informing him that Winthrop was a good friend of both Davies and Hearst and that she expected him to be treated as such.[4]

At the end of the ninety-day separation period between Winthrop and Bobo, a more permanent arrangement was put into place. At the April Brothers Meeting, Winthrop reported that he was searching for an acceptable apartment in which to relocate Bobo and Win Paul. He was also considering leasing 770 Park Avenue.[5] The final separation terms lay in the hands of lawyers. Winthrop retained Timothy N. Pfeiffer, while Bobo retained Messrs. Pross, Smith and Halpern, the first of many law firms and lawyers whose services Bobo employed throughout the separation and divorce proceedings. The near-constant turnover did little to help smooth the process. In early April, an agreement was struck for Bobo and Win Paul to move into an apartment at 53 East Ninety-First Street. Winthrop paid the lease of $7,000 (equivalent to $76,221 in 2020 dollars) from April 6 through to the end of September.[6] The property belonged to comedian Phil Baker, host of the quiz show *Take It or Leave It*, which later changed its name to *The $64,000 Question*.[7] Winthrop in addition agreed to pay Bobo $5,000 (equivalent to $54,444 in 2020 dollars) upon her move, along with the same amount on the first of each month until September. He also offered to pay for Win Paul's nurse, his medical expenses, and his bodyguard.[8] In May, Bobo sent Winthrop bills to pay that were not covered by their separation agreement. Winthrop sent them back with a letter of explanation and a copy of their separation agreement attached.[9]

At the May Brothers Meeting, the topic shifted from "Winthrop's separation" to "Winthrop's divorce."[10] This was easier said than done. From early on in the proceedings, Winthrop made it clear that he viewed the separation as merely a necessary first step in achieving his ultimate goal of obtaining a divorce as quickly as possible. Bobo saw things very differently. From the outset, she made it clear that she did not want a divorce, but rather sought a reconciliation with her husband. These two diametrically opposed positions produced a stalemate that made for a protracted end to the marriage.

In July 1950, Winthrop's annoyance was already apparent in a letter to Bobo in which he complained about her persistent refusal to address the issue of divorce. He informed Bobo that he intended to leave the country on an extended business trip and that in his absence his lawyer would represent him.[11] Winthrop also wrote to the Credit Bureau of New York requesting that it notify a number of commercial establishments, which continued to send him bills being run up by Bobo, that the couple were no longer together and that he was no longer responsible for her debts.[12] On August 11, Winthrop sailed to Caracas, Venezuela, on a work trip for Socony.[13] He told Robert W. Gumbel at the Rockefeller family office that he planned to be away from around four to six months and that his secretary Thelma Van Orden would join him there in mid-September. Bill Sylvan was authorized to manage Winthrop's business and civic affairs while he was out of the country.[14]

Bobo responded to these developments by vacating her apartment and taking Win Paul to stay with her parents on the family farm in Lowell. On September 18, Win Paul celebrated his second birthday there. The press reveled in the rags-to-riches-to-rags story of the Cinderella girl now abandoned by her Prince Charming. Dressed in a T-shirt and denim jeans, Bobo's hair was dyed from blonde to black, and her usually pale complexion was noticeably more tanned after seven weeks of outdoor work on the farm. She had been painting the barn and fence, shoveling gravel, chopping down trees, and tending the lawns and gardens. Bobo interrupted her painting to tell reporters, "I will never give him a divorce. I want him to suffer the way he has made me suffer; as he has humiliated me before the world." Speaking about Win Paul, Bobo was adamant: "I want him to grow up to be a man who knows both sides of life. . . . I want him to be a regular guy, not a snob in some private school." Bobo vowed to rebuff any attempts by her husband to remove Win Paul from her custody.

At Win Paul's birthday party, 120 guests "feasted on beer and a washtub of chop suey" as the children ate cake and ice cream.[15]

The respective relocations of Winthrop to Venezuela and Bobo to Lowell established the lines along which the couples' separation and divorce was fought. Winthrop, in keeping with Rockefeller family practice, looked to cloak himself in privacy and to say nothing, distancing himself from the unfolding drama as far as possible.[16] Bobo's approach was the exact opposite. Isolated, she had no powerful family or seemingly endless resources to draw upon. What she did have, as an actress and as someone who had made good friends in the theater, movies, and the media, was a sense of the dramatic and a keen understanding about the changing nature and emerging power of public relations, advertising, and celebrity culture in the 1950s. Developments in these areas were transforming the way the public received and processed information. Bobo intuited that she could harness and deploy the shifting communications landscape to her advantage by taking control of the story about the divorce and appealing to the court of public opinion. This proved a great leveler. The Rockefeller family's stance of saying nothing was fast becoming outdated and untenable. Bobo knew that garnering the maximum amount of publicity for her plight was precisely what the Rockefeller family did not want, and that it therefore afforded her the greatest leverage. The louder Bobo yelled, the more the Rockefellers winced. She expertly wielded this to her advantage.

Winthrop's life in Venezuela seemed a million miles away from the lives of his wife and son in Indiana. For the first couple of weeks, he stayed at the Hotel Avila.[17] Winthrop then rented a house near the Caracas Country Club, which belonged to Bill Woodson, the head of Standard Oil of Texas, who was taking his family on a four-month vacation to the United States. In his new home, Winthrop was busy entertaining friends, arranging dinners with influential Venezuelans, and dispatching his duties for Socony by investigating industrial relations in the country.[18] He reported to John, "The days seem to fly by, what with an endless series of interesting labor relations problems at the office, my daily Spanish lesson, and loads of such very pleasant people. The date of my return is still a little bit vague, but irrespective of cooperation or the continued lack thereof on Barbara's part, I expect to be here pretty much until Christmas."[19]

At the end of September, when the lease on Bobo's apartment expired, Isabel moved out her sister's belongings. There were few signs of any other developments. Winthrop's lawyer described conversations with Bobo about obtaining a divorce as being "a bit like the old broken record."[20] Winthrop was glad that Bobo had left the apartment without fuss, while bemoaning the fact that "the cold war goes on!"[21] Getting Bobo off the premises was one thing but, it turned out, cleaning up after her was quite another. The apartment was, according to Winthrop, trashed before it was vacated. He blamed Isabel for the wreckage.[22] No one, it seemed, had bothered to take an inventory of the house contents before Bobo moved in, which made matters even worse. Winthrop believed that some of the allegedly damaged items had in fact just been plain stolen. Initially, he insisted on getting the insurance company involved, since he put the total bill at an estimated $5,000 (equivalent to $54,444 in 2020 dollars) to $7,000 (equivalent to $76,221 in 2020 dollars).[23] In the end, Winthrop gave up on his pursuit of reparations, preferring to have the matter done with. He nevertheless remained frustrated that his distance from the situation prevented him from being able to do anything more about it.[24]

The same frustrations were evident in the way that the separation process was being handled more generally. Winthrop complained bitterly to Bill Sylvan that the people representing him in the family office were too slow at keeping him up to date on the latest developments.[25] In November, Bobo was busy doing the rounds in Hollywood. Winthrop's friend Bogart Rogers, a former World War I flying ace with the Royal Air Force, and now a movie writer and producer, noted that Bobo was a one-woman publicity show and acting like butter would not melt in her mouth. Bobo was generating headlines through interviews in city after city, with Win Paul constantly at her side. Rogers, who as a Hollywood mogul knew the power of the popular media, admitted that he was frustrated at how this made Winthrop look. He was convinced that Winthrop was losing the publicity war badly and advised, "You need a new defensive line and a completely new offensive team, from end to end to fullback."[26]

After a brief visit to the United States in mid-November, Winthrop arrived back in Venezuela with a new drama unfolding in Hollywood. Bobo and Win Paul were staying with Marion Davies and William Randolph Hearst in Beverly Hills. Bobo convinced Davies that the people loitering around outside her home were spies sent by Winthrop. Davies sent a telegram to Winthrop expressing her concerns and noting that such things did little to help the aged Hearst's ailing health.[27]

Winthrop confessed that he was totally nonplussed by the accusations. He told Davies not to believe the stories that Bobo was spinning in the press. True, he said, he had people keeping tabs on his son's whereabouts, but they were hardly henchmen. The real problem was that Bobo refused to admit that their marriage was over. As for her continual pleas about hardship, Winthrop noted that he had paid out close to $100,000 (equivalent to $1.1 million in 2020 dollars) in the past year to take care of his estranged wife and son. Bobo was, he told Davies, currently demanding a tax-free $125,000 (equivalent to over $1.3 million in 2020 dollars) per year from him. He found this unacceptable, but he was more than willing to come to a fair and amicable settlement. Winthrop believed that Bobo's posturing was about one thing only: extracting the highest possible payout to end the marriage. He sincerely apologized if the couple's wrangling had caused any upset or harm to Davies or Hearst.[28] Davies appeared to accept Winthrop's explanation and apology. She expressed regret that their longstanding friendship had been placed under such difficult strain.[29]

The episode appeared to have a salutatory effect on Bobo. As did, perhaps, the news that Hearst intended to direct one of his most trusted men, Walter Howey, to look into the private affairs of Winthrop and Bobo to establish exactly who was telling the truth. Howey was a formidable operator who had edited and managed a number of Hearst's publications. He was the inspiration behind the character of Walter Burns, a scheming, ruthless managing editor in the Ben Hecht and Charles MacArthur Broadway comedy *The Front Page*.[30] Certainly, the press headlines went quiet for a while. Winthrop felt safe enough to return to the United States from Venezuela in February 1951.[31] The return brought with it, a few months later, a change in jobs. At the end of May, Winthrop resigned his position at Socony, ending his twelve-year association with the company.[32]

On June 1, Winthrop took up a new position as elected chair of the board at the IBEC Housing Corporation.[33] IBEC grew out of Nelson's interest in Latin America and his desire to invest in the region. Founded in January 1947, it had a capitalization of $2 million (equivalent to $23.9 million in 2020 dollars), all of it coming from the five Rockefeller brothers. IBEC's first programs were launched in Brazil and involved "transportation, produce, fertilizer, hogs, reconstituted milk production, and the development of a hybrid seed corn business."[34] The IBEC Housing Corporation was founded as a separate concern in 1948. Wallace Harrison, the architect responsible for the Rockefeller Center and the United Nations Headquarters in New York, developed a cheap and simple method of producing concrete housing. He believed that this could be used to provide mass affordable accommodation in poorer countries. The first prototypes were constructed in the United States, and then in Iran and Iraq. But this was all on a small scale. When Winthrop became chair, the IBEC Housing Corporation was entering into its first large-scale project in Puerto Rico. The 1,665 three-bedroom homes in the Las Lomas project were sold within a year of construction.[35] As chair of the IBEC Housing Corporation,

Winthrop came into closer contact with family business interests. He moved back into an office in Room 5600 at 30 Rockefeller Plaza.[36]

Things remained relatively quiet between Winthrop and Bobo. When one news story slipped out in June 1951, Bobo was concerned enough to relay a message to Winthrop via Bogart Rogers that it was not her doing.[37] Later that month, Winthrop met up with Bobo and Win Paul in Chicago, the first time that he had seen either of them face-to-face since the December 1949 separation.[38] It still proved impossible to get Bobo to budge on the topic of obtaining a divorce.[39] That the Chicago meeting had not gone well was evidenced by Bobo's new outburst in the press. She contested a claim from Winthrop's lawyers that her husband had paid her a tax-free total of $128,000 (equivalent to $1.3 million in 2020 dollars) since their separation. Bobo said this was totally untrue. She still vehemently rejected any talk of a permanent marital breakup saying, "I love Winthrop. I always have. After all, he is the father of my first child. There's an old saying that a woman never forgets the father of her first-born. I'll never forget him."[40]

In August, at the age of seventy-seven, Junior married for a second and final time. His new wife, Martha Baird Allen, was twenty years younger than him, and a recent widow of Junior's Brown University classmate and lifelong friend, lawyer Arthur Moulton Allen.[41] Throughout the continuing trials and tribulations in Winthrop's marital breakup, Junior and the rest of the family tried to lend him the support that he needed, even as it pained them to witness what was occurring. When, in 1952, Junior made the final round of gifts to his progeny during his lifetime, Winthrop was included among the beneficiaries. Junior was hopeful that the "messy divorce might shock Winthrop into a more straight and narrow path."[42]

Junior gifted Winthrop $1.5 million (equivalent to $14.5 million in 2020 dollars). In addition, he set up a new trust at Chase National Bank worth $4.3 million (equivalent to $41.7 million in 2020 dollars), with restrictions in place that shielded the trust from any future divorce settlement. Winthrop and the Rockefeller Institute for Medical Research shared the income from the trust. For the children of the other four brothers, Junior set up a new series of trusts managed by the Fidelity Union Trust Company of New Jersey with combined assets of $42 million (the equivalent of over $407 million in 2020 dollars). Junior left it up to his four sons to decide the precise details of how to disburse this money to their children. Winthrop and Win Paul were not included in these trusts, since Junior had made separate arrangements for them given Winthrop's martial circumstances. Babs and her children were excluded altogether. Junior remained sour about Babs's behavior and attitude toward money.

She nevertheless benefited from her share of Abby's trust, through which she had already amassed a considerable fortune. Rockefeller family historians Harr and Johnson have calculated the value of the various financial transfers, including trusts and gifts, that Junior made to his children between 1934 and 1952. This breaks down on a 5 to 1 scale, with 5 being the highest, as follows: John 5.0; Nelson, Laurance, and David, 4.3; Winthrop 3.0; and Babs 2.4.[43]

The last remaining major asset of Junior's was the Pocantico Hills estate. In 1951, Junior created the Hills Realty Company and transferred his holdings into it.[44] The following year, he sold the stock to his five sons, although he still retained full control over the estate and paid the bills. In 1954, the brothers separated "the Park," the residential heart of the estate covering 249.5 acres, from the rest of "the open spaces," covering some 3,600 acres. They divided their shares in the Park unequally dependent upon their projected usage of it. Winthrop, who had by then moved most of his business interests to Arkansas, did not participate in the purchase. This meant that the Park was split unequally between the other four brothers, with Winthrop compensated for his one-fifth share.[45] It was not until 1970 that Winthrop sold the rest of his shares in the Hills Realty Company—those related to "the open spaces"—to his brothers.[46] Meanwhile, on April 27, 1953, Winthrop took on yet more new family responsibilities when he was elected chair of the board of trustees at Colonial Williamsburg.[47] John had held the position since 1941, but a difference of opinion with Junior about its future direction led to his resignation.[48]

In early 1953, Winthrop and Bobo were briefly back in the headlines. The Cholly Knickerbocker gossip column reported that Bobo was busy at work with a ghostwriter on an autobiography that threatened to expose all of the Rockefeller family's closely guarded secrets.[49] Two days later, in what was surely not an unrelated story, the New York Daily Mirror headlined, "Bobo Says Rockefeller Has Sent Her No Money for Year."[50]

The simmering tensions between Winthrop and Bobo came to an explosive head in June 1953 in a series of dramatic events. The opening salvo appeared innocuous enough. On June 3, Winthrop's lawyer Timothy N. Pfeiffer announced to the press that his client had set up a $1 million (equivalent to $9.6 million in 2020 dollars) trust fund for Bobo, which would pay an annual income of $20,000 (equivalent to $192,490 in 2020 dollars). This was in addition to the $1 million trust fund he had already set up for Win Paul in February 1952. Winthrop expressed the hope that in return Bobo would agree to allow him to have access to his son. Bobo instantly shot back, "My husband has always had visitation privileges. After all, we are neither separated nor divorced. Winthrop always has been welcome to see his son here in Lowell, but he has refused to come."[51] Bobo told *Time* magazine that Win Paul was "not a can of oil to be shipped over the country."[52]

On June 5, the press reported that the next Mrs. Winthrop Rockefeller, Jeannette Edris, was already waiting in the wings. Jeannette was born July 13, 1918, in Seattle, Washington. Her father, William "Bill" Edris, from Spokane, Washington, was described by *Time* magazine as a "logger's son" and "a four-times-married, hardfisted, carrot-topped entrepreneur who has amassed an estimated $10 million [equivalent to $96.2 million in 2020 dollars] by putting his hand to all sorts of ventures (hotels, race tracks, theaters, etc.) in the Pacific Northwest."[53] In November 1935, at the age of seventeen, Jeannette eloped with twenty-eight-year-old Nathan Barragar, an all-pro Green Bay Packers football player from Los Angeles. The marriage lasted only three months before the couple divorced the following year. In fall 1936, Jeannette enrolled in New York's Finch College. She left after one semester to travel, spending summer 1937 in Europe. After returning, Jeannette enrolled at the University of Washington. In July 1939, she interrupted her studies to marry Seattle attorney Bruce Bartley. The couple had two children, Bruce and Anne, before divorcing in 1948. In 1949, Jeannette married Donald McDonnell, a vice president in the New York investment firm Blyth and Company Inc. Two years later, she divorced again, and then became romantically linked with Winthrop.[54]

After moving to New York in 1950, Jeannette had worked with children in some capacity. She initially trained at the New York School of Social Work before working at Riverside Hospital, which was at the time a psychiatric clinic. She then moved to New York Hospital. It was there that she met Winthrop.[55] The newspapers alleged that Jeannette had already met with Junior, Martha, and the rest of the family, and that they approved of her.[56]

On June 6 came yet another bombshell. Winthrop announced that he was moving to Little Rock, Arkansas, to set up residence and open a business office. Winthrop's Little Rock lawyer Edwin E. Dunaway said that his client was already on his way to the state. He expected him to arrive the following week.[57] Winthrop put his 770 Park Avenue apartment up for sale.[58] In Little Rock, he moved into the penthouse suite at the Hotel Sam Peck on 625 W. Capitol Avenue.[59] Many people assumed that Winthrop's relocation to Arkansas was a cynical ploy to establish residency for a quick divorce. The state had some of the most liberal divorce laws in the country at the time, requiring only a sixty-day residence to qualify on the basis of two years' separation.[60] Winthrop never confirmed such stories. When asked directly by local reporters if that was the reason he had come to Arkansas, Winthrop somewhat ambiguously retorted, "That is the silliest question that's been asked yet."[61] Winthrop always maintained that it was Frank Newell more than anyone else who was responsible for his move to the state.[62] Winthrop had already made several reconnaissance trips to Arkansas earlier that year, and he was sold on a property that Newell had showed him on Petit Jean Mountain.[63]

Bobo wasted little time in launching her counteroffensive. She retained Louis Nizer, a lawyer who had become famous for receiving large settlements in high-profile and celebrity divorces.[64] The previous year he had won a $2 million (equivalent to $19.4 million in 2020 dollars) settlement for actress Marianne O'Brien Reynolds from her husband, the tobacco tycoon Richard J. Reynolds. He had also won Eleanor Holm Rose a record $7,000 (equivalent to $67,880 in 2020 dollars) per month alimony from her husband, showman and lyricist Billy Rose, while a final settlement was pending.[65] Nizer came up with a strategy for Bobo full of his trademark drama and panache.[66]

On late Friday afternoon, June 26, Bobo arrived at 770 Park Avenue along with Win Paul and her Indiana friend Viola Geanchos. They rode up to the penthouse together in the elevator. When the maid opened the door, Bobo jammed in her foot. The three newly arrived guests proceeded to occupy the apartment.[67] The following Monday, in a telephone interview, Bobo told the press that lawyers for both parties had agreed she could stay until the following day. The domestic help had vacated the premises, so she would have to do all the cooking and cleaning by herself, Bobo said, but she had enough food and money to last for a day or two. Later that afternoon, she agreed to meet the press in person downstairs in a room adjoining the lobby. Leaving Win Paul in the apartment with Geanchos, she dressed for the occasion, wearing a Chinese-red linen sheath dress with black trimming and gold pendant earrings. Bobo contended that she had innocently arrived in New York on Friday afternoon fully intending to stay at her sister's flat while she scouted nurseries for Win Paul. It had only then struck her that the penthouse was vacant.[68]

In a more belligerent interview with the *New York Journal-American*, Bobo told the reporter, "I feel the time has come for me to take a stand." Asserting that she would "not just sit quietly by ... while [her] husband pushes through a groundless divorce action in a state to which he has moved solely for that purpose," Bobo scoffed at the idea that he was "the barefoot boy type," who had "suddenly fallen in love with the heartland of America." To Bobo, Winthrop's move meant one thing alone: "He intends to high-pressure a quick, cheap mail-order divorce." An anonymous friend confided that Bobo's real purpose for inhabiting the apartment was "to show she never deserted her husband and was a good wife. She is trying to protect her own interests against Winthrop."[69]

This statement was seemingly confirmed in yet another interview, when

Bobo admitted to the *Daily News* that she had in fact taken over the apartment on the advice of her lawyer Louis Nizer. Bobo dismissed the million-dollar trust fund Winthrop had established for her as nothing more than a publicity stunt, noting that it was a revocable trust that could be canceled at any time. Seeking to take the high moral ground, Bobo said that the only reason she refused to divorce Winthrop was because of her son Win Paul. She stormed, "If people continue to regard divorce so casually, modern society will disintegrate."[70] As the Tuesday deadline for Bobo's eviction arrived, Nizer won an agreement for his client to stay in the apartment indefinitely. He declared that he was intent upon winning a "multimillion" settlement for her "without jokers." Part of the agreement that allowed Bobo to remain in the apartment involved her not making any further comments to the press.[71] Although this effectively placed negotiations behind closed doors, it did not prevent speculation about what was happening, nor did it stop the occasional public surfacing of disagreements.[72]

In August, talks appeared to have broken down again. Winthrop said Bobo was demanding a $10 million (equivalent to $96.2 million in 2020 dollars) settlement, with $7 million (equivalent to $67.3 million in 2020 dollars) for herself and $3 million (equivalent to $28.9 in 2020 dollars) for Win Paul. Bobo insisted upon having complete control over all the funds. When Winthrop declined the proposal, Bobo increased the stakes by filing in the New York State Supreme Court for a formal separation agreement.[73] Their respective lawyers agreed that she would hold the suit in abeyance while negotiations continued.[74] In late September, Winthrop appeared ready to walk away from negotiations altogether. He claimed that Bobo was demanding exclusive custody of Win Paul, that she was requesting an exorbitant amount of settlement money, and that she was constantly threatening smears against Winthrop and his family if they did not do her bidding. Winthrop maintained that gaining reasonable access to his son was his top priority and that he would not be coerced into a final divorce settlement. He pointed out that he had already offered Bobo $2 million (equivalent to $19.2 million in 2020 dollars) in trust funds, and that Bobo was currently receiving $2,250 (equivalent to $21,655 in 2020 dollars) in tax-free monthly payments, as well as staying at the 770 Park Avenue apartment rent-free.[75]

In October, it appeared that Winthrop and Bobo had finally agreed terms. Rumors of a $5.5 million (equivalent to $52.9 million in 2020 dollars) payout circulated in the press. *Life* magazine described it as "one of the world's record divorce settlements."[76] The reported October 1 agreement made Bobo's $1 million (equivalent to $9.6 million in 2020 dollars) trust irrevocable; provided her with a further $2 million (equivalent to $19.4 million in 2020 dollars) in cash; paid her an additional $70,000 (equivalent to $673,715 in 2020 dollars) of annual income or, as an alternative, an additional $500,000 (equivalent to $4.8 million in 2020 dollars) irrevocable trust; gave her the 770 Park Avenue apartment or a cash equivalent of $100,000 (equivalent to $962,449 in 2020 dollars); and established an irrevocable trust of $1 million for Win Paul, in addition to the $1 million trust fund Winthrop had already established for him. Finally, Bobo insisted upon a written assurance that Win Paul would be a guaranteed beneficiary of the substantial Rockefeller family trusts that had been established by Junior.[77] Winthrop's lawyer Edwin E. Dunaway said the settlement was contingent upon his client "having the right to have his son with him during half the summer school vacation and on special holidays."[78]

Things between Winthrop and Bobo could never be that simple. Bobo's lawyer Louis Nizer, who brokered the October 1 settlement, promised to have the final documents prepared expeditiously. Five months later, on March 1, 1954, Bobo's latest lawyer, Leo C. Fennelly, a former special assistant to the US attorney general, sent a draft of the proposed settlement. Before a response came, Bobo fired Fennelly and replaced him with Ephraim S. London, a former special investigator for the United Nations War Crimes Commission in postwar Germany. London sent another new draft settlement on March 16 that, according to Winthrop's lawyer Timothy N. Pfeiffer, did not accurately reflect the terms of the October 1 agreement. On May 6, after Bobo hired yet more lawyers, Messrs. Carb and Edelman, another draft settlement document was sent that again deviated significantly from the previously agreed terms. By that point, Winthrop had had enough. Pfeiffer drafted a letter to Bobo's attorneys informing them that June 1, 1954, was a take-it-or-leave-it deadline. If they refused to finalize the October 1 agreement by then, his client would revoke the offer.[79]

Apparently, the draft letter was never sent.[80] The threat alone appeared enough to convince Bobo that she had pushed Winthrop as far as she could. On June 17, Bobo's lawyer Ephraim S. London announced to the press that his client had accepted the terms of the October 1 settlement in full.[81] On June 19, Winthrop and Bobo separately signed the agreement in a New York hotel. Winthrop immediately boarded his private jet and flew back to Arkansas. Bobo refused to confirm the exact details to the press, telling them, "I frankly don't believe in revealing marriage settlements. Mine is one of the few privacies I have left."[82]

For the second time in her life, Bobo flew to Nevada to establish residency for a divorce. While there, she hired her final lawyer of record, former Nevada governor Edward P. Carville.[83] Bobo stayed at the famous Reno landmark the Mapes Hotel and started dating its millionaire owner, Charles W. Mapes Jr.[84] On August 3, 1954, at 9:14 on a sunny Reno morning, Bobo, happily chewing gum and accompanied by nine lawyers, two bankers, and a press agent, entered the judge's chambers. Fourteen minutes later, she emerged $5.5 million richer. The next evening, holding hands with her new beau, Mapes Jr., the couple attended a Hawaiian luau at the Lake Tahoe residence of Elsinore Machris Gilliland. Gilliland was the widow of oil magnate George Machris, founder and president of the Wilshire Oil Company, from whom she had inherited $20 million (equivalent to over $191 million in 2020 dollars). She had recently married another oil millionaire, C. Ray Gilliland.[85]

One of Bobo's first major purchases with her settlement money was a new five-story home at 13 East Sixty-Seventh Street in Manhattan. The property had a two-story drawing room, a squash court, three terraces, and an elevator.[86] Within a month, the news arrived that Bobo and Winthrop both intended to remarry: Bobo to Charles W. Mapes Jr., and Winthrop to Jeannette Edris.[87] Bobo and Mapes Jr. never did make it to the altar, although they came close. On February 7, 1962, a spokesperson for the then forty-one-year-old Mapes Jr. announced that the couple would wed soon.[88] Win Paul approved. He was said to be "crazy about Mapes," and believed that the "sugar doughnuts at the Mapes Hotel in Reno are the best sugar doughnuts in the world." Bobo finally wore the engagement ring that Mapes Jr. had bought her in 1954. The wedding was scheduled to take place within weeks.[89] With the date finally set for March 1, Bobo backed out at the last minute. She soon after announced that the engagement was off without any further explanation.[90] Bobo never married again.[91]

Winthrop and Jeannette did marry, on June 11, 1956, at her father's summer home in Hayden Lake, Idaho. Justice M. M. Humphrey officiated, with Jeannette escorted by her father and her daughter Anne. Winthrop's best man was Dr. Graham G. Hawks.[92] "This time," friends joked, "he's going to marry for money."[93] Jeannette had a personal fortune of $1 million (equivalent to $9.6 million in 2020 dollars) and was set to inherit another $10 million (equivalent to nearly $96 million in 2020 dollars) from her father.[94]

There was one final and very public postscript to the breakup of Winthrop and Bobo. On July 30, 1956, what *Time* magazine called "The Battle of Winrock" took place.[95] Win Paul was at Winrock Farms to spend his half of the summer with his father under the terms of the divorce settlement. Bobo sent a nurse along with him. Winthrop said that the person Bobo had sent was not in fact a registered nurse, as required by the settlement, but rather someone whom he had previously deemed unacceptable. When Winthrop dismissed the nurse, Bobo turned up at Winrock Farms with New York lawyers Aaron Danzig and Morton Bass, and the latter's wife, Mamie Bass, to take Win Paul back. In the account given by Winthrop's lawyer Edwin E. Dunaway, Bobo assured Winrock Farms staff that she was there simply to visit her son. Bobo then attempted to bundle Win Paul into her rental car before one of Winthrop's guards grabbed her keys.[96] The guard was Gene Smith, assistant police chief in Little Rock, who was on vacation. Winthrop had hired Smith to keep Win Paul safe over the summer.[97] Bobo said that Smith dragged her out of the car and tossed her ten feet into the air. She landed with a thud on hard gravel. Dunaway claimed that Bobo had been "loud and abusive."[98]

Toward the end of the day, local sheriff Marlin Hawkins arrived on the scene with his men and escorted Bobo and the rest of her party off the property. They were charged with disturbing the peace. Later that week, back in Manhattan and reportedly bedridden with nervous exhaustion, Bobo said that she was considering bringing assault charges against Winthrop and his employees.[99] The threatened charges never came. "The Battle of Winrock" turned out to be the last major public spat between Winthrop and Bobo. For many years afterward, Bobo kept her Upper East Side townhouse while also maintaining a home in Paris. She popped up in the press from time to time, always good for a quotable one-liner, but she generally kept a much lower profile.[100]

When *Saturday Evening Post* journalist Joe Alex Morris came to interview Winthrop at Winrock Farms for his article "The Hillbilly Rockefeller" just a couple of months later in September 1956, all the indications were that Winthrop's transformation from New Yorker to Arkansawyer was already well advanced. Bobo was off the scene, and Jeannette, along with her two children, Bruce and Anne Bartley, and Win Paul on the holidays, were his new family that defined his new Arkansas life.[101] Winthrop had divested most of his commitments in New York, and the now completed Winrock Farms formed the base from which he launched his Arkansas business, civic, philanthropic, and later political career. His initial projects were underway. He had been appointed head of the Arkansas Industrial Development Commission. He had set up the Rockwin Fund as a vehicle for his philanthropy. He had founded Winrock Enterprises as a venture-capital company to fund land development and local businesses. He had donated $100,000 (equivalent to $958,860 in 2020 dollars) to four colleges, two white, two Black, for student aid. He had given a further $50,000 (equivalent to $479,429 in 2020 dollars) to nine denominational colleges to pump-prime a fundraising campaign. He had provided $50,000 in

Winrock Farms atop Petit Jean Mountain, Arkansas, in the 1950s. *Winthrop Rockefeller Collection, UA Little Rock Center for Arkansas History and Culture.*

matching funds for a hospital addition. He had set in motion plans to construct a model school district in Morrilton. He had funded a model rural health clinic in Perry County. Many more projects were in the pipeline. In early 1956, when readers of the *Arkansas Democrat* voted Winthrop their "Man of the Year" for 1955, it signaled that his newly adopted state had embraced him as warmly as he had embraced it.[102] Winthrop was now in charge of his very own Rockefeller show, and he had at last discovered his very own stage to perform it on.

CHAPTER 1

1. Joe Alex Morris, "The Hillbilly Rockefeller," *Saturday Evening Post* (Philadelphia, PA), September 29, 1956, 23–25, 63–66; 63.

2. Morris, "Hillbilly Rockefeller." This and all following conversion rates in the book were obtained from https://www.usdinflation.com/.

3. Morris, "Hillbilly Rockefeller."

4. Morris, "Hillbilly Rockefeller."

5. John Winthrop, "A Model of Christian Charity" (1630), accessed online, https://www.winthropsociety.com/doc_charity.php.

6. See chapters 2, 3, and 4.

7. On the Standard Oil Company, see for example Tarbell, *History of the Standard Oil Company*; Gibb and Knowlton, *Resurgent Years*; Hidy and Hidy, *Pioneering in Big Business*; Manning, *Standard Oil Company*; and Chernow, *Titan*.

8. See chapters 5 and 6.

9. See chapter 6. On ExxonMobil and its history, see Coll, *Private Empire*.

10. See chapters 6, 7, 8, 9 and 10.

11. See chapters 10, 11 and 12.

12. See chapter 12.

13. See for example Collier and Horowitz, *Rockefellers*, 258; Moscow, *Rockefeller Inheritance*, 268; and Harr and Johnson, *Rockefeller Conscience*, 20.

14. Morris, "Hillbilly Rockefeller," 64.

15. On the Latin American trip and its impact, see chapter 6.

16. Morris, "Hillbilly Rockefeller," 63.

17. Chernow, *Titan*, 90.

18. Guy-Sheftall and Stewart, *Spelman*.

19. Chernow, *Titan*, 50.

20. Ernst, "Rockefeller Archive Center," 33–34.

21. "Rockefeller Family Activities in Civil Rights Field," memorandum from Dana S. Creel to John D. Rockefeller 3rd, September 17, 1964, series 2, box 34, folder 299, John D. Rockefeller 3rd Papers (FA108) (hereafter JDR3P), Office of the Messrs. Rockefeller Records, Rockefeller Archive Center, Sleepy Hollow, NY.

22. On the history of the National Urban League, see for example Parris and Brooks, *Blacks in the City*; Weiss, *National Urban League*; Moore, *Search for Equality*; and Reed, *Not Alms but Opportunity*.

23. "Rockefeller Family Activities in Civil Rights Field."

24. See chapter 6.

25. Morris, "Hillbilly Rockefeller," 63. See also "Rockefeller's Right-Hand Man," *Ebony*, August 1955, 17–24.
26. Fosdick, *Story of The Rockefeller Foundation*.
27. Ward, *Winthrop Rockefeller, Philanthropist*.
28. Fosdick, *Adventure in Giving*.
29. Ward, *Winthrop Rockefeller, Philanthropist*, 42–43.
30. On the Rockefeller Institute, see Corner, *History of the Rockefeller Institute*. On the RSC and the fight against hookworm, see Ettling, *Germ of Laziness*.
31. Ward, *Winthrop Rockefeller, Philanthropist*, 57–61.
32. On Abby's involvement in the founding of MoMA, see Kert, *Abby Aldrich Rockefeller*, chapter 20. On Abby's ongoing involvement with the museum, see Loebl, *America's Medicis*, chapter 6.
33. Ward, *Winthrop Rockefeller, Philanthropist*, 45–49. See also Loebl, *America's Medicis*, 328–330; and Lundgren, "Arts Advocate."
34. Kirk, "Southern Road Less Traveled," 177.
35. "Rockefeller Sees Danger of 'Gestapo,'" *Arkansas Gazette* (Little Rock), February 15, 1957, A7. On the Mississippi State Sovereignty Commission, for example, see Katagiri, *Mississippi State Sovereignty Commission*; and Irons, *Reconstituting Whiteness*.
36. On the 1957 Little Rock school crisis, see Kirk, *Redefining the Color Line*; Freyer, *Little Rock on Trial*; Jacoway, *Turn Away Thy Son*; and Anderson, *Little Rock*.
37. Don Cravens, "What Orval Hath Wrought," *Time*, September 23, 1957, accessed online, http://content.time.com/time/magazine/article/0,9171,893685-5,00.html. On Faubus, see Reed, *Faubus*.
38. On these issues, see Whayne et al., *Arkansas: A Narrative History*; and Johnson, *Arkansas in Modern America since 1930*.
39. Kirk, "Southern Road Less Traveled," 178.
40. Key, *Southern Politics in State and Nation*, 183–204.
41. Kirk, "Southern Road Less Traveled," 178.
42. On Jay Rockefeller, see Grimes, *Jay Rockefeller*. On the relationship between Jay and Winthrop, see also Collier and Horowitz, *Rockefellers*, 548–55.
43. Kirk, "Southern Road Less Traveled," 178.
44. Chernow, *Titan*, 39, 68–69.
45. Harr and Johnson, *Rockefeller Century*, 397–98.
46. On Nelson W. Aldrich, see Stephenson, *Nelson W. Aldrich*.
47. Kirk, "Southern Road Less Traveled," 178–79.
48. Kirk, "Southern Road Less Traveled," 179. On Junior's "The Rockefeller Credo" address, see chapter 7.
49. On Winthrop's two campaigns for governor, see Kirk, "Southern Road Less Traveled," 179–87.
50. On Winthrop's two terms in office as governor, see Urwin, *Agenda for Reform*; and Moscow, *Rockefeller Inheritance*, 289–96.
51. On Rockefeller and race, see Ward, *Arkansas Rockefeller*, chapter 10.
52. Brown, *Defining Moments*, 37–47.
53. See Urwin, *Agenda for Reform*.
54. On Bumpers, see Bumpers, *Best Lawyer in a One-Lawyer Town*.
55. Blair, "Big Three of Late Twentieth-Century Arkansas Politics."
56. See for example Clinton's comments on the back cover of Urwin, *Agenda for Reform*.
57. Moscow, *Rockefeller Inheritance*, 296.

58. Collier and Horowitz, *Rockefellers*, 444–49; Moscow, *Rockefeller Inheritance*, chapter 17; and Ward, *Arkansas Rockefeller*, chapter 13.

59. Ward, *Arkansas Rockefeller*.

60. Francis Irby Gwaltney, " 'Arkansas Rockefeller' Is Best Book Written on a State Subject," *Arkansas Gazette*, Sunday, May 28, 1978, F2.

61. Ward, *Arkansas Rockefeller*, 1–2.

62. Urwin, *Agenda for Reform*, 201.

63. Ward, *Winthrop Rockefeller, Philanthropist*.

64. Urwin, *Agenda for Reform*.

65. Kert, *Abby Aldrich Rockefeller*, 406.

66. Harr and Johnson, *Rockefeller Century*, 393.

67. Harr and Johnson, *Rockefeller Century*, 540–41.

68. Morris, *Those Rockefeller Brothers*; and Moscow, *Rockefeller Inheritance*.

69. "Winthrop Rockefeller Is Dead at 60," obituary, *New York Times*, February 23, 1973, 36.

70. Albin Krebs, "Abby Rockefeller Mauze, Philanthropist, 72, Is Dead," obituary, *New York Times*, May 29, 1976, 18.

71. Robert D. McFadden, "John D. Rockefeller 3d Is Killed in Auto Collision Near His Home," obituary, *New York Times*, July 11, 1978, B9.

72. Robert D. McFadden, "Rockefeller Is Dead at 70; Vice President Under Ford and Governor for 15 Years," obituary, *New York Times*, January 27, 1979, 1, 19.

73. Michael T. Kaufman, "Laurance S. Rockefeller, Passionate Conservationist and Investor, Is Dead at 94," obituary, *New York Times*, July 12, 2004, B7; and Jonathan Kandell, "David Rockefeller, Banker on a Global Mission, Dies at 101," obituary, *New York Times*, March 21, 2017, 1.

74. In addition to the other works cited below, see for example Josephson, *Federal Reserve Conspiracy*; Allen, *None Dare Call It Conspiracy*; Kutz, *Rockefeller Power*; and Allen, *Rockefeller File*.

75. See for example Morris, *Nelson Rockefeller*; Persico, *Imperial Rockefeller*; Reich, *Life of Nelson A. Rockefeller*; and Smith, *On His Own Terms*.

76. Harr and Johnson, *Rockefeller Century*; and Harr and Johnson, *Rockefeller Conscience*.

77. Winks, *Laurance S. Rockefeller*.

78. David Rockefeller, *Memoirs*.

79. Lundberg, *Rockefeller Syndrome*, 272.

80. Lundberg, *Rockefeller Syndrome*, 273 (first quote), 274 (second and third quotes).

81. Lundberg, *Rockefeller Syndrome*, 274.

82. Collier and Horowitz, *Rockefellers*, 222 (first quote), 576 (second quote), and 219 (third quote).

83. Harr and Johnson, *Rockefeller Century*, 5.

84. Persico, *Imperial Rockefeller*, 237.

85. David Rockefeller, interview by John A. Kirk, December 9, 2015, 146 East Fifty-Sixth Street, Manhattan, New York City (hereafter David Rockefeller interview).

86. Winthrop Rockefeller, interview by David Camelon, n.d., n.p., (hereafter Winthrop interview), transcript in record group 1, box 65, folders 2, 3, and 4, Winthrop Rockefeller Collection (UALR.MS.001) (hereafter WRC), University of Arkansas at Little Rock Center for Arkansas History and Culture, Bobby L. Roberts Library of Arkansas History and Art, Central Arkansas Library System.

87. "David Camelon, 52, a Magazine Writer," obituary, *New York Times*, May 4, 1956, 25.

88. Winthrop Rockefeller, with David Camelon, "A Letter to My Son," manuscript, record group 1, box 65, folder 5, WRC.

89. Winthrop interview.

90. Gonzales, *Rockefellers at Williamsburg*, 52.

91. Winthrop interview; and "Son to Winthrop Rockefeller," *New York Times*, September 18, 1948, 20.

92. Winthrop interview; Dr. Graham G. Hawks, interview by David Camelon, n.d., n.p., (hereafter Hawks interview), transcript in record group 1, box 65, folder 4, WRC; and Frank Newell, interview by David Camelon, n.d., n.p., (hereafter Newell interview), transcript in record group 1, box 65, folder 3, WRC.

93. John L. Ward to Donald Gonzales, January 15, 1970, record group 4, box 87, folder 1, WRC.

94. Ward, *Winthrop Rockefeller, Philanthropist*, 64–65.

95. "David Camelon, 52, A Magazine Writer."

96. Ward to Gonzales, January 15, 1970.

97. See https://arstudies.contentdm.oclc.org/digital/collection/findingaids/id/2086.

98. See https://rockarch.org/.

99. See the bibliography at the end of this book for a full list of sources.

100. Jane Bartlett, interview by Joseph W. Ernst, October 16, 1973, Little Rock, Arkansas, Parts 1 & 2, AV 9912 (hereafter Bartlett interview), Oral History and Audio Recordings Collection, Rockefeller Archive Center, Sleepy Hollow, NY.

CHAPTER 2

1. "State of New York Certificate and Record of Birth No. 23991, May 8, 1912," transcript copy produced April 6, 1927, record group 1, box 1, folder 1, WRC.

2. "People," *Time*, April 11, 1938, accessed online, http://content.time.com/time/magazine/article/0,9171,759473,00.html; Abels, *Rockefeller Billions*, 341; and Morris, *Those Rockefeller Brothers*, 108.

3. Johnson, *Winthrop W. Aldrich*, 4–5.

4. Kert, *Abby Aldrich Rockefeller*, chapter 20.

5. For the former view, see Nevins, *John D. Rockefeller*; and for the latter view, see most famously, Tarbell, *History of the Standard Oil Company*.

6. "Rockefeller Home Cut Off at Funeral," *New York Times*, March 15, 1915, 11.

7. Winthrop interview.

8. Winthrop interview.

9. Winthrop interview.

10. Barry W. Johnson and Martha Britton Eller, "Federal Taxation of Inheritance and Wealth Transfers," 10–11, accessed online, https://www.irs.gov/pub/irs-soi/1996-1997preprintar01.pdf.

11. Harr and Johnson, *Rockefeller Century*, 118; and Chernow, *Titan*, 623–24.

12. Chernow, *Titan*, 666.

13. On Junior's early life and career, see Harr and Johnson, *Rockefeller Century*, chapters 2–4.

14. Winthrop interview.

15. Collier and Horowitz, *Rockefellers*, 182–183.

16. Winthrop interview.

17. Collier and Horowitz, *Rockefellers*, 188.

18. On Abby's family background, early life, and marriage, see Kert, *Abby Aldrich Rockefeller*, chapters 1–7.

19. Ward, *Arkansas Rockefeller*, 81.

20. Kert, *Abby Aldrich Rockefeller*, 447.

21. Morris, *Those Rockefeller Brothers*, 108.

22. On these family dynamics, see Stasz, *Rockefeller Women*, 254–255; and Chernow, *Titan*, 627.

23. Stasz, *Rockefeller Women*, 176.

24. David Rockefeller, *Memoirs*, 16.

25. For details about the early lives of Babs and her brothers, see Moscow, *Rockefeller Inheritance*.

26. David Rockefeller, *Memoirs*.

27. David Rockefeller interview.

28. Winthrop interview.

29. Winthrop interview.

30. There is a very large literature on the subject of race in the United States during these years that covers many different aspects of white supremacy and racial discrimination. Two useful overviews and starting points are Wormser, *Rise and Fall of Jim Crow*; and Martinez, *Long Dark Night*.

31. Kert, *Abby Aldrich Rockefeller*, 208.

32. Kert, *Abby Aldrich Rockefeller*, 188.

33. Winthrop interview.

34. Winthrop interview.

35. Kert, *Abby Aldrich Rockefeller*, 154.

36. Winthrop interview.

37. Smith, *On His Own Terms*, 628.

38. Persico, *Imperial Rockefeller*, 50.

39. Smith, *On His Own Terms*, 28.

40. David Rockefeller, *Memoirs*, 26.

41. Ward, *Winthrop Rockefeller, Philanthropist*, 64.

42. Winthrop interview.

43. Ward, *Arkansas Rockefeller*, 58–59.

44. David Rockefeller, *Memoirs*, 27.

45. Reich, *Life of Nelson A. Rockefeller*, 30.

46. For Dewey's thoughts on education at the time, see Dewey, *Democracy and Education*.

47. David Rockefeller, *Memoirs*, 27.

48. Heffron, "Lincoln School," 148.

49. Persico, *Imperial Rockefeller*, 24.

50. David Rockefeller, *Memoirs*, 26.

51. Winthrop interview.

52. Winthrop interview.

53. Heffron, "Lincoln School," 148.

54. "Our Food Study by The Fourth Grade," 1922, class paper, record group 1, box 1, folder 6, WRC.

55. Annual Physical Examination, December 1926, conducted by Dr. Howard H. Mason, record group 1, box 1, folder 4, WRC.

56. David Rockefeller, *Memoirs*, 37.

57. David Rockefeller, *Memoirs*, 4.

58. Charles Dickens, "The Magic Fishbone," 1868, adapted class play, record group 1, box 1, folder 8a, WRC.

59. John to Winthrop, March 18, 1923, record group 1, box 50, folder 3, WRC.

60. Winthrop interview.

61. "We, the undersigned . . . ," n.d., class pledge, record group 1, box 3, folder 3, WRC.

62. Junior to Winthrop, December 27, 1926, record group 1, box 2, folder 1, WRC.

63. Winthrop to Junior, January 20, 1927; and Junior to Winthrop, December 27, 1926 (copy), both in record group 1, box 46, folder 7, WRC. A handwritten annotation on the copy of Junior's letter to Winthrop reads, "Note—May 1, 1933. Winthrop did not get the $2,500."

64. Morris, *Those Rockefeller Brothers*, 29; Collier and Horowitz, *Rockefellers*, 189; and Reich, *Life of Nelson A. Rockefeller*, 21.

65. David Mannes School, class reports, January 15, n.y., and May 15, n.y., both in record group 1, box 1, folder 4, WRC.

66. David Rockefeller, *Memoirs*, 27–28.

67. David Rockefeller, *Memoirs*, 29.

68. David Rockefeller, *Memoirs*, 29.

69. "Rockefellers Want to Be Better Neighbors; Give Family Dinner to the Town Board," *New York Times*, May 13, 1928, 1.

70. Winthrop interview.

71. John to Winthrop, September 10, 1922, record group 1, box 50, folder 3, WRC.

72. Winthrop interview.

73. David Rockefeller, *Memoirs*, 28.

74. Winthrop Rockefeller, "My Bicycle Rides," poem, record group 1, box 1, folder 8a, WRC.

75. Winthrop interview.

76. Karolevitz, *This Was Pioneer Motoring*, 167–68.

77. Winthrop interview.

78. Young M. Orsburn, "Museum of Automobiles," *Encylopedia of Arkansas History and Culture* accessed online, https://encyclopediaofarkansas.net/entries/museum-of-automobiles-4096/.

79. David Rockefeller interview.

80. Winthrop interview.

81. Chernow, *Titan*, 625.

82. David Rockefeller, *Memoirs*, 30–31.

83. David Rockefeller, *Memoirs*, 31.

84. David Rockefeller, *Memoirs*, 32; and Winthrop interview.

85. Winthrop interview.

86. Winthrop interview.

87. David Rockefeller, *Memoirs*, 32–33.

88. Winthrop interview.

89. On these activities, see for example Newhall, *Contribution to the Heritage of Every American*; Roberts, *Mr. Rockefeller's Roads*; Brown, *Pathmakers*; and Killion, *Cultural Landscape Report*.

90. Winthrop interview.

91. Reich, *Life of Nelson A. Rockefeller*, 30.

92. Winthrop interview.

93. Winthrop, "My Accident," July 30, 1924, diary entry, record group 1, box 2, folder 3b, WRC.

94. Abby to "Elsie," September 1, 1924, record group 1, box 43, folder 1, WRC; and Winthrop interview.

95. Junior to Winthrop, July 31, 1924, telegram, record group 1, box 46, folder 7, WRC; and Harr and Johnson, *Rockefeller Century*, 232.

96. Junior to Winthrop, August 3, 1924, record group 1, box 46, folder 7, WRC.

97. Winthrop interview.

98. Persico, *Imperial Rockefeller*, 160.

99. Winthrop interview.

100. Winthrop interview; Winthrop to Abby, n.d., 1925; Winthrop to Junior, August 14, 1925, both in record group 1, box 3, folder 1b; Junior to Winthrop, August 12, 1925, record group 1, box 46, folder 7, all in WRC; and Abby to Winthrop, August 14, 1925, box 5, folder 66, Abby Aldrich Rockefeller Papers (FA336) (hereafter AARP), Office of the Messrs. Rockefeller Records, Rockefeller Archive Center, Sleepy Hollow, NY.

101. Junior to Winthrop, August 21, 1925, record group 1, box 46, folder 7; David to Winthrop, Sunday 16, n.d., record group 1, box 50, folder 1; and Laurance to Winthrop, August 15, 1925, record group 1, box 50, folder 5, all in WRC.

102. Atta Albertson to Winthrop, August 17, 1927, record group 1, box 3, folder 2, WRC.

103. Winthrop to Anne Bartley, October 15, 1957, record group 1, box 49, folder 3, WRC.

104. Jess W. Caldwell to Winthrop, March 3, 1927, record group 1, box 3, folder 2, WRC; and Winthrop interview.

105. Winthrop interview.

106. For examples of this correspondence, see Leonard Sterling Jones to Winthrop, February 2, 1924; Henry Washington to Winthrop, January 9, 1925; and Leonard S. Jones to Winthrop, October 17, 1926, all in record group 1, box 3, folder 2, WRC.

107. Winthrop interview. On the history of International House, see https://www.ihouse-nyc.org/about-student-housing-in-ny/our-history/.

108. Winthrop interview.

109. "Social Notes," *New York Times*, June 14, 1925, 25.

110. David Rockefeller, *Memoirs*, 40–41. Quote on page 41.

111. Gonzales, *Rockefellers at Williamsburg*, 28–29.

112. David Rockefeller, *Memoirs*, 41–44. See also "Western Trip—1926," itinerary, record group 1, box 3, folder 4, WRC.

113. David Rockefeller, *Memoirs*, 44–46. See also "European Trip—1927," itinerary, record group 1, box 3, folder 4, WRC.

114. "Great Lakes Trip—1928," itinerary, record group 1, box 3, folder 4, WRC.

115. Junior to Dr. Jesse H. Newlon, September 12, 1928; and Dr. Jesse H. Newlon to Junior, September 19, 1928, both in box 4, folder 33, Winthrop Rockefeller Papers (FA403) (hereafter WRP), Office of the Messrs. Rockefeller Records, Rockefeller Archive Center, Sleepy Hollow, NY.

116. Abels, *Rockefeller Billions*, 343; and David Rockefeller, *Memoirs*, 63.

117. Kert, *Abby Aldrich Rockefeller*, 244.

118. On John's college career, see Harr and Johnson, *Rockefeller Century*, chapter 13; on Nelson's, see Smith, *On His Own Terms*, 56–76; and on Laurance's, see Winks, *Laurance S. Rockefeller*, 31–34.

119. David Rockefeller, *Memoirs*, chapter 6.

CHAPTER 3

1. Loomis Chaffee School, "History and Origins," accessed online, https://www.loomis chaffee.org/about-us/history-origins.
2. Nathaniel Horton Batchelder, "Comments of a Retiring Headmaster," October 25, 1949, record group 1, box 32, folder 2b, WRC.
3. Loomis Chaffee School, "History and Origins."
4. F. O. Grubbs to members of Newcomen Society of North America, April 1, 1964, address transcript, 11, record group 1, box 197, folder 5, WRC.
5. Winthrop interview.
6. F. O. Grubbs to members of Newcomen Society of North America, April 1, 1964.
7. Nathaniel Horton Batchelder to Junior, September 10, 1928, record group 1, box 3, folder 2, WRC.
8. Winthrop interview.
9. Nathaniel Horton Batchelder to Junior, July 27, 1931, record group 1, box 2, folder 2, WRC. On the left-handedness of the brothers, see Persico, *Imperial Rockefeller*, 27; Harr and Johnson, *Rockefeller Century*, 104; and Reich, *Life of Nelson A. Rockefeller*, 20.
10. Ward, *Winthrop Rockefeller, Philanthropist*, 35; David Rockefeller, *Memoirs*, 63; and Smith, *On His Own Terms*, xi.
11. A useful starting point in seeking to understand dyslexia is Shaywitz, *Overcoming Dyslexia*.
12. Ward, *Winthrop Rockefeller, Philanthropist*, 35.
13. Nathaniel Horton Batchelder to Junior, July 27, 1931.
14. Nathaniel Horton Batchelder to Junior, July 27, 1931.
15. Nathaniel Horton Batchelder to Junior, July 27, 1931.
16. Loomis School, Class Report, October 13, 1928, record group 1, box 2, folder 4, WRC.
17. John to Winthrop, October 21, 1928, record group 1, box 50, folder 3, WRC.
18. Winthrop to Abby and Junior, October 21, 1928, record group 1, box 3, folder 1b, WRC.
19. Winthrop to Abby and Junior, October 28, 1928, record group 1, box 3, folder 1b, WRC.
20. Urwin, *Agenda for Reform*, 121–123.
21. Junior to Winthrop, November 1, 1928, record group 1, box 46, folder 7, WRC.
22. Abby to Winthrop, November 1, 1928, box 5, folder 66, WRP.
23. Winthrop to Abby and Junior, October 28, 1928, record group 1, box 3, folder 1b, WRC.
24. Laurance to Winthrop, October 27, 1928, record group 1, box 50, folder 5, WRC.
25. Nathaniel Horton Batchelder to Junior, November 10, 1928, record group 1, box 2, folder 2, WRC.
26. Junior to David Newton, November 20, 1928, record group 1, box 2, folder 2, WRC.
27. Junior to Nathaniel Horton Batchelder, November 20, 1928, record group 1, box 2, folder 2, WRC.
28. "Extract from Mr. Jr.'s Letter to Dr. Newlon, November 21, 1928," box 4, folder 33, WRP.
29. Junior to Winthrop, November 20, 1928, record group 1, box 46, folder 7, WRC.
30. Loomis School, Class Report, November 24, 1928, record group 1, box 2, folder 4, WRC.
31. Loomis Institute, Junior Class Report, December 20, 1928, record group 1, box 2, folder 2, WRC.
32. David Newton to Junior, December 22, 1928, record group 1, box 2, folder 2, WRC.
33. Junior to Nathaniel Horton Batchelder, December 26, 1928, record group 1, box 2, folder 2, WRC.

34. Loomis Institute, Class Report, February 2, 1929; Loomis Institute, Class Report, February 23, 1929; and Loomis Institute, Class Report, Winter, March 21, 1929, all in record group 1, box 2, folder 4, WRC.

35. Junior to Nathaniel Horton Batchelder, April 11, 1929, record group 1, box 2, folder 2, WRC.

36. Junior to Winthrop, April 11, 1929, record group 1, box 46, folder 7, WRC.

37. Winthrop to Abby and Junior, n.d., 1929, record group 1, box 3, folder 1a, WRC.

38. Junior to Winthrop, April 19, 1929, record group 1, box 46, folder 7, WRC.

39. Winthrop to Abby and Junior, n.d., 1929, record group 1, box 3, folder 1a, WRC.

40. Junior to Winthrop, April 24, 1929, record group 1, box 46, folder 7, WRC; and Junior to Edwin V. Spooner, April 24, 1929, box 4, folder 33, WRP.

41. Loomis Institute, Transcript of Marks, 1928–29, record group 1, box 2, folder 4, WRC.

42. Junior to Winthrop, May 29, 1929, record group 1, box 46, folder 7, WRC.

43. Junior to Dr. Jesse H. Newlon, June 5, 1929, record group 1, box 2, folder 2, WRC.

44. Dr. Jesse H. Newlon to Junior, July 1, 1929, record group 1, box 2, folder 2, WRC.

45. Winthrop to Abby and Junior, n.d., 1929, record group 1, box 3, folder 1a, WRC.

46. Loomis Institute, Class Report, October 12, 1929; and Loomis Institute, Class Report, November 13, 1929, both in record group 1, box 2, folder 4, WRC.

47. Nathaniel Horton Batchelder to Junior, September 9, 1929, record group 1, box 3, folder 2; Nathaniel Horton Batchelder to Junior, December 12, 1929, record group 1, box 46, folder 7; and Junior to Winthrop, December 14, 1929, record group 1, box 46, folder 7, all in WRC.

48. Nathaniel Horton Batchelder to Winthrop, August 22, 1929, record group 1, box 3, folder 2, WRC.

49. Morris, *Those Rockefeller Brothers*, 108; and Smith, *On His Own Terms*, 39.

50. Winthrop interview.

51. Nathaniel Horton Batchelder to Junior, November 18, 1929, record group 1, box 2, folder 2, WRC.

52. Loomis Institute, Class Report, December 14, 1929, record group 1, box 2, folder 4, WRC.

53. Winthrop to Robert Hunter, May 25, 1957, record group 1, box 121, folder 7, WRC.

54. Junior to Winthrop, January 28, 1930, box 1, folder 6, WRP.

55. Junior to Winthrop, February 14, 1930, record group 1, box 46, folder 5, WRC.

56. Nathaniel Horton Batchelder to Junior, February 21, 1930, record group 1, box 2, folder 2, WRC.

57. Loomis Institute, Class Report, March 1, 1930; and Loomis Institute, Class Report, March 27, 1930, both in record group 1, box 2, folder 4, WRC.

58. Junior to Howard A. Morse, April 22, 1930, record group 1, box 2, folder 2, WRC.

59. Junior to Winthrop, April 20, 1930, box 4, folder 33, WRP.

60. John to Winthrop, April 25, 1930, box 4, folder 33, WRP.

61. Winthrop interview.

62. Winthrop interview.

63. Junior to Winthrop, May 3, 1930, record group 1, box 46, folder 5, WRC.

64. Loomis Institute, Junior Class Report, June 5, 1930, record group 1, box 2, folder 4, WRC.

65. College Entrance Examination Board Results, June 16–21, 1930, record group 1, box 2, folder 3a; and Nathaniel Horton Batchelder to Junior, July 11, 1930, record group 1, box 2, folder 2, both in WRC.

66. "Miss Mary Clark to Wed Tomorrow," *New York Times*, June 22, 1930, N4; "N. A. Rockefeller Weds Mary Clark," *New York Times*, June 24, 1930, 1; and "Western Trip—1930," itinerary, record group 1, box 3, folder 4, WRC.

67. Nathaniel Horton Batchelder to Winthrop, August 4, 1930, record group 1, box 3, folder 2; and Junior to Winthrop, August 23, 1930, record group 1, box 46, folder 5, both in WRC.

68. Winthrop interview.

69. Winthrop to Abby and Junior, n.d., 1930, record group 1, box 3, folder 1a, WRC.

70. Roxbury School Report, August 19, 1930; Roxbury School Report, August 26, 1930; and Roxbury School Report, September 2, 1930, all in record group 1, box 2, folder 4, WRC.

71. Nathaniel Horton Batchelder to Junior, September 26, 1930, record group 1, box 2, folder 2; and Robert N. Corwin to Winthrop, October 13, 1930, record group 1, box 3, folder 3, both in WRC.

72. Junior to Winthrop, October 3, 1930, record group 1, box 46, folder 5, WRC.

73. Winthrop interview.

74. Winthrop to Endowment Fund Committee, August 11, 1930, record group 1, box 3, folder 2, WRC.

75. Winthrop interview.

76. Winthrop to Robert Hunter, May 25, 1957, record group 1, box 121, folder 7, WRC.

77. Nathaniel Horton Batchelder to Junior, September 26, 1930, record group 1, box 2, folder 2, WRC.

78. Junior to Winthrop, October 10, 1930, record group 1, box 46, folder 5, WRC.

79. Loomis Institute, Class Report, November 8, 1930, record group 1, box 2, folder 4, WRC.

80. Loomis Institute, Class Report, October 11, 1930; Loomis Institute, Class Report, November 8, 1930; Loomis Institute, Class Report, November 19, 1930; and Loomis Institute, Class Report, December 13, 1930, all in record group 1, box 2, folder 4, WRC.

81. Junior to Winthrop, January 15, 1931, record group 1, box 46, folder 5, WRC.

82. Junior to Winthrop, January 28, 1931, record group 1, box 46, folder 5, WRC.

83. John to Winthrop, February 3, 1931, record group 1, box 50, folder 3, WRC.

84. Nelson to Winthrop, May 8, 1931, record group 1, box 51, folder 1, WRC.

85. Loomis Institute, Class Report, February 21, 1931; Loomis Institute, Class Report, May 2, 1931, both in record group 1, box 2, folder 4; and Loomis Institute, Class Report, June 6, 1931, record group 1, box 6, folder 2, all in WRC.

86. "Commencement Exercises, The Loomis School, Saturday June Sixth 1931," program, record group 1, box 2, folder 3a; Junior to Nathaniel Horton Batchelder, June 16, 1931, record group 1, box 2, folder 2; and Junior to Winthrop, June 16, 1931, record group 1, box 46, folder 5, all in WRC.

87. Nathaniel Horton Batchelder, "Report on Standard Senior Tests," June 1931, record group 1, box 6, folder 2, WRC.

88. John to Winthrop, October 1, 1971, record group 1, box 382, folder 2, WRC.

89. Kert, *Abby Aldrich Rockefeller*, 310.

90. Kert, *Abby Aldrich Rockefeller*, 247–48.

91. Nathaniel Horton Batchelder to Winthrop, July 4, 1931, record group 1, box 6, folder 2, WRC.

92. Kert, *Abby Aldrich Rockefeller*, 310.

93. Junior to Nathaniel Horton Batchelder, July 6, 1931, record group 1, box 2, folder 2, WRC.
94. Junior to Nathaniel Horton Batchelder, August 26, 1931, record group 1, box 2, folder 2; and Nathaniel Horton Batchelder to Winthrop, September 11, 1931, record group 1, box 6, folder 2, both in WRC.
95. Winthrop interview.

CHAPTER 4

1. On the history of Yale, see Kelly, *Yale: A History*. On Angell's years as president, see chapter 18.
2. Winthrop interview.
3. Percy T. Walden to Winthrop, November 19, 1931, record group 1, box 7, folder 5a, WRC.
4. Samuel B. Hemmingway to Junior, November 24, 1931, box 1, folder 4, WRP.
5. Junior to Samuel B. Hemmingway, November 28, 1931, box 1, folder 4, WRP.
6. Nathaniel Horton Batchelder to Winthrop, November 27, 1931, record group 1, box 6, folder 2, WRC.
7. The Freshman Year, Yale University, December 17, 1931, report, box 1, folder 4, WRP.
8. Percy T. Walden to Winthrop, January 8, 1932, box 1, folder 4, WRP.
9. Junior to Percy T. Walden, January 11, 1932, box 1, folder 4, WRP.
10. Percy T. Walden to Junior, January 12, 1932, box 1, folder 4, WRP. On dyslexia symptoms, see Shaywitz, *Overcoming Dyslexia*.
11. Samuel B. Hemmingway to Winthrop [copied to Junior], February 2, 1932, and Junior to Samuel B. Hemmingway, February 8, 1932, both in record group 1, box 46, folder 6, WRC.
12. Junior to Samuel B. Hemmingway, February 15, 1932, record group 1, box 46, folder 6, WRC.
13. Abby to Winthrop, February 16, 1932, box 5, folder 66, AARP.
14. The Freshman Year of Yale University, March 5, 1932, report, box 1, folder 4, WRP; and The Freshman Year of Yale University, June 11, 1932, report, record group 1, box 46, folder 6, WRC.
15. Junior to Samuel B. Hemmingway, July 6, 1932, record group 1, box 46, folder 6, WRC.
16. Samuel B. Hemmingway to Junior, July 25, 1932, record group 1, box 46, folder 6, WRC.
17. Junior to Winthrop, July 21, 1932, record group 1, box 46, folder 6, WRC.
18. Winthrop interview.
19. Philip Cobb to Winthrop, September 8, 1932, record group 1, box 4, folder 6, WRC.
20. Junior to Winthrop, August 8, 1932, record group 1, box 46, folder 5, WRC.
21. "J. D. Rockefeller 3D Is to Marry Soon," *New York Times*, August 28, 1932, 23.
22. Junior to Samuel B. Hemmingway, September 2, 1932, record group 1, box 46, folder 6, WRC.
23. Richard Brooks to Junior, September 30, 1932, record group 1, box 7, folder 5b, WRC.
24. Junior to James R. Angell, October 4, 1932, record group 1, box 46, folder 6, WRC.
25. Percy T. Walden to Junior, October 6, 1932, and James R. Angell to Junior, October 6, 1932, memorandum, both in record group 1, box 46, folder 6, WRC.

26. James R. Angell to Junior, October 13, 1932, record group 1, box 46, folder 6, WRC.

27. Junior to Winthrop, October 6, 1932, box 1, folder 6, WRP.

28. Winthrop interview.

29. "Sonny Tufts, 59, Actor In Movies," obituary, *New York Times*, June 6, 1970, 31.

30. Winthrop to Marcelle Baum, November 6, 1945, record group 1, box 17, folder 1, WRC.

31. Winthrop interview.

32. Winthrop interview.

33. Collier and Horowitz, *Rockefellers*, 256.

34. David Rockefeller interview.

35. Moscow, *Rockefeller Inheritance*, 282–83, 289–90. Quote on p. 283.

36. Murthy, "Facing Addiction in the United States."

37. Nelson to Winthrop, October 7, 1932, record group 1, box 51, folder 1, WRC.

38. Nelson to Winthrop, October 25, 1932, record group 1, box 51, folder 1, WRC.

39. Junior to Winthrop, January 9, 1933, box 1, folder 11, WRP.

40. Junior to Winthrop, January 4, 1933, box 1, folder 6, WRP.

41. Winthrop to Junior, n.d., record group 1, box 46, folder 5, WRC.

42. Junior to Winthrop, January 13, 1933, and Winthrop to Junior, February 6, 1933, both in record group 1, box 46, folder 5, WRC.

43. Junior to Winthrop, February 9, 1933, record group 1, box 46, folder 5, WRC.

44. Junior to Winthrop, February 16, 1933, record group 1, box 46, folder 5, WRC.

45. Junior to Winthrop, April 25, 1933, box 1, folder 6, WRP.

46. Winthrop to Junior, n.d., record group 1, box 46, folder 5, WRC.

47. Junior to Winthrop, May 16, 1933, box 1, folder 11, WRP.

48. Junior to Nelson, May 12, 1933, box 4, folder 33, WRP, and Nelson to Winthrop, May 13, 1933, record group 1, box 51, folder 1, WRC. On the Rockefeller Center, see David G. Loth, *City Within a City*; Krinsky, *Rockefeller Center*; Karp, *Center*; Okrent, *Great Fortune*; and Roussel, *Art of Rockefeller Center*.

49. John to Winthrop, May 17, 1933, record group 1, box 50, folder 3, WRC.

50. John to Winthrop, May 22, 1933, record group 1, box 50, folder 3, WRC.

51. John to Winthrop, May 23, 1933, record group 1, box 50, folder 3, WRC.

52. Nelson to Winthrop, May 23, 1933, record group 1, box 51, folder 1, WRC.

53. Winthrop interview.

54. "Rockefeller's Son in Job," *New York Times*, June 20, 1933, 21; and "People," *Time*, July 3, 1933, accessed online, http://content.time.com/time/magazine/article/0,9171,745749,00.html.

55. "New Rockefeller Job," *New York Times*, July 6, 1933, 23.

56. Junior to Winthrop, July 20, 1933, box 1, folder 6, WRP.

57. Junior to Winthrop, July 28, 1933, box 1, folder 6, WRP; and Junior to Winthrop, August 4, 1933, record group 1, box 46, folder 5, WRC.

58. "Guard Rockefeller's Son," *New York Times*, August 19, 1933, 12.

59. Winthrop interview.

60. "Guard Rockefeller's Son."

61. "Rockefeller's Son Flies Home from Texas, Laughs at Kidnap Report, but Has Escort," *New York Times*, August 20, 1933, 1.

62. "Rockefeller's Grandson Runs Out of Gasoline," *New York Times*, August 29, 1933, 38; and "People," *Time*, September 11, 1933, accessed online, http://content.time.com/time/magazine/article/0,9171,746043,00.html.

63. Robert L. Blaffer to Junior, September 5, 1933, box 4, folder 33, WRP.

64. Junior to Robert L. Blaffer, August 25, 1933, box 4, folder 33, WRP.

65. Junior to Winthrop, September 11, 1933, box 1, folder 6, WRP.

66. Junior to Winthrop, September 9, 1933, box 1, folder 6, WRP.

67. Winthrop interview.

68. Junior to Winthrop, September 27, 1933, record group 1, box 46, folder 5, WRC.

69. Hollon A. Farr to Winthrop, June 30, 1933, record group 1, box 7, folder 5a, WRC.

70. A. K. Merritt to Junior, October 7, 1933, telegram, record group 1, box 46, folder 6, WRC.

71. Clarence W. Mendel to Junior, October 9, 1933, record group 1, box 46, folder 6, WRC.

72. James R. Angell to Junior, October 10, 1933, telegram, record group 1, box 46, folder 6, WRC.

73. James R. Angell to Junior, October 12, 1933, record group 1, box 46, folder 6, WRC.

74. Junior to Winthrop, October 7, 1933, telegram, record group 1, box 46, folder 3, WRC.

75. Winthrop to Abby and Junior, n.d., record group 1, box 46, folder 3, WRC.

76. Winthrop interview.

77. Clarence W. Mendel to Junior, February 2, 1934, record group 1, box 46, folder 3, WRC.

78. Junior to Winthrop, May 31 [no year], record group 1, box 46, folder 5; and "Report of Induction of Selective Service Man," January 22, 1941, 2, record group 1, box 54, folder unnumbered and untitled, both in WRC.

79. Winthrop interview.

80. Junior to James R. Angell, January 31, 1934, record group 1, box 46, folder 3, WRC.

81. James R. Angell to Junior, January 29, 1934, record group 1, box 46, folder 3, WRC.

82. Junior to Clarence W. Mendel, February 5, 1934, record group 1, box 46, folder 3, WRC.

83. "W. A. Rockefeller Resigns from Yale," *New York Times*, February 6, 1934, 23.

84. Harr and Johnson, *Rockefeller Century*, 390.

85. See for example Reich, *Life of Nelson A. Rockefeller*, 155; and Chernow, *Titan*, 660.

86. Harr and Johnson, *Rockefeller Century*, 539n15.

87. Harr and Johnson, *Rockefeller Century*, 539n15.

88. John to Faith Rockefeller, February 21, 1934, series 1, subseries 2, box 33, folder 305, JDR3P.

CHAPTER 5

1. Winthrop interview.

2. Winthrop interview.

3. Junior to Bill Alton, February 19, 1934, record group 1, box 1, folder 6, WRC.

4. Junior to Bill Alton, February 19, 1934.

5. Junior to Winthrop, February 19, 1934, record group 1, box 1, folder 6, WRC.

6. Junior to Winthrop, February 20, 1934, record group 1, box 1, folder 6, WRC.

7. Winthrop to Junior, March 26, 1934, record group 1, box 6, folder 14a, WRC.

8. Winthrop interview.

9. Junior to Senior, February 17, 1934, in Ernst, *"Dear Father"/"Dear Son"*, 190–92.

10. Winthrop to Abby, February 20, 1934, telegram, record group 1, box 6, folder 14b, WRC. For background on the Texas oil industry, see for example Larson and Porter, *History of Humble Oil and Refining Company*; Olien and Olien, *Oil in Texas*; Sterling and Kilman, *Ross Sterling, Texan*; and Burrough, *Big Rich*.

11. Smith, *On His Own Terms*, 49.

12. Winthrop interview.

13. Winthrop interview; and Morris, *Those Rockefeller Brothers*, 110.

14. Junior to Winthrop, June 29, 1934, record group 1, box 46, folder 4, WRC.

15. Winthrop interview.

16. Winthrop interview; and Junior to Winthrop, February 28, 1934, record group 1, box 1, folder 6, WRC.

17. "Extract from letter from Winthrop Rockefeller to Mr. and Mrs. John D. Rockefeller, Jr., dated March 15, 1934," box 1, folder 9, WRP.

18. "Extract from letter . . . dated March 15, 1934."

19. Winthrop interview.

20. "Extract from letter from Winthrop Rockefeller to Mr. and Mrs. John D. Rockefeller, Jr., dated March 15, 1934," box 1, folder 9, WRP.

21. "Extract from letter . . . dated March 15, 1934."

22. "Excerpts from letter from John D. Rockefeller, Jr. to Winthrop Rockefeller, March 20, 1934," box 1, folder 9, WRP.

23. Abby to Winthrop, March 20, 1934, box 5, folder 66, AARP.

24. Nelson to Winthrop, April 11, 1934, record group 1, box 51, folder 1, WRC.

25. Wallace E. Pratt to William S. Farish II, March 14, 1934, box 4, folder 33, WRP; and Winthrop interview.

26. D. P. Carlton to Winthrop, May 7, 1934; and Wallace E. Pratt to Winthrop and Bill Alton, June 12, 1934, both in record group 1, box 5, folder 5, WRC.

27. Wallace E. Pratt to Winthrop and Bill Alton, June 12, 1934, record group 1, box 5, folder 5, WRC.

28. Winthrop to Abby and Junior, May 5, 1934, record group 1, box 6, folder 14a, WRC.

29. Winthrop interview.

30. Winthrop to Abby and Junior, April 30, 1934, record group 1, box 6, folder 14a, WRC.

31. Winthrop interview. On the term *roustabout*, see Larson and Porter, *History of Humble Oil and Refining Company*, 122–23.

32. Winthrop interview.

33. Winthrop to Abby and Junior, June 6, 1934, record group 1, box 6, folder 14a, WRC.

34. Winthrop interview.

35. Winthrop interview.

36. Winthrop interview. On Edgar Gardner Tobin, see Franks and Dempsey, *American Aces of World War I*, 82, 87.

37. Winthrop interview.

38. Winthrop to Abby and Junior, June 10, 1934, record group 1, box 6, folder 14a, WRC.

39. C. E. Shaw to Abby, July 13, 1934, record group 1, box 46, folder 3, WRC.

40. Winthrop to Junior, July 15, 1934, series 3, subseries 2, box 33, folder 305, JDR3P.

41. Winthrop to Abby and Junior, April 22, 1934, record group 1, box 6, folder 14a, WRC.

42. Winthrop interview.

43. Winthrop interview.

44. Junior to Winthrop, June 29, 1934, record group 1, box 46, folder 4, WRC.

45. Junior to Winthrop, June 29, 1934, WRC.

46. Winthrop to Abby and Junior, July 6, 1934, record group 1, box 6, folder 14a, WRC.

47. Winthrop to Abby and Junior, July 14, 1934, record group 1, box 6, folder 14a, WRC.

48. "L.S. Rockefeller Weds Miss French," *New York Times*, August 16, 1934, 14; and Kert, *Abby Aldrich Rockefeller*, 368.

49. Winthrop to Abby and Junior, October 7, 1934, record group 1, box 6, folder 14a,

WRC; and Winthrop interview. On the term *roughneck*, see Larson and Porter, *History of Humble Oil and Refining Company*, 121–22.

50. Winthrop interview.

51. Winthrop interview.

52. Winthrop to Abby and Junior, November 17, 1934, record group 1, box 6, folder 14a, WRC; and "A Rockefeller's New Job," *New York Times*, February 9, 1935, 10.

53. Winthrop interview; and "Business: Oil Week," *Time*, February 1, 1937, accessed online, http://content.time.com/time/magazine/article/0,9171,788678,00.html.

54. Winthrop interview.

55. Winthrop interview.

56. Junior to Winthrop, March 6, 1935, record group 1, box 46, folder 4, WRC.

57. Winthrop to Abby and Junior, December 19, 1934, record group 1, box 6, folder 14a, WRC. See also Johnson, *Winthrop W. Aldrich*, 193.

58. Nelson to Winthrop, n.d., record group 1, box 51, folder 1, WRC.

59. Winthrop to Abby and Junior, December 19, 1934, record group 1, box 6, folder 14a, WRC.

60. Junior to Winthrop, December 19, 1934, box 1, folder 6, WRP.

61. Junior to Winthrop, December 26, 1934, box 1, folder 6, WRP.

62. "Copy of letter from Winthrop Rockefeller to Laurance S. Rockefeller, Jennings, La., January 14, 1935," box 1, folder 9, WRP.

63. David Rockefeller, *Memoirs*, 73–75.

64. Stasz, *Rockefeller Women*, 274.

65. David Rockefeller, *Memoirs*, 73–75.

66. Harr and Johnson, *Rockefeller Century*, 358–61.

67. Winthrop to Junior, February 12, 1935, box 1, folder 6, WRP; and "A Rockefeller's New Job," *New York Times*, February 9, 1935, 10.

68. Winthrop to Abby and Junior, February 11, 1935, record group 1, box 6, folder 14a, WRC.

69. Winthrop interview.

70. Junior to Winthrop, February 6, 1935, box 1, folder 6, WRP.

71. Junior to Winthrop, March 2, 1935, box 1, folder 6, WRP.

72. Winthrop to Abby and Junior, March 13, 1935, record group 1, box 6, folder 14a, WRC.

73. Junior to Winthrop, March 6, 1935, record group 1, box 46, folder 4, WRC.

74. Winthrop to Abby and Junior, March 13, 1935.

75. Junior to Winthrop, March 16, 1935, box 1, folder 6, WRP.

76. "Not Rockefeller to Him," *New York Times*, April 4, 1935, 3; and "Winthrop Rockefeller Fined $10," *New York Times*, April 5, 1935, 17.

77. Wallace E. Pratt to Junior, March 9, 1935, box 4, folder 33, WRP.

78. Junior to Winthrop, March 11, 1935, record group 1, box 46, folder 4, WRC; and Junior to Winthrop, June 28, 1935, box 1, folder 6, WRP.

79. Winthrop interview.

80. Winthrop interview.

81. Winthrop interview.

82. Dalzell and Dalzell, *House the Rockefellers Built*, 181.

83. Winthrop interview.

84. Winthrop interview.

85. Brown, *Rockefeller Medicine Men*, 148–49.

86. On Julius Rosenwald, the Rosenwald Fund, and race, see for example Ascoli, *Julius Rosenwald*; Schulman, *Force for Change*; Deutsch, *You Need a Schoolhouse*; Perkins,

Edwin Rogers Embree; Diner, *Julius Rosenwald;* and Johnson-Jones, *African American Struggle for Library Equality.*

87. Winthrop interview.

88. Gamble and Brown, "Midian Othello Bousfield." See also Gamble, *Making a Place for Ourselves.*

89. Winthrop interview.

90. Winthrop interview.

91. Winthrop interview.

92. Winthrop interview.

93. Ward, *Arkansas Rockefeller,* chapter 10.

94. Winthrop interview.

95. Winthrop interview.

96. Winthrop interview.

97. Junior to Winthrop, January 7, 1937, box 1, folder 6, WRP.

98. Junior to Winthrop, January 14, 1937, box 1, folder 6, WRP; "A Rockefeller Quits Job," *New York Times,* January 19, 1937, 25; and "Winthrop Rockefeller Ends Oil Fields Apprenticeship," *Wall Street Journal,* January 19, 1937, 3.

99. "Extract from letter of Mr. David B. Harris, Houston, Texas, to Mr. John D. Rockefeller, Jr., dated March 16, 1935," box 1, folder 9, WRP.

100. Nelson to Winthrop, n.d., box 51, folder 1, WRP.

101. Junior to Winthrop, December 23, 1935, box 1, folder 6, WRP.

102. Wallace E. Pratt to Junior, February 4, 1937, record group 1, box 46, folder 3, WRC.

CHAPTER 6

1. Junior to Winthrop, February 10, 1937, box 1, folder 6, WRP.

2. Junior to Kenneth R. Kingsbury, January 29, 1937, record group 1, box 46, folder 3, WRC.

3. Winthrop to Abby, February 1, 1937, record group 1, box 6, folder 14a, WRC.

4. "Winthrop," itinerary, box 5, folder 41, WRP.

5. Winthrop to Abby and Junior, telegram, February 20, 1937, record group 1, box 6, folder 14a, WRC.

6. Winthrop to Abby and Junior, telegram, February 24, 1937, record group 1, box 6, folder 14a, WRC.

7. Junior to Winthrop, February 25, 1937, record group 1, box 46, folder 2, WRC.

8. Winthrop to Abby and Junior, telegram, March 2, 1937, record group 1, box 6, folder 14a, WRC. On Frank A. Vanderlip, see Mack, *Frank A. Vanderlip.*

9. Junior to Winthrop, March 16, 1937, box 1, folder 6, WRP.

10. Winthrop to Abby and Junior, telegram, March 15, 1937, record group 1, box 6, folder 14a, WRC.

11. Ralph K. Davies to Kenneth R. Kingsbury, memorandum, March 8, 1937, record group 1, box 46, folder 3, WRC.

12. Collier and Horowitz, *Rockefellers,* 207–10.

13. Collier and Horowitz, *Rockefellers,* 207–10.

14. "Notes of Social Activities in New York and Elsewhere," *New York Times,* March 31, 1937, 27; and Winthrop interview.

15. Winthrop interview.

16. "Final Revised Itinerary South American Trip, Itinerary for Mr. Nelson A. Rockefeller and Party, March 18, 1937," box 5, folder 41, WRP.

17. Collier and Horowitz, *Rockefellers*, 210.

18. "Final Revised Itinerary South American Trip."

19. Winthrop to Abby and Junior, n.d., record group 1, box 6, folder 14a, WRC.

20. "Final Revised Itinerary South American Trip."

21. Winthrop interview.

22. "Final Revised Itinerary South American Trip."

23. Winthrop interview.

24. "Final Revised Itinerary South American Trip."

25. "Rockefeller Party Safe in Plane Crash in Peru," *New York Times*, May 21, 1937, 5.

26. Winthrop to John Susman, June 8, 1937, record group 1, box 44, folder 4, WRC.

27. "Son and Family Remain Secluded," *New York Times*, May 24, 1937, 10.

28. Collier and Horowitz, *Rockefellers*, 210–14.

29. Morris, *Those Rockefeller Brothers*, 224.

30. Collier and Horowitz, *Rockefellers*, 210–14.

31. Durr, *Rodman Rockefeller*, 10.

32. Durr, *Rodman Rockefeller*, 12.

33. Smith, "Rockefeller Brothers," 199.

34. For a more sympathetic account of Nelson's involvement in Latin America, see for example Rivas, *Missionary Capitalist*; and for a more critical account, see for example Colby and Dennet, *Thy Will Be Done.*

35. Winthrop interview.

36. "Memorandum Re: Texas Ranch from WR and Nelson, July 20, 1937," record group 1, box 51, folder 1, WRC.

37. Persico, *Imperial Rockefeller*, 284; and Colby and Dennet, *Thy Will Be Done*, 298.

38. Winthrop to Winthrop Aldrich, July 19, 1937, record group 1, box 49, folder 3, WRC.

39. Winthrop Aldrich to Winthrop, July 22, 1937, record group 1, box 49, folder 3, WRC.

40. Charles C. Huitt to Winthrop, September 9, 1937, record group 1, box 9, folder 2a, WRC.

41. James Hudson, interview by Linda Edgerly, May 1, 1973, Room 5600, 30 Rockefeller Plaza, New York, New York, Part 1, AV 9910 (hereafter Hudson interview, part 1), Oral History and Audio Recordings Collection, Rockefeller Archive Center, Sleepy Hollow, NY.

42. Charles C. Huitt to Winthrop, September 9, 1937, record group 1, box 9, folder 2a, WRC.

43. Hudson interview, part 1; and Morris, *Those Rockefeller Brothers*, 122.

44. Winthrop to Charles C. Huitt, September 13, 1937, record group 1, box 9, folder 2a, WRC.

45. Morris, *Those Rockefeller Brothers*, 122.

46. Hudson interview, part 1. On the Dunbar Apartments, see Reed, *Not Alms but Opportunity*, 48–58.

47. Junior to Winthrop, November 6, 1937, box 1, folder 6, WRP.

48. Winthrop interview.

49. Harr and Johnson, *Rockefeller Century*, 391.

50. Winthrop interview.

51. Winthrop interview.

52. Winthrop interview.

53. Winthrop interview.

54. Harr and Johnson, *Rockefeller Century*, 391.

55. Winthrop interview.

56. Harr and Johnson, *Rockefeller Century*, 391.

57. Hudson interview, part 1.

58. "Confidential Notes for Mr. Winthrop Rockefeller on the New York Urban League, November 4, 1940," record group 1, box 6, folder 7, WRC.

59. Winthrop's activities with Air Youth of America are documented in record group 1, box 10, folders 1a and 1b, WRC. See also Morris, *Those Rockefeller Brothers*, 104, 114.

60. Winthrop interview.

61. Winthrop interview.

62. Winthrop interview. On Saudi Arabia and Aramco, see for example Yergin, *Prize*; Brown, *Oil, God and Gold*; and Wald, *Saudi, Inc.*

63. Winthrop interview.

64. Othman, *With their Bare Hands*, 33.

65. Winthrop interview.

66. Winthrop interview.

67. Winthrop interview.

68. Kington, *Forgotten Summers*, 180.

69. "Plattsburgh Posts Sought By 1,933," *New York Times*, June 25, 1940, 12.

70. "Plattsburgh Lists 800 For Training," *New York Times*, June 29, 1940, 32.

71. "Life Goes to Plattsburgh Barracks," *Life*, July 29, 1940, 87.

72. "Plattsburgh Lists 800 For Training."

73. On Patterson and the war effort, see Eiler, *Mobilizing America*.

74. Collier and Horowitz, *Rockefellers*, 255.

75. "Plattsburgh 'Army' Begins Its Training," *New York Times*, July 6, 1940, 8.

76. Junior to Winthrop, July 8, 1940, box 22, folder 6, WRP.

77. "David Rockefeller Will Marry Margaret McGrath of Mt. Kisco," *New York Times*, July 10, 1940, 16.

78. "Joe" to Winthrop, July 12, 1940, record group 1, box 6, folder 4, WRC.

79. Kert, *Abby Aldrich Rockefeller*, 436–37.

80. "Copy of letter from Winthrop Rockefeller to Mr. and Mrs. John D. Rockefeller, Jr., on letterhead 'Plattsburg Barracks, New York," July 22, 1940, box 1, folder 9, WRP.

81. "Life Goes to Plattsburgh Barracks," 87.

82. Winthrop interview; and Junior to Winthrop, July 25, 1940, box 1, folder 6, WRP.

83. Kennedy, *Freedom From Fear*, 459.

84. Winthrop interview; and Gonzales, *Rockefellers at Williamsburg*, 21.

85. Harr and Johnson, *Rockefeller Century*, 393.

86. David Rockefeller, *Memoirs*, chapter 9; and Harr and Johnson, *Rockefeller Conscience*, 14.

87. Harr and Johnson, *Rockefeller Conscience*, 14–15. Quote on p. 15.

88. "Rockefeller Son to Go into Army," *New York Times*, January 2, 1941, 14.

89. "310 Inducted Here Under Third Call," *New York Times*, January 21, 1941, 28.

CHAPTER 7

1. "Persecution of the Rich," *Time*, Monday, February 3, 1941, accessed online, http://content.time.com/time/magazine/article/0,9171,765196,00.html.

2. "Persecution of the Rich"; and "Rockefeller Son in the Army Now," *New York Times*, January 23, 1941, 14. All quotes from the *New York Times* article.

3. "Rockefeller Son in the Army Now."

4. Winthrop interview.

5. "Rockefeller Son in the Army Now."

6. "Persecution of the Rich."

7. Morris, *Those Rockefeller Brothers*, 115.

8. "Persecution of the Rich."

9. Nelson to Winthrop, January 24, 1941, record group 1, box 51, folder 2, WRC.

10. John to Winthrop, February 7, 1941, series 3, subseries 2, box 33, folder 305, JDR3P.

11. Laurance to Winthrop, February 8, 1941, record group 1, box 50, folder 5, WRC.

12. Junior to Winthrop, February 7, 1941, box 1, folder 7, WRP.

13. "No Reason Why the Normal Should Be Notable," *Visalia Times-Delta* (Visalia, CA), February 14, 1941, clipping in record group 1, box 55, folder 3, WRC.

14. Winthrop interview.

15. Marshall Newton, " 'Mr.' Rockefeller Is Not at Fort Dix," January 24, 1941, *New York Times*, 10.

16. "Rockefeller Ends Duty at Fort Dix," *New York Times*, January 25, 1941, 8; and Winthrop interview.

17. Winthrop interview.

18. Winthrop to Abby and Junior, January 27, 1941, box 4, folder 67, AARP.

19. Winthrop to Abby and Junior, January 27, 1941.

20. Winthrop interview.

21. Morris, *Those Rockefeller Brothers*, 115.

22. Winthrop to Abby and Junior, January 27, 1941, box 5, folder 67, AARP.

23. Winthrop to Abby and Junior, February 14, 1941, box 5, folder 67, AARP.

24. Winthrop to Abby and Junior, February 27, 1941, box 5, folder 67, AARP.

25. Winthrop interview.

26. Winthrop interview.

27. Winthrop to Abby and Junior, March 20, 1941, box 5, folder 67, AARP.

28. "Copy of letter from Lt. General H. A. Drum, Commanding General, First Army, Governors Island, New York, to Junior, April 8, 1941," box 1, folder 9, WRP.

29. Winthrop to Joseph Rovensky, April 28, 1941, record group 1, box 16, folder 4, WRC.

30. Winthrop interview.

31. George Ross, "Private Rockefeller Drops 24 pounds at Fort Devens," *Washington D.C. News*, May 21, 1941, clipping in record group 1, box 55, folder 3, WRC.

32. "ARMY: Colonel T.R.," *Time*, May 5, 1941, accessed online, http://content.time.com/time/magazine/article/0,9171,795174,00.html.

33. Winthrop interview.

34. "Army's Richest Private to Celebrate—On Payday," *Daily News* (Chicago), May 29, 1941, clipping in record group 1, box 55, folder 3, WRC; and Winthrop interview.

35. "Rockefeller Gives His Family's Creed," *New York Times*, July 9, 1941, 1. See "The Credo of John D. Rockefeller, Jr.," accessed online, https://library.brown.edu/create/rock50/the-credo-of-john-d-rockefeller-jr/.

36. "Rockefeller Gives His Family's Creed."

37. Junior to Winthrop, July 10, 1941, box 1, folder 7, WRP.

38. "Troops Are Back from Army Games," *New York Times*, August 15, 1941, 15.

NOTES 211

39. Winthrop to Abby and Junior, July 14, 1941, box 5, folder 67, WRP.

40. Junior to Winthrop, July 14, 1941, box 1, folder 7, WRP.

41. Winthrop to Abby and Junior, July 14, 1941, box 5, folder 67, AARP.

42. Winthrop to Abby and Junior, July 27, box 5, folder 67, AARP.

43. Winthrop to Abby and Junior, July 30, 1941, box 5, folder 67, AARP.

44. Winthrop interview.

45. "Troops Are Back From Army Games."

46. "People: War and Defense," *Time*, August 25, 1941, accessed online, http://content
.time.com/time/magazine/article/0,9171,766004,00.html.

47. Junior to Winthrop, August 27, 1941, box 1, folder 7, WRP.

48. Capt. J. W. Bowen to Junior, August 29, 1941, box 3, folder 21, WRP.

49. Junior to Winthrop, September 10, 1941, box 1, folder 7, WRP.

50. Winthrop interview.

51. "Winthrop Rockefeller Advanced," *New York Times*, January 24, 1942, 9; and "People:
Uniforms," *Time*, February 2, 1942, accessed online, http://content.time.com/time
/magazine/article/0,9171,849760,00.html.

52. Nelson to Winthrop, February 9, 1942, record group 1, box 51, folder 2, WRC.

53. Junior to Winthrop, February 17, 1942, box 1, folder 7, WRP.

54. Winthrop interview.

55. Winthrop interview.

56. Winthrop interview; and Smith, *On His Own Terms*, 145–46.

57. Men, *Ours to Hold It High*, 7.

58. Men, *Ours to Hold It High*, 1. For an overview of the division's record in World War I,
see pp. 1–4.

59. Prefer, *Leyte 1944*, 212.

60. "Winthrop Rockefeller, Army History," record group 1, box 10, folder 2, WRC.

61. Men, *Ours to Hold It High*, 25; and Winthrop interview.

62. Men, *Ours to Hold It High*, 22–23.

63. Winthrop interview. For more on Newell's background, see Charles T. Davies, "Frank
Newell: He Watches the Tides," *Arkansas Gazette*, Sunday, October 21, 1951, F5.

64. Newell interview.

65. Kert, *Abby Aldrich Rockefeller*, 447–48.

66. Newell interview.

67. "Graham Hawks, Physician and Professor, 85," obituary, *New York Times*, March 25,
1997, B7.

68. Ria Hawks and Graham Hawks Jr., interviewed by Sara Bost, July 2, 2018, Little Rock,
Arkansas (hereafter R. Hawks and G. Hawks interview).

69. Winthrop interview.

70. Men, *Ours to Hold It High*, 23–24.

71. "Dimes to Dollars," *New York Times*, January 3, 1943, E2; and Men, *Ours to Hold It
High*, 25.

72. Winthrop interview.

73. "Dimes to Dollars"; and Men, *Ours to Hold It High*, 25.

74. Winthrop interview.

75. Junior to Winthrop, January 19, 1943, box 1, folder 7, WRP.

76. Newell interview.

77. Newell interview.

78. Winthrop interview.

79. Winthrop to Marie Galloway Lewis, April 9, 1943, record group 1, box 17, folder 2, WRC.

80. Winthrop interview.

81. West et al., *Second to None*, 28.

82. Winthrop interview.

83. Men, *Ours to Hold It High*, 26–28.

84. "A Rockefeller on Army Manoeuvers," *New York Times*, March 18, 1943, 10.

85. Junior to Winthrop, March 24, 1943, box 1, folder 7, WRP.

86. Junior to Winthrop, March 30, 1943, box 1, folder 7, WRP.

87. Junior to Winthrop, April 12, 1943, box 1, folder 7, WRP.

88. Winthrop to Marie Galloway Lewis, April 9, 1943, record group 1, box 17, folder 2, WRC.

89. Men, *Ours to Hold It High*, 30–31.

90. Men, *Ours to Hold It High*, 31–32.

91. Winthrop to Abby and Junior, July 16, 1943, box 3, folder 21, WRP.

92. Men, *Ours to Hold It High*, 31–32.

93. Winthrop to Abby and Junior, July 4, 1943, box 3, folder 21, WRP.

94. Newell interview.

95. Winthrop interview.

96. West et al., *Second to None*, 54.

97. Winthrop interview.

98. Moscow, *Rockefeller Inheritance*, 201.

99. Kert, *Abby Aldrich Rockefeller*, 441–42.

100. Abby to Winthrop, September 3, 1943, record group 1, box 42, folder 2, WRC; and Junior to Winthrop, September 10, 1943, box 1, folder 7, WRP.

101. Winthrop to Marie Galloway Lewis, September 10, 1943, record group 1, box 17, folder 2, WRC.

102. Winthrop interview.

103. "Rockefeller Son Stops for Rest in Denver," *Denver Post*, September 4, 1943; and "Captain Rockefeller Is in Denver to Rest," *Rocky Mountain News* (Denver, CO), September 4, 1943, clippings both in box 55, folder 3, WRP.

104. Winthrop interview.

105. "Copy of letter from Winthrop Rockefeller to Laurance S. Rockefeller," October 28, 1943, box 1, folder 9, WRP.

106. Winthrop interview.

107. Winthrop to Marie Galloway Lewis, November 26, 1943, record group 1, box 17, folder 2, WRC.

108. Men, *Ours to Hold It High*, 34–36.

109. Winthrop interview.

110. Winthrop interview.

111. "W. Rockefeller a Major," *New York Times*, January 4, 1944, 9.

112. Junior to Winthrop, February 21, 1944, box 1, folder 7, WRP.

113. Kert, *Abby Aldrich Rockefeller*, 447; and Winthrop interview.

114. Winthrop to Marcelle Baum, January 9, 1944, record group 1, box 17, folder 1, WRC.

115. Winthrop interview.

116. Winthrop interview.

117. Winthrop to Marie Galloway Lewis, March, n.d., 1944, record group 1, box 17, folder 2, WRC.

118. Winthrop interview.

119. Hawks interview.

120. West et al., *Second to None*, 94.

121. Men, *Ours to Hold It High*, 40.

122. West et al., *Second to None*, 95.

123. Winthrop interview.

124. Men, *Ours to Hold It High*, 41; and West et al., *Second to None*, 95–96.

125. Winthrop to Abby and Junior, March 1944, box 3, folder 21, WRP.

CHAPTER 8

1. Heinrichs and Gallicchio, *Implacable Foes*, 10.

2. Heinrichs and Gallicchio, *Implacable Foes*, chapters 1 and 2.

3. Winthrop interview.

4. West et al., *Second to None*, 98.

5. Winthrop interview.

6. West et al., *Second to None*, 99.

7. Abby to Winthrop, May 18, 1944, box 1, folder 5, WRP.

8. Junior to Winthrop, April 12, 1944, box 1, folder 7, WRP.

9. Dr. Graham G. Hawks to Abby, April 5, 1944, record group 1, box 42, folder 1, WRC.

10. Winthrop to Abby and Junior, April 16, 1944, box 3, folder 21, WRP.

11. Men, *Ours to Hold It High*, 41.

12. Winthrop to Abby and Junior, May 2, 1944, box 3, folder 21, WRP.

13. Winthrop interview.

14. West et al., *Second to None*, 100.

15. Winthrop interview.

16. Winthrop interview.

17. Newell interview.

18. Winthrop interview.

19. Winthrop interview.

20. Winthrop interview; and Winthrop to Abby and Junior, May 6, 1944, box 3, folder 21, WRP.

21. Winthrop to Abby and Junior, May 17, 1944; and Winthrop to Abby and Junior, May 21, 1944, both in box 3, folder 21, WRP.

22. Winthrop to Abby and Junior, May 2, 1944, box 3, folder 21, WRP.

23. Winthrop to Marcelle Baum, May 7, 1944, record group 1, box 17, folder 1, WRC.

24. Winthrop to Abby and Junior, May 12, 1944, box 3, folder 21, WRP.

25. Winthrop to Abby and Junior, June 6, 1944, box 3, folder 21, WRP.

26. Abby to Winthrop, June 15, 1944, record group 1, box 42, folder 3, WRC.

27. On Eleanor Roosevelt, see Michaelis, *Eleanor: A Life*.

28. Winthrop interview.

29. Winthrop to Marcelle Baum, May 27, 1944, record group 1, box 17, folder 1, WRC.

30. Winthrop to Marcelle Baum, June 12, 1944, record group 1, box 17, folder 1, WRC; Winthrop to Abby and Junior, June 14, 1944, box 3, folder 21, WRP; and Heinrichs and Gallicchio, *Implacable Foes*, 94.

31. Junior to Winthrop, June 29, 1944, box 1, folder 11, WRP.

32. Junior to Winthrop, June 15, 1944, box 1, folder 7, WRP.

33. Winthrop to Marcelle Baum, June 16, 1944, record group 1, box 17, folder 1, WRC.

34. Winthrop interview.

35. Men, *Ours to Hold It High*, 43.

36. Heinrichs and Gallicchio, *Implacable Foes*, 93.

37. On the Saipan campaign see Heinrichs and Gallicchio, *Implacable Foes*, 92–125.

38. Winthrop interview.

39. Winthrop to Abby and Junior, n.d. [postmarked July 24, 1944], box 3, folder 21, WRP.

40. Men, *Ours to Hold It High*, 43.

41. On the early history of Guam, see Gailey, *Liberation of Guam*, 9–27.

42. Heinrichs and Gallicchio, *Implacable Foes*, 125–26. Quote on p. 126.

43. Heinrichs and Gallicchio, *Implacable Foes*, 126–27.

44. West et al., *Second to None*, 112.

45. Winthrop interview.

46. Winthrop interview.

47. Winthrop interview.

48. "Saved by a Rockefeller," *New York Times*, August 12, 1944, 5; and "Rockefeller Saves Soldier," *Tarrytown Daily News*, August 12, 1944, clipping in record group 1, box 12, folder 4, WRC.

49. Winthrop interview.

50. Winthrop to Marie Galloway Lewis, October 1, 1944, record group 1, box 17, folder 2, WRC.

51. Winthrop interview.

52. On the Guam campaign, see Heinrichs and Gallicchio, *Implacable Foes*, 125–37. For a more detailed account, see Gailey, *Liberation of Guam*.

53. Winthrop to Marie Galloway Lewis, October 1, 1944, record group 1, box 17, folder 2, WRC.

54. Heinrichs and Gallicchio, *Implacable Foes*, 124–25.

55. Winthrop to Abby and Junior, August 30, 1944, box 3, folder 21, WRP.

56. Winthrop to Abby and Junior, September 11, box 3, folder 21, WRP.

57. Junior to Winthrop, September 26, 1944, box 1, folder 7, WRP.

58. Abby to Winthrop, August 15, 1944, record group 1, box 42, folder 3, WRC.

59. Winthrop interview.

60. Junior to Winthrop, September 14, 1944, box 1, folder 7, WRP.

61. Winthrop interview.

62. Winthrop to Marcelle Baum, September 21, 1944, record group 1, box 17, folder 1, WRC.

63. West et al., *Second to None*, 121.

64. Winthrop interview.

65. Abby to Winthrop, October 31, 1944, record group 1, box 42, folder 3, WRC.

66. Junior to Winthrop, November 2, 1944, box 1, folder 7, WRP.

67. Winthrop interview.

68. Hawks interview.

69. Winthrop interview.

70. Winthrop interview.

71. On Betty Hutton, see Hutton, *Backstage, You Can Have*.

72. Winthrop to Marcelle Baum, October 29, 1944, record group 1, box 17, folder 1, WRC; and Winthrop interview.

73. Winthrop interview.

74. Winthrop interview.

75. West et al., *Second to None*, 124.

76. Winthrop to Abby and Junior, October 29, 1944, box 3, folder 21, WRP.

77. Abby to Winthrop, November 14, 1944, record group 1, box 42, folder 3, WRC; and Junior to Winthrop, November 15, 1944, box 1, folder 7, WRP.

78. Winthrop to Laurance, n.d., series 1, box 5, folder 65, Laurance S. Rockefeller Papers (FA433) (hereafter LSRP), Office of the Messrs. Rockefeller Records, Rockefeller Archive Center, Sleepy Hollow, NY; Winthrop interview; and Heinrichs and Gallicchio, *Implacable Foes*, 204.

79. Heinrichs and Gallicchio, *Implacable Foes*, 193.

80. On the Battle of Leyte Gulf, see for example Woodward, *Battle for Leyte Gulf*; Stewart, *Battle of Leyte Gulf*; Cutler, *Battle of Leyte Gulf*; Friedman, *Afternoon of the Rising Sun*; Willmott, *Battle of Leyte Gulf*; and Thomas, *Sea of Thunder*.

81. Heinrichs and Gallicchio, *Implacable Foes*, 204–5.

82. Winthrop to Laurance, n.d., box 5, folder 65, LSRP; and Winthrop interview.

83. Winthrop interview.

84. Winthrop interview.

85. Winthrop interview.

86. Men, *Ours to Hold It High*, 141.

87. Heinrichs and Gallicchio, *Implacable Foes*, 205.

88. Winthrop interview.

89. Winthrop interview; and Men, *Ours to Hold It High*, 141.

90. Winthrop interview.

91. Hawks interview; and Men, *Ours to Hold It High*, 141.

92. Winthrop to Junior, November 25, 1944, box 1, folder 11, WRP.

93. Winthrop interview; and Heinrichs and Gallicchio, *Implacable Foes*, 205.

94. Winthrop interview.

95. Winthrop to Marie Galloway Lewis, November 28, 1944, record group 1, box 17, folder 2, WRC.

CHAPTER 9

1. Winthrop interview.

2. Winthrop interview.

3. Morris, *Those Rockefeller Brothers*, 119.

4. On segregation, the military, and World War II, see Kryder, *Divided Arsenal*; Morehouse, *Fighting in the Jim Crow Army*; Phillips, *War! What Is It Good For?*; and Knauer, *Let Us Fight as Free Men*.

5. Morris, *Those Rockefeller Brothers*, 120.

6. Heinrichs and Gallicchio, *Implacable Foes*, 195.

7. Heinrichs and Gallicchio, *Implacable Foes*, 195–205.

8. Winthrop interview.

9. Winthrop interview; and Heinrichs and Gallicchio, *Implacable Foes*, 205.

10. Winthrop to Abby and Junior, December 12, 1944, box 3, folder 21, WRP; and Winthrop interview.

11. Winthrop interview.

12. Winthrop to Abby and Junior, December 12, 1944, box 3, folder 21, WRP; and Winthrop interview.

13. Winthrop interview.

14. Winthrop interview; and Heinrichs and Gallicchio, *Implacable Foes*, 206.

15. Heinrichs and Gallicchio, *Implacable Foes*, 206.

16. Winthrop interview.

17. Heinrichs and Gallicchio, *Implacable Foes*, 207–8.

18. Winthrop interview.

19. Hawks interview.

20. Phillips, *Winthrop Tour of Duty Map*, Winthrop Rockefeller Institute.

21. Heinrichs and Gallicchio, *Implacable Foes*, 209.

22. Winthrop interview.

23. Winthrop to Abby and Junior, December 23, 1944, box 1, folder 11, WRP.

24. Winthrop to Abby and Junior, December 25, 1944, box 1, folder 11, WRP.

25. Winthrop interview.

26. Winthrop interview.

27. Hawks interview.

28. Winthrop to Lt. Peter Waldo, September 12, 1946, record group 1, box 53, folder 1a, WRC.

29. Winthrop interview.

30. West et al., *Second to None*, 135.

31. Winthrop interview.

32. Winthrop interview.

33. Winthrop interview.

34. Winthrop interview.

35. Winthrop to Abby and Junior, February 6, 1945, record group 1, box 45, folder 11; and Winthrop to Marcelle Baum, record group 1, box 17, folder 1, both in WRC.

36. Winthrop to Abby and Junior, January 19, 1945, record group 1, box 45, folder 11, WRC.

37. Winthrop to Abby and Junior, February 6, 1945, record group 1, box 45, folder 11, WRC.

38. Monserrat S. Del Gallego, "Rockefeller aided Leyte folk in 1944," n.d., clipping in record group 1, box 55, folder 3, WRC.

39. Col. Vincent J. Tanzola to Winthrop, memorandum, February 25, 1945, record group 1, box 12, folder 4, WRC.

40. Winthrop to Marcelle Baum, February 15, 1945, record group 1, box 17, folder 1, WRC.

41. Winthrop to Junior, December 16, 1944, record group 1, box 12, folder 4, WRC.

42. Winthrop to Junior, December 16, 1944.

43. Ralph K. Davies to Junior, February 12, 1945, record group 1, box 12, folder 4, WRC.

44. Winthrop to Junior, February 17, 1945, record group 1, box 12, folder 4, WRC.

45. Junior to Ralph K. Davies, February 16, 1945, telegram, record group 1, box 12, folder 4, WRC.

46. Junior to Winthrop, February 16, 1945, record group 1, box 12, folder 4, WRC.

47. Abby to Winthrop, February 20, 1945, record group 1, box 12, folder 4, WRC.

48. Newell interview.

49. Winthrop to Abby and Junior, March 1, 1945, record group 1, box 12, folder 4, WRC.

50. Junior to Winthrop, March 6, 1945, box 1, folder 7, WRP.

51. Junior to Winthrop, March 15, 1945, box 1, folder 7; and Winthrop to Abby and Junior, March 15, 1945, box 1, folder 11, both in WRP.

52. Winthrop to Abby and Junior, March 15, 1945, box 1, folder 11, WRP.

53. Winthrop to Abby and Junior, March 18, 1945, box 1, folder 11, WRP.

54. Winthrop to Marie Galloway Lewis, March 19, 1945, record group 1, box 17, folder 2, WRC.

55. Winthrop to Marcelle Baum, March 24, 1945, record group 1, box 17, folder 1, WRC.
56. Winthrop to Abby and Junior, March 31, 1945, box 1, folder 11, WRP.
57. Men, *Ours to Hold It High*, 223; and Heinrichs and Gallicchio, *Implacable Foes*, 365–67.
58. Heinrichs and Gallicchio, *Implacable Foes*, 367.
59. Heinrichs and Gallicchio, *Implacable Foes*, 370.
60. Men, *Ours to Hold It High*, 253.
61. Winthrop interview.
62. Winthrop interview.
63. Winthrop interview; and Heinrichs and Gallicchio, *Implacable Foes*, 370.
64. Winthrop interview.
65. Winthrop interview.
66. Winthrop interview.
67. Hawks interview.
68. Winthrop interview; and Heinrichs and Gallicchio, *Implacable Foes*, 370.
69. Winthrop interview.
70. Winthrop interview.
71. Hawks interview.
72. Hawks interview.
73. Winthrop interview; and R. Hawks and G. Hawks interview.
74. Winthrop interview.
75. Winthrop interview.
76. Dr. Thomas M. Rivers to Junior, April 10, 1945, box 3, folder 22, WRP.
77. Winthrop to Abby and Junior, April 7, 1945, box 1, folder 11, WRP; and Winthrop interview.
78. Junior to Winthrop, April 18, 1945, box 1, folder 7, WRP; and Winthrop interview.
79. Winthrop to Junior, April 15, 1945, box 1, folder 11, WRP; and Winthrop interview.
80. Winthrop interview.
81. "Major Rockefeller Burned in Guam Raid," *New York Times*, April 18, 1945, 3; and "Maj. Winthrop Rockefeller Hurt in Japanese Raid off Okinawa," *New York Herald Tribune*, April 18, 1945, clipping in box 1, folder 9, WRP. See also "People: Family Circles," *Time*, April 30, 1945, accessed online, http://content.time.com/time/magazine/article/0,9171,797415,00.html.
82. Dr. Thomas M. Rivers to Junior, April 16, 1945, box 3, folder 22, WRP.
83. Dr. Thomas M. Rivers to Junior, April 24, 1945, box 3, folder 22, WRP; and Winthrop interview.
84. Winthrop to Abby and Junior, April 24, 1945, box 1, folder 11, WRP.
85. Winthrop interview.
86. Winthrop to Abby and Junior, May 4, 1945, box 1, folder 11, WRP; and Winthrop interview.
87. Dr. Thomas M. Rivers to Junior, May 1, 1945, box 3, folder 22, WRP.
88. Dr. Thomas M. Rivers to Junior, May 7, 1945, box 3, folder 22; and Winthrop to Abby and Junior, May 7, 1945, box 1, folder 11, both in WRP.
89. Dr. Thomas M. Rivers to Junior, May 7, 1945, box 3, folder 22, WRP.

CHAPTER 10

1. Winthrop to Marie Galloway Lewis, May 14, 1945, box 17, folder 2, WRP.
2. Winthrop to Abby and Junior, May 17, 1945, box 1, folder 11, WRP.

3. Dr. Thomas M. Rivers to Junior, May 20, 1945, box 3, folder 22, WRP.

4. Winthrop to Abby and Junior, May 13, 1945, box 1, folder 11, WRP.

5. Winthrop to Abby and Junior, May 17, 1945, box 1, folder 11, WRP.

6. Winthrop to Marie Galloway Lewis, June 1, 1945, record group 1, box 17, folder 2, WRC.

7. Winthrop to Abby and Junior, May 22, 1945, box 1, folder 11, WRP.

8. Winthrop to Junior, May 26, 1945, box 1, folder 11, WRP; and Winthrop to Marie Galloway Lewis, June 1, 1945, record group 1, box 17, folder 2, WRC.

9. Winthrop to Marcelle Baum, July 3, 1945, record group 1, box 17, folder 1, WRC.

10. Frank Newell to Abby, June 11, 1945, record group 1, box 42, folder 3, WRC.

11. Winthrop to Abby and Junior, June 16, 1945, folder 21, box 3, WRP.

12. Winthrop to Marie Galloway Lewis, record group 1, box 17, folder 2, WRC.

13. Winthrop to Abby and Junior, July 1, 1945, box 3, folder 21, WRP.

14. Winthrop to Abby and Junior, July 1, 1945.

15. Abby to Winthrop, June 18, 1945, box 1, folder 5, WRP.

16. Abby to Winthrop, June 20, 1945, box 1, folder 5, WRP.

17. Winthrop to Abby and Junior, July 1, 1945, box 3, folder 21, WRP.

18. Junior to Winthrop, July 16, 1945, box 1, folder 7, WRP.

19. Abby to Winthrop, July 13, 1945, box 1, folder 5, WRP.

20. Winthrop to Marcelle Baum, August 22, 1945, record group 1, box 17, folder 1, WRC.

21. For a discussion on the end of the war in the Pacific, see Heinrichs and Gallicchio, *Implacable Foes*, chapters 12 and 13. The footnotes in these chapters provide a gateway to exploring the voluminous secondary literature on the topic.

22. Winthrop to Abby and Junior, August 15, 1945, box 3, folder 21, WRP.

23. Junior to Winthrop, August 15, 1944, box 1, folder 7, WRP.

24. "Excerpts from letter from Nelson A. Rockefeller to Winthrop Rockefeller, September 3, 1945," box 1, folder 9, WRP.

25. Winthrop to Abby and Junior, August 23, 1945, box 3, folder 21, WRP.

26. Winthrop to Marie Galloway Lewis, August 25, 1945, record group 1, box 17, folder 2, WRC. Cary Reich suggests that Nelson pulled strings to have Winthrop sent home. But the dates in the sources he cites fall after the decision was made. More likely, this represents a confusion with the role that Nelson did later play in having his brother transferred to New York after Winthrop arrived back in the United States. See Reich, *Life of Nelson A. Rockefeller*, 377.

27. Winthrop to Marcelle Baum, September 5, 1945, record group 1, box 17, folder 1, WRC.

28. Winthrop to Abby and Junior, September 19, 1945, box 3, folder 21, WRP.

29. Winthrop to Marcelle Baum, November 6, 1945, record group 1, box 17, folder 1, WRC.

30. "Sonny Tufts, 59, Actor in Movies," obituary, *New York Times*, June 6, 1970, 31.

31. Winthrop to Marcelle Baum, November 6, 1945, record group 1, box 17, folder 1, WRC.

32. Winthrop to Frank Newell, October 13, 1945, record group 1, box 40, folder 5, WRC.

33. Winthrop to Marcelle Baum, November 6, 1945, record group 1, box 17, folder 1, WRC.

34. Abby to Winthrop, September 6, 1945, box 1, folder 5, WRP.

35. "Copy of letter from John D. Rockefeller Jr. to H. D. Collier, 225 Bush Street, San Francisco, California, October 9, 1945," box 1, folder 9; and Junior to Brig. Gen. R. G. Devoe, October 10, 1945, box 3, folder 21, both in WRP.

36. Winthrop to Marcelle Baum, November 6, 1945, record group 1, box 17, folder 1, WRC.

37. Winthrop to Maj. Gen. A. D. Bruce, October 18, 1945, record group 1, box 14, folder 3c, WRC.

38. Winthrop to Frank Newell, October 13, 1945, record group 1, box 40, folder 5, WRC.

39. Winthrop to Marcelle Baum, November 6, 1945, record group 1, box 17, folder 1, WRC.

40. Winthrop to Maj. Gen. A. D. Bruce, October 18, 1945, record group 1, box 14, folder 3c, WRC.

41. Winthrop to Marcelle Baum, November 6, 1945, record group 1, box 17, folder 1, WRC.

42. Winthrop to Marcelle Baum, November 6, 1945; and Moscow, *Rockefeller Inheritance*, 204.

43. "Winthrop Rockefeller, May 1948," box 5, folder 35, WRP; and "To Study 'Vet' Problems," *New York Times*, November 27, 1945, 8.

44. Hudson interview, part 1.

45. Hudson interview, part 1.

46. Hudson interview, part 1; and Morris, *Those Rockefeller Brothers*, 122–123.

47. Junior to Winthrop, February 28, 1946, box 1, folder 8, WRP.

48. Lt. Col. D. J. Rogers to Winthrop, May 23, 1946, record group 1, box 53, folder 4a, WRC.

49. Winthrop to Lt. Peter Waldo, September 12, 1946, record group 1, box 53, folder 1a; and Francis A. Jamieson to Winthrop, October 30, 1951, memorandum, record group 1, box 40, folder 1, both in WRC.

50. Winthrop to D. R. Delap, September 30, 1946, record group 1, box 14, folder 1, WRC.

51. Morris, *Those Rockefeller Brothers*, 122–23.

52. Winthrop Rockefeller, "Report on Veterans' Readjustment," July 18, 1946, 25–26, record group 1, box 13, folder 8a, WRC.

53. Robert P. Patterson to Winthrop, August 22, 1946, record group 1, box 53, folder 1a, WRC.

54. "Minutes of Rockefeller Brothers Meeting Held at the Playhouse, Pocantico Hills, 8:00 p.m., September 12, 1946," record group 1, box 11, folder 12, WRC.

55. "Patterson Backs a Veteran 'Czar'," *New York Times*, December 6, 1946, 26.

56. Winthrop to Col. George Fays, March 20, 1947, record group 1, box 38, folder 5, WRC.

57. Maj. Gen. A. D. Bruce to Winthrop, February 1, 1946, record group 1, box 14, folder 3c, WRC.

58. Capt. L. C. Sutton Jr. to Winthrop, July 22, 1946, record group 1, box 53, folder 1a, WRC.

59. Robert W. Gumbel to Thelma Irby, April 27, 1961, box 5, folder 35, WRP.

60. Winthrop to Frank Newell, March 20, 1947, record group 1, box 40, folder 5, WRC.

61. Moscow, *Rockefeller Inheritance*, 204.

62. "Minutes of Rockefeller Brothers Meeting Held at the Playhouse, Pocantico Hills, 8:00 p.m., September 12, 1946," record group 1, box 11, folder 12, WRC.

63. Collier and Horowitz, *Rockefellers*, 255.

64. Winthrop to Nathaniel Horton Batchelder, February 11, 1947, record group 1, box 32, folder 2a, WRC.

65. Moscow, *Rockefeller Inheritance*, 205.

66. "Minutes of Rockefeller Brothers Meeting Held at the Playhouse, Pocantico Hills, 8:00 p.m., September 12, 1946," record group 1, box 11, folder 12, WRC. On domestic civil rights in the Cold War era, see for example Horne, *Communist Front?*; Dudziak, *Cold War Civil Rights*; Lewis, *White South and the Red Menace*; Woods, *Black Struggle, Red Scare*; Lent and Gower, *Opinions of Mankind*; Swindall, *Path to the Greater, Freer, Truer World*; and Zeigler, *Red Scare Racism and Cold War Black Radicalism*.

67. Winthrop to Lester B. Granger, January 1, 1949, record group 1, box 33, folder 1b, WRC.

68. Lester B. Granger to Winthrop, February 23, 1943, record group 1, box 6, folder 7, WRC.

69. Lester B. Granger to Winthrop, September 12, 1946, record group 1, box 6, folder 7, WRC; "Urban League to Meet," *New York Times*, September 15, 1946, 9; "Asks Race Accord for Nation's Unity," *New York Times*, September 26, 1946, 37; "Urban League Meet to Open on Job Bias," *New York Times*, September 28, 1946, 4; and "Nation's Notables at Urban League Meet," *New York Times*, October 5, 1946, 21.

70. "Rockefeller Plea Heard by Group," *Detroit Times*, June 22, 1948, clipping in record group 1, box 33, folder 1b, WRC.

71. *Chicago Defender*, photograph, October 13, 1951, 4; and *New York Amsterdam News*, photograph, October 27, 1951, 25.

72. Winthrop Rockefeller, "Ask Government Jobs for Negroes," September 4, 1952, speech, record group 1, box 33, folder 1, WRC.

73. Hazel Garland, "Things to Talk About: Urban League Slates Annual Meet," *Pittsburgh Courier*, January 17, 1953, 12; Toki Schalk Johnson, "Toki Types: You're Never Too Old," *Pittsburgh Courier*, January 31, 1953, 10; "Rockefeller at League Luncheon," *Pittsburgh Courier*, February 7, 1953, 1; Hazel Garland, "Things to Talk About: Don't Forget these Dates," *Pittsburgh Courier*, February 14, 1953, 15; and "Winthrop Rockefeller to Address Urban League Annual Luncheon," *Pittsburgh Courier*, February 28, 1953, 2.

74. Winthrop to Henry Luce, February 18, 1947; and Gerald Swope to Henry Luce, April 1, 1947, both in record group 1, box 6, folder 7, WRC. See also "Luce Heads Drive of Urban League," *New York Times*, February 20, 1947, 20; "Henry R. Luce Heads Urban League Drive," *New York Amsterdam News*, February 22, 1947, 20; "To Aid Urban League Fund," *New York Times*, April 18, 1947, 23; and "Rockefeller Heads Urban League Fund Industrial Unit," *Chicago Defender*, April 26, 1947, 11.

75. Winthrop to Henry Ford II, December 8, 1948; Winthrop to John Hay Whitney, December 20, 1948, both in record group 1, box 33, folder 1a; and see also general correspondence in record group 1, box 6, folder 7, all in WRC. On John Hay Whitney, see Kahn, *Jock*.

76. "Minutes Meeting of Commerce and Industry Council National Urban League The Links Club 36 East Sixty-second Street, January 10, 1950," record group 1, box 33, folder 2a, WRC. See also *Chicago Defender*, photograph, September 9, 1950, 11; and "The Urban League Makes Another Important Move," *Pittsburgh Courier*, June 14, 1952, 8.

77. Winthrop to Robert A. Thompson, Jr., October 2, 1946, record group 1, box 6, folder 7; and Winthrop to John Seal, April 21, 1948, record group 1, box 33, folder 1b, both in WRC.

78. "350 Attend League Party at Rockefeller Rainbow Room," *Chicago Defender*, August 14, 1948.

79. " 'Amateur Artists' Exhibit To Benefit Urban League," *Chicago Defender*, September 18, 1948, 16; "Joe Louis, Lena Horne to Exhibit Paintings for Urban League Fund," *New York Amsterdam News*, September 18, 1948, 12; "Notables' Art on View," *New York Times*, September 28, 1948, 29; and "Amateur Painters Assist Urban League," *New York Amsterdam News*, October 2, 1948, 4.

80. Winthrop to Robert W. Dowling, December 12, 1952; and Philip F. Keebler to Winthrop, December 17, 1952, both in record group 1, box 29, folder 8a, WRC.

81. Philip F. Keebler to Winthrop, December 30, 1952, record group 1, box 29, folder 8a, WRC.

82. "Urban League Buys New Bldg.; Sells Old One," *New York Amsterdam News*, May 28, 1955, 1; and "League Opens New N.Y. Office," *Daily Defender* (Chicago), June 23, 1956, 10.

83. Lester B. Granger to Winthrop, December 29, 1948, record group 1, box 33, folder 2c, WRC.

84. Winthrop to Lester B. Granger, January 1, 1949, record group 1, box 33, folder 1b, WRC.

85. Lillian Scott, "What Do the Rockefellers Think About the Negro?: Winthrop, Family's Expert on Harmony, Tells Defender, " *Chicago Defender*, October 30, 1948, 1, 12.

86. Scott, "What Do the Rockefellers Think About the Negro?"

87. "W. Rockefeller Honored," *New York Amsterdam News*, December 22, 1948, 21; and "Winthrop Rockefeller was honored by the Harlem Mobilization Committee," *Chicago Defender*, January 1, 1949, 2.

88. "Defender Cites 17 Citizens, 9 Groups on Honor Roll," *Chicago Defender*, January 8, 1949, 1.

89. "Negro Paper Puts 17 on Honor Role," *New York Times*, January 2, 1949, 41.

90. Nelson to Winthrop, January 4, 1949, record group 1, box 51, folder 2, WRC.

91. "Elected Board Chairman of New Medical Center," *New York Times*, January 12, 1949, 20; and "Biographical and Other Information," October 29, 1951, record group 1, box 54, folder unnumbered and untitled, WRC.

92. "Drive for Education Set," *New York Times*, May 21, 1947, 27; "Loomis Institute Elects," *New York Times*, October 2, 1951, 25; and "Hospitals Board Member Elected to N.Y.U. Council," *New York Times*, May 1, 1952, 31.

93. "Biographical and Other Information," October 29, 1951, record group 1, box 54, folder unnumbered and untitled, WRC; and Harr and Johnson, *Rockefeller Century*, 183.

94. "W. Rockefeller Quits Socony-Vacuum Post," *New York Times*, June 1, 1951, 16. See also Press Release, June 1, 1951, series 7, box 57, folder 575, Rockefeller Family Public Relations Department Papers (FA789A) (hereafter RFPRP), Rockefeller Archive Center, Sleepy Hollow, NY.

95. "Heads Board of Trustees of Colonial Williamsburg," *New York Times*, April 28, 1953, 15.

96. Francis A. Jamieson to Winthrop, October 30, 1951, memorandum, record group 1, box 40, folder 1, WRC.

97. Harr and Johnson, *Rockefeller Century*, 391.

98. Moscow, *Rockefeller Inheritance*, 205–206. On the nightclub scene in Manhattan at the time, see for example Kaytor, *"21"*; Kriendler, 21; and Blumenthal, *Stork Club*.

99. David Rockefeller interview.

100. Moscow, *Rockefeller Inheritance*, 206; and Persico, *Imperial Rockefeller*, 51.

101. David Rockefeller interview.

102. Reich, *Life of Nelson A. Rockefeller*, 392. On Mary Martin, see Martin, *My Heart Belongs*; and Kaufman, *Some Enchanted Evenings*.

103. Collier and Horowitz, *Rockefellers*, 256.

104. Moscow, *Rockefeller Inheritance*, 206.

CHAPTER 11

1. Winthrop to Junior and Abby, March 26, 1947, record group 1, box 36, folder 6, WRC.
2. Patricia Bronte, "The Truth About Bobo Rockefeller," *Daily News* (Chicago), September 1, 1953, clipping in record group 1, box 55, folder 6, WRC.
3. Bronte, "Truth About Bobo Rockefeller," September 1.
4. Bronte, "Truth About Bobo Rockefeller," September 1; "The Story of Jievute Paulekiute," *Life*, February 23, 1948, 29; and "Manners & Morals: The Bride Wore Pink," *Time*, February 23, 1948, accessed online, http://content.time.com/time /magazine/article/0,9171,798211,00.html.
5. Bronte, "Truth About Bobo Rockefeller," September 1.
6. Bronte, "Truth About Bobo Rockefeller," September 1; and "Rockefeller Son Will Wed Tonight," *New York Times*, February 13, 1948, 23.
7. Bronte, "Truth About Bobo Rockefeller," September 1.
8. Bronte, "Truth About Bobo Rockefeller," September 1.
9. Bronte, "Truth About Bobo Rockefeller," September 1.
10. Patricia Bronte, "The Truth About Bobo Rockefeller," *Daily News*, September 2, 1953, clipping in record group 1, box 55, folder 6, WRC; and "Rockefeller Son Will Wed Tonight."
11. Bronte, "Truth About Bobo Rockefeller," September 2.
12. "Rockefeller Son Will Wed Tonight."
13. Bronte, "Truth About Bobo Rockefeller," September 2; and "Rockefeller Son Will Wed Tonight."
14. Bronte, "Truth About Bobo Rockefeller," September 2; and "Rockefeller Son Will Wed Tonight."
15. Bronte, "Truth About Bobo Rockefeller," September 2.
16. Dorothy M. Diemer to Winthrop, February 5, 1946, record group 1, box 14, folder 6b, WRC.
17. "Bobo and the Prince," *Newsweek*, February 23, 1948, 21.
18. Laurance to Winthrop, October 31, 1947, series 1, box 5, folder 65, LSRP.
19. Laurance to Winthrop, October 31, 1947.
20. Laurance to Winthrop, October 31, 1947.
21. Bronte, "Truth About Bobo Rockefeller," September 2.
22. Frederick Graham, "Crippled Over Sea, Plane Carrying 69 Lands in Safety," *New York Times*, February 8, 1948, 1, 62.
23. On Eastern Airlines, see Serling, *From the Captain to the Colonel*; and Russell, *Eastern Airlines*.
24. Graham, "Crippled Over Sea, Plane Carrying 69 Lands in Safety."
25. Civil Aeronautics Board, "Accident Investigation Report," October 20, 1949, 1, record group 1, box 28, folder 2, WRC.
26. Civil Aeronautics Board, "Accident Investigation Report"; and Graham, "Crippled Over Sea, Plane Carrying 69 Lands in Safety."
27. Frank Newell to Winthrop, February 9, 1948, record group 1, box 40, folder 5, WRC.
28. Harr and Johnson, *Rockefeller Century*, 468.
29. Bronte, "Truth About Bobo Rockefeller," September 2.
30. Harr and Johnson, *Rockefeller Conscience*, 20.
31. "Story of Jievute Paulekiute."
32. "Bobo and the Prince."

33. "Manners & Morals: The Bride Wore Pink."
34. "Bobo and the Prince."
35. Kert, *Abby Aldrich Rockefeller*, 467.
36. "Manners and Morals: The Bride Wore Pink."
37. Bronte, "Truth About Bobo Rockefeller," September 2.
38. "Bobo and the Prince."
39. Bronte, "Truth About Bobo Rockefeller," September 2.
40. Abby to Susan Sears, February 20, 1948, record group 1, box 42, folder 4, WRC.
41. Susan Sears to Abby, n.d., 1948, record group 1, box 42, folder 4, WRC.
42. Bronte, "Truth About Bobo Rockefeller," September 2.
43. Bronte, "Truth About Bobo Rockefeller," September 2.
44. "Bobo and the Prince."
45. Moscow, *Rockefeller Inheritance*, 207.
46. Junior to Laurance, February 20, 1948, series 1, box 5, folder 65, LSRP.
47. "Rockefeller Marries Mrs. Sears in a Midnight Florida Ceremony," *New York Times*, February 14, 1948," 1.
48. "Manners and Morals: The Bride Wore Pink."
49. "Rockefeller Son Will Wed Tonight"; and "Rockefellers Off on Wedding Trip," *New York Times*, February 15, 1948, 54.
50. Bronte, "Truth About Bobo Rockefeller," September 2.
51. Bobo to Junior, March 1, 1948, telegram, record group 1, box 45, folder 5, WRC.
52. Harr and Johnson, *Rockefeller Century*, 474–75.
53. Patricia Bronte, "The Truth About Bobo Rockefeller," *Daily News*, September 3, 1953, clipping in record group 1, box 55, folder 6, WRC.
54. Kert, *Abby Aldrich Rockefeller*, 471–73.
55. Moscow, *Rockefeller Inheritance*, 208.
56. Kert, *Abby Aldrich Rockefeller*, 471–73. Kert mistakenly dates Abby's death as April 4, not April 5.
57. Junior to Bobo, September 16, 1948, record group 1, box 45, folder 5, WRC. See also "Family Affairs," *Time*, May 3, 1948, accessed online, http://content.time.com/time/magazine/article/0,9171,798534,00.html.
58. Junior to Winthrop, May 26, 1948, box 1, folder 8, WRP.
59. "W. Rockefeller Asks 'Patience' For Peace," *New York Times*, May 9, 1948, 56.
60. Winthrop to Jerry Drew [*sic*] and Dean Martin, June 2, 1948, record group 1, box 39, folder 1, WRC.
61. Junior to Winthrop, May 10, 1948, box 1, folder 8, WRP.
62. Winthrop to Bill Sylvan, n.d., record group 1, box 37, folder 8, WRC.
63. Bill Sylvan to Winthrop, June 12, 1948, record group 1, box 37, folder 8, WRC.
64. Junior to Bobo, May 19, 1948, record group 1, box 45, folder 5; Winthrop to Junior, August 17, 1948, record group 1, box 36, folder 6; Winthrop to Stacey Way, August 26, 1948, record group 1, box 38, folder 8; and Winthrop to Frederick W. Gehle, June 1, 1948, record group 1, box 39, folder 5, all in WRC.
65. Bronte, "Truth About Bobo Rockefeller," September 3.
66. Harr and Johnson, *Rockefeller Century*, 544.
67. "Winthrop Hits Report Of Rift," *New York Journal-American*, June 20, 1948, clipping in series 7, box 57, folder 575, RFPRP.
68. Bronte, "Truth About Bobo Rockefeller," September 3.

69. "Winthrop Jr. Is Born to Bobo Rockefeller," *Daily News*, September 18, 1948, clipping in series 7, box 57, folder 575, RFPRP.

70. "Son to Winthrop Rockefeller," *New York Times*, September 18, 1948, 20.

71. Bobo to Junior, September 22, 1948, record group 1, box 45, folder 5, WRC.

72. Bronte, "Truth About Bobo Rockefeller," September 3.

73. Junior to Bobo, September 30, 1948, record group 1, box 45, folder 5, WRC.

74. Winthrop to Olga Wise, October 8, 1948, record group 1, box 41, folder 4, WRC.

75. Winthrop to Philip Broun, October 19, 1948, record group 1, box 39, folder 3, WRC.

76. Winthrop to Mr. and Mrs. Nathaniel Horton Batchelder, November 8, 1948, record group 1, box 32, folder 2a, WRC.

77. Winthrop to Bill Sylvan, December 3, 1948, record group 1, box 37, folder 8, WRC.

78. Winthrop to Clara Schiller, January 11, 1949, record group 1, box 41, folder 3, WRC.

79. "Elected Board Chairman of New Medical Center," *New York Times*, January 12, 1949, 20; and "N.Y.U.-Bellevue Plan Grows, With Cost at $32,744,000," *New York Times*, January 17, 1949, 1.

80. Nelson to Winthrop, January 12, 1949, record group 1, box 51, folder 2, WRC.

81. Bill Sylvan to Winthrop, January 20, 1949; and Winthrop to Douglas Gibbons & Co., Inc., February 11, 1949, both in record group 1, box 37, folder 8, WRC.

82. Winthrop to Frank Newell, February 11, 1949, record group 1, box 40, folder 5; and Winthrop to Clara Schiller, April 22, 1949, record group 1, box 41, folder 3, both in WRC.

83. Junior to Bobo and Winthrop, February 25, 1949, record group 1, box 45, folder 5, WRC.

84. Junior to Bobo, April 4, 1949, record group 1, box 45, folder 3, WRC.

85. Bronte, "Truth About Bobo Rockefeller," September 3.

86. Junior to Winthrop, April 8, 1949, record group 1, box 45, folder 3, WRC.

87. Winthrop to Frederick W. Gehle, April 20, 1949, record group 1, box 39, folder 5, WRC.

88. Winthrop to Clara Schiller, April 22, 1949, record group 1, box 41, folder 3, WRC.

89. Junior to Winthrop, July 15, 1949, record group 1, box 45, folder 3, WRC.

90. Harr and Johnson, *Rockefeller Century*, 522.

91. Junior to Winthrop, July 19, 1949, telegram, record group 1, box 45, folder 3, WRC.

92. "Mrs. W. Rockefeller in Hospital," *New York Times*, August 2, 1949, 22.

93. Winthrop to Robert W. Gumbel, September 6, 1949, box 4, folder 34, WRP.

94. Bobo to Junior, September 1, 1949, record group 1, box 45, folder 5, WRC.

95. Bronte, "Truth About Bobo Rockefeller," September 3.

96. "Minutes of Rockefeller Brothers Meeting Held at the Playhouse, Pocantico Hills, 5:00 p.m., Saturday, October 22, 1949," record group 1, box 35, folder 9, WRC.

97. "Minutes of Rockefeller Brothers Meeting Held at Laurances's Apartment, New York City, 8:00 p.m., Sunday, January 15, 1950," record group 1, box 35, folder 9, WRC.

98. Bronte, "Truth About Bobo Rockefeller," September 3.

99. Charles Ventura, "Next Mrs. Winnie Rockefeller May Wear Horn-Rimmed Glasses," *World and Telegram and Sun* (New York), June 5, 1953, clipping in record group 1, box 134, folder 4, WRC; and Bronte, "Truth About Bobo Rockefeller," September 3.

100. Marion Davies and William Randolph Hearst to Winthrop, December 8, 1949, telegram, record group 1, box 30, folder 2, WRC.

101. Winthrop to Marion Davies and William Randolph Hearst, December 8, 1949, telegram, record group 1, box 30, folder 2, WRC.

102. "Minutes of Rockefeller Brothers Meeting Held at the Playhouse, Pocantico Hills, 10:30 a.m., Sunday, December 18, 1949," record group 1, box 35, folder 9, WRC.

103. Junior to Winthrop, December 28, 1949, record group 1, box 45, folder 3, WRC.

CHAPTER 12

1. "Minutes of Rockefeller Brothers Meeting Held at Laurance's Apartment, New York City, 8:00 p.m., Sunday, January 15, 1950," record group 1, box 35, folder 9, WRC.

2. Winthrop to Marion Davies, January 13, 1950, record group 1, box 30, folder 2, WRC.

3. Marion Davies to Winthrop, January 17, 1950, record group 1, box 30, folder 2, WRC.

4. Marion Davies to Paul Schoenstein, January 17, 1950, record group 1, box 30, folder 2, WRC.

5. "Minutes of Rockefeller Brothers Meeting Held at the Playhouse, Pocantico Hills, Saturday, April 1, 1950, 8:00 p.m.," record group 1, box 35, folder 9, WRC.

6. Timothy N. Pfeiffer to Messrs. Pross, Smith & Halpern, April 2, 1950, record group 2, box 41, folder 2, WRC.

7. Bronte, "Truth About Bobo Rockefeller," September 3.

8. Timothy N. Pfeiffer to Messrs. Pross, Smith & Halpern, April 2, 1950, record group 2, box 41, folder 2, WRC.

9. Winthrop to Bobo, May 5, 1950, record group 2, box 41, folder 2, WRC.

10. "Minutes of Rockefeller Brothers Meeting Held Abby's [Babs's] Apartment, One Beekman Place, 8:30 p.m., May 5, 1950, New York City," record group 1, box 35, folder 9, WRC.

11. Winthrop to Bobo, July 18, 1950, record group 2, box 41, folder 2, WRC.

12. Winthrop to Mr. Bowdre, July 18, 1950, record group 2, box 41, folder 2, WRC.

13. Winthrop to Junior, August 7, 1950, record group 1, box 36, folder 6, WRC.

14. Winthrop to Robert W. Gumbel, August 9, 1950, record group 1, box 39, folder 5, WRC.

15. " 'I'll Never Give Rockefeller A Divorce': Bobo," *Chicago Tribune*, September 21, 1950, clipping in record group 1, box 55, folder 6, WRC.

16. Bill Sylvan to Winthrop, September 21, 1950, record group 1, box 37, folder 8, WRC.

17. Durr, *Rodman Rockefeller*, 8.

18. Winthrop to Junior, October 5, 1950, record group 1, box 36, folder 6; and Winthrop to Philip Broun, October 5, 1950, record group 1, box 39, folder 3, both in WRC.

19. Winthrop to John, October 16, 1950, series 3, subseries 2, box 33, folder 305, JDR3P.

20. Francis A. Jamieson to Winthrop, October 5, 1950, record group 1, box 40, folder 1, WRC.

21. Winthrop to Philip Broun, October 5, 1950, record group 1, box 39, folder 3, WRC.

22. Winthrop to Bill Sylvan, October 10, 1950, record group 1, box 37, folder 8, WRC.

23. Winthrop to Bill Sylvan, October 11, 1950, record group 1, box 37, folder 8, WRC.

24. Winthrop to Bill Sylvan, October 31, 1950, record group 1, box 37, folder 8, WRC.

25. Winthrop to Bill Sylvan, November 1, 1950, record group 1, box 37, folder 8, WRC.

26. Bogart Rogers to Winthrop, November 6, 1950, record group 1, box 40, folder 4, WRC.

27. Marion Davies to Winthrop, telegram, November 14, 1950, record group 1, box 30, folder 2, WRC.

28. Winthrop to Marion Davies, telegram, November 14, 1950, record group 1, box 30, folder 2, WRC.

29. Marion Davies to Winthrop, November 22, 1950, record group 1, box 30, folder 2, WRC.

30. Francis A. Jamieson to Winthrop, December 7, 1950, record group 1, box 40, folder 1, WRC.

31. Junior to Winthrop, January 11, 1951, box 1, folder 8, WRP.

32. "Minutes of Rockefeller Brothers Meeting Held at David's House, Tarrytown, New York, June 12, 1951, 8 p.m.," record group 1, box 35, folder 9, WRC.

33. "W. Rockefeller Quits Socony-Vacuum Post," *New York Times*, June 1, 1951, 39; and press release, June 1, 1951, series 7, box 57, folder 575, RFPRP.

34. Durr, *Rodman Rockefeller*, 15.

35. Durr, *Rodman Rockefeller*, 45–47; and "Rockefeller Program Bears Fruit in Puerto Rico," *New York Times*, February 27, 1955, F7.

36. "Minutes of Rockefeller Brothers Meeting Held at David's House, Tarrytown, New York, June 12, 1951, 8 p.m.," record group 1, box 35, folder 9, WRC.

37. Bogart Rogers to Winthrop, June 4, 1951, record group 1, box 40, folder 4, WRC.

38. "Mrs. W. Rockefeller Gets Million Trust," *New York Times*, June 4, 1953, 25; and Harry Ober, "Bobo Gets a Million, Yield is 20G a Year," *New York Daily Mirror*, June 4, 1953, clipping in record group 1, box 55, folder 6, WRC.

39. "Minutes of Rockefeller Brothers Meeting Held at David's House, Tarrytown, New York, June 12, 1951, 8 p.m.," record group 1, box 35, folder 9, WRC.

40. "People," *Time*, June 23, 1952, accessed online, http://content.time.com/time/magazine/article/0,9171,859803,00.html.

41. Stasz, *Rockefeller Women*, 299–300.

42. Harr and Johnson, *Rockefeller Century*, 522.

43. Harr and Johnson, *Rockefeller Century*, 522–23.

44. Winks, *Laurance S. Rockefeller*, 189.

45. Harr and Johnson, *Rockefeller Century*, 527–29; and Harr and Johnson, *Rockefeller Conscience*, 494–95.

46. Harr and Johnson, *Rockefeller Conscience*, 498.

47. "Heads Board of Trustees of Colonial Williamsburg," *New York Times*, April 28, 1953, 15.

48. Gonzales, *Rockefellers at Williamsburg*, 51–52.

49. Cholly Knickerbocker, "The Smart Set," *Times Herald* (Norristown, PA), March 10, 1953, clipping in record group 1, box 55, folder 6, WRC.

50. "Bobo Says Rockefeller Has Sent Her No Money for Year," *New York Daily Mirror*, March 12, 1953, clipping in record group 1, box 55, folder 6, WRC.

51. "Mrs. W. Rockefeller Gets Million Trust."

52. "People," *Time*, June 15, 1953, accessed online, http://content.time.com/time/magazine/article/0,9171,818563,00.html.

53. "People," *Time*, September 6, 1954, accessed online, http://content.time.com/time/magazine/article/0,9171,820097,00.html.

54. On Jeannette's early life see Lundgren, "Arts Advocate," chapter 1.

55. Jeannette Rockefeller, interview by Joseph W. Ernst, April 22, 1974, 1 East End Avenue, New York, New York, AV 9918, Oral History and Audio Recordings Collection, Rockefeller Archive Center, Sleepy Hollow, NY.

56. Ventura, "Next Mrs. Winnie Rockefeller May Wear Horn-Rimmed Glasses."

57. "Winthrop Rockefeller to Set Up Residence in Arkansas," *New York Times*, June 7, 1953, 26.

58. Charles McHarry and Neal Patterson, "Bobo Coup Revealed as Divorce Roadblock," *Daily News* (Chicago), July 1, 1953, record group 1, box 55, folder 6, WRC. The

apartment was sold December 22, 1955, to Kenneth C. Tower for $80,000. See "Agreement of Sale, December 22, 1955," record group 1, box 11, folder 3, WRC.

59. Ward, *Arkansas Rockefeller*, 1.

60. "Report Bobo Seeks Multi-Million Fund," *New York Journal-American*, July 1, 1953, clipping in record group 1, box 55, folder 6, WRC.

61. "Bobo Faces Eviction," *New York Journal-American*, n.d., clipping in record group 1, box 55, folder 6, WRC.

62. "Far, Far From Bobo: Winnie Rockefeller's Ranching in Arkansas," *New York Journal-American*, December 27, 1953, clipping in record group 1, box 55, folder 6, WRC.

63. Moscow, *Rockefeller Inheritance*, 268–69.

64. Eric Pace, "Louis Nizer, Lawyer to the Famous, Dies at 92," obituary, *New York Times*, November 11, 1994, B7. See also Nizer, *My Life in Court*.

65. "Report Bobo Seeks Multi-Million Fund."

66. McHarry and Patterson, "Bobo Coup Revealed as Divorce Roadblock."

67. "Bobo Takes Over Rockefeller's Park Ave. Home," *New York Daily Mirror*, June 29, 1953, clipping in record group 1, box 55, folder 6, WRC.

68. Gabriel Pressman and Luman H. Long, "No Intruder, Merely a Mother, Bobo Says," *New York World Telegram and Sun*, June 29, 1953, clipping in record group 1, box 55, folder 6, WRC.

69. "Bobo Camps in Mate's Apartment," *New York Journal-American*, June 29, 1953, clipping in record group 1, box 55, folder 6, WRC.

70. "Bobo Seizes Winthrop's Castle," *Daily News*, June 29, 1953, clipping in record group 1, box 55, folder 6, WRC.

71. "Report Bobo Seeks Multi-Million Fund."

72. John to Winthrop, July 31, 1953, series 3, subseries 2, box 33, folder 305, JDR3P; and Babs to Winthrop, July 24, 1953, record group 1, box 49, folder 6, WRC.

73. Draft Press Release, August 5, 1953, series 7, box 57, folder 580, RFPRP.

74. "Draft of Statement by Dunaway, 9/17/53," series 7, box 57, folder 580, RFPRP.

75. Draft Press Release, September 21, 1953, series 7, box 57, folder 580, RFPRP.

76. "Life on the Newsfronts of the World," *Life*, October 26, 1953, 59. See also "People," *Time*, October 26, 1953, accessed online, http://content.time.com/time/magazine/article/0,9171,818988,00.html.

77. "Mrs. Rockefeller Shuns 5 1/2 Million," *New York Times*, January 6, 1954, 12. For further details of the divorce settlement see "Bobo Rockefeller Seeking $10 Million, Dunaway Says," *Arkansas Gazette*, January 6, 1954, clipping in record group 1, box 55, folder 6, WRC.

78. "Bobo Rockefeller Seeking $10 Million, Dunaway Says."

79. Copy of draft letter from Hilbank, Tweed, Hope & Hadley to Ephraim S. London, Esq., Messrs. London, Simpson & London, May 14, 1954, series 7, box 57, folder 580, RFPRP.

80. Copy of draft letter from Hilbank, Tweed, Hope & Hadley to Ephraim S. London. The letter contains the pencil notation "Not Sent Out."

81. "W. Rockefellers Agree on Divorce," *New York Times*, June 18, 1954, 18.

82. "Rockefellers Agree," *New York Times*, June 20, 1954, 28.

83. "Rockefellers Agree"; and "Bobo Decides to Accept."

84. "Waiting for Her Divorce," n.d., clipping in record group 1, box 55, folder 6, WRC.

85. "People," *Time*, August 16, 1954, accessed online, http://content.time.com/time/magazine/article/0,9171,820007,00.html.

86. "Mrs. Rockefeller Buys 5-Story Home on 67th St.," *New York Times*, October 27, 1955, 56.
87. *Daily Express* (London, United Kingdom), September 4, 1954, transcribed and untitled newspaper article, record group 1, box 55, folder 6, WRC. See also "People," *Time*, September 6, 1954, accessed online, http://content.time.com/time/magazine /article/0,9171,820097,00.html; and "People," *Time*, September 13, 1954, accessed online, http://content.time.com/time/magazine/article/0,9171,820176,00.html.
88. "Barbara Rockefeller to Wed," *New York Times*, February 7, 1962, 8.
89. "Society by Suzy: Bobo's Son is Glad to be a Member of the Wedding," *New York Daily Mirror*, February 8, 1962, clipping in record group 1, box 55, folder 6, WRC. See also "People," *Time*, February 16, 1962, accessed online, http://content.time .com/time/magazine/article/0,9171,829048,00.html.
90. "Rockefeller Wedding Off," *New York Times*, March 9, 1962, 13.
91. "Barbara Sears Rockefeller, 91, Actress With a Famous Divorce Settlement," obituary, *New York Times*, May 21, 2008, 27.
92. "Winthrop Rockefeller Weds Jeanette [*sic*] Edris," *New York Times*, June 12, 1956, 40.
93. "People," *Time*, September 6, 1954.
94. "People," *Time*, September 6, 1954; and Charles Ventura, "Rockefeller Wedding Vane Is Multi-Carat Diamond," *New York World-Telegram and Sun*, March 7, 1956, clipping in record group 1, box 55, folder 5, WRP.
95. "People," *Time*, August 13, 1956.
96. "Bobo Goes to Winrock Farm, Arrested During Hectic Day," *Arkansas Gazette*, July 31, 1956, 1, 2.
97. "Bobo Spends Day Telling all to The Tabloids," *Arkansas Gazette*, August 1, 1956, 1, 2.
98. "Bobo, Friends Charged in Ruckus at Winrock," *Arkansas Democrat*, July 31, 1956, 1, 2.
99. "People," *Time*, August 13, 1956. Sheriff Marlin Hawkins recounts these events in his autobiography, Hawkins, *How I Stole Elections*, 224–30.
100. "Barbara Sears Rockefeller, 91, Actress With a Famous Divorce Settlement."
101. Morris, "Hillbilly Rockefeller."
102. Moscow, *Rockefeller Inheritance*, 269, 274–76.

PRIMARY SOURCES

Manuscript Collections

ROCKEFELLER ARCHIVE CENTER, SLEEPY HOLLOW, NEW YORK.

Moscow, Alvin. Papers (FA066).
Office of the Messrs. Rockefeller Records, Record Group 2.
    Mauze, Abby Rockefeller. Papers (FA337).
    Rockefeller, Abby Aldrich. Papers (FA336).
    Rockefeller, David. Papers (FA436).
    Rockefeller, John D., 3rd. Papers (FA108).
    Rockefeller, John D., Jr. Personal Papers (FA335).
    Rockefeller, Laurance S. Papers (FA433).
    Rockefeller, Nelson A. Papers (FA343).
    Rockefeller, Winthrop. Papers (FA403).
Oral History and Audio Recordings Collection (FA1444).
Rockefeller Family Public Relations Department Papers (FA789A).
Winthrop Rockefeller Foundation Records (FA248).

UNIVERSITY OF ARKANSAS AT LITTLE ROCK CENTER FOR ARKANSAS HISTORY AND CULTURE, BOBBY L. ROBERTS LIBRARY OF ARKANSAS HISTORY AND ART, CENTRAL ARKANSAS LIBRARY SYSTEM, LITTLE ROCK, ARKANSAS.

Hawks Family Collection of Rockefeller Family Materials (UALR.MS.0218).
Rockefeller, Winthrop. Collection (UALR.MS.001).

Interviews

Bartlett, Jane. Interview by Joseph W. Ernst, October 16, 1973, Little Rock, Arkansas. Parts 1 & 2, AV 9912, Oral History and Audio Recordings Collection, Rockefeller Archive Center, Sleepy Hollow, New York.
Hawks, Dr. Graham G. Interview by David Camelon, n.d., n.p. Transcript in record group 1, box 65, folder 4, Winthrop Rockefeller Collection, University of Arkansas at Little Rock Center for Arkansas History and Culture, Bobby L. Roberts Library of Arkansas History and Art, Central Arkansas Library System, Little Rock, Arkansas.
Hawks, Ria and, Graham Hawks Jr. Interviewed by Sara Bost, July 2, 2018, Little Rock,

Arkansas, accessed online, https://arstudies.contentdm.oclc.org/digital/collection /p15532coll1/id/14879/rec/6, Hawks Family Collection of Rockefeller Family Materials, University of Arkansas at Little Rock Center for Arkansas History and Culture, Bobby L. Roberts Library of Arkansas History and Art, Central Arkansas Library System, Little Rock, Arkansas.

Hudson, James. Interview by Linda Edgerly, May 1, 1973, Room 5600, 30 Rockefeller Plaza, New York, New York. Part 1, AV 9910, and Part 2, AV 9911, Oral History and Audio Recordings Collection, Rockefeller Archive Center, Sleepy Hollow, New York.

Newell, Frank. Interview by David Camelon, n.d., n.p. Transcript in record group 1, box 65, folder 3, Winthrop Rockefeller Collection, University of Arkansas at Little Rock Center for Arkansas History and Culture, Bobby L. Roberts Library of Arkansas History and Art, Central Arkansas Library System, Little Rock, Arkansas.

Rockefeller, David. Interview by John A. Kirk, December 9, 2015, 146 East Fifty-Sixth Street, Manhattan, New York City. Interview in author's possession.

Rockefeller, Jeannette. Interview by Joseph W. Ernst, April 22, 1974, 1 East End Avenue, New York, New York. AV 9918, Oral History and Audio Recordings Collection, Rockefeller Archive Center, Sleepy Hollow, New York.

Rockefeller, Winthrop. Interview by David Camelon, n.d., n.p. Transcript in record group 1, box 65, folders 2, 3, and 4, Winthrop Rockefeller Collection, University of Arkansas at Little Rock Center for Arkansas History and Culture, Bobby L. Roberts Library of Arkansas History and Art, Central Arkansas Library System, Little Rock, Arkansas.

Newspapers and Magazines

Arkansas Democrat (Little Rock)
Arkansas Democrat-Gazette (Little Rock)
Arkansas Gazette (Little Rock)
Chicago Defender
Chicago Tribune
Daily Defender (Chicago, Illinois)
Daily Express (London, United Kingdom)
Daily News (Chicago, Illinois)
Denver Post
Detroit Times
Ebony (Chicago, Illinois)
Life (New York)
Los Angeles Times
New York Amsterdam News
New York Daily Mirror
New York Herald Tribune
New York Journal-American
New York Sun
New York Times
New York World-Telegram and Sun
Newsweek (New York)
Pittsburgh Courier

Rocky Mountain News (Denver, Colorado)
Saturday Evening Post (Philadelphia, Pennsylvania)
Time (New York)
Times Herald (Norristown, Pennsylvania)
Visalia Times-Delta (Visalia, California)
Wall Street Journal (New York)
Washington D.C. News
Washington Post

Map

Phillips, Dale. *Winthrop Tour of Duty Map*. 1951. Winthrop Rockefeller Institute, 1 Rockefeller Drive, Petit Jean Mountain, Morrilton, Arkansas.

Sermon

Winthrop, John. "A Model of Christian Charity." 1630. Accessed online, https://www .winthropsociety.com/doc_charity.php.

SECONDARY SOURCES

Abels, Jules. *The Rockefeller Billions: The Story of the World's Most Stupendous Fortune*. New York: Macmillan, 1965.

Allen, Gary. *None Dare Call It Conspiracy: The Inside Story of the Rockefellers*. Rossmoor, CA: Concord Press, 1971.

———. *The Rockefeller File*. Seal Beach, CA: '76 Press, 1976.

Alsop, Stewart J. O. *Nixon and Rockefeller: A Double Portrait*. Garden City, NY: Doubleday, 1960.

Anderson, Karen. *Little Rock: Race and Resistance at Central High School*. Princeton, NJ: Princeton University Press, 2010.

Ascoli, Peter M. *Julius Rosenwald: The Man Who Built Sears, Roebuck and Advanced the Cause of Black Education in the American South*. Bloomington: Indiana University Press, 2006.

Berman, Edward H. *The Influence of the Carnegie, Ford, and Rockefeller Foundations on American Foreign Policy*. Albany: State University of New York Press, 1983.

Betts, Robert B. *Along the Ramparts of the Tetons: The Saga of Jackson Hole, Wyoming*. Boulder, CO: Colorado Associated University Press, 1978.

Blair, Diane D. "The Big Three of Late Twentieth-Century Arkansas Politics: Dale Bumpers, Bill Clinton, and David Pryor." *Arkansas Historical Quarterly* 54 (Spring 1995): 53–79.

Blumenthal, Ralph. *Stork Club: America's Most Famous Nightspot and the Lost World of Café Society*. Boston: Little, Brown, 2000.

Broehl, Wayne G., Jr. *The International Basic Economy Corporation*. Washington, DC: International Planning Association, 1968.

Brown, Anthony Cave. *Oil, God and Gold: The Story of Aramco and the Saudi Kings*. New York: Houghton Mifflin, 1999.

Brown, E. Richard. *Rockefeller Medicine Men: Medicine and Capitalism in America*. Berkeley: University of California Press, 1979.

Brown, Margaret Coffin. *Pathmakers: Cultural Landscape Report for the Historic Hiking Trail System of Mount Desert Island: Acadia National Park, Maine: History, Existing Conditions and Analysis*. Boston: National Park Service, Olmstead Center for Landscape Preservation, 2006.

Brown, Robert L. "Winthrop Rockefeller: 1967–1971." In *Defining Moments: Historic Decisions by Arkansas Governors from McMath Through Huckabee*, 37–47. Fayetteville: University of Arkansas Press, 2010.

Bullock, Mary Brown. *An American Transplant: The Rockefeller Foundation and Peking Union Medical College*. Berkeley: University of California Press, 1980.

Bumpers, Dale. *The Best Lawyer in a One-Lawyer Town*. Fayetteville: University of Arkansas Press, 2004.

Burrough, Bryan. *The Big Rich: The Rise and Fall of the Greatest Texas Oil Fortunes*. New York: Penguin, 2009.

Calkins, Frank. *Jackson Hole*. New York: Alfred A. Knopf, 1973.

Capello, Ernesto. "Latin America Encounters Nelson Rockefeller: Imagining the Gringo Patrón in 1969." In *Human Rights and Transnational Solidarity in Cold War Latin America*, edited by Jessica Stites Mor, 48–73. Madison: University of Wisconsin Press, 2013.

Chase, Mary Ellen. *Abby Aldrich Rockefeller*. New York: Macmillan, 1950.

Chernow, Ron. *Titan: The Life of John D. Rockefeller, Sr*. New York: Random House, 2008.

Colby, Gerald, and Charlotte Dennet. *Thy Will Be Done: The Conquest of the Amazon; Nelson Rockefeller and Evangelism in the Age of Oil*. New York: Harper Collins, 1995.

Coleman, James S. "Professorial Training and Institution Building in the Third World: Two Rockefeller Foundation Experiences." *Comparative Education Review* 8 (May 1984): 180–202.

Coll, Steve. *Private Empire: ExxonMobil and American Power*. New York: Penguin, 2012.

Collier, Peter, and David Horowitz. *The Rockefellers: An American Dynasty*. New York: Holt, Rinehart and Winston, 1976.

Corner, George W. *A History of the Rockefeller Institute, 1901–1953; Origins and Growth*. New York: Rockefeller Institute Press, 1964.

Cueto, Marcos, ed. *Missionaries of Science: The Rockefeller Foundation and Latin America*. Bloomington: Indiana University Press, 1994.

Cutler, Thomas. *The Battle of Leyte Gulf, 23–28 October 1944*. Annapolis, MD: Naval Institute Press, 1994.

Dalrymple, Martha. *The AIA Story: Two Decades of International Cooperation*. New York: American International Association for Economic and Social Development, 1968.

Dalzell, Robert F., Jr., and Lee Baldwin Dalzell. *The House the Rockefellers Built: A Tale of Money, Taste, and Power in Twentieth-Century America*. New York: Henry Holt, 2007.

Daugherty, John. *A Place Called Jackson Hole: The Historic Resource Study of Grand Teton National Park*. Moose, WY: Grand Teton National Park, 1999.

Day, Paula, and Tom Pyle. *Pocantico: Fifty Years on the Rockefeller Domain*. New York: Duell, Sloan and Pierce, 1964.

Desmond, James. *Nelson Rockefeller: A Political Biography*. New York: Macmillan, 1964.

Deutsch, Stephanie. *You Need a Schoolhouse: Booker T. Washington, Julius Rosenwald, and the Building of Schools for the Segregated South*. Evanston, IL: Northwestern University Press, 2011.

Dewey, John. *Democracy and Education: An Introduction to the Philosophy of Education*. New York: Macmillan, 1916.

Dillard, Tom W. "Winthrop Rockefeller, 1967–1971." In *The Governors of Arkansas: Essays in Political Biography*, edited by Timothy P. Donovan, Willard B. Gatewood Jr., and Jeannie M. Whayne, 226–34. 2nd ed. Fayetteville: University of Arkansas Press, 1995.

Diner, Hasia R. *Julius Rosenwald: Repairing the World*. New Haven, CT: Yale University Press, 2017.

Dolkart, Andrew S. *Morningside Heights: A History of Its Architecture and Development*. New York: Columbia University Press, 1998.

Dudziak, Mary L. *Cold War Civil Rights: Race and the Image of American Democracy*. Princeton, NJ: Princeton University Press, 2000.

Durr, Kenneth D. *Rodman Rockefeller and the International Basic Economy Corporation, 1947–1984: A Company with a Mission*. Rockville, MD: Montrose Press, 2006.

Eiler, Keith. *Mobilizing America: Robert P. Patterson and the War Effort, 1940–1945*. Ithaca, NY: Cornell University Press, 1997.

Elmer, Isabel Lincoln. *Cinderella Rockefeller: An Autobiography*. New York: Freundlich Books, 1987.

Ernst, Joseph W., ed. *"Dear Father"/"Dear Son:" Correspondence of John D. Rockefeller and John D. Rockefeller, Jr.* New York: Fordham University Press in cooperation with the Rockefeller Archive Center, 1994.

———. "The Rockefeller Archive Center: A Reservoir of Information." *Journal of Thought* 17 (Winter 1982): 28–38.

———, ed. *Worthwhile Places: Correspondence of John D. Rockefeller, Jr. and Horace M. Albright*. New York: Fordham University Press for the Rockefeller Archive Center, 1991.

Ettling, John. *The Germ of Laziness: Rockefeller Philanthropy and Public Health in the New South*. Cambridge, MA.: Harvard University Press, 1981.

Fosdick, Raymond B. *Adventure in Giving: The Story of the General Education Board*. New York: Harper and Row, 1962.

———. *John D. Rockefeller, Jr., A Portrait*. New York: Harper and Brothers, 1956.

———. *The Story of The Rockefeller Foundation*. New York: Harper and Brothers, 1952.

Franks, Norman, and Harry Dempsey. *American Aces of World War I*. Oxford, UK: Osprey, 2001.

Frei, Terry. *Horns, Hogs, and Nixon Coming: Texas vs. Arkansas in Dixie's Last Stand*. New York: Simon and Schuster, 2002.

Freyer, Tony A. *Little Rock on Trial: Cooper v. Aaron and School Desegregation*. Lawrence: University Press of Kansas, 2007.

Friedman, Kenneth. *Afternoon of the Rising Sun: The Battle of Leyte Gulf*. Novato, CA: Presidio, 2001.

Gailey, Harry. *The Liberation of Guam, 21 July-10 August 1944*. Novato, CA: Presidio Press, 1988.

Gamble, Vanessa Northington. *Making A Place for Ourselves: The Black Hospital Movement, 1920–1945*. New York: Oxford University Press, 1995.

Gamble, Vanessa Northington, and Theodore M. Brow. "Midian Othello Bousfield: Advocate for the Medical and Public Health Concerns of Black Americans." *American Journal of Public Health* 99 (July 2009): 1186.

Gates, Frederick T. *Chapters in My Life*. New York: Free Press, 1977.

Gibb, George Sweet, and Evelyn H. Knowlton. *The Resurgent Years: History of the Standard Oil Company (New Jersey), 1911–1927*. New York: Harper and Brothers, 1956.

Gonzales, Donald J. *The Rockefellers at Williamsburg: Backstage with the Founders, Restorers, and World-Renowned Guests*. McLean, VA: EPM Publications, 1991.

Gray, George W. *Education on an International Scale: A History of the International Education Board, 1923–1938.* New York: Harcourt, Brace, 1941.

Grimes, Richard. *Jay Rockefeller: Old Money, New Politics.* Parsons, WV: McClain, 1984.

Guy-Sheftall, Beverly, and Jo Moore Stewart. *Spelman: A Centennial Celebration, 1881–1981.* Atlanta, GA: Spelman College, 1981.

Hanson, Elizabeth. *The Rockefeller University Achievements: A Century of Science for the Benefit of Humankind, 1901–2001.* New York: Rockefeller University Press, 2000.

Harr, John Ensor, and Peter J. Johnson. *The Rockefeller Century: Three Generations of America's Greatest Family.* New York: Charles Scribner's Sons, 1988.

———. *The Rockefeller Conscience: An American Family in Public and in Private.* New York: Charles Scribner's Sons, 1991.

Hathorn, Billy B. "Friendly Rivalry: Winthrop Rockefeller Challenges Orval Faubus in 1964." *Arkansas Historical Quarterly* 53 (Winter 1994): 446–73.

Hawke, David Freeman. *John D.: The Founding Father of the Rockefellers.* New York: Harper and Row, 1980.

Hawkins, Marlin, with C. Fred Williams. *How I Stole Elections: The Autobiography of Sheriff Marlin Hawkins.* Morrilton, AR: n.p., 1991.

Heffron, John M. "The Lincoln School of Teachers College: Elitism and Educational Democracy." In *"Schools of Tomorrow," Schools of Today: What Happened to Progressive Education,* edited by Susan F. Semel and Alan R. Sadovnik, 141–70. New York: Peter Lang, 1999.

Heinrichs, Waldo, and Marco Gallicchio. *Implacable Foes: The War in the Pacific, 1944–1945.* New York: Oxford University Press, 2017.

Hidy, Ralph, and Muriel B. Hidy. *Pioneering in Big Business: History of the Standard Oil Company (New Jersey), 1882–1911.* New York: Harper and Brothers, 1955.

Hiebert, Ray Eldon. *Courtier to the Crowd: The Story of Ivy Lee and the Development of Public Relations.* Ames: Iowa State University Press, 1966.

Hoffman, Carl. *Savage Harvest: A Tale of Cannibals, Colonialism, and Michael Rockefeller's Tragic Quest.* New York: William Morrow, 2014.

Horne, Gerald. *Communist Front? The Civil Rights Congress, 1946–1956.* London: Associated University Press, 1988.

Humelsine, Carlisle H. *Recollections of John D. Rockefeller, Jr. in Williamsburg, 1926–1960.* Williamsburg, VA: Colonial Williamsburg Foundation, 1985.

Hutton, Betty, with Carl M. Bruno and Michael H. Mayer. *Backstage, You Can Have: My Own Story.* Palm Springs, CA: Betty Hutton Estate, 2009.

Irons, Jenny. *Reconstituting Whiteness: The Mississippi State Sovereignty Commission.* Nashville: Vanderbilt University Press, 2010.

Jacoway, Elizabeth. *Turn Away Thy Son: Little Rock, the Crisis that Shocked a Nation.* New York: Free Press, 2007.

Johnson, Arthur M. *Winthrop W. Aldrich: Lawyer, Banker, Diplomat.* Boston: Harvard University Press, 1968.

Johnson, Barry W., and Martha Britton Eller. "Federal Taxation of Inheritance and Wealth Transfers." Internal Revenue Service. https://www.irs.gov/pub/irs-soi/1996-1997preprintar01.pdf.

Johnson, Ben F., III. *Arkansas in Modern America since 1930.* 2nd ed. Fayetteville: University of Arkansas Press, 2019.

Johnson, Haynes, and David S. Broder. *The System: The American Way of Politics at the Breaking Point.* Boston: Little, Brown, 1996.

Johnson-Jones, Aisha M. *The African American Struggle for Library Equality: The Untold Story of the Julius Rosenwald Fund Library Program.* Lanham, MD: Rowman and Littlefield, 2019.

Jonas, Gerald. *The Circuit Riders: Rockefeller Money and the Rise of Modern Science.* New York: W.W. Norton, 1989.

Jones, Merrill Anway. "A Rhetorical Study of Winthrop Rockefeller's Political Speeches, 1964–1971 (Arkansas)." PhD diss., Louisiana State University and Agricultural and Mechanical College, 1984.

Josephson, Emanuel M. *The Federal Reserve Conspiracy and the Rockefellers: Their Gold Corner.* New York: Chedney, 1968.

Joyce, Henry. *Tour of Kykuit: The House and Gardens of the Rockefeller Family.* Tarrytown, NY: Historical Hudson Valley Press, 1994.

Kahn, E. J., Jr. *Jock: The Life and Times of John Hay Whitney.* New York: Doubleday, 1981.

Karolevitz, Robert F. *This Was Pioneer Motoring—An Album of Nostalgic Automemorabilia.* Seattle, WA: Superior, 1968.

Karp, Walter. *The Center: A History and Guide to Rockefeller Center.* New York: American Heritage, 1982.

Katagiri, Yasuhiro. *The Mississippi State Sovereignty Commission: Civil Rights and States' Rights.* Jackson: University Press of Mississippi, 2001.

Kaufman, David. *Some Enchanted Evenings: The Glittering Life and Times of Mary Martin.* New York: St. Martin's, 2016.

Kaytor, Marilyn. *"21": The Life and Times of New York's Favorite Club.* New York: Viking, 1975.

Kelly, Brooks Mather. *Yale: A History.* New Haven, CT: Yale University Press, 1974.

Kennedy, David M. *Freedom from Fear: The American People in Depression and War, 1929–1945.* New York: Oxford University Press, 1999.

Kert, Bernice. *Abby Aldrich Rockefeller: The Woman in the Family.* New York: Random House, 1993.

Key, V. O., Jr. *Southern Politics in State and Nation.* New York: Alfred A. Knopf, 1949.

Killion, Jeffrey. *Cultural Landscape Report for the Historic Motor Road System, Acadia National Park.* Boston: National Parks Service, Olmstead Center for Landscape Preservation, 2007.

Kington, Donald M. *Forgotten Summers: The Story of the Citizens' Military Training Camps, 1921–1940.* San Francisco: Two Decades, 1995.

Kirk, John A. *Redefining the Color Line: Black Activism in Little Rock, Arkansas, 1940–1970.* Gainesville: University Press of Florida, 2002.

———. "A Southern Road Less Traveled: The 1966 Arkansas Gubernatorial Election and (Winthrop) Rockefeller Republicanism in Dixie." In *Painting Dixie Red: When, Where, Why, and How the South Became Republican,* edited by Glenn Feldman, 172–97. Gainesville: University Press of Florida, 2011.

Knauer, Christine. *Let Us Fight as Free Men: Black Soldiers and Civil Rights.* Philadelphia: University of Pennsylvania Press, 2014.

Kramer, Michael, and Sam Roberts. *"I Never Wanted to be Vice-President of Anything:" An Investigative Biography of Nelson Rockefeller.* New York: Basic Books, 1976.

Kriendler, H. Peter, with H. Paul Jeffers. *21: Every Day Was New Year's Eve, The Memoirs of a New York Saloonkeeper.* Dallas, TX: Taylor, 1999.

Krinsky, Carol Herselle. *Rockefeller Center.* New York: Oxford University Press, 1978.

Kryder, Daniel. *Divided Arsenal: Race and the American State during World War II.* New York: Cambridge University Press, 2000.

Kutz, Myer. *Rockefeller Power: America's Chosen Family*. New York: Simon and Schuster, 1974.

Larson, Henrietta M., and Kenneth Wiggins Porter. *History of Humble Oil and Refining Company: A Study in Industrial Growth*. New York: Harper and Brothers, 1959.

Lent, Richard, and Karla K. Gower. *The Opinions of Mankind: Racial Issues, Press, and Propaganda in the Cold War*. Columbia: University of Missouri Press, 2010.

Lewis, George. *The White South and the Red Menace: Segregationists, Anticommunism, and Massive Resistance*. Gainesville: University of Florida Press, 2004.

Lewis, W. David. *Eddie Rickenbacker: An American Hero in the Twentieth Century*. Baltimore: Johns Hopkins University Press, 2005.

Lisenby, Foy. "Winthrop Rockefeller and the Arkansas Image." *Arkansas Historical Quarterly* 43 (Summer 1984): 143–52.

Loebl, Suzanne. *America's Medicis: The Rockefellers and their Astonishing Cultural Legacy*. New York: HarperCollins, 2010.

Loth, David G. *The City Within a City; the Romance of Rockefeller Center*. New York: William Morrow, 1966.

Lundberg, Ferdinand. *America's Sixty Families*. New York: Vanguard, 1937.

———. *The Rich and the Super-Rich: A Study in the Power of Money Today*. New York: Lyle Stuart, 1968.

———. *The Rockefeller Syndrome*. Secaucus, NJ: Lyle Stuart, 1975.

Lundgren, Kaye M. "Arts Advocate: Jeannette Edris Rockefeller and the Founding of the Arkansas Arts Center." Master's thesis, University of Arkansas at Little Rock, 2014.

Machlin, Milton. *The Search for Michael Rockefeller*. New York: Putnam, 1972.

Mack, Vicki. *Frank A. Vanderlip: The Banker Who Changed America*. Palos Verdes Estates, CA: Pinale, 2013.

Malczewski, Joan. "Weak State, Stronger Schools: Northern Philanthropy and Organizational Change in the Jim Crow South." *Journal of Southern History* 75 (November 2009): 963–1000.

Manchester, William R. *A Rockefeller Family Portrait, from John D. to Nelson*. Boston: Little, Brown, 1959.

Manning, Thomas G. *The Standard Oil Company: The Rise of a National Monopoly*. New York: Holt, Reinhart, and Winston, 1962.

Martin, Mary. *My Heart Belongs*. New York: William Morrow, 1976.

Martinez, J. Michael. *A Long Dark Night: Race in America from Jim Crow to World War II*. Lanham, MD: Rowman and Littlefield, 2016.

Men Who Were There. *Ours to Hold It High: The History of the 77th Infantry Division in World War II*. Nashville, TN: Battery Press, 1947.

Michaelis, David. *Eleanor: A Life*. New York: Simon and Schuster, 2020.

Moore, Jesse Thomas, Jr. *A Search for Equality: The National Urban League, 1910–1961*. University Park: Pennsylvania State University Press, 1981.

Morehouse, Maggi. *Fighting in the Jim Crow Army: Black Men and Women Remember World War II*. New York: Rowman and Littlefield, 2000.

Morgan, Mary Rockefeller. *Beginning with the End*. New York: Vantage Point, 2012.

Morris, Joe Alex. *Nelson Rockefeller, A Biography*. New York: Harper and Brothers, 1960.

———. *Those Rockefeller Brothers: An Informal Biography of Five Extraordinary Young Men*. New York: Harper and Brothers, 1953.

Morrow, Lance. *The Chief: A Memoir of Fathers and Sons*. New York: Random House, 1984.

Moscow, Alvin. *The Rockefeller Inheritance*. Garden City, NY: Doubleday, 1977.

Murthy, Vivek H. "Facing Addiction in the United States: The Surgeon General's Report of Alcohol, Drugs and Health." *Journal of the American Medical Association* 317 (January 2017): 133–34.

Nevins, Allen. *John D. Rockefeller: The Heroic Age of American Enterprise*. 2 vols. New York: Charles Scribner's Sons, 1940.

———. *Study in Power: John D. Rockefeller, Industrialist and Philanthropist*. 2 vols. New York: Charles Scribner's Sons, 1953.

Newhall, Nancy Wynne. *Contribution to the Heritage of Every American: The Conservation Activities of John D. Rockefeller, Jr.* New York: Alfred A. Knopf, 1957.

Nizer, Louis. *My Life in Court*. New York: Doubleday, 1961.

Okrent, Daniel. *Great Fortune: The Epic of Rockefeller Center*. New York: Viking Press, 2003.

Olien, Diana Davids, and Roger M. Olien. *Oil in Texas: The Gusher Age, 1895–1945*. Austin: University of Texas Press, 2002.

Othman, Nassar al-. *With their Bare Hands: The Story of the Oil Industry in Qatar*. Translated and edited by Ken Whittingham. London: Longman, 1984.

Parris, Guichard, and Lester Brooks. *Blacks in the City, A History of the National Urban League*. Boston: Little, Brown, 1971.

Perkins, Alfred. *Edwin Rogers Embree: The Julius Rosenwald Fund, Foundation Philanthropy, and American Race Relations*. Bloomington: Indiana University Press, 2011.

Persico, Joseph E. *The Imperial Rockefeller*. New York: Simon and Schuster, 1982.

Phillips, Kimberley L. *War! What Is It Good For? Black Freedom Struggles and the U.S. Military from World War II to Iraq*. Chapel Hill: University of North Carolina Press, 2012.

Pierson, Mary Louise, and Ann Rockefeller. *The Rockefeller Family Home, Kykuit*. New York: Abbeville Press, 1998.

Prefer, Nathan N. *Leyte 1944: The Soldiers' Battle*. Havertown, PA: Casemate Publishers, 2012.

Rasmussen, Anne-Marie. *There Was Once a Time of Islands, Illusions, and Rockefellers*. New York and London: Harcourt Brace, 1975.

Read, Florence Mathilda. *The Story of Spelman College*. Princeton, NJ: Princeton University Press, 1961.

Reed, Roy. *Faubus: The Life and Times of an American Prodigal*. Fayetteville: University of Arkansas Press, 1997.

Reed, Touré F. *Not Alms but Opportunity: The Urban League and the Politics of Racial Uplift, 1910–1950*. Chapel Hill: University of North Carolina Press, 2008.

Reich, Cary. *The Life of Nelson A. Rockefeller: Worlds to Conquer, 1908–1958*. New York: Doubleday, 1996.

Rickenbacker, Eddie. *Rickenbacker: An Autobiography*. Englewood Cliffs, NJ: Prentice Hall, 1967.

Ringer, Andrea. " 'Purely Personal and Philosophical': Governor Winthrop Rockefeller's Death Sentence Commutations." *Arkansas Historical Quarterly* 74 (Summer 2015): 130–46.

Rivas, Darlene. *Missionary Capitalist: Nelson Rockefeller in Venezuela*. Chapel Hill: University of North Carolina Press, 2002.

Roberts, Ann Rockefeller. *Mr. Rockefeller's Roads: The Untold Story of Acadia's Carriage Roads and Their Creator*. Camden, ME: Down East Books, 1990.

Rockefeller, Abby A. *Abby Aldrich Rockefeller's Letters to Her Sister Lucy*. New York: John D. Rockefeller, Jr., 1957.

Rockefeller, David. *Memoirs*. New York: Random House, 2002.

Rockefeller, Eileen. *Being a Rockefeller, Becoming Myself: A Memoir*. New York: Blue Rider Press, 2013.

Rockefeller, John D. *Random Reminiscences of Men and Events*. New York: Doubleday, 1908.

Rockefeller, John D., 3rd. *The Second American Revolution: Some Personal Observations*. New York: Harper and Row, 1973.

Rockefeller, John D., Jr. *The Personal Relation in Industry*. New York: Albert and Charles Boni, 1923.

Rodgers, William A. *Rockefeller's Follies: An Unauthorized View of Nelson A. Rockefeller*. New York: Stein and Day, 1966.

Roussel, Christine. *The Art of Rockefeller Center*. New York: W. W. Norton, 2006.

Russell, David Lee. *Eastern Airlines: A History, 1926–1991*. Jefferson, NC: McFarland, 2013.

Saarinen, Aline B. "The One Luxury: The Rockefellers." In *The Proud Possessors: The Lives, Times and Tastes of Some Adventurous American Art Collectors*, 344–95. New York: Random House, 1958.

Schenkel, Albert F. *The Rich Man and the Kingdom: John D. Rockefeller, Jr., and the Protestant Establishment*. Minneapolis: Fortress Press, 1995.

Schriftgiesser, Karl. "The Rockefellers: Oil to Radio City." In *Families*, 367–405. New York: Howell, Soskin, 1940.

Schulman, Daniel. *A Force for Change: African American Art and the Julius Rosenwald Fund*. Evanston, IL: Northwestern University Press, 2009.

Serling, Robert J. *From the Captain to the Colonel. An Informal History of Eastern Airlines*. New York: Dial, 1980.

Shapiro, Marsha Rose. "Wealth, Gender, and Inheritance Among the U.S. Elite: The Rockefellers and Binghams." In *Family Welfare: Gender, Property, and Inheritance Since the Seventeenth Century*, edited by David R. Green and Alastair Owens, 121–42. Westport, CT: Praeger, 2004.

Shaplen, Robert. *Toward the Well-Being of Mankind: Fifty Years of the Rockefeller Foundation*. New York: Doubleday, 1964.

Shaywitz, Sally. *Overcoming Dyslexia: A New and Complete Science-Based Program for Reading Problems at Any Level*. 2nd ed. New York: Vintage Books, 2020.

Silk, Leonard, and Mark Silk. *The American Establishment*. New York: Basic Books, 1980.

Sloan, Bill. *The Ultimate Battle: Okinawa 1945—The Last Epic Struggle of World War II*. New York: Simon and Schuster, 2007.

Smith, Richard Austin. "The Rockefeller Brothers." In *The Art of Success*, edited by the editors of *Fortune*, 199–225. Philadelphia: J. B. Lippincott, 1956.

Smith, Richard Norton. *On His Own Terms: A Life of Nelson Rockefeller*. New York: Random House, 2014.

Smith, S. L. *Builders of Goodwill: The Story of the State Agents of Negro Education in the South, 1910–1950*. Nashville: Tennessee Book Company, 1950.

Stasz, Clarice. *The Rockefeller Women: Dynasty of Piety, Privacy, and Service*. New York: St. Martin's, 1995.

Stephenson, Nathaniel Wright. *Nelson W. Aldrich: A Leader in American Politics*. New York: Charles Scribner's Sons, 1930.

Sterling, Ross, and Ed Kilman. Edited and revised by Don Carleton. *Ross Sterling, Texan:*

A Memoir by the Founder of the Humble Oil and Refining Company. Austin: University of Texas Press, 2007.

Stevenson, Russell, and Virginia O. Locke. *The Agricultural Development Council, A History*. Morrilton, AR: Winrock International Institute for Agricultural Development, 1989.

Stewart, Adrian. *The Battle of Leyte Gulf*. London: Hale, 1979.

Swindall, Lindsey R. *The Path to the Greater, Freer, Truer World: Southern Civil Rights and Anticolonialism, 1937–1955*. Gainesville: University of Florida Press, 2014.

Tarbell, Ida. *The History of the Standard Oil Company*. 2 vols. New York: Macmillan, 1905.

Thomas, Evan. *Sea of Thunder: Four Commanders and the Last Great Naval Campaign, 1941–1945*. New York: Simon and Schuster, 2006.

Thurber, Timothy N. "Goldwaterism Triumphant? Race and the Republican Party, 1965–1968." *Journal of the Historical Society* 7 (September 2007): 349–84.

Urwin, Cathy Kunzinger. *Agenda for Reform: Winthrop Rockefeller as Governor of Arkansas, 1967–1971*. Fayetteville: University of Arkansas Press, 1991.

———. "'Noblesse Oblige' and Practical Politics: Winthrop Rockefeller and the Civil Rights Movement." *Arkansas Historical Quarterly* 54 (Spring 1995): 30–52.

Vego, Milan. *The Battle for Leyte, 1944: Allied and Japanese Plans, Preparations, and Execution*. Annapolis, MD: Naval Institute Press, 2006.

Wald, Ellen R. *Saudi, Inc.: The Arabian Kingdom's Pursuit of Profit and Power*. New York: Pegasus Books, 2018.

Ward, John L. *The Arkansas Rockefeller*. Baton Rouge: Louisiana State University Press, 1978.

———. *Winthrop Rockefeller, Philanthropist: A Life of Change*. Fayetteville: University of Arkansas Press, 2004.

Warren, Aldice G., ed. *Catalogue of the Delta Kappa Epsilon Fraternity*. New York: Delta Kappa Epsilon Council, 1910.

Weiss, Nancy J. *The National Urban League, 1910–1940*. New York: Oxford University Press, 1974.

West, Charles O., and Philip C. Wood, Neil F. Wender, and Harold R. Butler, eds. *Second to None: The Story of the 305th Infantry in World War II*. Washington, DC: Infantry Journal Press, 1949.

Whayne, Jeannie, and Thomas A. DeBlack, George Sabo III, and Morris M. Arnold. *Arkansas: A Narrative History*. 2nd ed. Fayetteville: University of Arkansas Press, 2013.

Willmott, H. P. *The Battle of Leyte Gulf: The Last Fleet Action*. Bloomington: Indiana University Press, 2005.

Winks, Robin W. *Laurance S. Rockefeller: Catalyst for Conservation*. Washington, DC: Island Press, 1997.

Wirges, Gene. *Conflict of Interests: The Gene Wirges Story*. North Little Rock, AR: Riverboat, 1992.

Woods, Jeff. *Black Struggle, Red Scare: Segregation and Anti-Communism in the South, 1948–1968*. Baton Rouge: Louisiana State University Press, 2004.

Woodward, Colin. "'There's a Lot of Things That Need Changin': Johnny Cash, Winthrop Rockefeller, and Prison Reform in Arkansas." *Arkansas Historical Quarterly* 79 (Spring 2020): 40–58.

Woodward, C. Vann. *The Battle for Leyte Gulf: The Incredible Story of World War II's Largest Navy Battle*. New York: Macmillan, 1947.

Wormser, Richard. *The Rise and Fall of Jim Crow*. New York: St. Martin's, 2003.

Wye, Deborah, and Audrey Isselbacher. *Abby Aldrich Rockefeller and Print Collecting: An Early Mission for MoMA.* New York: Museum of Modern Art, 1999.

Yergin, Daniel. *The Prize: The Epic Quest for Oil, Money and Power.* New York: Simon and Schuster, 1990.

Young, Edgar B. *Lincoln Center: The Building of an Institution.* New York: New York University Press, 1980.

Zeigler, James. *Red Scare Racism and Cold War Black Radicalism.* Jackson: University Press of Mississippi, 2015.

Italicized page numbers refer to illustrations.

Hope, Bob, 129
Horowitz, David, 15, 16, 57
Hotel Avila, Venezuela, 88, 181
Hotel Roosevelt, New York, 173
Hotel Sam Peck, Arkansas, 186
Houston Negro Hospital, Texas, 78, 80
Houston, Texas: oil industry in, 60, 61;
    Winthrop Rockefeller based in, 72,
    77, 78–81, 163; Winthrop Rockefeller
    and race relations in, 78–80; Winthrop
    Rockefeller travels to, 61, 69, 75
Howard University, Washington, DC, 79
Howard University School of Medicine,
    Washington, DC, 79
Howey, Walter, 183
Hudson, Hortense, 90, 156
Hudson, James "Jimmy": background
    of, 90; and Greater New York Fund
    (GNYF) campaign, 92; Hortense
    Hudson, wife of, 90; Winrock
    road named after, 90; Winthrop
    Rockefeller, interviews and hires
    as assistant, 89–90; Winthrop
    Rockefeller, places in charge of ren-
    ovations at 770 Park Avenue, 157;
    Winthrop Rockefeller, and "Report
    on Veterans' Readjustment," 155–56;
    Winthrop Rockefeller, as bridge
    to Black community for, 92, 156;
    Winthrop Rockefeller, moves to
    Arkansas with, 8, 90; World War II,
    Coast Guard service in, 155–56
Huitt, Charles C., 89, 90
Humble Oil Company: buys Waters-
    Pierce Oil Company, 81; David B.
    Harris, head of industrial relations
    at, 72; Harry Weiss, vice president of,
    77; head office of, 68, 69; Wallace E.
    Pratt, chief geologist of, 70; Winthrop
    Rockefeller, as alleged spy for, 73–74;
    Winthrop Rockefeller, resigns from,
    81; Winthrop Rockefeller, works for,
    60, 61, 62, 68, 69–81, 83
Humphrey, Hubert, 159
Humphrey, M. M., 190
Hungary, 95
Hunter Liggett, USS, 156
Huston, Angelica, 165

Huston, John, 165
Huston, Walter, 165
Hutton, Betty, 128–29, 154
Hypoluxo, Florida, 31

Indiana, 169, 187
Indiantown Gap Military Reservation,
    Pennsylvania, 114, 119
Industrial Relations Counselors Inc., 160
International Basic Economy Corporation
    (IBEC), 160, 183–85
International House, New York, 36
Ipil, Leyte, 134, 135
Iran, 183
Iraq, 94, 183
Iraq oil fields, 95
Iraq Petroleum Company, 94
Istanbul, Turkey, 95, 166
"It Couldn't Be Done" (poem by Edgar
    Albert Guest), 35, 64
Italy, 94, 167
Iwo Jima, Japan, 142

Jack Tar (sailboat), 32
Jacksonville, Florida, 169
Jamaica, 176
James Melton Museum, Florida, 31
Jamieson, Frank, 167
Japan: and Battle of Leyte Gulf, 130; and
    Guam, 122, 123, 124; and Imabori
    Detachment, 135; and Okinawa, 142,
    143; and Pearl Harbor, 108, 117; and
    Philippines, 130, 133, 135, 136, 137; and
    US military strategy in Pacific, 117, 121;
    and World War II, kamikaze attacks of
    during, 5, 133, 143–44; and World War
    II, surrender, 153. See also Iwo Jima;
    Kerama Retto Islands; Kyushu Island;
    Ryukyu Islands
Jennings, Louisiana, 75–77
Jenny (tavern owner), 105
John Price Jones Corporation (consul-
    tancy firm), 46, 91
Johnson, James D., 10
Johnson, Joe, 57
Johnson, Peter J.: Barbara Sears
    Rockefeller, claims pregnant at time
    of marriage to Winthrop Rockefeller,

Morrilton, Arkansas, 3, 8, 192
Morris, Frank, 111
Morris, Joe Alex, 3, 13, 191
Morris, Newbold, 97
Moscow, Alvin, 13, 19, 57, 113
Mosul oil fields, Iraq, 94
Moton, Robert Russa, 45–46
Mount Desert Island, Maine, 32
Mount Vernon, Virginia, 36
Muir, James I., 97
Museum of Automobiles, Arkansas, 31
Museum of Fine Arts, Arkansas, 8
Museum of Modern Art (MoMA), New
    York, 8, 21
Mutt and Jeff (comic strip), 29

Naples, Italy, 94
National Aeronautic Association
    (NAA), 94
National City Bank of New York, 84
National Defense Act (1920), 96
National Fund for Medical Education, 160
National Guard, 96
National Negro Insurance Association, 79
National Recovery Administration
    (NRA), 71
National Resources Planning Board
    (NRPB), 164
National Urban League (NUL), 7–8, 83,
    92, 158–59
Naval Medical Research Unit No. 2
    (NAMRU 2), 146, 147
Navy: on Carolina maneuvers, 107;
    and Guam, 122, 126, 146; John D.
    Rockefeller, World War II service
    in, 98, 155; and kamikaze attack on
    USS *Henrico*, 143, 144; Laurence S.
    Rockefeller, World War II service in,
    98–99, 155; Richard Sears Jr., World
    War II service in, 164; Winthrop
    Rockefeller, involvement in 1948 air-
    plane incident, 168. *See also* Bureau of
    Naval Personnel
Near Eastern Development Company
    (NEDC), 5, 94
Netherlands, 94
Nevada, 113, 165, 190
Neveckas, Peter (father-in-law), 164, 169

Nevins, Allen, 107
Newark Bay, New Jersey, 61
New Caledonia, 130, 131
New Deal, 71, 105
Newell, Frank: and Abigail Aldrich
    Greene Rockefeller, 109, 151; in
    Hawaii, 119, 120; in Leyte, 134; in
    Okinawa, 150–51; Twenty-Fourth
    Corps, assigned to, 119; Winthrop
    Rockefeller, comments on appear-
    ance, 112, 151; Winthrop Rockefeller,
    comments on 1948 airplane incident,
    168; Winthrop Rockefeller, comments
    on relationship with Rockefeller
    family, 110, 140; Winthrop Rockefeller,
    friendship with, 18, 109, 115, 120,
    157; Winthrop Rockefeller, role in
    assignment as S-4, 111; Winthrop
    Rockefeller, role in move to Arkansas,
    186–87
New Guinea, 117
New Hampshire, 37
New Haven, Connecticut, 53, 55, 57
New Jersey. *See* Fidelity Union Trust
    Company; Princeton University;
    Standard Oil of New Jersey; *and
    names of individual locations*
New Left, 16
Newlon, Jesse H., 43, 45
New Mexico, 70
Newton, David, 42, 43–44
New York City. *See names of individual
    locations*
New York City Council, 97
New York Daily Mirror, 185
New York Hospital, 186
New York Journal-American, 17, 179, 187
New York Life Insurance Company, 138
New York School of Social Work, 186
New York State. *See names of individual
    locations*
New York State Supreme Court, 188
New York Times, 21, 61, 96
New York University Council, 160
New York University School of Medicine,
    109
New York University–Bellevue Medical
    Center, 160, 175–76

190–91; Charles W. Mapes Jr., relationship with, 190; early life of, 163–64; Hollywood, moves to, 165; Lowell, moves to family farm in, 180; Manhattan, purchases apartment in, 190; movies, career in, 165; New York, moves to, 166; nicknamed Bobo, 165; photograph of, *171*; postnatal illness of, 173, 176; Richard Sears Jr., divorce from, 165, 166; Richard Sears Jr., marriage to, 164; Rockefeller family, life as a member of, 172; 770 Park Avenue, occupies, 187–88; Susan Sears, relationship with, 165–66, 170; views on separation and divorce, 180; Winthrop Paul Rockefeller, difficult pregnancy with, 173; Winthrop Paul Rockefeller, gives birth to, 174; Winthrop Paul Rockefeller, in custody of during separation and divorce, 18; Winthrop Paul Rockefeller, pregnant with, 6, 169, 173; and Winthrop Paul Rockefeller stay with William Randolph Hearst and Marion Davies in Beverley Hills, 182–83

—and Winthrop Rockefeller: approach to separation and divorce from, 181; dates, 166; divorce from, 6, 188–90; feared dead in a plane crash with, 166–67; hires attorneys for separation and divorce from, 179, 187, 189, 190; honeymoon with, 172; marital difficulties with, 173–74; marriage to, 6, 168–72; meets, 165; relationship with, 19; rumors of marriage to, 166, 167; rumors of separation from, 173–74; separation from, 6, 176–80; speaks to press about separation from, 180; views on marriage to, 173, 174; views on move to Arkansas, 187; visits Montego Bay with, 176; visits Paris with, 177; and Winthrop Paul Rockefeller, family life with, 174–75

Rockefeller, Blanchette Ferry Hooker (sister-in-law), 56

Rockefeller, David (brother): Abby Aldrich Greene Rockefeller, and death of, 172; Atta Albertson, governess of, 35; attributes of, 25; baptism of, 27; Barbara Sears Rockefeller, and Margaret McGrath, vacations with, 177; Chase Manhattan Bank, as chair and CEO of, 25; death of, 13; dyslexia of, 40; Harvard University, admitted to, 4, 56; James Hudson, employs, 156; John D. Rockefeller Jr., comments on Colonial Williamsburg restoration, 36; John D. Rockefeller Jr., comments on relationship with Abby Aldrich Greene Rockefeller, 24; John D. Rockefeller Jr., receives check from for not smoking, 30; left-handedness of, 40; Lincoln School, complaints about, 37; Lincoln School, roller-skates to, 28; Margaret McGrath, engagement and marriage to 97; memoir of, 15, 32; photographs of, *14*, *20*; and race relations, 120; and Rockefeller family, financial affairs of, 76, 184–85; Rockefeller family, place in, 25; and Rockefeller family trips, 36–37; Seal Harbor, recalls visits to, 32, 33; World War II, Army service in, 98; World War II, returns from, 155

—and Winthrop Rockefeller: comments on attractiveness to women, 161; comments on drinking, 57; comments on friends of, 31; comments on participation in New York nightlife, 161; comments on place in Rockefeller family history, 17; investigates rumors of death in plane crash, 167; and marriage to Barbara Sears Rockefeller, 169; relationship, 25

Rockefeller, Faith (cousin), 65

Rockefeller, Jeannette Edris (second wife): background of, 186; finances of, 190; and Museum of Fine Arts, 8; and Winrock Farms, 191; Winthrop Rockefeller, divorce from, 12; Winthrop Rockefeller, marriage to, 8, 190; Winthrop Rockefeller, meets, 186

Rockefeller, John Davison 3rd (brother): attributes of, 24–25; biography of, 15; Blanchette Ferry Hooker, marriage to, 56, 58; Browning School, attendance

at, 27–28; Colonial Williamsburg, chair of board at, 185; death of, 13; Laurance S. Rockefeller, as playmate of, 33; Loomis Institute, attendance at, 37, 39–40; Nelson A. Rockefeller, as playmate of, 33; photographs of, *14, 20*; Princeton University, attendance at, 4, 37; and Rockefeller family, financial affairs of, 76, 184–85; Rockefeller family, place in, 24–25; World War II, Navy service in, 96, 108, 155
—and Winthrop Rockefeller: arranges summer work experience in oil industry, 53, 60–61; comments on enlistment in Army, 102–3; correspondence with, 42, 43, 48, 51, 181; dismisses rumors of engagement to Betty Shallcross, 65; jealous of Loomis Institute award, 51; sent to Yale University to investigate whereabouts of, 55

Rockefeller, John Davison, IV "Jay" (nephew), 10

Rockefeller, John Davison, Jr. "Junior" (father): advocacy of fresh air and exercise, 28; Abigail Aldrich Greene Rockefeller, and death of, 172–73; Abigail Aldrich Greene Rockefeller, meeting and courtship of, and engagement and marriage to, 23–24; Abigail Aldrich Greene Rockefeller, relationship with, 24; Abeyton Lodge, builds the Playhouse at, 30; Abigail Aldrich Rockefeller, views on divorce of, 113; Abigail Rockefeller Milton, and birth of, 37; and Acadia National Park, 33; aversion to suggestion of special favors, 40; background and characteristics of, 22–23; and Barbara Sears Rockefeller, 173, 174, 176; biography of, 15; and Colonial Williamsburg, 36–37, 185; Dunbar Apartments, helps fund construction of, 90; Dunbar National Bank, founder of, 89; and the Eyrie, 32; Greater New York Fund (GNYF), as a founder of, 91; Industrial Relations Counselors Inc., founder of, 160; International House, cofounder

of, 36; and Jeannette Edris Rockefeller, 186; John D. Rockefeller Sr., as only son of, 22; John D. Rockefeller Sr., transfer of wealth from, 22–23; John D. Rockefeller 3rd, chooses Loomis Institute for preparatory education of, 39–40; John D. Rockefeller 3rd, grooms as heir, 24–25; Laurance S. Rockefeller, mutual interests in conservation, 25; and left-handedness of sons Nelson A. Rockefeller, Winthrop Rockefeller, and David Rockefeller, 40; and Lincoln School, 28, 37, 43, 45; Martha Baird Allen, marriage to, 184; Nathaniel Horton Batchelder, correspondence with, 39, 43, 44, 46, 50, 51; and National Urban League (NUL), 8; Nelson A. Rockefeller, permits to trade Standard Oil shares, 85; offers money to his children not to smoke, 29–30; permits his children to sell garden produce to household, 30; philanthropy of, 23; photograph of, *20*; Prohibition, support of, 32, 42, 43; and religion, 27; and Republican Party, 10; Richard E. Byrd, funds expedition of to Antarctica, 29; Richard E. Byrd, funds expedition of to North Pole, 29; Rockefeller Center, construction of, 59–60; "Rockefeller Credo," 10, 106; as Rockefeller family disciplinarian, 23, 26; and Rockefeller family office, 5, 29, 83, 110; and Rockefeller family trips, 35–37; Seal Harbor, projects in, 33; Seal Harbor, spends summers in, 32–35, 153; and the United Negro College Fund (UNCF), 7, 120; William Alton, hires to keep Winthrop Rockefeller company at the Eyrie, 69; and Winthrop Paul Rockefeller, 173, 174, 176; work with United Service Organizations (USO), 106, 129
—and Winthrop Rockefeller: agrees to apprenticeship at Chase Bank, 89; approves of participation in Citizens' Military Training Camp, 97; arranges treatment at Rockefeller Institute for Medical Research, 154; birth of,

Rockefeller, Margaret Dulany "Peggy" (niece), 172

Rockefeller, Margaret McGrath "Peggy" (sister-in-law), 97, 167, 169, 175

Rockefeller, Martha Baird (stepmother), 184, 186

Rockefeller, Mary Billings French (sister-in-law), 74

Rockefeller, Mary Todhunter Clark "Tod" (sister-in-law), 49, 86, 87, 174

Rockefeller, Nelson Aldrich (brother): American International Association for Economic Development (AIA), founder of, 88; attributes of, 25; biographies of, 15, 16, 27; Chase Bank, apprenticeship at, 75, 85; Creole Petroleum Company, joins board of, 85; Dartmouth College, attendance at, 4, 37; death of, 13; Department of State, leaves, 155; dyslexia of, 40; Europe, travels in, 85; Greater New York Fund (GNYF), declines to participate in, 91; Harlem, claims to have gone to school in, 28; Hotel Avila, construction of in Caracas, Venezuela, 88; International Basic Economy Corporation (IBEC), founder of, 160, 183–84; James Hudson, employs, 156; James Hudson, helps secure job at Bendix Aviation Corporation, 156; John D. Rockefeller Jr., receives check from for not smoking, 30; John D. Rockefeller Sr., attends funeral of, 88; John D. Rockefeller 3rd, playmate of, 33; and John D. Rockefeller 3rd, wedding of, 58; Latin America, interest in, 88–89, 209n34; Laurance S. Rockefeller, best man at wedding to Mary Billings French, 74; Laurance S. Rockefeller, friendship with, 25, 33; left-handedness of, 40; Lincoln School, complaints about, 37; Lincoln School, roller-skates to, 28; Mary Todhunter Clark, marriage to, 49; New York, elected governor of, 11; and oil industry, 86, 88; photographs of, 14, 20, 87; President Eleazar Lopez Contreras of Venezuela, meets with,

86; President Franklin D. Roosevelt, appointed as Coordinator of Inter-American Affairs by, 88; and race relations, 159; ranches owned by, 7, 89; and Rockefeller brothers, receives most public attention of, 26–27; and Rockefeller family, financial affairs of, 23, 76, 184–85; Rockefeller family, place in, 25; as Rockefeller family politician, 25; and Rockefeller family trips, 36–37; and Rockefeller Institute for Medical Research, 30; Theodore Roosevelt Sr., bounced on knee by, 27; Act of Chapultepec, helps negotiate, 88; Venezuelan Development Company (VDC), founder of, 88; William Alton, best friends with at Lincoln School and Dartmouth College, 69; and World War II draft, 98; World War II, works in government during, 99

—and Winthrop Rockefeller: assists in transfer to Rockefeller Institute for Medical Research, 154, 219n26; bullying of, 26, 27, 29, 33; correspondence with, 43, 51, 70, 75, 82, 102, 108, 153, 160, 176; discusses Army career with, 108; helps find Army division to serve in, 108–9; and marriage to Barbara Sears Rockefeller, 170; mutual interests in ranching, 86, 89; plans for summer vacation from Yale University, 59–60; recommends nurse for Winthrop Paul Rockefeller, 174; relationship, 27; trip to Latin America with, 7, 83, 85–88; visits in oil fields, 75

Rockefeller, William Avery, Jr. (great-uncle), 109

Rockefeller, Winthrop Paul "Win Paul" (son): Barbara Sears Rockefeller, comments on, 180–81, 186, 188; Barbara Sears Rockefeller, in custody of during separation, 18, 177, 179, 180, 182; Barbara Sears Rockefeller, divorce settlement arrangements for custody of, 188; Barbara Sears Rockefeller, moves to Lowell family farm with, 180; Barbara Sears Rockefeller, occupies

Jackson, South Carolina, 109–111; promoted to captain, 110; assigned as 305th Infantry Regiment supply officer (S-4) 111; on maneuvers in Louisiana, 111; on maneuvers in Arizona and California, 111–13; visits sister Abigail Aldrich Rockefeller in Nevada, 113; attends Command and General Staff School at Fort Leavenworth, Kansas, 113; mountain training in Elkins, West Virginia, 114–15; amphibious training at Camp Bradford, Virginia, 115; promoted to major; 115; at Camp Stoneman, California, 115–16; sails overseas from San Francisco to Hawaii, 116–18

—Army life from Hawaii to New York: at Camp Pauli, Hawaii, 118–21; sails from Hawaii to Eniwetok, 121–23; sails from Eniwetok to Guam, 123; participates in Battle of Guam, 123–39; participates in assault landings in Guam, 123–24; based in Guam, 124–31; entertains Betty Hutton, 129; sails from Guam to Manus Island, 131; sails from Manus Island to Leyte, 131; participates in Battle of Leyte, 131–37; participates in assault landings in Ipil, Leyte, 134; participates in the capture of Ormoc, Leyte, 135; advances through the Ormoc Valley, Leyte, 135–36; in Matag-ob, Leyte, 136–37; in Palompon, Leyte, 137–39; awarded Bronze Star Medal, 139; on Tarragona Beach, Leyte, 139–42; considers offer of petroleum attaché job in London, United Kingdom, 139–41; develops bronchial pneumonia, 141–42; contracts hepatitis A, 142; rejoins the 305th Infantry Regiment in the Kerama Retto Islands, 142; sails from Kerama Retto Islands aboard the USS *Henrico*, 142–43; kamikaze attack on the USS *Henrico*, 143–45; sails to Guam for medical treatment, 145–46; recovers from injuries in Guam, 146–49; awarded Purple Heart, 149; flies from Guam to Okinawa, 149; based in

Okinawa, 149–52; assigned as Seventy-Seventh Infantry Division personnel and morale officer (G-1), 149–50; disagreements with parents about Army service and postwar life, 151–52; contracts hepatis A for a second time, 152; transferred from Okinawa to Cebu, Philippines, 152; hospitalized in Cebu, 152–53; end of the Pacific War, 153; sails from Cebu to Los Angeles, 153; at Camp Hahn, California, 153–54; transfers from Camp Hahn to Halloran General Hospital, New York, 154–55; transfers from Halloran General Hospital to Rockefeller Institute for Medical Research, New York, 155; reunites with James Hudson, 155–56; works on "Report on Veterans' Readjustment," 155–57; promoted to lieutenant colonel, 156; war decorations, 156; discharged from Army, 156

—postwar life in New York: moves into 770 Park Avenue apartment, 157; returns to work at Socony-Vacuum Oil Company, 157–58; works with National Urban League (NUL), 158–59; interviewed by *Chicago Defender*, 159; listed in *Chicago Defender* 1948 "honor roll of democracy," 160; postwar involvement in education, health, and Rockefeller family operations, 160; postwar New York social life, 160–61; meets Barbara Sears Rockefeller, 165; dates Barbara Sears Rockefeller, 166; feared dead in plane crash with Barbara Sears Rockefeller, 166–67; 1948 airplane incident, 168; proposes to Barbara Sears Rockefeller, 168–69; marries Barbara Sears Rockefeller, 170–72; honeymoon with Barbara Sears Rockefeller, 172; marital difficulties with Barbara Sears Rockefeller, 173–74; birth of son Winthrop Paul Rockefeller, 174–75; separation from Barbara Sears Rockefeller, 176–80; works for Socony-Vacuum Oil Company in Venezuela, 180–83; returns to New York from Venezuela,

career prior to, 5; and Winthrop Rockefeller manuscript "A Letter to My Son," 18; Winthrop Rockefeller, personal life after, 18; Winthrop Rockefeller, return from, 17, 57; Winthrop Rockefeller, service in, 6, 19, 84

Yale University: history of, 52; James Rowland Angell, president of, 51–52, 53, 56, 63, 64–65; Winthrop Rockefeller, admitted to, 52; Winthrop Rockefeller, adrift at, 84; Winthrop Rockefeller, attempts to gain entry to, 50, 51, 52; Winthrop Rockefeller, attendance at, 19, 53–66; Winthrop Rockefeller, begins drinking at, 57–58; Winthrop Rockefeller, decision to attend, 45; Winthrop Rockefeller, friendship with Bowen Charlton Tufts III at, 57, 154; Winthrop Rockefeller, friendship with George Henry at, 57, 163; Winthrop Rockefeller, majors in history at, 54; Winthrop Rockefeller, myth of expulsion from, 65–66; Winthrop Rockefeller, resignation from, 4, 65; Winthrop Rockefeller, runs into former friend from while on Manus Island, 131; Winthrop Rockefeller, summer vacations from, 55–56, 59–63
Yale, Elihu, 53
Yankee Stadium, New York, 92
Yap Islands, 141
Yosemite National Park, California, 85
You Can't Take It with You (play by George S. Kaufman and Moss Hart), 164
Yuma, Arizona, 111

About the Author

John A. Kirk is the George W. Donaghey Distinguished Professor of History at the University of Arkansas at Little Rock and the author or editor of ten books, including *Beyond Little Rock: The Origins and Legacies of the Central High Crisis* and *Race and Ethnicity in Arkansas: New Perspectives.*